Los Angeles & Disneyland® For Dummies, 1st Edition

Cheat Sheet

Los Angeles Freeways

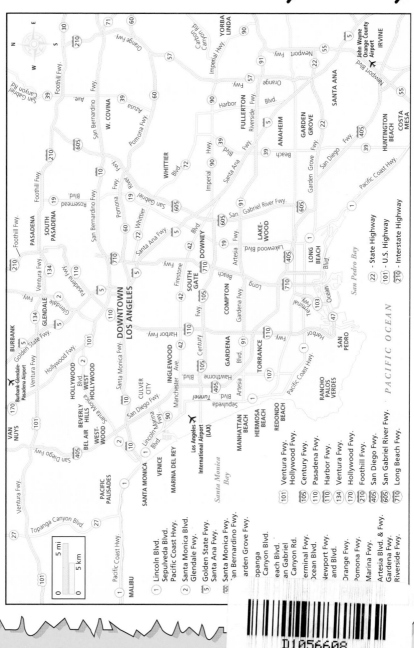

Scale: 5 mi / 5 km

Key:
- 22 - State Highway
- 101 - U.S. Highway
- 210 - Interstate Highway

1 Pacific Coast Hwy.
1 Lincoln Blvd.
1 Sepulveda Blvd.
1 Pacific Coast Hwy.
2 Santa Monica Blvd.
2 Glendale Fwy.
5 Golden State Fwy.
5 Santa Ana Fwy.
10 Santa Monica Fwy.
10 San Bernardino Fwy.
[ ]arden Grove Fwy.
[ ]opanga Canyon Blvd.
[ ]each Blvd.
[ ]an Gabriel Canyon Rd.
[ ]erminal Fwy.
Ocean Blvd.
Newport Fwy. and Blvd.
Orange Fwy.
Marina Fwy.
Artesia Blvd. & Fwy.
Gardena Fwy.
Riverside Fwy.

101 Ventura Fwy.
101 Hollywood Fwy.
105 Century Fwy.
110 Pasadena Fwy.
110 Harbor Fwy.
134 Ventura Fwy.
170 Hollywood Fwy.
210 Foothill Fwy.
405 San Diego Fwy.
605 San Gabriel River Fwy.
710 Long Beach Fwy.

For Dummies: Bestselling Book Series for Beginners

Los Angeles & Disneyland® For Dummies® 1st Edition

Cheat Sheet

Universal City & Studio Tours

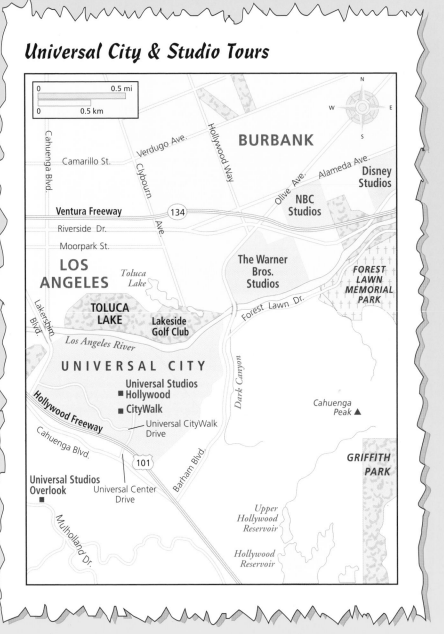

0 — 0.5 mi
0 — 0.5 km

N
W — E
S

BURBANK

Cahuenga Blvd.

Camarillo St.

Verdugo Ave.

Clybourn

Hollywood Way

Olive Ave.

Alameda Ave.

Disney Studios

NBC Studios

Ventura Freeway 134

Ave.

Riverside Dr.

Moorpark St.

LOS ANGELES

Toluca Lake

The Warner Bros. Studios

FOREST LAWN MEMORIAL PARK

TOLUCA LAKE

Lakeside Golf Club

Forest Lawn Dr.

Lakershim Blvd.

Los Angeles River

UNIVERSAL CITY

Universal Studios
■ Hollywood
■ CityWalk

Dark Canyon

Cahuenga Peak ▲

Universal CityWalk Drive

Hollywood Freeway

Cahuenga Blvd.

101

Universal Center Drive

Universal Studios Overlook
■

Barham Blvd.

GRIFFITH PARK

Mulholland Dr.

Upper Hollywood Reservoir

Hollywood Reservoir

For Dummies: Bestselling Book Series for Beginners

Los Angeles & Disneyland® FOR DUMMIES®

1ST EDITION

by Mary Herczog

Wiley Publishing, Inc.

Best-Selling Books • Digital Downloads • e-Books • Answer Networks
e-Newsletters • Branded Web Sites • e-Learning

Los Angeles & Disneyland® For Dummies¸ 1st Edition

Published by
Wiley Publishing, Inc.
909 Third Avenue
New York, NY 10022
www.wiley.com

For general information on our other products and services or to obtain technical support, please contact our Customer Care Department within the U.S. at 800-762-2974, outside the U.S. at 317-572-3993, or fax 317-572-4002.

Wiley also publishes its books in a variety of electronic formats. Some content that appears in print may not be available in electronic books.

Library of Congress Cataloging-in-Publication Data:

Library of Congress Control Number: 2002108107

ISBN: 0-7645-6611-3

ISSN: 1537-8152

Manufactured in the United States of America

10 9 8 7 6 5 4 3 2

About the Author

Mary Herczog is a relative anomaly in Los Angeles, a second-generation native. Her mom sat next to Norma Jean Baker in home room, and since Norma Jean went on to become Marilyn Monroe, this clearly gives Mary ample authority to talk about Los Angeles and, of course, celebrity scandals. She also writes *Frommer's New Orleans, Frommer's Las Vegas,* and *Las Vegas For Dummies,* plus one half of *California For Dummies,* and when she's not doing that, she works in the film industry.

Dedication

To my father who moved here and my mother who lived here, and who together gave me this city.

Author's Acknowledgments

Extra special hard core thanks to Lisa Derrick (for endlessly cheerful and ridiculously thorough research, and fine writing to boot) and Heidi Siegmund Cuda (for knowing all about L.A. nightlife and willingness to tell) — this book would not exist without them, or if it did, it wouldn't be as good.

Great thanks to Alexis Lipsitz Flippin and Frommer's, for sweetly putting up with me, and giving me the sort of job that makes others totally jealous.

Thanks to Rick Garman for always answering the phone, Sioux Sandberg for jokes, and to Suzanne and Henry Zumbrunnen for being Disneyland Resort test subjects and splendid travel companions.

Living in L.A. is greater fun and evermore a joy because I do it with Steve Hochman.

Publisher's Acknowledgments

We're proud of this book; please send us your comments through our Dummies online registration form located at www.dummies.com/register/.

Some of the people who helped bring this book to market include the following:

Editorial

Editors: Kathleen A. Dobie, Alexis Lipsitz Flippin

Copy Editor: Greg Pearson, Mary Fales

Cartographer: Elizabeth Puhl

Editorial Manager: Christine Meloy Beck

Editorial Assistant: Melissa Bennett

Senior Photo Editor: Richard Fox

Assistant Photo Editor: Michael Ross

Production

Project Coordinator: Regina Snyder

Layout and Graphics: Sean Decker, Laurie Petrone, Julie Trippetti, Jacque Schneider

Proofreaders: John Bitter, TECHBOOKS

Indexer: TECHBOOKS

Publishing and Editorial for Consumer Dummies

Diane Graves Steele, Vice President and Publisher, Consumer Dummies

Joyce Pepple, Acquisitions Director, Consumer Dummies

Kristin A. Cocks, Product Development Director, Consumer Dummies

Michael Spring, Vice President and Publisher, Travel

Brice Gosnell, Publishing Director, Travel

Suzanne Jannetta, Editorial Director, Travel

Publishing for Technology Dummies

Andy Cummings, Acquisitions Director

Composition Services

Gerry Fahey, Executive Director of Production Services

Debbie Stailey, Director of Composition Services

Contents at a Glance

Cartoons at a Glance

By Rich Tennant

page 7

page 249

page 33

page 303

page 93

page 271

page 115

page 161

Cartoon Information:
Fax: 978-546-7747
E-Mail: richtennant@the5thwave.com
World Wide Web: www.the5thwave.com

Maps at a Glance

Table of Contents

Introduction

• •

*L*otus Land. La-La Land. Swimming pools. Movie stars. Fruits, nuts, and flakes. And 350 cloudless days a year.

Face it: That's what you conjure up when you think of Los Angeles. You figure that everyone runs around sporting sunglasses and spouting New Age aphorisms while heading off to lunch on granola with Mel and Gwyneth. Well, that's just so untrue. For one thing, Mel and Gwyneth won't take our phone calls. For another, it's been weeks, *weeks*, since we were last at the Bodhi Tree (New Age bookstore nonpareil). And finally, we so hate granola.

But that's just us. In truth, all those things you think about L.A. aren't terribly far off the mark, in one form or another. And yet, mere clichés don't do the town justice. Let's add to your list, shall we? Los Angeles also features bougainvillea and roses blooming year-round, pretty little Spanish and Craftsman bungalows, flea markets, sunsets and Sunset Boulevard, art at the Getty, hiking in Griffith Park, surfing at Zuma Beach, shopping on Third Street, first-run movies, palm trees, summer-evening concerts at the Santa Monica Pier, and all types of ethnic food from A (Armenian) to Z (zabaglione). And that's not even getting into in-line skating, UCLA, driving up Pacific Coast Highway, the Museum of Television and Radio and the Museum of Jurassic Technology, performance art at Highways and opera at the Dorothy Chandler Pavilion, the Rose Parade, baseball games at Dodger Stadium, wild parrots, celebrity grave-hunting, author signings at Dutton's Books, concerts at the Greek Theater, nighttime club hopping, Zankou Chicken, and the Laurel Canyon dog park. Oh, yeah, and the weather, which allows us to play softball in our T-shirts and shorts in January and go to the beach on Christmas Day.

There is, you see, quite a bit more to La Pueblo de la Seignora, la Reigna de Los Angeles ("The City of Our Lady, Queen of the Angels") — the full and proper name of the place you usually call L.A. — than you may first think. There is even more to its very name. If you follow us, here in the very first *Los Angeles & Disneyland For Dummies*, you may not see it all, but you shall have a very good start, indeed. And we dare say you'll have a ripping good time in the process. Sure, there may be sunglasses, granola, and even a Mel or Gwyneth sighting (if you're lucky) involved, but that certainly won't be the whole of it.

About This Book

This book is designed to get you quickly acclimated to Los Angeles and provide you with the best, most essential ingredients for a great vacation. And, in our humble opinion, you won't find a better source of travel expertise than that gleaned from informed insiders — seasoned travel pros who happen to call L.A. home. That would be us, of course. We are happy to say we live here, work here, eat here, and even play here. We also *know* a few people, if you get our drift. To create *Los Angeles & Disneyland For Dummies,* we have not only scoured the city for our favorite places to recommend but we've enlisted friends and fellow Angelenos to offer up the same. All to make it easier for you, the reader, who, if you're like us, hasn't the time to thumb through traditional travel tomes that drown you in too much information — leaving you high and dry, trying to make sense of it all.

Here, we've done the legwork for you, offering our expertise and frank opinion to help you make savvy, informed decisions while you plan your trip. What you *won't* find here is a numbing, phone-book-style directory of every single place to eat, sleep, and do your laundry in Los Angeles or statistics of people who have registered satisfaction with a particular restaurant or attraction. Frankly, those kinds of guidebooks make our eyes glaze over. In *Los Angeles & Disneyland For Dummies,* we cut to the chase. We chose our favorites in many categories and put them into a form you can easily access and use to make your own decisions.

The book is designed to help you flip to the exact parts you want at any given moment. You'll even find pages in the back for you to use for notes, along with worksheets to help you plan your budget and itinerary.

Plus, we give you a whole section on traveling to Disneyland, with advice on how to most easily navigate the parks, find great deals on hotels and restaurants, and discover the latest attractions off Disneyland Drive.

 Please be advised that travel information is subject to change at any time — and this is especially true of prices. I therefore suggest that you write or call ahead for confirmation when making your travel plans. The authors, editors, and publisher cannot be held responsible for the experiences of readers while traveling.

Foolish Assumptions

In writing this book, we've made some of the following assumptions about you, the reader:

✔ You may be an inexperienced traveler who is interested in Los Angeles and wants a no-nonsense guide on when to go, how to arrange your trip, and what to expect.

✔ You may be an experienced traveler who has visited the region before, but you're looking for a guide full of lively, informed opinions to help you plan your vacation. You want to know what's new, and you want to be able to quickly access information with a minimum of fuss and muss.

✔ You're a busy, on-the-go consumer, who doesn't want to waste time absorbing the mind-numbing details of traditional guides and micromanaging your trip. You want a book that gives you frank, informed opinions on planning the perfect, hassle-free trip.

If any of these ring a bell with you, then *Los Angeles & Disneyland For Dummies* is your guidebook of choice. You realize that hundreds of thousands of visitors come to sunny L.A. every year. We want to give you the tools to make your own, unique choices in Los Angeles so that you aren't simply following the crowds from place to place.

Conventions Used in This Book

In this book, we have included lists of hotels, restaurants, and attractions. As we describe each, we often include abbreviations for commonly accepted credit cards. Take a look at the following list for an explanation of each:

✔ AE – American Express

✔ DC – Diners Club

✔ DISC – Discover

✔ MC – MasterCard

✔ V – Visa

We also include some general pricing information to help you as you decide where to unpack your bags or dine on the local cuisine. We have used a system of dollar signs to show a range of costs for one night in a hotel (the price refers to a double-occupancy room) or a meal at a restaurant (included in the cost of each meal is soup or salad, an entrée, dessert, and a non-alcoholic drink). Check out the following table to decipher the dollar signs:

Cost	Hotel	Restaurant
$	Under $100	Under $20
$$	$100–$200	$20–$30
$$$	$200–$275	$30–$40
$$$$	$275 and up	$40–$50
$$$$$		over $50

How This Book Is Organized

This book is divided into eight parts, and together they cover all of the major aspects of planning and enjoying your trip. The Table of Contents at a Glance and complete Table of Contents that preceded this chapter are perfect tools for finding general and specific information. At the back of the book, you'll find worksheets and quick listings of helpful service information and phone numbers, as well as the index, the most useful tool for navigating this book.

Part I: Getting Started

Here's where that old proverbial ball gets rolling with some information on when to plan a trip to L.A., some events to keep in mind, and a framework for establishing your budget. Here, you'll also discover a preliminary list of good reasons why Los Angeles is so much fun to visit.

Part II: Ironing Out the Details

Details, details. What kind of lodging is right for you? How can you get the best bang for your buck? Should you buy travel insurance? Do you need traveler's checks? And, perhaps most important, here is where you discover our favorite hotels and places to stay in Los Angeles so that you can make an informed opinion on where to base yourself.

Part III: Settling in to Los Angeles

Arriving in a new city and getting acclimated is one of the great joys of travel, and this section makes it easy. Here's where you really get to know the City of Angels, neighborhood by neighborhood. You'll discover the myriad of ways to get from the airport to your hotel, the smartest ways to get around the city, and where to get cash.

Part IV: Dining, Los Angeles Style

Here we give you the lowdown on dining in L.A., with our favorite restaurants, spots for quick, delicious bites, and tips on cutting down the cost of your food budget.

Part V: Exploring Los Angeles

Here you discover what we consider the best sights and attractions in Los Angeles, as well as the best museums, sports events, movie tours, kid-friendly venues, and downtown delights. Here, too, is a select shopper's guide to L.A., with tips on how to make the shopping scene, whether you're strolling in a glittering supermall or taking it to the streets at funky flea markets. For the reader looking for a variety of L.A. experiences, we offer a variety of unique itineraries. You'll also find invaluable tips on organizing your time in order to explore the city more efficiently.

Part VI: Living It Up After the Sun Goes Down

Los Angeles has no dearth of nightlife, and here you get the lowdown on how to get tickets to hot shows, where to go to see theater, dance, and more, and where to find the nightclub or bar of your (L.A.) dreams.

Part VII: A Trip to Disneyland

Here we tell you how to get to Disneyland Drive, when to come to avoid the peak tourist season, how to avoid long lines, where to stay and dine in the Disneyland area, and what's new and exciting in the Disney park system.

Part VIII: The Part of Tens

Here we have fun throwing our opinions around on such topics as the messiest intersections in the city, places to spot the city's celebrated celebrities, and venues where you can have an out-of-L.A. experience.

Icons Used in This Book

We scatter several icons around the book to alert you to special cases or particularly useful information.

The Bargain Alert icon tells you when you're about to save a bundle, or suggests ways that you can cut costs.

The Heads Up icon tells you when you should be especially aware of a situation that may be potentially dangerous, a tourist trap, or, more likely, a rip-off. In other words, you should be especially alert when you encounter these situations.

Families with kids in tow will appreciate the Kid Friendly icon, which identifies places and attractions that are welcoming and/or particularly suited to kids.

Helpful hints to make your experience easier and/or less stressful are marked with the Remember icon.

Especially created for this book, the Star Spotting icon directs you to those places where you have the best chance to spot celebrities.

The Tip icon delivers some inside information and advice on things to do or ways to best handle a specific situation, helping you to save time or money.

Where to Go From Here

Fly, drive, run, or walk. Just come. The bougainvillea is in bloom. The sand is warm and tawny, and the surf is up at Zuma. With *Los Angeles & Disneyland For Dummies* by your side, the City of Angels is yours for the taking.

Part I
Getting Started

The 5th Wave   By Rich Tennant

"Here we go, boys. Heck—even if they can't help us at least we won't feel so dern out of place."

In this part . . .

This first part introduces you to Los Angeles — the sprawling, sparkling, scintillating City of Angels. In this part we help you decide the best time to go, plot out your itinerary, and budget for your trip. We include a calendar of the city's top events, festivals, and happenings, and provide extra planning tips for people with kids, seniors, travelers with disabilities, and members of the gay community.

Chapter 1

Discovering the Best of Los Angeles

"This town is our town, this town is so fabulous. Bet you'd live here if you could and be one of us," sang L.A.'s very own Go-Go's back in their heyday, and all the natives sang along lustily.

*W*e love L.A. — we really, really do, but that's because we know how to best find and experience its admittedly subtle charms. Yeah, it's got smog (though increasingly less), and yes, it's got traffic (alas, more than ever), and yes, much of the distinctive architecture has been torn down thanks to an utter disinterest in preservation. And yes, it's far-flung, and public transportation stinks, so you absolutely have to buck that aforementioned heavy traffic to get anywhere to enjoy anything.

But. Here's a place where you can surf and ski on the same day. Here's a place where your sightseeing is enhanced by the 350 cloudless days a year. Here's a place where movie-star footprints are enshrined, and the Getty family gave a great deal of money to amass one of the finest art collections in the world. Here's a place where you can enjoy the L.A. Philharmonic (and other internationally known artists) out in the fragrant night air at the gorgeous Hollywood Bowl. Here's a place where just a 1-mile stretch of Hollywood Boulevard peacefully holds Thai, Mexican, Romanian, Armenian, Vietnamese, and Persian restaurants, all of them with some of the most wonderful food you've ever tasted, for a bargain price. Here's a place where weirdness and eccentricity are embraced — and of course, if you can turn it into a sitcom, so much the better. Here's a place where you can grocery shop right next to the actors who star in those very sitcoms, just like they were regular folks. Here's a place where you can take a ride in a spinning teacup.

And when you get past the snarling traffic, the smog, the freeway signs, the steel-and-glass behemoths, and you happen upon L.A. on one of those gin-clear days when the Santa Ana winds have blown away the smog, you'll see that the sky is a memorable blue, and the mountains stand out so sharply they seem cut out of glass. The impossibly blooming bougainvillea flaunts a floozy pink, and the air smells of gardenia. You're in your shirt sleeves, enjoying the sun on your face as you sip some coffee, and you think to yourself, "It's January?" . . . well, we'd be surprised if you didn't find yourself loving L.A., too.

Let us introduce you to our city and its sly charms. We give you the highlights of Los Angeles and Disneyland, the sights and attractions that make it one of the country's top destinations.

A little history

El Pueblo de la Señora, la Reina de Los Angeles ("the city of Our Lady, Queen of the Angels") was founded by the Spanish in 1781— and take that, all you Easterners who think L.A. doesn't have a history. But truth be told, L.A. really wasn't on the map until the movie folks came out here, in search of outdoor locations that didn't suffer from snow. By World War I, the movie business had a hold on the town, and in the 1920s and '30s, folks came here in droves, seeking their fortunes on and off the silver screen. Very few of them were "discovered" sipping sodas in malt shops, à la Lana Turner, but that didn't stop anyone from trying.

That crush of people came with cars, and as early as 1940, the Arroyo Seco Parkway, the first freeway, was opened. The automobile business solidified L.A.'s total dependence on cars by crushing the then quite handy public transport (the "Little Red Cars" trolley system). More freeways followed, and more people came to work in the thriving aerospace industry (lead by McDonnell Douglas) and the new television industry. It didn't hurt that every year, Pasadena put on the glorious Rose Parade under inevitably clear blue skies, causing snowbound Midwesterners and others to throw everything in the car and come to permanently join the balmy fun. In no time at all, L.A. became an urban sprawl of impossible dimensions.

And they keep on a'comin', though a few events have quenched migration enthusiasm, at least briefly. In 1971, a 6.2 earthquake rocked nearby Sylmar, but though it loomed in legend for more than 20 years, it was nothing compared with the "Biggish One" in 1994, the 6.8 Northridge quake that left nearly 60 people dead and a portion of the 10 freeway collapsed. Riots in the wake of the Rodney King verdict shut the city down for several days, as homes and businesses burned and the National Guard came out to restore order. And then there was the O.J. trial. But thanks to its blessedly short memory, floods, fires, and even football players haven't managed to stop this town.

Which Way's the Beach?

To many people, Los Angeles is one big beach party, with Frankie and Annette riding an eternal surfboard against a picture-perfect blue sky. To some extent, you can find a piece of that *Beach Blanket Bingo* vibe at places like the **Santa Monica Pier,** where you can stroll among the motley collection of souvenir shops, old carny rides, and a 1930s-era merry-go-round, or the **Venice Ocean Front Walk,** where the boys preen at Muscle Beach and pony-tailed, gals zoom by on their in-line skates — both genders have more tattoos than they did back in the '50s. But, if you want to enjoy the ocean in a more pristine setting, head north into the **Pacific Palisades** and **Malibu,** where the waves get bigger and the houses get ritzier. North of that is **Zuma,** with its wild, cold waters.

All the Stars in Heaven

The days of studio moguls like Louis B. Mayer and his stable of MGM stars may be long gone, but the city of Los Angeles remains synonymous with high-wattage celebrity. Of course, these days Hollywood proper is more a state of mind than a place where movies are made and film stars prance around in ermine and silk. That's because the motion-picture industry isn't based in Hollywood, and truth be told, never really was. If you want to see stars — and they're out there, to be sure — you need to trek to the nether reaches of Malibu coffee shops and Beverly Hills clothing stores. In the following chapters, we tell you our favorite places to spot celebrities in their native habitat. (Chapter 25 lists the best of the best.)

You may not find filmmakers in Hollywood, but you still have a number of fine reasons to visit, such as **Grauman's Chinese Theatre.** What began in 1927 as a publicity stunt (heck, it's still a publicity stunt) has gotten a facelift, which removed some of its more endearingly eccentric stylings (neon dragons!) but left the glorious interior (pomp and gilt!) intact. But of course, you go to see the footprints, handprints, and other body prints of stars past. Have fun comparing your foot size with that of Mary Pickford or nose length with Jimmy Durante's proboscis print. Shoppers and mall fanciers will want to head to the **Hollywood-Highland Complex**, new home of the Academy Awards (in the Kodak Theatre) and a mega shopping center with major shops, movie theaters, a couple of nightclubs, several restaurants, and the brand-new **Hollywood Motion Picture Museum,** home of such Tinseltown artifacts as Dorothy's gingham dress from *Wizard of Oz*. And of course, there's **Sunset Boulevard**, the city's main artery and witness to any number of sordid "Hollywood Babylon" stories. And of course, savvy shoppers will want to head to **Melrose Avenue,** where funky stores and hip dining spots abound.

City of Museums

L.A. has a number of museums with very high-quality collections, along with a few of the quirkier sort that folks like us tend to patronize. The big ones, of course, are the **Getty,** which specializes in Greek and Roman antiquities and European paintings; the **Los Angeles County Museum of Art (LACMA),** which is undergoing a redesign and holds masterpieces by Rembrandt, Degas, and Magritte as well as one of the finest collections of Islamic art in the world; and the **Museum of Contemporary Art (MOCA) at the Geffen Contemporary,** which has two locations and a collection that includes Warhol, Pollack, and De Kooning, plus conceptual installations.

Then there are the specialty museums, such as the **Autry Museum of Western Heritage,** the legacy of the Singing Cowboy himself; the **Japanese American National Museum,** which includes a moving reconstruction of an actual building from a Japanese relocation camp; the **Museum of Tolerance,** which offers a look at prejudice and intolerance through the ages; the **California ScienCenter,** a wonderful hands-on science museum; and the **Petersen Automotive Museum,** a paean to the freeway's favorite accessory, the car.

Pillow Talk and Fast Food

Los Angeles is spread out, so no matter where you stay, you'll probably be driving (or taking some other means of transportation) to get to the major sightseeing spots. Unlike quainter places, such as Santa Fe or New Orleans, Los Angeles has few atmospheric B&Bs or cunning little inns. What it does have are many standard-issue hotel rooms. You can find a measure of individuality, however, by staying at one of the venerable Old Hollywood establishments (such as the **Hollywood Roosevelt**, said to be haunted by Marilyn Monroe) or such hipster spots as West Hollywood's the **Standard** (where you can schedule a tattoo). Or, if you have buckets of money, you can stay where the movie stars stay, in the cream-colored suites with the champagne on ice, the 300-thread-count sheets, and the Egyptian-cotton towels. Or not.

As for food, we are happy as punch to tell you that you don't have to *spend* like a movie star to eat like a movie star. Oh, sure, you can spring for a four-star meal at **Spago Beverly Hills** or **Matsuhisa,** but you can eat very well in any number of inexpensive places all over the city — and often brilliantly. Among our favorites are **Zankou Chicken,** a hole-in-the-wall joint with perfect roast chicken, **Sanamluang Cafe,** for scrumptious Thai noodles, and **Pink's,** a famously dumpy little hot-dog stand in West Hollywood, where a line of people stand day and night to get their hands on one of the divine hot dogs. And L.A. wouldn't be L.A. without the quintessential **old-school restaurants,** where you can order a ring-a-ding-ding martini and a slab of red meat from crusty old waiters in dark wood-paneled environs. Need we say: Meet us at **Musso & Frank.**

Let Me Entertain You

L.A. truly rocks. Nightlife in the City of Angels ranges from family-style sporting events like an evening at the **Staples Center** cheering on the world champion L.A. Lakers, to classical concerts under the stars at the **Hollywood Bowl** (the Beatles played here!), to finding your way past the velvet ropes into club land. Rock historians will have a field day in L.A., visiting such seminal '60s and '70s clubs as the **Roxy, the Whisky a Go-Go,** and **the Troubadour.** You'll find saucy places to dance to any kind of music, as well as elegant cocktail lounges and real dive bars (but look who's sitting on the barstool next to you!). And don't forget the opportunities to see major plays and musicals (**the Music Center, the Mark Taper Forum, the Actors' Gang**), symphony (**the Los Angeles Philharmonic,** in its new home at the Walt Disney Concert Hall), and opera (**the Los Angeles Opera,** at the Dorothy Chandler Pavilion).

The Happiest Place on Earth

Walt's Folly, they called it, and while it isn't as shiny and sprawling as its sister resort in Orlando, it's still here, the original Disney park, sprung from the fertile imagination of cartoonist Walt Disney back in 1955. And it's now the **Disneyland Resort,** a formidable enterprise consisting of two theme parks (including the latest, **California Adventure**), three hotels, a big shopping center, and lots of interesting restaurants. We'll give you the lowdown on where to stay, where to eat, which rides are still the most fun (and which your daredevil kids will brag most about), and how to avoid showing up with the rest of the Western World.

Chapter 2

Deciding When to Go

● ●

In This Chapter

▶ Los Angeles in fall, winter, spring, and summer

▶ L.A. calendar of events

● ●

*T*here really isn't a bad time to visit L.A. — you can expect 350 cloudless, comfortable days a year. But deciding *when* you want to visit likely depends on factors other than mere weather conditions. You may want to breeze into town when the big events are on, or when hotel rates are at their most reasonable, or when you simply need a respite from the winter blahs. But no matter what time of year you come to L.A., you'll have no trouble finding plenty of activities and events to entertain you.

The Secrets of the Seasons

People are fond of complaining that Los Angeles has no seasons. Sure, certain flowers bloom all year long, but the seasonal changes are there — they're just subtle, that's all. In the winter, the trees are bare (well, not the palm trees), and spring looks like spring almost anywhere.

If it's going to rain — and odds are, it won't, unless another El Niño snakes its way out of the tropics — it's most likely going to happen in spring. Even then, heavy rainstorms are unusual.

It can get nippy in winter — oh, not Minnesota, 40-degrees-below-zero nippy — but it can get down in the 20s at night, so bring a coat if you visit in the cool months. A light wrap is always a good idea, thanks to temperatures that can flit annoyingly from 80 during the day to 50 at night.

Fall can bring the *Santa Anas,* the surprisingly strong, warm winds that are a bane to firefighters. And summer brings the real heat, and with that often real smog. Get in the car and head to the beach along with everyone else.

Note also that the Westside neighborhoods (Santa Monica, Brentwood, Pacific Palisades, and even Westwood) always seem to be 20 degrees (or more) cooler than Hollywood, Pasadena, and the Valley (the latter two are the hottest places in the metropolitan area). We've spent many a day sweltering in 90-degree weather on the Eastside and then traveled west, only to find it 62 and foggy. Go figure. Thank the ocean breezes.

Autumn serenade

Autumn is a fine time to consider a trip to Los Angeles because

- ✔ The tourist season slows down around the end of September and remains that way for some months to come.
- ✔ Rain is virtually nonexistent.

But on the other hand

- ✔ Summer doesn't really end until after September (and sometimes it pops up again in October), which means that it can be quite hot. We mean triple-digit hot — sometimes a record heat of 115 degrees.
- ✔ Fall brings the strong *Santa Anas* winds, which play havoc with fire.

Winter wonderland

Winter is an absolutely wonderful time to come to Los Angeles because

- ✔ It's a slow time, tourist-wise, and hotel rates can be a bargain.
- ✔ The weather is fabulous: crisp and clear. Okay, it can rain, and there can be wind, but those elements just blow away the smog and haze, leaving the landscape looking crisp and perfect.

  The mountains appear to be cut from glass, and the palm trees stand stark against the sky, which is blue blue blue, except when puffy cloud formations add to the extraordinary look of things. This is the time for mountains-to-the-sea views.

  It can get a bit nippy, yes, but that's relative, and besides, within a day or two, it might be in the 80s again. Or at least in the 70s. If you experience an L.A. winter, you'll understand why so many people moved here in the first place, and why they are loathe to leave.

- ✔ It's whale-watching season! The Pacific gray whales make their annual migration, providing many opportunities to watch 'em frolic.
- ✔ Cold or even drizzly weekdays are the best time to visit theme parks like Disneyland — you can practically have the place to yourself!

But keep in mind that

- ✔ The notorious Santa Ana winds, which crop up from October through February, are likely to hit their peak during this season, with gusts up to 50 mph in some places and maybe even higher in the Santa Ana mountain foothills. The winds make some people nuts, because they're warm yet breezy and can make travel into other parts of Southern California tricky. In fact, they've been known to blow over semis in certain mountain passes.

- ✔ The Pacific is never very temperate, but that matters more on cold days than when steamy triple-digit temperatures are in play. And the winter ocean may well be fogbound much of the day, anyway. So you can forget about swimming in the ocean.

- ✔ Although the tourist season is slow, it does pick up during Christmas and the New Year's holidays (when you may be more likely to travel, especially if you have kids), because lots of people come to town for the Tournament of Roses Parade and the Rose Bowl. And you will likely have to contend with passels of school-children visiting museums and so forth.

Spring in your step

Spring is another delightful time in Los Angeles because

- ✔ It's Oscar time! The Academy Awards, in its new home at the Kodak Theatre, honors the best in film with a high-wattage display of star power every year around the end of March or early April.

- ✔ Temperatures are moderate, and so are the crowds.

- ✔ Blooms are bustin' out all over, not the least of which are the jacaranda trees with their light purple blossoms. They bloom in May, turning into purple puffballs and raining purple snow, a sight that regularly reconciles even the grouchiest driver to the slow-ness of her commute. Plus, the hills are green, and birds are out in abundance.

- ✔ There still can be snow up in the mountains, which means that you can ski in your bikini. Really. Or you can just go to watch snow bunnies ski in their bikinis. Really.

On the other hand

- ✔ It never rains in southern California, except when it *does,* and when it does, the streets can (and often do) flood, traffic snarls, and it's darn wet. Yes, it is. And it's more likely to happen at this time of year.

- ✔ Speaking of weather, because summer lasts so long, it's only rea-sonable that it shouldn't start too soon, and many unsuspecting tourists may find themselves shivering in what locals call the "June gloom." It's cold. Foggy. Unfair.

Summer in the city

Summer is our least favorite time but perhaps the best for you because

- ✔ The kids are out of school, so when else can you travel?
- ✔ It's warm, and you did come here to go to the beach, didn't you?

But then again

- ✔ Heavens above, can it be hot. Dry heat, sure, but who cares? This isn't predictable, and it may only be a few days during the entire summer, but sheesh. . . .
- ✔ With summer comes the smog — in inescapable layers. Blech. In fact, entire mountain ranges can disappear in the haze. Los Angeles looks pretty tawdry this time of year.
- ✔ Almost everyone heads to the beach to escape the heat. Expect to battle for towel space on the sand.
- ✔ Speaking of everyone, that includes everyone with kids. Crowds. Lots of 'em.

Los Angeles Calendar of Events

Los Angeles is a festive place any time of year, but some extra-special occasions stand out. Here are some of the city's biggest events to mark on your calendar.

January

The granddaddy of all parades is the **Tournament of Roses Parade,** and New Year's Day is Pasadena's moment to shine — and bloom — because all the floats are constructed out of natural products, mostly flowers. The parade features marching bands, costumed horseback riders, and other entries, but it's the floats that matter. And if you've seen them only on TV, honestly, you've never really seen them. It's well worth coming to L.A. just to witness this spectacle in person, but you won't be alone; a million or more folks line up on the parade route, many of them spending the night to secure their patch of sidewalk, which makes for one noisy, memorable New Year's Eve party. Call ☎ 626-449-4100 or check out www.tournamentofroses.com for more details. January 1.

March

Twenty-six miles and it's a hoot; sure, the guys (and gals) out front are streamlined and serious, but behind them are thousands of participants, some dressed like Elvis or in other pieces of whimsy. You can run or walk the **Los Angeles Marathon;** some even bike it or just line the route (which starts in downtown L.A. and hits most of Hollywood and other scenic bits) and cheer everyone on. Call ☎ **310-444-5544** or go to www. lamarathon.com for information. Early March.

Just an hour or so north of L.A. lies the Antelope Valley California Poppy Reserve, where, during the springtime **California Poppy Blooming Season,** miles of hillside blaze with vibrant, dazzling color. Visit during the **California Poppy Festival,** usually held in April. For information and directions, call ☎ **805-724-1180** or go to www.poppyfestival.com. Mid-March through mid-May.

The **Academy of Motion Picture Arts and Sciences Awards** — that's the Oscars to you and me — is held in March. For its biggest, most self-congratulatory day, the town turns topsy-turvy, so don't expect to get any attention from any serious facialist, manicurist, stylist, or clothier, and don't look to get a really good hotel room, either (but if you do find one, you can bet that you'll have some cover-boy neighbors). The Academy's new home is the Kodak Theatre, in the Hollywood-Highland Complex. Go to www.oscars.org and read all about it. Last Sunday in March.

April

Look both ways before you cross the street in Long Beach, because Indy-level drivers from around the world race in and through the streets during the **Toyota Grand Prix.** For information, call ☎ **888-82-SPEED** (888-827-7333) or 562-981-2600, or go to www.longbeachgp.com. Mid-April.

May

The **Venice Art Walk** is a festival of art and music, with self- and docent-guided tours of local studios, galleries, and even collectors' homes, plus installations, auctions, and receptions. Proceeds benefit the Venice Family Clinic. Call ☎ **310-392-8630** or go to www.vfc.net. Mid-May.

June

West Hollywood, also known as "Christopher Street West," rivals the Castro in San Francisco for the size of its gay and lesbian community. For more than 30 years, the celebration of **Gay & Lesbian Pride Day** has gotten bigger and bigger. (Local gays complain that it's turned into Gay Pride Week.) The parades, dance tents, food booths, costumes, and general revelry must be seen to be believed. Call ☎ **323-658-8700.** Last weekend in June.

July

For more than 60 years, the **Festival of the Arts** and **Pageant of the Masters** have been held in Laguna Beach. The incredible Pageant of the Masters re-creates works of art using live people; it sounds goofy, but it's also astonishing. The Festival of the Arts is a juried (meaning that the artists are chosen by a selection committee) fine-arts show, with 150 exhibitors.

Across the street, local artists and craftspeople are showcased all summer long at the **Sawdust Art Festival** (Internet: www.sawdustart festival.org). Tickets for the Festival of the Arts and the Pageant of the Masters must be arranged in advance; call ☎ **800-487-FEST** (800-487-3378) or 949-494-1145, or go to www.foapom.com. July through August.

August

For more than 30 years, in an effort (and a successful one) to promote neighborhood harmony, the **Sunset Junction Street Fair** (located at 3600 through 4200 Sunset Boulevard) has brought together all the disparate elements of Silver Lake into one music-loving, snack-chewing, mingling, sweaty, harmonious whole. The Latino gang members and homosexual leather boys, not to mention artists, punks, and ordinary families, all come together for two days to enjoy three stages of local music, carnival rides, and 200 booths of crafts, food (fabulous Mexican, wonderful Thai, and our new favorite, bacon-wrapped hot dogs; see Chapter 15), and community service and outreach. It gets really crowded later in the day, and it's almost always hot, but it's a hoot. (You can find street parking, but it fills up, so you may have a hike to the actual site. Plus, the later in the day, the more crowded it gets.) For more information, call ☎ **323-661-7771** or go to www.sunsetjunction. org. Toward the end of August.

September

It's got pig races. Oh, and agriculture and cake-baking contests, and all that sort of thing, only on a massive scale, at the **Los Angeles County Fair,** one of the largest county fairs in the world. It's held in Pomona, which is 30 miles east of downtown Los Angeles. Call ☎ **909-623-3111** or go to www.fairplex.com. Throughout September.

October

The American Film Institute's **Los Angeles International Film Festival** is not quite as prestigious and groundbreaking as it used to be (or so hardcore film buffs sniff), but it's still a must for those with an interest in cinema, and it usually features early viewings of major works. Call ☎ 323-856-7707 or go to www.afifest.com. Late October or early November.

November

It's the *other* Pasadena parade. Started as a response to the Tournament of Roses Parade on New Year's Day, the **Doo Dah Parade** features such memorable entries as the Synchronized Marching Briefcase Drill Team, the Precision BBQ Team, the Hello Dalai Lamas, Queen Tequila Mockingbird, and the Little Old Ladies from Hooters. An utter, utter hoot. Call ☎ **626-440-7379.** Usually Thanksgiving weekend.

As kids, we would stay up late to catch Santa, who always brought up the rear of the **Hollywood Christmas Parade.** Now we watch the parade to mock the B-level celebs who ride in it. Call ☎ **323-469-2337.** Sunday after Thanksgiving.

Chapter 3

Planning Your Budget

• •

In This Chapter

▶ Building a budget for your trip to L.A.

▶ Using traveler's checks and credit cards

▶ Discovering cost-cutting tips for the savvy traveler

• •

*L*os Angeles isn't a breathtakingly expensive town. But hotel rooms can be costly (though we provide some economical alternatives; see Chapter 8), and dining out can take a bite out of your wallet (but you can enjoy some great cheap eats; see Chapters 14 and 15). In this chapter, we lay out the major expenditures for your trip to Los Angeles. Now it's up to you to decide how you want to spend your money. (The budget worksheet at the back of the book can help.)

Adding Up the Elements

Your major, hard-to-avoid costs come in the form of hotel rooms, restaurants, transportation, and admissions to certain high-priced attractions (check out Part VII for info on one of the major attractions — Disneyland). Keep on the alert for "hidden" costs, such as **state and city hotel taxes** that range from 12% to 17% in southern California), **sales tax** (8% in the state), and **parking charges** (which we explain in the "Transportation" section later in this chapter).

Accommodations

A constant theme in your trip planning will be "the Internet is your friend." Many hotels (and other establishments) offer special deals available only through the Web, and we strongly advise that you check there before booking a room. You can also use the information you find to bargain a room price down, especially during the slow seasons — which is when you ought to come to L.A. anyway, because prices drop dramatically. And if you aren't bringing children along, you may want to consider staying Downtown, where very nice hotel rooms go for considerably less than rooms in other areas on weekend nights.

Transportation

The costs for getting into the city vary according to your mode of transportation. From Los Angeles International Airport (LAX), you either drive yourself in a **rental car,** take a **cab, car service,** or **shuttle,** or take **public transportation.** Cabs charge an airport fee of $2.50 in addition to a $2 pickup fee and $2 per mile (plus tip). The shuttles and vans that operate to and from the airport charge on a per-person basis: from LAX to Santa Monica, for example, it's $18 (plus a $2 tip). A car service typically charges fares of around $40 to $45 (including a $1.50 airport pickup fee), depending on where you are dropped off. You can also take public transportation on the Metropolitan Transit Authority (MTA) combination light rail/bus system to and from LAX for less than $2.

Transportation around the city is a little bit tricky. We recommend **renting a car.** Finding the best rental-car deal just means putting in some time — call travel agents, search the Web, call car-rental companies yourself, and pit them all against each other.

But even if you get a good deal, you're still going to have **parking costs** — lots around town charge from $2 to $20, depending on location and time of day or night. Keep in mind that some lots, near or directly connected with certain attractions, offer discounts in the form of rebates: If you bring back a ticket from the attraction, you can get $2 or so back. (A current example is a lot north of Hollywood on Las Palmas, on the west side of the street, which offers rebates following screenings at the Egyptian Theatre.)

Read signs carefully, try to drive about and compare and contrast options, or just park a ways away and hoof it (which may not work well at night in Downtown, where it's dark and creepy, or in West Hollywood, where the parking restrictions are fierce). Or you can just be brave and try to rely entirely on **public transportation.** This is a fine idea if you plan on doing limited travel around the city; the buses work great in Santa Monica, and the subway works swell between Hollywood, Universal City, and Downtown. You can also do some advance trip planning through the Metropolitan Transit Authority's Web site (Internet: www.mta.net) or by giving them a call (☎ 800-COMMUTE/266-6883). On the Web site, just plug in when and where you want to go, and your designated route pops up, complete with bus and subway lines. In Downtown, in addition to the subway, you can take the DASH, a commuter bus that flits around the entire area and costs only 25¢ one way, including one transfer.

If you intend to rely on cabs to get around, keep in mind that cabs charge a $2 pickup fee and then $2 per mile, and the meter keeps ticking if you get stuck in traffic, a common occurrence. Plus, you should give your cab driver a 10% to 15% tip.

Dining

Food in L.A. need not set your budget back; we constantly assert that the best food in town comes in the form of cheap ethnic places and other hole-in-the-wall joints. We've made a number of suggestions in Chapters 14 and 15, but you can also consider purchasing *Hungry? Los Angeles: A Guide to the City's Greatest Diners, Dives, Cafeterias and Coffee Shops!* edited by Kristin L. Petersen (Really Great Books), a handy guide to all the eateries that are affordable and savory in a town that has an incredible variety of dining cultures.

Attractions

Prices for attractions vary, of course. The behemoth **Disneyland** is pretty costly (more on that in Part VII), but check the park Web site at http://disney.go.com/Disneyland before you go. As we write this book, multi-day Hopper Passes are being offered at a substantial discount, and other offers come up all the time. It's practically worth designing a trip around the times these great deals come up. Package tours can help with that expense as well. Also, **Universal Studios** (Internet: www.universalstudioshollywood.com), itself none too cheap, is currently offering, for $10 over regular admission, a month-long pass that includes admission to a number of local sights. It pays for itself with just one visit to the Gene Autry Museum, for example.

But not all local attractions hit the middle double digits. In fact, some are downright cheap. One of the city's top attractions, the **Getty Museum,** is free, though there is a $5-per-car parking fee. Only the fit can walk up to the museum, but you can take advantage of the free park-and-ride service from a lot at Sepulveda Boulevard and Constitution Avenue (located just north of Wilshire Boulevard). A couple of local bus lines also service it (but by then, depending on how many people you're paying for, you may as well take your car in). The **California ScienCenter** is free, and so are the **La Brea Tar Pits,** though the museum attached is not. The **Museum of Jurassic Technology** costs a mere $4 for adults over 21, and kids under 18 are only charged $1 at the Los Angeles County Museum of Art.

And speaking of free, the **beach** is, though nearby parking is not. So just walk from your hotel or your street parking a few blocks away. The **Venice Boardwalk** and **Santa Monica Pier** are also free, and Thursday nights during the summer, free concerts are held at the latter. All summer long, mostly at night, but not exclusively, free concerts are held at the **California Plaza** near the Museum of Contemporary Art. Again, parking will likely be problematic, so just take the MetroRail. And way-high-up seats for many summertime **Hollywood Bowl** concerts cost only $2. (All these prices are subject to change, of course, but not by too terribly much.)

Shopping

This category depends entirely on you, your budget, and those things you absolutely can't live without. You can pay full price here almost anytime of the year, but know that the major department stores and malls tend to have sales most holiday weekends (Labor Day, President's Day, Memorial Day, and so forth) and back-to-school events beginning mid-August. The *Los Angeles Times* is crammed with full-page ads just before these events, often with coupons that promise still more discounts.

The biggest shopping event of the year is the **Divine Design sale,** held the first week in December. Hundreds of clothing, housewares, and accessory designers donate extra goods and samples, which are then offered to the public at steep discounts that sharply decline each day. Nervy shoppers try to stick it out as long as they can, watching the prices plummet from 20% discounts to 75% off by the last day; call ☎ **323-845-1800** for more information.

If you're looking for unique bargains, check out the flea markets and vintage-wear shops throughout the city. Even the **Farmer's Market** has many stands that feature wonderful fresh breads, prepared foods, and even clothing to take home.

Nightlife

This category depends on how much nightlife you want to pursue when you're in town. If you plan to attend any big events, such as the symphony, opera, or major theater offerings, keep in mind that if you purchase your tickets through Ticketmaster, you pay a hefty per-ticket handling fee that can be anywhere from $2 to $15 extra per ticket.

Cover prices vary from nightclub to nightclub (from $5 to $20), but remember that parking rates get steeper as the week progresses, and you can expect to pay up to $30 on the Sunset Strip Friday and Saturday nights. Taking a cab might be the smarter way to visit clubland.

Paying Your Way

Most travelers these days use a combination of traveler's checks, plastic, or cash to cover their expenses in L.A. Certainly, having a credit card makes sense if you plan to reserve a hotel room or rent a car (although we list some rental-car companies that don't require credit cards; see Chapter 9). And with the prevalence of ATMs throughout the city, cash is easy to access on the spot. Here is a quick look at all the options at your disposal to pay for your vacation. (For more on ATMS and getting cash where you need it in Los Angeles, see Chapter 12.)

Traveler's checks

Traveler's checks are something of an anachronism from the days before ATMs made cash accessible at any time. Traveler's checks used to be the only sound alternative to traveling with dangerously large amounts of cash. They were as reliable as currency but, unlike cash, could be replaced if lost or stolen.

These days, traveler's checks don't seem as necessary, because most cities have 24-hour ATMs that allow you to withdraw cash as needed. However, you're likely to be charged an ATM withdrawal fee if the bank is not your own, so if you're withdrawing money every day, you may be better off with traveler's checks — provided that you don't mind showing identification every time you want to cash one.

You can get traveler's checks at almost any bank. **American Express** offers denominations of $20, $50, $100, $500, and (for cardholders only) $1,000. You pay a service charge ranging from 1% to 4%. You can also get American Express traveler's checks over the phone by calling ☎ **800-221-7282;** American Express Gold and Platinum cardholders who use this number are exempt from the 1% fee. AAA members can obtain checks without a fee at most AAA offices.

Visa offers traveler's checks at Citibank locations nationwide, as well as at several other banks. The service charge ranges between 1.5% and 2%. Call ☎ **800-732-1322** for information. **MasterCard** also offers traveler's checks. Call ☎ **800-223-9920** for a location near you.

Credit cards

Credit cards are invaluable when traveling. They are a safe way to carry money and provide a convenient record of all your expenses. You can also withdraw cash advances from your credit cards at any bank (though you'll start paying hefty interest on the advance the moment you receive the cash). At most banks, you don't even need to go to a teller; you can get a cash advance at the ATM if you know your PIN access number. If you've forgotten your PIN number, or if you didn't know you had one, call the number on the back of your credit card and ask the bank to send it to you. It usually takes 5 to 7 business days, though some banks will provide the number over the phone if you tell them your mother's maiden name or pass some other kind of security clearance.

Cutting Costs

Even those of us with very deep pockets don't like to throw money away. There's a little cost-cutter in everyone. Here are some savvy money-saving tips for chipping away at your vacation budget.

✔ **Visit the city during the slower seasons.** The time of year you decide to visit may affect your bargaining power more than anything else. During the peak season — basically summer — when a hotel is booked, management is less likely to extend discount rates or value-added package deals. In the slower season — winter — when capacity is down, they're often willing to negotiate.

✔ **Take advantage of membership programs.** AAA, AARP, or frequent flier/traveler programs often qualify you for discounted rates. You may also qualify for corporate, student, or senior discounts even if you're not an AARP member (though we highly recommend joining; see Chapter 4 for details). Members of the military or those with government jobs may also qualify for price breaks.

✔ **Ask about package deals.** Even if you're not traveling on an all-inclusive package, you may be able to take advantage of packages offered by hotels and condos directly. See Chapter 5 for more details on package tours.

✔ **Call the hotel direct in addition to going through central reservations.** See which one gives you the better deal. Sometimes, the local reservation clerk knows about packages or special rates that the hotel may neglect to tell the central booking line.

✔ **Surf the Web to save.** A surprising number of hotels advertise great value packages via their Web sites, and some hotels offer Internet-only special rates. In addition to surfing individual hotel sites, check out the many Internet reservations services that have cropped up. For recommended reservations services, see Chapter 7.

✔ **Consult a reliable travel agent.** A travel agent is often able to negotiate a better price with certain hotels and assemble a complete travel package that is a better value than you can get on your own. Even if you book your own airfare, you may want to contact a travel agent to price your hotel. On the other hand, hotels, condos, and even B&Bs are sometimes willing to discount your rate as much as 30% — the amount they'd otherwise pay an agent in commissions — if you book direct. For more advice on the pros and cons of using a professional go-between, see Chapter 5.

✔ **Book your rental car at weekly rates when possible.** Weekly rates are generally considerably lower than daily rates. See Chapter 9 for details.

✔ **Ask if the kids can stay in your room.** A room with two double beds usually doesn't cost any more than one with a king-size bed, and most hotels don't charge an extra-person rate if the additional person is your kid.

✔ **Include hidden costs in your budget.** Don't forget to budget for tips for service providers like cab drivers and bellhops, tacked-on hotel taxes (12% to 18%), state and county sales tax (8.25%), and little incidentals like soft drinks or newspapers.

Chapter 4

Planning Ahead for Special Travel Needs

• •

In This Chapter

▶ Traveling to L.A. with the family

▶ Discovering special deals for seniors

▶ Enabling the disabled

▶ Finding gay-friendly resources and communities

• •

*L*os Angeles puts out the welcome mat for visitors of all stripes, sizes, and ages. This chapter gives you some special travel tips and invaluable resource information for travelers with special needs or preferences.

Advice for Families

You can relax; Los Angeles is a fine place to bring children. After all, it offers, among so many other things, a really big beach, a pier, a few amusement parks (including one called Disneyland), a nice zoo, and recreational parks galore. Yes, L.A. is kid-friendly, and if you bring children, you won't be alone; babies are the new hip accessories here!

Note: Throughout this book, we mark the best hotels, restaurants, and activities for children with a Kid Friendly icon.

Most kids, unless they loathe water, will want to spend a great deal of time at the **beach.** You can vary this potentially dull routine with jaunts to the **Santa Monica Pier,** with its shops, food stalls, and mini-amusement park, plus one delightful merry-go-round. You can also stroll on the **Venice Ocean Front Walk,** which does have its freak quotient (from street musicians to hippies hawking wares), but the oddballs are harmless, and they add to the people-watching fun. Plus, it's a great place for roller/in-line skating, biking, and more.

Los Angeles has quite a few **parks,** from some small municipal ones (the best are in Santa Monica and Beverly Hills; try www.citysearch.com for a complete list of options or go to www.ci.la.ca.us/RAP for the City of Los Angeles's Department of Parks and Recreations individual listing) to giant places like Griffith Park, the largest municipal park in the country. In addition to acres of Santa Monica mountains to hike through, Griffith Park has a lovely merry-go-round and Travel Town, a place where kids ride little trains and sometimes ponies.

Of course, there is **Disneyland;** its appeal to kids is so massive and legendary that it's hard to sum up in a few pithy words. Suffice to say that every kid ought to go at least once, as part of his or her birthright. (The chapters in Part VII explore this attraction.)

Your kid may or may not be into **museums,** but keep in mind that the Getty has an *entire section* devoted to children's activities (some hands-on approaches to art), while the California Science Center is designed just for kids. The Natural History Museum is getting a bit musty, but the Discovery Room is still great fun and contains live snakes.

Families are probably better off basing themselves in **Santa Monica;** it's more pedestrian friendly (to say nothing of beach-accessible), and you'll see as many locals (accompanied by kids themselves, likely as not) as tourists, whereas Hollywood is mostly tourists (and few kids), and West Hollywood is more for the shopper or well-dressed mom seeking her yoga and cappuccino fix. Downtown really isn't for families.

Keep in mind that L.A. is spread out, and it does take a bit of driving to get from, say, Santa Monica to Hollywood (and Disneyland takes at least an hour), distances that can seem like an eternity to kids. So prep them for a certain amount of driving time as best you can, and be sure to have on hand their favorite toys, games, and road snacks.

Advice for Seniors

Oh, the jokes we can make about seniors in L.A. (like "they were outlawed along with smoking"), but we won't. It's true that people here don't seem to age properly, thanks in part to a religious commitment to exercise and healthy diet, but even more so to a commitment to keeping plastic surgeons in business. You may feel that you're the oldest person in L.A., but that's only because the woman next to you, who looks 40, is keeping up appearances through the magic of special effects. She's really 80.

But by and large, L.A. is a perfectly enjoyable destination for the visiting senior, apart from the heartbreak of how the town has neglected its heritage. Too many fantastic monuments to the Golden Age of Hollywood are gone, and there is always that moment of shock as you read off names on the Walk of Fame or slip your foot into a cement print at Grauman's, and you hear a teen or twenty-something ask, "So who's John Wayne?" But then you notice the sun and how good it feels on your skin, and you think, "Oh, whatever."

Seniors have a wealth of travel resources to choose from in Los Angeles. Most attractions in the city offer senior discounts, as do public transportation and movie theaters. Members of **AARP** (601 E St. NW, Washington, DC 20049; ☎ **800-424-3410** or 202-434-2277; Internet: www.aarp.org) get discounts on hotels, airfares, and car rentals. Anyone over 50 can join.

A variety of intriguing and entertaining senior study trips are offered by the **Center for Studies of the Future,** a local affiliate of **Elderhostel** (☎ **877-426-8056;** Internet: www.elderhostel.org), the well-known nonprofit organization that arranges study programs for those aged 55 and over (and a spouse or companion of any age) in the United States and in more than 80 countries around the world. Most courses last from five to seven days and may include airfare, accommodations in hotels or university dormitories (during the summer), meals, and tuition.

Grand Circle Travel (☎ **800-221-2610** or 617-350-7500; Internet: www.gct.com) offers package deals for the 50-plus market, mostly of the tour-bus variety, with free trips thrown in for those who organize groups of 10 or more.

Advice for Travelers with Disabilities

Los Angeles is a very, *very* politically correct town, so every place, but *every place,* is handicap accessible. Sidewalks have dips at the curb to ease wheelchair movement; restaurants and hotels all come properly equipped. Those in wheelchairs more or less have to deal with just the usual problems, plus, of course, the drag of being in a crowd.

The main problem is that this is not a pedestrian-friendly town; you have to rely on a car to get everywhere. To this end, we suggest staying in Santa Monica or Beverly Hills, where the sightseeing is less reliant on cars. The Third Street Promenade in Santa Monica is an outdoor street closed to vehicular traffic, and most pleasant to be on, while both Santa Monica and Venice have sidewalks and pathways along the beaches.

Disabled travelers can get more general information from the **Society for Accessible Travel and Hospitality** (☎ **212-447-7284;** Fax: 212-725-8253; Internet: www.sath.org), which offers travel resources for all types of disabilities and informed recommendations on destinations, access guides, travel agents, tour operators, vehicle rentals, and companion services. Annual membership costs $45 for adults and $30 for seniors and students. **The American Foundation for the Blind** (☎ **800-232-5463;** Internet: www.afb.org) provides information on traveling with Seeing Eye dogs. **The Moss Rehab Hospital** (☎ **215-456-9603;** Internet: www.mossresourcenet.org) provides friendly, helpful phone assistance to all disabled travelers through its **Travel Information Service.**

For customized tours, **Flying Wheels Travel** (☎ 800-535-6790; Internet: www.flyingwheelstravel.com) offers escorted tours and cruises that emphasize sports and private tours in minivans with lifts.

Mobility International USA (☎ 541-343-1284; Internet: www.miusa.org) publishes *A World of Options,* a 658-page book of resources, covering everything from biking trips to scuba outfitters, and a biannual newsletter, *Over the Rainbow.* Annual membership is $35.

Advice for Gay and Lesbian Travelers

Los Angeles probably ranks behind only New York City and San Francisco (and then only barely) on the gay-friendly meter. In fact, the city of **West Hollywood,** located right in the heart of Los Angeles, is predominantly gay (and known as Christopher Street West, after the longtime heart of gay Manhattan). Here you find the bulk of the gay bars, restaurants, shopping, and resources, and it is here that an annual Gay Pride Parade of considerable dimensions is held. The nightlife in West Hollywood is quite fabulous, as you can well imagine.

Other gay-friendly neighborhoods include the **Silverlake** area, just east of Hollywood and north of Downtown; **Studio City/North Hollywood**, in the San Fernando Valley; and portions of **Long Beach.** But really, you can feel free to hold hands anywhere you're likely to go in the city.

The **Los Angeles Gay and Lesbian Center** (1625 N. Schrader Blvd., Los Angeles; ☎ 323-993-7400; Internet: www.laglc.org/home.htm; open from 9 a.m. to 9 p.m. weekdays) can provide a full range of services, from finding the most popular nightclub to counseling and HIV assistance.

After that, your best bet for finding what's going on in Los Angeles is to pick up one of the free local gay publications such as *Frontiers, In,* and *Odyssey.* They're packed with directories, events, maps, and more, and you can find them at most of the gay bars in town.

Online, start at www.westhollywood.com, a fairly comprehensive compendium of events, directories, classifieds, and more. You can also visit the *Los Angeles Times* at www.latimes.com/extras/outinla/index.html. The paper's "Out in LA" section is certainly not as "complete" as they bill it to be, but it's a good place to start.

For more general travel information and packages, the **International Gay & Lesbian Travel Association** (IGLTA) (☎ 800-448-8550 or 954-776-2626; Fax: 954-776-3303; Internet: www.iglta.org) links travelers up with gay-friendly hoteliers, tour operators, and airline and cruise-line representatives. It offers monthly newsletters, marketing mailings, and a membership directory that's updated once a year. Membership is $150 yearly, plus a $100 administration fee for new members.

Part II
Ironing Out the Details

The 5th Wave   By Rich Tennant

"The closest hotel room to the Santa Monica Pier I can get you for that price is in Bakersfield."

In this part . . .

*H*ere we discuss all your travel options: choosing a method of transportation, working with a travel agent, whether to go the package-tour route, and finalizing those little last-minute details like making dinner reservations at hot local restaurants, packing the right clothes, and weighing your travel insurance options. No glamour here — but it's all necessary.

Chapter 5

Getting to Los Angeles

• •

• •

*Y*ou've bought the *Risky Business* shades, and you've perfected the hipster slouch. You may have even changed your name to oh, say, Stone or Tiffany. Hey, now all you gotta do is get here! This chapter gives you all you need to know about finding your way to Los Angeles, along with a wealth of travel resources to help you arrive with little muss or fuss.

Finding a Travel Agent You Can Trust

A good travel agent is like a good mechanic or plumber — hard to find, but invaluable once you get the right person. Any travel agent can help you find a bargain airfare, hotel, or rental car. But a good travel agent will stop you from ruining your vacation by trying to save a few dollars. The best travel agents can tell you how much time you should budget for each destination, find you a cheap flight that doesn't require you to change planes three times on your way to Los Angeles, get you a hotel room with a view for the same price as a lesser room, arrange for a competitively priced rental car, and even give recommendations on restaurants.

In the past few years, more and more airlines and resorts have begun limiting or eliminating travel agent commissions altogether. The immediate result has been that travel agents don't bother booking these services unless the customer specifically requests them. In the long run, it may mean that travel agents will have to start charging customers for their services.

To track down the travel agent of your dreams, use these tips:

✔ **Ask friends.** Your best bet, of course, is a personal referral. If you have friends or relatives who have a travel agent they're happy with, start there.

✔ **Go with what you know.** If you're pleased with the service you get from the agency that books business travel at your workplace, ask if it also books personal travel. Also, because business travel tends to be booked in volume, a lot of the agencies that specialize in this kind of business act as consolidators for certain airlines or have access to other discounts that they can extend to you for your personal travel.

✔ **Go to the travel agent source.** If you can't get a good personal or business referral, contact the **American Society of Travel Agents** (Internet: www.astanet.com), the world's largest association of travel professionals, which can refer you to one of its local member agents. ASTA asks that all its member agents uphold a code of ethics, and it has its own consumer affairs department to handle complaints and help travelers mediate disputes with ASTA member agencies.

To narrow the field you may want to

✔ Look for an agent who specializes in planning vacations to your destination.

✔ Choose an agent who has been in business a while and has an established client base.

✔ Consider everything about the agent, from the appearance of his or her office to the agent's willingness to listen and answer questions.

The best agents want to establish a long-term relationship with a client, not just make one sale.

Choosing a Package Tour

Package tours are not the same thing as escorted tours. *Package tours* are simply a way to buy the airfare, accommodations, and other elements of your trip (such as car rentals, airport transfers, and sometimes even activities) at the same time and often at discounted prices — kind of like one-stop shopping.

Package tours do have their advantages — someone else does most of the arranging for you, and you almost always save money. But among the disadvantages are limited choices, such as where you stay (the hotels will be fine but unremarkable and are usually located more for the packager's convenience than for yours), or a fixed itinerary that doesn't allow for an extra day of shopping. Some packages offer a better class of hotels than others. Some offer the same hotels for lower prices than their competitors. Some offer flights on scheduled airlines while others book charters. In some packages, your choices of travel days may be limited. Some packages let you choose between escorted vacations and independent vacations; others allow you to add on a few guided excursions or escorted day trips (also at prices lower than if you booked them yourself) without booking an entirely escorted tour.

How to tell the deals from the duds

Once you start looking at packages, you're going to find that the sheer number of choices may overwhelm you — but don't let them. Use these tips to help you figure out the right package for you.

- ✔ **Do your homework.** Read through this guide and decide what attractions you want to visit and what type of accommodations you think you'll like. Compare the rack rates that we list in Chapter 6 against the discounted rates being offered by the packagers to see if you're actually being given a substantial savings.

- ✔ **Read the fine print.** Make sure that you know exactly what's included in the price you're being quoted, and what's not. Some packagers include airfare plus lots of extra discounts on restaurants and activities, while others don't even include airfare in the price.

- ✔ **Know what you're getting yourself into — and if you can get yourself out of it.** Before you commit to a package, make sure that you know how much flexibility you have. Some packagers require ironclad commitments, while others charge minimal fees for changes or cancellations. Ask about the packagers' restrictions and cancellations policies upfront.

Where to find the packager for you

The best place to start looking is the **travel section of your local Sunday newspaper.** Also check the ads in the back of **national travel magazines** like *Travel & Leisure, National Geographic Traveler,* and *Condé Nast Traveler.* Then call a few package tour companies and ask them to send you their brochures. The biggest **hotel chains** also offer packages. If you already know where you want to stay, call the hotel and ask if it offers land/air packages.

Airlines also often package their flights together with accommodations. Although you can book most airline packages directly with the airline itself, your local travel agent can also do it for you. Prices are usually comparable to what you can get from other packagers.

When you pick an airline, choose one that allows you to accumulate frequent-flier miles. Most airline packages reward you with miles based not only on the flight but also on all the dollars you spend — which can really add up and earn you credit toward your next vacation.

Package deals to Los Angeles

The following offer specific L.A. package deals. There are some bargains to be had, but you should always call and find out rates beforehand to make sure that the package is the more economical way to go.

✔ **American Airlines Vacations:** California packages have included Los Angeles and the beaches, with accommodations for two or more nights and optional sightseeing tours of Disneyland, Catalina, and Hollywood. Car rental and airport/hotel transfers are available (☎ 800-321-2121; Internet: www.aav1.aavacations.com).

✔ **American Express Vacation Packages:** American Express offers custom packaging through any of its retail outlets, or you can ask your American Express agent about special southern California packages (☎ 800-346-3607; Internet: www.americanexpress.com/travel).

✔ **Amtrak Vacations:** L.A. package includes round-trip Amtrak coach rail, moderate lodging for 2 nights, and a 4-hour sightseeing tour. Available options include Universal Studios Hollywood, Disneyland, and rental car (☎ 800-321-8684; Internet: www.amtrak.com).

✔ **Continental Airlines Vacations:** Includes round-trip airfare from select cities, hotel accommodations, economy rental car, plus discounts on admission to Autry Museum of Western Heritage, Movieland Wax Museum, and Ripley's Believe It or Not Museum. Optional features include Catalina Island Adventure Tour and admission to Universal Studios Hollywood, Disneyland, and Knott's Berry Farm (☎ 800-634-5555; Internet: www.coolvacations.com).

✔ **Southwest Airlines Vacations:** Packages include round-trip airfare, hotel accommodations for 2 to 14 nights, an Alamo economy rental car, and a FunBook discount coupon booklet. Optional features include airport/hotel transfers and passes for Universal Studios Hollywood and Disneyland (☎ 800-423-5683; Internet: www.southwestairlines.com).

✔ **United Vacations:** United Vacations offers a wide array of lodging options to fit individual taste and budget. California vacation packages include hotel accommodations, Alamo 2-door economy car rental, 10% off food, beverages, and merchandise, plus VIP seating at Planet Hollywood. Optional features include airport/hotel transfers and admission to Universal Studios Hollywood and Disneyland (☎ 888-854-3899; Internet: www.unitedvacations.com).

✔ **Universal Studios Hollywood Vacations:** Each package includes unlimited admission to Universal Studios Hollywood for the entire length of your stay; VIP priority entrance to Jurassic Park-The Ride, Back to the Future-The Ride, Backdraft, The E.T. Adventure, and the Backlot Tram Tour; hotel accommodations; and a Universal City Coupon Book. Optional airfare and rental car features are available. *Note:* This package may be a particularly good option for families, given how much kids tend to love Universal (☎ 800-224-3838; Internet: www.universalstudios.com).

✔ **US Airways Vacations:** Southern California packages include round-trip airfare, hotel accommodations for 2 to 21 nights, an Alamo rental car with upgrade, and lunch at Planet Hollywood with VIP seating (☎ 800-455-0123; Internet: www.usairways vacations.com).

Making Your Own Arrangements

A package tour may be just dandy for some folks. But others wouldn't dream of letting anyone else plan their trip. If you're a do-it-yourselfer, the following information can help you plot the perfect trip all on your own.

Who flies there?

The City of Angels is an international hub and thus is served by most major commercial airlines. Of the five airports in the Los Angeles area, most visitors fly in to Los Angeles International Airport (LAX) (☎ 310-646-5252; Internet: www.lawa.org/lax/laxframe.html).

Within North America

Airlines that fly within North America on regularly scheduled flights to and from Los Angeles at LAX are

✔ **Air Canada** (☎ 888-247-2262; Internet: www.aircanada.ca), which flies from Vancouver, Toronto, and Montreal

✔ **Alaska Airlines** (☎ 800-426-0333; Internet: www.alaskaair.com)

✔ **American Airlines** (☎ 800-433-7300; Internet: www.aa.com)

✔ **American Trans Air** (☎ 800-225-2995; Internet: www.ata.com)

✔ **America West Airlines** (☎ 800-235-9292; Internet: www.americawest.com)

✔ **Continental Airlines** (☎ 800-525-0280; Internet: www.continental.com)

✔ **Delta Air Lines** (☎ 800-221-1212; Internet: www.delta.com)

✔ **Frontier Airlines** (☎ 800-432-1359; Internet: `www.frontier airlines.com`)

✔ **Hawaiian Airlines** (☎ 800-367-5320; Internet: `www.hawaiian air.com`)

✔ **Midwest Express** (☎ 800-452-2022; Internet: `www.midwest express.com`)

✔ **Northwest Airlines** (☎ 800-225-2525; Internet: `www.nwa.com`)

✔ **Southwest Airlines** (☎ 800-435-9792; Internet: `www.southwest.com`)

✔ **Spirit Airlines** (☎ 800-772-7117; Internet: `www.spiritair.com`)

✔ **United Airlines** (☎ 800-241-6522; Internet: `www.united.com`)

✔ **US Airways** (☎ 800-428-4322; Internet: `www.usairways.com`)

International flights

From **Great Britain,** you can get regularly scheduled flights to Los Angeles on **American Airlines** and **United,** (contact information for both is in the preceding section), as well as the following:

✔ **British Airways** (☎ 800-247-9297 in the continental U.S. and ☎ 0345/222-111 or 0845/77-333-77 in Britain; Internet: `www.british-airways.com`)

✔ **Virgin Atlantic Airways** (☎ 800-862-8621 in the continental U.S and ☎ 0293/747-747 in Britain; Internet: `www.virgin-atlantic.com`)

✔ **Air New Zealand** (☎ 800-262-1234 or 800-262-2468 in the U.S.; ☎ 800-663-5494 in Canada; ☎ 0800/737-767 in New Zealand; Internet: `www.airnewzealand.com`)

From **Australia,** you can get regularly scheduled flights to Los Angeles from **Sydney** on carriers mentioned previously in this chapter, such as **American Airlines United** and **Air New Zealand,** as well as **Qantas** (☎ 800-227-4500 in the U.S. and ☎ 612/9691-3636 in Australia; Internet: `www.qantas.com`). From Melbourne, you can take **American Airlines** and **Qantas.** From **New Zealand,** you can get regularly scheduled flights to Los Angeles on **Air New Zealand, United,** and **Qantas.**

From **Canada,** you can get regularly scheduled flights to Los Angeles from **Vancouver** on **Air Canada, United, Alaska,** and **Northwest.** From **Toronto,** you can take **American Airlines** and **Air Canada.** From **Montreal,** you can take **Air Canada.** (Contact information for all these carriers is listed earlier in this chapter.)

Tips for getting the best airfare

These days, with a little know-how and advance planning, the independent traveler should have no trouble snagging a deal on airline tickets. Through the Internet alone, consumers have more options than ever in locating the best airfares, whether from airline Web sites or online travel and booking sites such as Travelocity. Here are some tips on how to get the best prices on airline tickets.

- **Book in advance and be flexible.** Passengers who can book their tickets long in advance, who can stay over Saturday night, or who are willing to travel on a Tuesday, Wednesday, or Thursday after 7 p.m., for example, will pay a fraction of the full fare. If your schedule is flexible, say so — ask if you can secure a cheaper fare by staying an extra day, by flying midweek, or by flying at less-trafficked hours. Buying in advance makes a big difference, as well: If you can book your airfare more than 21 days in advance, you may be able to snag supersaver seats.

- **Shop around for seasonal or promotional specials.** You'll almost never see a sale during the peak summer vacation months of July and August or during the Thanksgiving or Christmas seasons; but in periods of low-volume travel, look for sales or fare wars, when airlines periodically lower prices on their most popular routes. Check the travel section of your Sunday newspaper for advertised discounts or call the airlines directly and ask if any **promotional rates** or special fares are available. If you already hold a ticket when a sale breaks, it may even pay to exchange your ticket, which usually incurs a $100 to $150 charge. Keep in mind that the lowest-priced fares are often nonrefundable, require advance purchase of one to three weeks and a certain length of stay, and carry penalties for changing dates of travel.

- **Use the Internet.** The benefits of researching your trip online can be well worth the effort. Airlines often offer discounts on fares or incentives like extra frequent-flier miles just for booking online. **Last-minute specials,** such as weekend deals or Internet-only fares, are also offered by airlines to fill empty seats. Most of these are announced on Tuesday or Wednesday and must be purchased online. Most are only valid for travel that weekend, but some can be booked weeks or months in advance. Sign up for weekly e-mail alerts at airline Web sites or check mega-sites that compile comprehensive lists of last-minute specials, such as **Smarter Living** (Internet: http://smarterliving.com) or **WebFlyer** (Internet: www.webflyer.com).

- **Travelocity** (Internet: www.travelocity.com or www.frommers.travelocity.com) and **Expedia** (Internet: www.expedia.com) are among the most popular travel planning and booking sites, each offering an excellent range of options. Travelers search by destination, dates, and cost. **Orbitz** (Internet: www.orbitz.com) is a popular site launched by United, Delta, Northwest, American, and Continental Airlines. **Priceline** (Internet: www.priceline.com) lets you "name your price" for airline tickets, hotel rooms, and rental cars. For airline tickets, you can't say what time you want to fly — you have to accept any flight between 6 a.m. and 10 p.m. on the dates you've selected, and you may have to make one or more stopovers. Tickets are nonrefundable, and no frequent-flier miles are awarded.

✔ **Use consolidators.** Also known as bucket shops, consolidators are a good place to find low fares. Consolidators buy seats in bulk from the airlines and then sell them back to the public at prices usually below even the airlines' discounted rates. Their small ads usually run in Sunday newspaper travel sections. Be aware that bucket shop tickets are usually nonrefundable or rigged with stiff cancellation penalties, often as high as 50% to 75% of the ticket price. Do some comparison shopping before you buy by searching for fares on airline Web sites to make sure you are indeed paying the lowest prices. **The TravelHub** (☎ 888-AIR-FARE; Internet: www.travelhub.com) represents nearly 1,000 travel agencies, many of whom offer consolidator and discount fares. Other reliable consolidators include **1-800-FLY-CHEAP** (Internet: www.1800flycheap.com); **TFI Tours International** (☎ 800-745-8000 or 212-736-1140; Internet: www.lowestprice.com), which serves as a clearinghouse for unused seats; or "rebators," such as **Travel Avenue** (☎ 800-333-3335; Internet: www.travelavenue.com) and the **Smart Traveller** (☎ 800-448-3338 in the U.S. or 305-448-3338), which rebate part of their commissions to you.

✔ **Join frequent-flier clubs.** It's best to accrue miles on one program so you can rack up free flights and achieve elite status faster. But it makes sense to open as many accounts as possible, no matter how seldom you fly a particular airline. It's free, and you often get the best choice of seats, faster response to phone inquiries, and prompter service if your luggage is stolen, your flight is canceled or delayed, or if you want to change your seat.

Spinning wheels: Getting to Los Angeles by car, train, or bus

Flying may be the quickest way to get to Los Angeles, especially if you're coming from far away, but you can make a real adventure out of your travel time by driving, riding the rails, or hopping a bus. Here are the alternative ways to get to L.A.

By car

Drive, of course. Los Angeles is accessible from a number of freeways — after all, it was once on the much-missed Route 66 and is still on the

Christopher Columbus Trans-Continental Highway, otherwise known as the 10, which runs pretty much straight across the southern part of the United States. Just point your car west and be sure to hit the brakes when you see the ocean.

By train

But now that you've thought of planes and automobiles, you want to remember trains. Los Angeles is serviced by the national passenger railway **Amtrak** and is accessible from any U.S. city that has rail service. For schedules and rate information, call ☎ **800-USA-RAIL** (800-872-7245) or check online at www.amtrak.com.

By bus

Greyhound serves Los Angeles, with connections to other cities throughout the country. The main station for arriving buses is downtown at 1716 E. Seventh St., east of Alameda (☎ **800-231-2222;** Internet: www.greyhound.com).

Chapter 6

Deciding Where to Stay

• •

• •

*A*fter going on and on about the variety that Los Angeles has to offer in so many areas, we come to this section on hotels and begin to mumble and shuffle our feet while staring at the ground. Truth is, Los Angeles has two kinds of hotels — expensive and basic. This isn't New Orleans, where you have dozens of atmospheric or quaint old B&Bs and small hotels, or Las Vegas, which has behemoth themed hotels. Oh sure, if you're a movie star, or someone similarly well-heeled, you have quite a range to choose from — discreet luxury, quiet luxury, unctuous luxury, hip luxury, or eccentric luxury. For the rest of us, there are basic hotels.

The absence of cunning B&Bs is probably due to Los Angeles's lack of reverence for its original architecture (so many likely B&B candidates have long ago been turned into parking lots) and equal lack of reverence for commercial zoning laws. Plus, the most interesting hotels have to charge quite a bit in order to support their prime locations and interior-design costs. But we've tried, really tried, to locate those little gems and sensible spots where you trade a certain level of glitz and glamour for reasonable rates — and, believe it or not, we found a few. You can look them up in the hotel listings in Chapter 8.

Location, Location, Location

The one area, accommodations-wise, where Los Angeles *does* offer great variety is location. The neighborhoods we focus on are each very different visually and in what they have to offer. This variety brings up a whole new set of problems, however. As we mention over and over, Los Angeles is quite large. Consequently, there is no single central location or neighborhood that gives you the perfect base from which to handle all your sightseeing needs. Unless yours is a short trip with a very specific purpose in mind (beach-going, say), no matter where you stay, you're going to be nowhere near many of the things you really want to see and do.

Los Angeles Neighborhoods

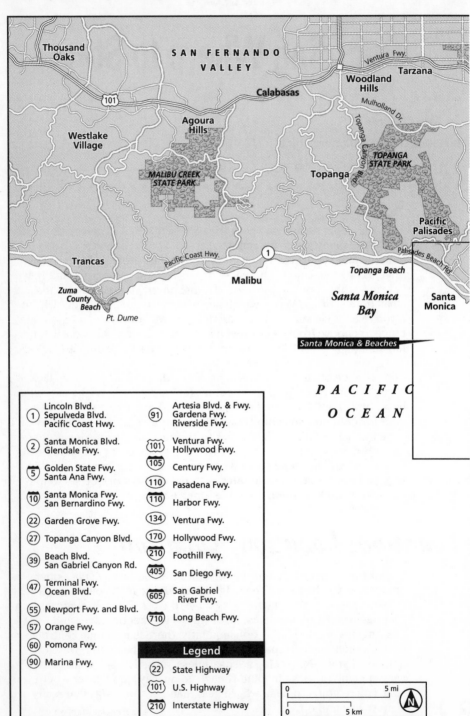

Thousand Oaks

SAN FERNANDO VALLEY

Ventura Fwy.

Woodland Hills

Tarzana

101

Calabasas

Agoura Hills

Mulholland Dr.

Westlake Village

MALIBU CREEK STATE PARK

TOPANGA STATE PARK

Topanga

Topanga Canyon Blvd.

Pacific Palisades

Trancas

Pacific Coast Hwy.

1

Palisades Beach Rd.

Topanga Beach

Malibu

Zuma County Beach

Santa Monica Bay

Santa Monica

Pt. Dume

Santa Monica & Beaches

PACIFIC OCEAN

Legend

(1)	Lincoln Blvd. Sepulveda Blvd. Pacific Coast Hwy.	(91)	Artesia Blvd. & Fwy. Gardena Fwy. Riverside Fwy.
(2)	Santa Monica Blvd. Glendale Fwy.	(101)	Ventura Fwy. Hollywood Fwy.
(5)	Golden State Fwy. Santa Ana Fwy.	(105)	Century Fwy.
(10)	Santa Monica Fwy. San Bernardino Fwy.	(110)	Pasadena Fwy.
(22)	Garden Grove Fwy.	(110)	Harbor Fwy.
(27)	Topanga Canyon Blvd.	(134)	Ventura Fwy.
(39)	Beach Blvd. San Gabriel Canyon Rd.	(170)	Hollywood Fwy.
(47)	Terminal Fwy. Ocean Blvd.	(210)	Foothill Fwy.
(55)	Newport Fwy. and Blvd.	(405)	San Diego Fwy.
(57)	Orange Fwy.	(605)	San Gabriel River Fwy.
(60)	Pomona Fwy.	(710)	Long Beach Fwy.
(90)	Marina Fwy.		

Legend

(22)	State Highway
(101)	U.S. Highway
(210)	Interstate Highway

0 _____ 5 mi

0 _____ 5 km

N

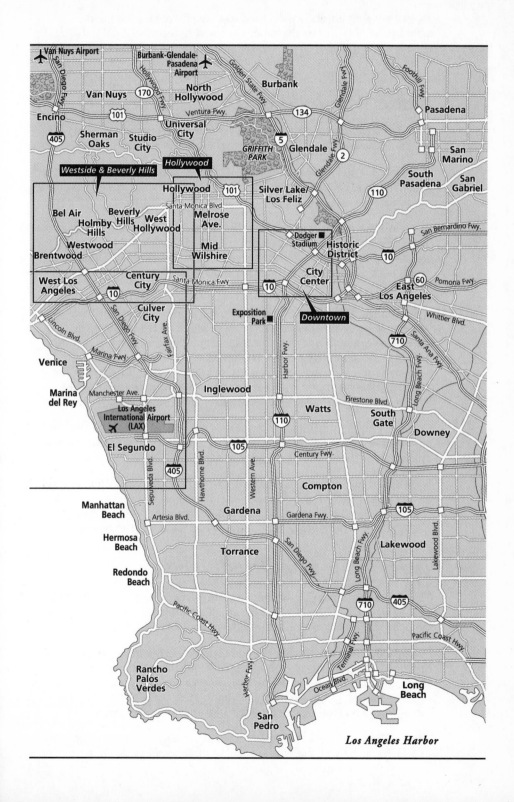

Los Angeles Harbor

So, in choosing hotels, we decided to concentrate on the main neighborhoods — ones that offer the most in terms of sights, dining, and shopping. And although Los Angeles is not a walking town, most of these hotels have some of these very elements within just a few blocks.

Santa Monica/Venice

The area around Santa Monica and Venice is the number-one area for any tourist, and why not? It's the beach, for Pete's sake.

It's lovely, for sure, but it does have its drawbacks, not the least of which is price. Except for certain chic locales, you find the highest hotel rates here — and the closer you get to the water, the more you'll pay.

Santa Monica also offers the nicest walking opportunities — pretty residential neighborhoods full of palm trees and Spanish architecture, great shopping (especially on the pedestrian, blocks-long Third Street Promenade), and outdoor dining options galore.

Plus, the weather is the best in the city; the ocean air keeps the sky clear and the air fresh, with temperatures nearly always temperate — you rarely need an air conditioner on this side of town. However, that same temperate air adds up to some interesting meteorological phenomena; it can be foggy, overcast, and downright chilly in Santa Monica and Venice, even when it's sunny and warm elsewhere in the city. Don't be surprised if it's too foggy to sunbathe or too chilly to have a good ocean swim — at least part of the time.

Crime is minimal, although pickpockets are around. You may also be approached by homeless people (the nice weather makes this a desirable area for them) asking for spare change.

Note also that few hotels are actually right on the beach; there is actually a large street (Ocean Avenue) and, in places, a large grassy park (Palisades Park) between "seaside" hotels and the Pacific. Expect to pay more for a hotel room that actually has a view of the ocean.

West Hollywood/Hollywood

The area around West Hollywood and Hollywood is a mixed bag, but it's probably your best bet if you want anything close to a central location, because this area is about midway between just about everything in L.A.

Many hotels in both neighborhoods (but especially in Hollywood and on Sunset Strip — the stretch of Sunset Boulevard between Doheny Drive and Crescent Heights Boulevard) offer what can be, depending on the weather, gorgeous hill and mountain views. The taller hotels facing south may offer, smog permitting, sweeping city vistas.

Parts of West Hollywood (WeHo) are dull visually but trendy and thus expensive; nearly all are within walking distance of great shopping and dining, however. Several streets (most notably Melrose and Third) are full of cafes and boutiques, which makes for great strolling.

Hollywood proper is not the Hollywood of legend and lore; real celebs, for reasons we can't quite explain, are far more likely to be found noshing and shopping in West Hollywood than hanging around the fabled corner of Hollywood and Vine. These days, however, Hollywood is an up-and-comer, and a lot of money is being thrown around to clean up its slightly seedy self — plus staying here puts you closer to several sights and the Metro rail. Crime is greater here, but, it's mostly of the "don't go down that dark alley alone at night" sort.

Beverly Hills

Yes, Beverly Hills is expensive, but if you look hard enough, you can find some deals here. The problem is that even if you are able to find affordable lodgings, everything around it is dear. Restaurants cost more here (and they aren't that interesting), and the shopping is some of the priciest in the world (you have heard, perhaps, of Rodeo Drive?).

Beverly Hills is also old-money stodgy (when it's not new-money excessive) and too chic for the likes of our wrinkled wardrobe. But it is wonderful for walking, being flat and aesthetically appealing. You can go snooping on foot outside the home of many a legendary — but also probably very dead — movie star on palm tree-lined streets.

Beverly Hills has several very nice (if a bit intimidatingly groomed) parks, and it is one of the safest neighborhoods in the city, thanks to a most zealous police force. Plus, you can yawn and say to the folks, "Oh, I stayed in Beverly Hills." What's that worth to you?

Downtown

Okay, here's the thing: Downtown Los Angeles is seedy, yes, but in an urban-center sort of way: lotsa homeless people with varying grasps on reality; views from hotel windows are mostly of the claustrophobic, gee-there's-another-window-right-there sort; and we wouldn't walk around there much at night. *But,* downtown L.A. is on the cusp of experiencing a renaissance, thanks to some very brisk development and renovations. On weekends, hotel business drops tremendously, and so do the prices. We're talking quite nice hotel rooms for under (okay, in some cases, just under, but still) $100.

The cultural opportunities are greater and more varied here than in most other sections of the city, what with Chinatown, Olvera Street (and other Hispanic oriented-portions), and Little Tokyo in the mix. Plus, you have the Music Center for theater, opera, and classical music, not to mention the upcoming Disney Hall, several museums (including the contemporary arts-centered Museum of Contemporary Art/MOCA), and some of the best bargain shopping in town.

The DASH, the downtown bus system, which costs 25¢ one way, makes it easy to get around the area, and there are several Metro rail stops, making it a snap to get to Hollywood and Universal City. If you're coming to town for just a short stay, want to save some money, don't need an ocean or mountain view, prefer an urban setting, and don't want to rely on a car to get around, this is a perfect location.

Burbank

For convenience to the main studios, the Metro rail, and Universal City, we tossed in a couple of hotels from Burbank. But otherwise, it's dull.

Airport area

You stay here only because you want a place near the airport. It's ghastly, and there is nothing to see.

Price, Price, Price

The following list gives you the breakdown on hotel prices. The $ symbols accompanying each listing in Chapter 8 are based on the hotel's posted rack rates for a standard room. (Suites are more expensive.) Keep in mind that rates fluctuate, and rack rates are generally at the top of a hotel's price schedule. For tips on how to get discounts on lodgings, see Chapter 7.

- ✔ **$ (Under $100).** This gets you basically a bed and motel-room furniture — unless, of course, you scored a good deal on an otherwise pricey room usually found in a higher category. Towels are likely to be of the depressingly thin variety, and don't expect top-brand toiletries. Remind yourself that you are there for the sunshine.

- ✔ **$$ ($100–$200).** This is a mixed-bag category. You could have a very nice (though perhaps generic-looking) hotel room, in a fine establishment with all the amenities. Or it could be even posher. Or it could be less so. *Check each listing carefully.*

- ✔ **$$$ ($200–$275).** Now we're talkin'. The service may be snooty, but the linens are soft, plus you get bathrobes and high-end amenities (nice shampoo, lotion, shoe buffer). And we bet the grounds are fabulously landscaped.

- ✔ **$$$$ ($275 and up).** In theory, you should have everything your little heart could desire in this category, but this is L.A., and sometimes you pay that price just for the privilege of staying somewhere that pampers Jennifer Lopez. You not being Jennifer Lopez, you may wonder what the fuss is all about.

Chapter 7

Booking Your Room

You've done your homework; you're ready to play ball and book a room. Here are some of the many ways to save on lodging costs and avoid being stuck with the rack rate.

Uncovering the Truth about Rack Rates

The **rack rate** is the maximum rate that a hotel charges for a room. It's the rate you'd get if you walked in off the street and asked for a room for the night. We can't stress this enough: Rack rates are just a guideline. For the most part, you won't have to pay them. (Occasionally, you'll have to pay more, though. Blech.) How to avoid paying rack rates? Start by planning your trip during the off-season — early December, January, and February. Be sure to check the Internet, starting with hotel Web sites, because most establishments have their best rates available there. For Downtown-area hotels, go on the weekends; prices drop precipitously because it's a business-oriented neighborhood and many hotels have rooms begging for guests when the workweek ends.

Getting the Best Room at the Best Rate

Frankly, rates around Los Angeles seem so willy-nilly — with rack rates at certain chain hotels equal to the ones at posher places — that trying to figure out rhyme and reason behind them is exhausting. Think instead about what is important to you: Character? Location? Hip-quotient? Room size? Go from there, and pay accordingly, using the following tips to help find the best rates.

✔ **Don't be afraid to bargain.** Most rack rates include commissions of 10% to 25% for travel agents, which some hotels may be willing to reduce if you make your own reservations and haggle a bit. Always ask whether a room that is less expensive than the first one quoted is available, or whether any special rates apply to you. You may qualify for corporate, student, military, senior citizen, or other discounts. Be sure to mention membership in **AAA, AARP, frequent-flier programs, or trade unions,** which may entitle you to special deals, as well. Find out the hotel policy on children, if necessary. Do kids stay free in the room, or does the hotel offer a special rate?

✔ **Use the Internet.** Many hotels offer discounted rates if you book directly from their Web sites or online reservations services.

✔ **Dial direct.** When booking a room in a chain hotel, compare the rates offered by the hotel's local line with that of the toll-free number. Also check with an agent and online. A hotel makes nothing on a room that stays empty, so the local hotel reservations desk may be willing to offer a special rate unavailable elsewhere.

✔ **Rely on a qualified professional.** Certain hotels give travel agents discounts in exchange for steering business their way, so if you're shy about bargaining, an agent may be better equipped to negotiate discounts for you.

✔ **Remember the law of supply and demand.** Resort hotels are most crowded, and therefore most expensive, on weekends, so discounts are usually available for midweek stays. Business hotels in downtown locations are busiest during the week, so you can expect big discounts over the weekend. Avoid high-season stays whenever you can: Planning your vacation just a week before or after official peak season can mean big savings.

✔ **Look into group or long-stay discounts.** If you come as part of a large group, you should be able to negotiate a bargain rate, because the hotel can then guarantee occupancy in a number of rooms. Likewise, if you're planning a long stay (at least five days), you may qualify for a discount. As a general rule, expect one night free after a seven-night stay.

✔ **Avoid excess charges.** When you book a room, ask whether the hotel charges for parking. Many hotels charge a fee just for dialing out on the phone in your room. Find out whether your hotel imposes a surcharge on local and long-distance calls. A pay phone, however inconvenient, may save you money, though many calling cards charge a fee when you use them on pay phones. Finally, ask about local taxes and service charges, which can increase the cost of a room by 25% or more.

✔ **Watch for coupons and advertised discounts.** Scan ads in the travel section of your local Sunday newspaper, an excellent source for up-to-the-minute hotel deals.

✔ **Consider a suite.** If you're traveling with your family or another couple, you can pack more people into a suite (which usually comes with a sofa bed) and thereby reduce your per-person rate. Keep in mind that some places charge for extra guests.

✔ **Book an efficiency.** A room with a kitchenette allows you to shop for groceries and cook your own meals. This is a big money saver, especially for families on long stays.

✔ **Join hotel frequent-visitor clubs.** Even if you don't stay in the hotels much, you'll be more likely to get upgrades and other perks.

✔ **Ask about frequent-flier points.** Many hotels offer frequent-flier points, so ask for yours when you check in.

Surfing the Web for Hotel Deals

Many hotel deals are offered on the Internet at lodging sites with multiple listings. In addition to the online sites listed below, the major travel booking sites (such as Travelocity, Expedia, and Orbitz) also offer hotel booking. Some lodging sites may specialize in a particular type of accommodations. Others, such as TravelWeb (contact information is in the following bulleted list), offer weekend deals on major chain properties, which cater to business travelers and have more empty rooms on weekends.

A sampling of lodging sites on the Internet includes

✔ Although the name **All Hotels on the Web** (Internet: www.all-hotels.com) is something of a misnomer, the site *does* have tens of thousands of listings for hotels throughout the world. Bear in mind that each hotel has paid a small fee (of $25 and up) to be listed, so it's less an objective list and more like a book of online brochures.

✔ **Places to Stay** (Internet: www.placestostay.com) lists one-of-a-kind places in the United States that you might not find in other directories, with a focus on resort accommodations. Again, the listing is selective — this isn't a comprehensive directory, but it can give you a sense of what's available at different destinations.

✔ **TravelWeb** (Internet: www.travelweb.com) lists more than 26,000 hotels in 170 countries, focusing on chains such as Hyatt and Hilton, and you can book almost 90%of these online. TravelWeb's Click-It Weekends, updated each Monday, offers weekend deals at many leading hotel chains.

Using Reservations Services

Reservations services usually work as consolidators, buying up or reserving rooms in bulk and then dealing them out to customers at a profit. You can get 10% to 50% off; but remember that these discounts apply to inflated rack rates that savvy travelers rarely end up paying. You may get a decent rate, but always call the hotel, as well, to see if you can do better.

Among the more reputable reservations services, offering both telephone and online bookings, are **Accommodations Express** (☎ 800-950-4685; Internet: www.accommodationsexpress.com), **Hotel Reservations Network** (☎ 800-715-7666; Internet: www.hotel discounts.com or Internet: www.180096HOTEL.com), and **Quikbook** (☎ 800-789-9887, includes fax-on-demand service; Internet: www.quikbook.com). Online, try booking your hotel through **Arthur Frommer's Budget Travel** (Internet: www.frommers.com). **Microsoft Expedia** (Internet: www.expedia.com) features a "travel agent" that will also direct you to affordable lodgings.

Chapter 8

The Best Hotels in Los Angeles

In This Chapter

▶ A complete breakdown of the best lodgings in L.A.

▶ Accommodations by price and location

▶ Where to go if the best hotels are booked solid

Sure, Los Angeles has plenty of standard-issue hotels and motels. But it wouldn't be L.A. without the standout spots, from venerable Old Hollywood establishments to hip new upstarts; from lodgings with character to independent-minded places that offer perfectly nice rooms at sensible rates.

Note that we don't include every single hotel in town. That would defeat the purpose of giving you some helpful advice and saving you precious time and energy, now wouldn't it? Instead, we send you directly to our favorite places to stay, at the same time providing a range of choices in cost, location, and amenities. You can quickly and easily find out which hotels are closest to shopping, nightlife, and museums; which hotels can be counted on for smart service at reasonable rates; and which hotels flat-out have the hottest ambience or star-spotting potential.

If you're coming to the L.A. area with children in tow, look for the Kid Friendly icons throughout the chapter, which point out the lodgings that are especially good for families.

The following list gives you the breakdown on hotel prices. The $ symbols accompanying each listing in this chapter are based on the hotel's posted rack rates for a standard room. (Suites are much more expensive.) Keep in mind that rates fluctuate, and rack rates are generally at the top of a hotel's price schedule. For tips on how to get considerable discounts on lodgings, see Chapter 7.

$	Under $100
$$	$100–$200
$$$	$200–$275
$$$$	$275 and up

Top Los Angeles Hotels from A to Z

Alta Cienega Motel
$ West Hollywood

The Alta Cienega is famous around the world as the spot where Doors singer Jim Morrison often crashed in bacchanalian contemplation in a room above the motel driveway. This room, number 32, now bears a plaque on the door stating "Home of Jim Morrison" and is available for a maximum of $58 per night, plus tax — the same rate you'd pay for any other room at this no-frills joint, which is painted in pea-green, orange, and white. And what do you get for the lowest hotel rate in the city of West Hollywood? Well, not a lot. The soda and ice machine are vintage and may be the same ones the Lizard King used, if he was so inclined. The rooms have wood-toned Formica furniture, small TVs, and no phones, though there are two pay phones conveniently located in the parking lot. Morning coffee and pastries, served in the office, are free. The Alta Cienega is full during the summer months, when American and European rock fans haunt the motel, trying to relive and revive Jim's spirit, as demonstrated by the ghostly graffiti on the walls of room 32.

1005 N. La Cienega Blvd. (near the Sunset Strip). ☎ **310-652-5797.** *Fax: 310-652-5797. Rack rates: $55–$58. AE, DC, DISC, MC, V.*

Argyle
$$$$ West Hollywood

Built in 1929 as the Sunset Towers apartment house, this Art Deco masterpiece has had starring roles in movies, including *The Player, Get Shorty,* and *Wayne's World 2,* and has been mentioned in literary works by Raymond Chandler, among others. Howard Hughes, John Wayne, Marilyn Monroe, Paulette Goddard, Zasu Pitts, and gangster Bugsy Siegel kept apartments here. Now, as a hotel, the Argyle still hosts celebrities in well-appointed suites, with masterpieces of Deco perfection and meticulous historical detail that reflect the glamour that was Hollywood (the carpet was woven especially for the stars!). Of course, the glamour doesn't come cheap; the least expensive suite starts at $260, and we spied at least one room that had evidence of shabby neglect, for shame. The hotel has a health club, as well as 24-hour room service, complimentary continental breakfast, and the restaurant Fenix, which becomes a club/lounge featuring hip-hop on Friday nights and jazz on Saturday nights. Luckily, the building is soundproofed and strikingly quiet, buffered from the noise of the club and the Sunset Strip.

8358 Sunset Blvd. (at Kings Rd.). ☎ **800-225-2637** *or 323-654-7100. Fax: 323-654-9287. E-mail:* rez@argylehotel.com. *Internet:* www.argylehotel.com. *Rack rates: $260–$595 per night. AE, DC, DISC, JCB, MC, V.*

Avalon Hotel

$$$ Beverly Hills

Mae West and Marilyn Monroe lived here when it was an apartment building, and Lucy and Ricky Ricardo stayed here when they went to Hollywood in *I Love Lucy*. Now, it's a small, chic hotel, aggressively styled and inadvertently harkening back to the 1950s/Jetsons' futurism — look for the green polished concrete and atom-age emblems. Rooms are spare but oh so comfortable — Frette linens! Philosophy-brand bathroom amenities! CD players and VCRs! The bathrooms are smallish, with inexplicable bamboo poles (for stripper practice?). The pool demands a good bathing suit and a figure to match, and the on-site restaurant, **Blue on Blue,** has a signature drink that looks like a glass of toilet-bowl cleaner. Not too surprisingly, they look for business and fashion-industry clientele.

9400 W. Olympic Blvd. (at Cañon Dr.). ☎ *800-534-4715 or 310-277-5221. Fax: 310-277-4928. Internet:* www.Avalon-hotel.com. *Rack rates: $235–$475 double. AE, DC, DISC, MC, V.*

Best Western Hollywood Hills Hotel

$$ Hollywood

Famous for the huge sign declaring this to be the "Last Cappuccino before the 101" and for the coffee shop (now under new ownership and design and renamed the **101 Coffee Shop**) that was featured in the movie *Swingers*, this motel is usually crowded with local musicians, actors, and lounge-abouts digging on the hearty, reasonably priced food. The rooms are good-sized, the large pool is tiled and heated, and the location is good for public transportation and excellent for driving. There are star-spotting spots within walking distance (Victor's Deli and Café, Mayfair Market, Bourgeois Pig, and Cosmopolitan Books and Music), Universal Studios is 5 minutes away on the freeway, Hollywood is just down the hill, and Dodger Stadium, Griffith Park, and the Los Angeles Zoo are around the corner, making this a great choice for kids. The rooms are large, with marble counters, comfy beds, and recently updated bathrooms. Redecoration is underway to eliminate the maroon, mauve, and green theme that predominates. The most expensive rooms, the executive kings, feature a wet bar and seating area. Room service from 7 a.m. to midnight is from the coffee shop, which is open until 3 a.m.

6141 Franklin Ave. (between Vine and Gower Sts.). ☎ *800-528-1234 or 323-464-5181. Fax: 323-962-0536. Internet:* www.bestwestern.com/hollywoodhillshotel. *Rack rates: $79–$129 double. AE, DC, DISC, MC, V.*

Best Western Ocean View Hotel

$$ Santa Monica

A Best Western, but a top-of-the-line one, so if you're looking for a standard modern hotel with a slippery marble foyer/lobby, this is it. Rooms

Santa Monica Accommodations

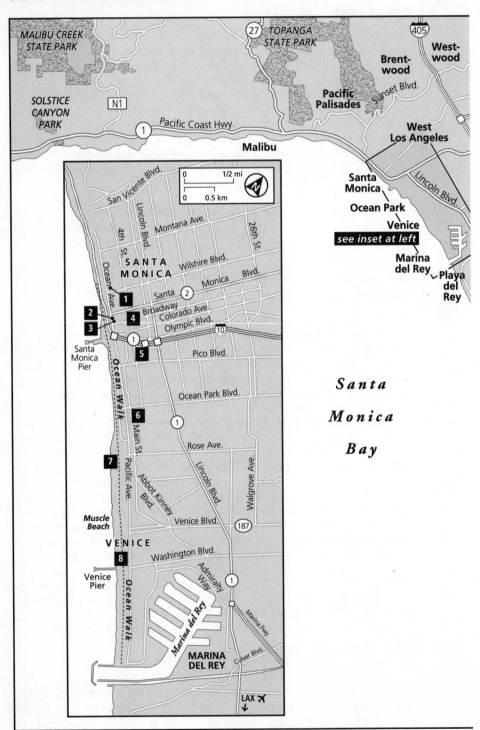

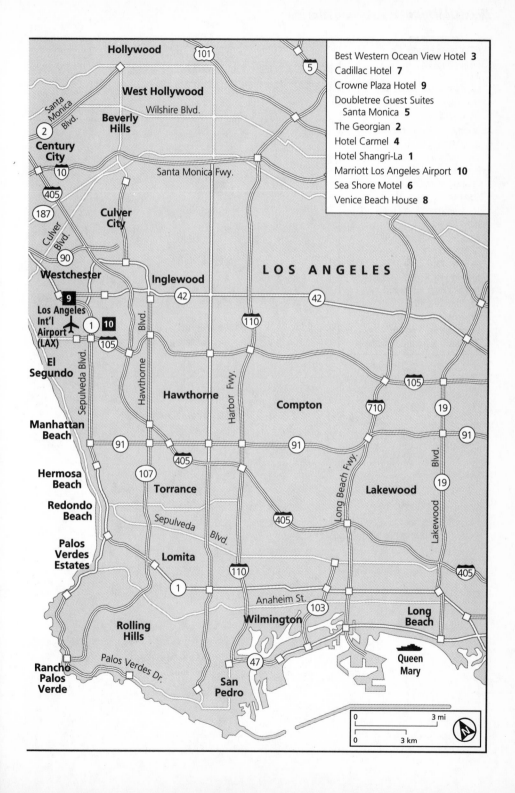

Best Western Ocean View Hotel **3**
Cadillac Hotel **7**
Crowne Plaza Hotel **9**
Doubletree Guest Suites
   Santa Monica **5**
The Georgian **2**
Hotel Carmel **4**
Hotel Shangri-La **1**
Marriott Los Angeles Airport **10**
Sea Shore Motel **6**
Venice Beach House **8**

West Hollywood Accommodations

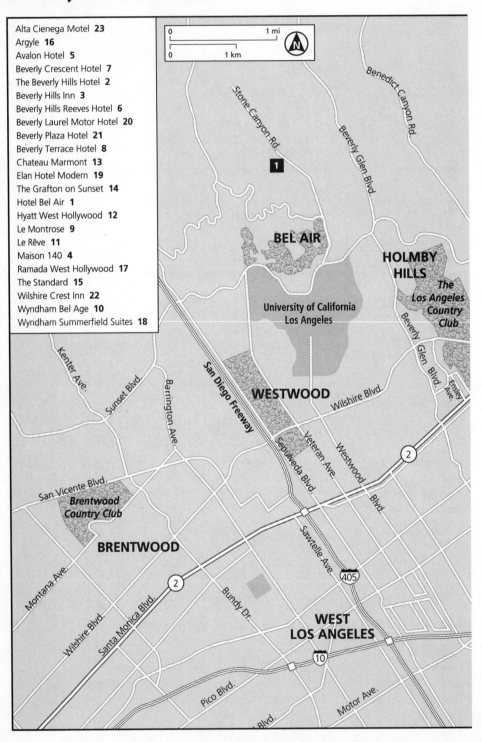

Alta Cienega Motel **23**
Argyle **16**
Avalon Hotel **5**
Beverly Crescent Hotel **7**
The Beverly Hills Hotel **2**
Beverly Hills Inn **3**
Beverly Hills Reeves Hotel **6**
Beverly Laurel Motor Hotel **20**
Beverly Plaza Hotel **21**
Beverly Terrace Hotel **8**
Chateau Marmont **13**
Elan Hotel Modern **19**
The Grafton on Sunset **14**
Hotel Bel Air **1**
Hyatt West Hollywood **12**
Le Montrose **9**
Le Rêve **11**
Maison 140 **4**
Ramada West Hollywood **17**
The Standard **15**
Wilshire Crest Inn **22**
Wyndham Bel Age **10**
Wyndham Summerfield Suites **18**

0   1 mi
0   1 km

BEL AIR

HOLMBY HILLS

The Los Angeles Country Club

University of California
Los Angeles

Benedict Canyon Rd.

Stone Canyon Rd.

Beverly Glen Blvd.

Beverly Glen Blvd.

Ensley Ave.

WESTWOOD

Wilshire Blvd.

Kenter Ave.

Sunset Blvd.

Barrington Ave.

San Diego Freeway

Sepulveda Blvd.

Veteran Ave.

Westwood Blvd.

San Vicente Blvd.

Brentwood Country Club

BRENTWOOD

Montana Ave.

Wilshire Blvd.

Santa Monica Blvd.

Bundy Dr.

Sawtelle Ave.

WEST LOS ANGELES

Pico Blvd.

Motor Ave.

Blvd.

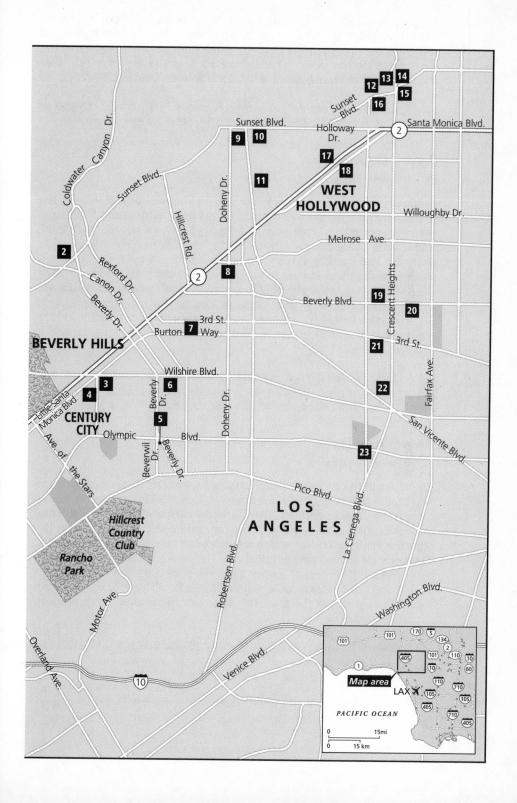

are medium-sized, comfortable, heavy on the pinky-goldy color scheme, and instantly forgettable (though some rooms do have ocean views, and some are handicapped accessible, which isn't always the case in the older Santa Monica hotels). Palisades Park is across the street; the Pier and Third Street Promenade are but a block or so away.

1447 Ocean Ave. (across the street from Palisades Park). ☎ *800-452-4888 or 310-458-4888. Fax: 310-458-0848. Rack rates: $99–$149 (depending on season).*

Beverly Crescent Hotel
$$ Beverly Hills

Originally used as an auxiliary building for Paramount Pictures (in the 1920s, when the studio was located in this area, actors used it for naps between scenes) and currently undergoing a renovation, this delightful, secret little European-style hotel in the heart of Beverly Hills is quite charming and friendly. Rooms are both elegant and cute, and there are plans to make them appear more spacious (something about a frosted glass wall between the sleeping area and the bathroom). The baths are showers only, but they have Aveda products, plus robes and slippers. Other niceties include down comforters, bottles of water, complimentary continental breakfast, plans for flat-screen TVs in every room, and a lobby restaurant.

403 N. Crescent Dr. (at Brighton Way). ☎ *800-451-1566 or 310-247-0505. Fax: 310-247-9053. Internet:* www.beverlycrescenthotel.com. *Rack rates: $159–$239 (ask about discounts). AE, DC, DISC, MC, V.*

Beverly Hills Inn
$$$ Beverly Hills

The inn is in the process of tranforming its somewhat chain-hotel looks into that of a more boutique, European-style hotel. This ultimately means a concierge, maid service without a bulky cart, and pets are welcome. Budget-minded businesspeople stay here and take their meetings at the adjacent Peninsula Hotel, which is fancier and considerably more costly. The beds are remarkably comfortable, the amenities are nice, and each room has a little recessed vanity area. The pool is heated to 85 degrees year-round, and there is an on-site restaurant, with room service from 7 a.m. to 11 p.m. For the area, this is a reasonable alternative to more expensive venues.

125 S. Spalding Dr. (south of Wilshire Blvd.) ☎ *800-463-4466 or 310-278-0303. Fax: 310-278-2723. E-mail:* inn@beverlyhillsinn.com. *Internet:* www.innatbeverlyhills.com. *Rack rates: $189–$429 double. AE, DC, DISC, MC, V.*

Beverly Hills Reeves Hotel
$ Beverly Hills

This is the cheapest hotel in Beverly Hills, so if you want to maximize your shopping dollar and still tell the folks back home that you stayed in that famous burg, this is the place to do it. We wouldn't go so far as to say that this hotel is shabby, but it's definitely not chic. Small rooms with older 13-inch TVs (albeit with satellite channels) and a continental breakfast of canned orange juice and doughnuts make for super-low tariffs. If you want to go ultra economical, you can request one of the rooms with a shared bathroom and biweekly maid service ($45 a night!). All rooms in this *very* basic hotel have air-conditioning, small electric space heaters, microwaves, and refrigerators, and most of the tiny bathrooms have showers, though you can request a tub. The Reeves is popular with foreign tour groups, students, and budget travelers who appreciate its location and access to public transportation; the hotel is within walking distance of Rodeo Drive and all its glitz.

120 S. Reeves Dr. (half a block from Wilshire Blvd.). ☎ *310-271-3006. Fax: 310-271-2276. E-mail:* Reservations@bhreeves.com.. *Internet:* www.bhreeves.com. *Rack rates: $45–$75 per day, $225–$420 per week. AE, DC, DISC MC, V.*

Beverly Laurel Motor Hotel
$ West Hollywood

Built in 1964, the Beverly Laurel has plenty of kitschy charm, especially in the elevator, which is paneled with tiki-styled faux wood. It has a heated pool and cable TV; rooms — all of which face the pool — feature fridges and microwaves, along with Vargas prints and electric-blue walls. Larger rooms have kitchenettes with a ministove. Pets are welcome with a $10-per-day charge. There's no room service, but the hip diner **Swingers** is right downstairs. It's a favorite with porn stars, who actually sleep rather than work here! The motel has an arrangement with Easton's Gym across the street, and guests can get a reduced rate at the health club. Bus tours to see the sights can be arranged; it's close to the Farmers Market, as well. Free parking.

8018 Beverly Blvd. (between Fairfax Ave. and La Cienega Blvd.). ☎ *800-962-3824 or 323-651-2441. Fax: 800-962-3824. Rack rates: $80–$84 double. AE, DC, MC, V.*

Beverly Plaza Hotel
$$$ West Hollywood

Third Street in West Hollywood is a glorious riot of antiques shops, boutiques, and restaurants, and it's walking distance from the Beverly Center mall. Right there in the thick of it is the Beverly Plaza Hotel. This European-style hotel features 24-hour room service, large rooms that have bathrobes, coffeemakers, and daily newspaper delivery, plus $10 a day in taxicab vouchers. Best of all, for those who crave a luxurious vacation, it has the most reasonably priced hotel spa in Los Angeles (half-hour massage, $45; half-hour facial with Dermalogica products, $45; eyebrow wax, $15), with a well-appointed fitness room (dry sauna, whirlpool, treadmills, stair machines, and weights), fitness excursions (mountain biking, for example, or hiking), and personal trainers available by appointment. You'll also find a heated pool and sundeck, and the acclaimed tapas bar/Spanish–California restaurant/jazz club **Cava.**

8384 Third St. (near the Beverly Center mall). ☎ *800-624-6835 or 323-658-6600. Fax: 323 653-3464. E-mail:* info@beverlyplazahotel.com. *Internet:* www.beverlyplazahotel.com. *Rack rates: $219–$272. AE, DC, DISC, MC, V.*

Beverly Terrace Hotel
$$ Beverly Hills

This is the best hotel deal in Beverly Hills. It's located 6 (long) blocks from the heart of Beverly Hills and is about a steep quarter-mile hike from Sunset Strip. The exterior is fabulous 1950s glamour; the interior has a cozy, tropical feel and a pair of cockatiels. The entire hotel is nonsmoking, though you can puff poolside next to the lush jungle murals. The rooms, all of which come with refrigerators, are not large, and that's being kind. Most rooms feature showers only, though you can request a tub room. Complimentary continental breakfast is served poolside daily, and the restaurant **Amici Italian** is located on-site.

469 North Doheny Dr. (at Santa Monica Blvd.). ☎ *310-274-8141. Fax: 310-385-1998. Rack rates: $95–$145. AE, DISC, MC, V.*

Bevonshire Lodge
$ Hollywood

Oh, this motel is very inexpensive, the pool is unheated year-round, which can make for a really brisk morning swim, and rooms are basic and unfancy. But each room has a fridge, and some come with kitchenettes. A huge, famous rubber tree — taking up a ridiculous amount of space, bless it — grows in the lobby. The owner is a former employee who saved up money and bought the place; he also owns the (slightly) pricier **Beverly Inn** a block west, which is a fine but utterly basic value given the price and easy access to the Farmers Market and CBS. If you're looking for function over form, and a convenient location (with free parking!), this is the motel for you. If you want the same idea, but with slightly fresher paint, check out the Beverly Inn (7701 Beverly Blvd.; ☎ 323-931-8109), a block away.

7575 Beverly Blvd. (at Curson Ave.). ☎ *323-936-6154. Fax: 323-934-6640. Rack rates: $50–$63. AE, DC, DISC, MC, V.*

Cadillac Hotel

$ Venice

Built in 1905 as Charlie Chaplin's residence, this hotel is funky but cheap, a sort of Southern California version of the classic European pensione. Yes, some of the paint is peeling in the lobby; yes, there can be homeless people lurking around the (don't forget free!) parking lot; yes, services are basic (you can access the Internet by dropping quarters into a machine), *but* all the rooms are clean, easy on the eyes, and come with an ocean view (though it may be a strain in some cases). Plus, the staff will arrange tours for you, and the location is right on the beach. Right there. I mean, *Baywatch* has filmed here. And there's a piece of the Berlin Wall in the lobby — we don't know why, but isn't that charming? Rooms vary in size but are quite comfortable. Exercise machines are in the basement next to the laundry, which tells you a lot, but the hotel is also just a couple blocks from the happening part of Main Street — and did we mention that it's right on the beach?!

8 Dudley Ave. (at Speedway). ☎ *310-399-8876. Fax: 310-399-4536. Internet:* www.thecadillachotel.com. *Rack rates: $79–$110 (Sept 1–May 31), $89–$130 (June 1–Aug 31). AE, MC, V.*

Celebrity Hotel

$ Hollywood

Smack dab in the heart of what the Chamber of Commerce desperately hopes will be a rejuvenated Hollywood, this family-owned and -operated bed-and-breakfast is humble, friendly, funky, well-meaning, and the place to stay if you prefer to spend your money on souvenirs. Rooms aren't anything fabulous, but they do have murals featuring (not always recognizable) movie stars. Quiet, clean, and pet-friendly (the owners' dog is on the premises) — consider it a mom-and-pop alternative to Motel 6.

1775 Orchid Ave., between Hollywood Blvd. and Franklin Ave. ☎ *800-222-7017 or 323-850-6464. Fax: 323-850-7667. Rack rates: $69–$99. AE, DISC, MC, V.*

Chateau Marmont

$$$$ Hollywood/West Hollywood

Though its most notorious fame comes from John Belushi's overdose death (in Bungalow 2 in 1982), this is a fabulously romantic, slightly spooky old hotel much favored by celebs who value naturally acquired style and quirkiness. The whole place looks like a setting for a Raymond Chandler–style mystery, to say nothing of discreet assignations, which is probably why the legendary studio boss Harry Cohn famously said, "If you must get into trouble, do it at the Chateau Marmont." It was once a residence hotel (and many long-time occupants still live there), so the rooms can often be ridiculously large, especially the suites, which were originally intended as apartments. The furnishings and style in said rooms may put you in mind of the slighty faded Art Deco grandeur of the Coen Brothers' movie, *Barton Fink* (though beds are modern and comfortable). The tree-rimmed pool area is gorgeous and, along with the 1920s Spanish Mission lobby, is a hot spot for star spotting. The celebrity list, past and present, goes on and on, but suffice to say that we were just there and so were Nicole Kidman and Ben Stiller. Jim Morrison once fell out of a window here. Okay, so the price may not be in your budget, and your idea of honeymoon bliss may require more pristine, conventional surfaces, but at least come by for a drink on the grounds and be sure to keep your eyes open.

8221 Sunset Blvd. (near Laurel Canyon Blvd.). ☎ *800-CHATEAU (800-242-8328) or 323-656-1010. Fax: 323-655-5311. Internet:* www.designhotels.com. *Rack rates: $280 and up (double). AE, DC, MC, V.*

Crowne Plaza Hotel
$$$ Airport

The Crowne Plaza Hotel is situated a block closer to Los Angeles Airport than the Marriott, with slightly larger rooms, Krispy Kreme doughnuts, and a fitness room that has a great view and plenty of equipment, doubles on all cardio machines, plus a free-weight bench and a weight machine. Rates are flexible, and there are suites as well as standard rooms with a king or two doubles. You won't find any room safes or minibars, but you can rent a fridge. The multilingual staff speaks Chinese, English, French, German, Italian, and Spanish. The hotel offers currency exchange, tours for sightseeing and to local attractions, room service, handicapped-accessible rooms, a pool, free transportation to and from the airport, and who can forget those Krispy Kreme doughnuts?

5985 W. Century Blvd. (near the airport). ☎ *800-227-6963 or 310-642-7500; TTY 310-348-9061. Fax: 310-417-3608. Internet:* www.crowneplaza.com. *Rack rates: $179–$450. AE, DC, DISC, MC, V.*

Elan Hotel Modern
$$–$$$ West Hollywood

Sleek, chic, and not that cheap, the elegant Elan prides itself on service and discretion. Room furnishings are clean-lined and modern, with touches like Irish linen bathrobes, fresh flowers, and Wolfgang Puck coffee for the coffeemakers. Instead of calling room service, you can order from Jan's Coffee Shop across the street from 6 a.m. to 2 a.m., and they'll jaywalk it over for you (because the crosswalk is too far away). The hotel serves complimentary continental breakfast daily, and as of this writing, there's a nightly manager's wine and cheese reception for guests. The small on-site health club features free weights, a universal weight machine, a cross-trainer, and a treadmill; if that doesn't suit you, arrangements can be made for you at Beverly Hills Fitness just a few blocks away. Or just walk over to the Beverly Center, two blocks east, and power shop.

8435 Beverly Blvd. (at La Cienega Blvd.). ☎ ***888-661-0398*** *or 323-658-6663. Fax: 323-658-6640. Internet:* www.elanhotel.com. *Rack rates: $165–$215 double (ask about corporate discounts). AE, DC, DISC, JCB, MC.*

The Georgian
$$$ Santa Monica

For our money, because we value atmosphere above all, we find the Georgian your best pricey bet in Santa Monica. Though it dates from the 1930s (it's a National Trust Historic Hotel), the hotel is more Edwardian than Georgian, and oh, is it stately. It's well maintained, too, by a polite staff. Basic rooms are good-sized (the difference in price depends on what sort of bed is within), romantic, and cozy thanks to furniture that seems to know its place. Suites are expensive but look almost straight out of a 1930s screwball comedy. Bathrooms veer towards quaint (read: not ultramodern), which doesn't bother us but may concern you. You'll find a bar and restaurant called the **Speakeasy** featuring American cuisine — Clark Gable ate here! — plus a health club, room service (for breakfast only, alas), and the ocean across the street. We initially want more, but then we look at the place and get over it.

1415 Ocean Ave. (across the street from Palisades Park). ☎ **310-395-9945.** *Fax: 310-451-3374. Internet:* www.georgianhotel.com. *Rack rates: $235–$400 double (rates slightly higher in summer). AE,DC, DISC, JCB, MC, V.*

Hollywood Bungalows
$ Hollywood

If you are a free-spirited, bohemian, backpacking, young-at-heart type, Hollywood Bungalows is the hotel/hostel for you. Many visitors are international travelers and students from around the world (though there *was* that 90-year-old woman last year). This rambling complex features primarily dorm-style rooms, housing from 4 to 14 guests in bunk beds. These rooms feature personal, secure lockers for belongings, with one bathroom per cottage, and start at $17 per night. If you'd rather have a more private room, with its own bath and TV set, you can get one for $59. There's a snack/coffee bar, a gym, a common kitchen where you can whip up a meal, pool tables, an Internet cafe, a swimming pool, an arcade, and a large-screen TV room with satellite, videos, and DVDs, plus a rooftop dance floor. The hotel offers a variety of daily tours of Los Angeles, featuring stops at the George Michael toilet and a cruise through South Central and downtown, as well as Venice beach and Melrose. There are daily shuttles to Hollywood and Universal Studios, as well as a 24-hour bus line just outside the door. During the summer, the busiest time at the Bungalows, the staff throws together theme nights, like Las Vegas Night and the Aluminum Foil Party, where guests create costumes from rolls of the shiny stuff. Great wacky fun for those who like to get into the spirit of things.

Hollywood Accommodations and Dining

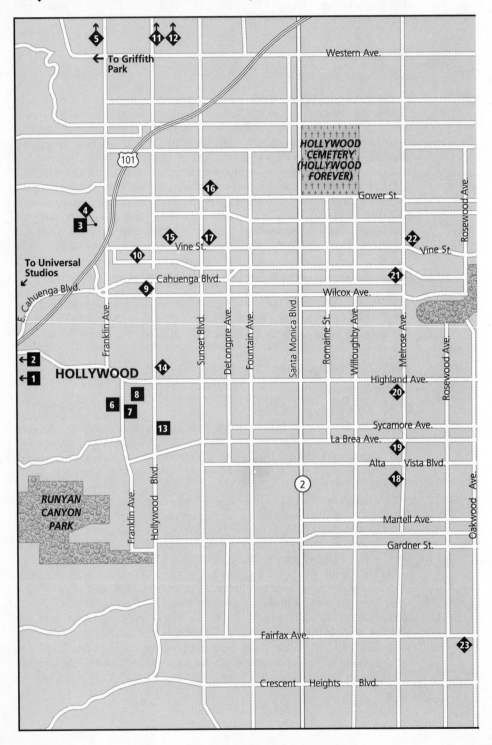

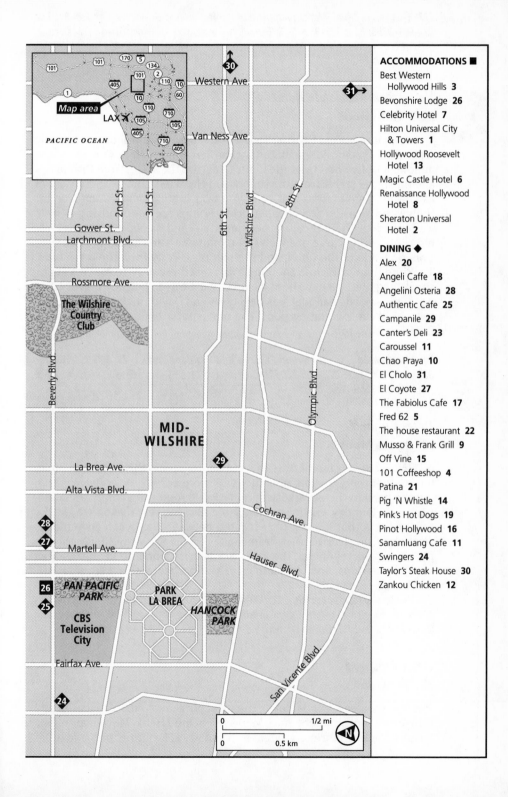

ACCOMMODATIONS ■

Best Western
  Hollywood Hills **3**
Bevonshire Lodge **26**
Celebrity Hotel **7**
Hilton Universal City
  & Towers **1**
Hollywood Roosevelt
  Hotel **13**
Magic Castle Hotel **6**
Renaissance Hollywood
  Hotel **8**
Sheraton Universal
  Hotel **2**

DINING ◆

Alex **20**
Angeli Caffe **18**
Angelini Osteria **28**
Authentic Cafe **25**
Campanile **29**
Canter's Deli **23**
Caroussel **11**
Chao Praya **10**
El Cholo **31**
El Coyote **27**
The Fabiolus Cafe **17**
Fred 62 **5**
The house restaurant **22**
Musso & Frank Grill **9**
Off Vine **15**
101 Coffeeshop **4**
Patina **21**
Pig 'N Whistle **14**
Pink's Hot Dogs **19**
Pinot Hollywood **16**
Sanamluang Cafe **11**
Swingers **24**
Taylor's Steak House **30**
Zankou Chicken **12**

2775 Cahuenga Blvd. West. (just north of the Hollywood Bowl). ☎ *888-259-9990 or 323-969-9155. Fax: 323-969-9678. E-mail:* hwres@hollywoodbungalows.com. *Internet:* www.hollywoodbungalows.com. *Rack rates: $17–$59 per night. AE, DISC, MC, V.*

Hollywood Roosevelt Hotel

$$$ Hollywood

This is a fabulous old Roaring Twenties Deco/Mission wonder, beautifully restored and reputedly haunted by Marilyn Monroe. It lies smack in the middle of Hollywood Upgrade Central (across the street from Grauman's and down the street from the Hollywood-Highland Complex; the Walk of Fame runs right in front of it), and you won't get more style and a better Hollywood location at a cheaper price. Rooms are good-looking — well, we could do without the floral bedspreads — and the smallish baths have old-school tile. There are views of mountains and the Hollywood sign from one side of the hotel, and the rest of the city from the other side. The long-time jazz club, the Cinegrill, closed recently to make way for something that, we have been assured, will be even better. The very first Academy Awards banquet was held here, and David Hockney painted the bottom of the swimming pool. You may spot a big name or two here. Great for kids, too.

7000 Hollywood Blvd. (between La Brea and Highland Aves.). ☎ *800-950-7667 or 323-466-7000. Fax: 323-469-7006. Internet:* www.hollywoodroosevelt.com. *Rack rates: $159–$299 double. AE, DC, DISC, MC, V.*

Hotel Carmel

$$ Santa Monica

A 75-year-old veteran of the beachside hotel scene, this Italianate building is admittedly low on amenities (no room service or coffeemakers), but the beds in the otherwise unremarkable rooms are comfy, and dataports and laundry service are available. But the real reason we list the hotel here is that it's perfectly located between the beach (two blocks away) and the Third Street Promenade (one block away). Plus, though it's hardly hostel-cheap, the rates are very reasonable for beach-area accommodations, and you simply can't find a hostel this well situated.

201 Broadway (at Second St.). ☎ *800-445-8695 or 310-451-2596. Fax: 310-393-4180. E-mail:* HotlCarmel@aol.com. *Internet:* www.hotelcarmel.com. *Rack rates: $100–$190 suite. AE, DC, DISC, MC, V.*

Hotel Figueroa

$$ Downtown

The Figueroa has, hands down, the most gorgeous public spaces of any Downtown hotel: decor in a Moorish theme (think Moroccan meets Spanish), exotic fabrics, wrought-iron and wood furniture, tiles and other decorative bits of fancy, and soaring ceilings — how the heck did this place land here? Rooms are not quite as splashy, but boy, did somebody try, successfully tarting up what was probably a dumpy old hotel by painting the walls with bold faux-finish paint and adding more of that exotic furniture and fabric. Too bad the acoustical tile ceilings and antiquated TVs remain. Rooms vary in size; 25s and 09s have cunning archways, and 30s are the biggest. With its desert succulents and splashing fountains, the pool area is *so* Palm Springs — who would expect to find such a quiet, secluded spot right in the middle of downtown? The across-the-street location from the Staples Center sports complex means that this is a favorite meeting-up spot for Lakers and Clippers fans (so, do pop in to the lobby for a drink or a bite at one of the two restaurants). Given that you can get similarly priced (at least, on weekends), more up-to-date rooms at the Wyndham Checkers, this may not be the place for you, but note that a former top executive with a national hotel chain volunteered that this is the only place he stays when he's in town, and that can tell you a great deal.

939 S. Figueroa St. (at Olympic Blvd.). ☎ 800-421-9092 or 213-627-3971. Fax: 213-689-0305. Internet: www.figueroahotel.com. *Rack rates: $104–$136 double. AE, MC, V.*

Hotel Shangri-La

$$$ Santa Monica

Miami-Deco fabulous, at least on the outside, the Shangri-La is a venerable Santa Monica establishment that is 90% one-bedroom suites. Some of the living room/bedroom combos come with sundecks, and all the rooms are filled with minimalist modern furniture that strives to maintain (but doesn't entirely achieve) that Deco feel. In truth, for the price, it's a bit more tacky than you may expect. This apparently does not bother the often upscale guests (rich musicians like Madonna and a number of actors) who doubtless enjoy the fact that they are staying directly across from Palisades Park and, thus, the ocean, access to which makes up for the lack of pool. Continental breakfast and a simple afternoon tea are included in the price.

1301 Ocean Ave. (2 blocks from Third Street Promenade). ☎ 800-345-STAY (800-345-7829) or 310-394-2791. Fax: 310-451-3351. Internet: www.shangrila-hotel.com. *Rack rates: $170–$550 double (ask about AAA discounts). AE, DISC, JCB, MC, V.*

Hyatt West Hollywood

$$$ West Hollywood

You've seen the rooftop pool in the movies *This is Spinal Tap* and *Almost Famous*; you've read the stories about the famous "Riot House" — no self-respecting 1970s rock star could claim that title unless he'd lobbed a TV out its windows. Nowadays, the Hyatt is a bit more sedate, darn it, but it still vibrates with energy (and the occasional metal guitarist), much like the trippy op-art carpeting in the hallways. Many rooms (done up in good corporate hotel style, but rock-star hangovers could get a workout from all the patterns) have aquariums or balconies with hillside or Sunset Strip views. A fitness center has all the necessary equipment; the gift shop sells bathing suits in case you've left yours behind. You get room service from 6 a.m. till midnight, a bar, a restaurant (with pan-urban cuisine), money-exchange services, and fabulous views — though no longer of Robert Plant declaring that he is a golden god.

8401 Sunset Blvd. (at Kings Rd.). ☎ *323-656-1234. Fax: 323-650-7024. Internet:* www.hyatt.com. *Rack rates: $195–$390 double (ask about AAA and senior discounts). AE, DC, DISC, MC, V.*

Le Montrose
$$$ West Hollywood

Discreetly tucked onto a residential side street south of the Sunset Strip (which makes one feel a tad safer, especially with kids in tow) and one block from Beverly Hills, Le Montrose offers quiet European-style comfort amid Art Nouveau decor in the lobby and elevators (which are something to see, honest), plus a restaurant, a health club, and a rooftop tennis court and pool. All rooms are suites with sunken living rooms, with fireplaces, fax machines, and twice-daily maid service; most come with kitchenettes. Free bicycles (adult size only) and tennis rackets are available for guests. Compared with equivalent places in the area, this is reasonably priced. Because it also has bed-and-breakfast packages, and children under 14 aren't generally charged, this isn't a bad upscale choice for families.

900 Hammond St. (at Sunset Blvd.). ☎ *800-766-0666 or 310-855-1115. Fax: 310-657-9192. Internet:* www.lemontrose.com. *Rack rates: $149–$950 per night. AE, DC, DISC, JCB, MC, V.*

Le Rêve
$$ West Hollywood

Located in a residential neighborhood and within walking distance from the Sunset Strip, Le Rêve is a small European-style hotel with a rooftop pool and spa, 24-hour room service, a decent fitness room, and best of all, fireplaces in almost every room. All rooms are suite-style, with a separate sitting area, fax machine, HBO, coffeemaker, and minibar; most rooms come with kitchenettes. The room furnishings are cheery, the staff is pleasant, and guests receive a complimentary fruit basket at check-in. Massages can be scheduled, and there's same-day laundry and dry cleaning. The only (minor) drawback is that the hotel is two blocks from the main fire station for the City of West Hollywood, so sirens may pierce your sleep. But the gamble is worth taking if you want a good hotel at a reasonable price (for Los Angeles) in a prime location. And golfers find the guaranteed tee times, transportation, and other golf amenities an extra bonus.

8822 Cynthia St. (off San Vicente Blvd.). ☎ ***800-835-7997*** *or 310-854-1114. Fax: 310-657-2623. Internet:* www.lerevehotel.com. *Rack rates: $149–$290. AE, DC, DISC, MC, V.*

Magic Castle Hotel
$$ Hollywood

The Magic Castle is a long-time clubhouse hangout for magicians and is impossible to get into unless you're a member (or invited by one) or unless you stay at this former dump now transformed into a nice bit of lodging. The gray-and-green spanking-clean new rooms (embellished with magician showbills) have plenty of elbow room; many rooms even have kitchenettes (grocery-shopping services are available). The on-site pool is square and situated in the middle of the courtyard, but you also have access to the curvy number up the street at the hotel's sister establishment, the all-suites **Hollywood Hills Hotel Apartments** (1999 N. Sycamore; ☎ **323-874-5089;** same rates and also worth checking out). The immediate surroundings are pulpy — as opposed to seedy — but it does have security parking, which is good, because you'll need a car; this hotel isn't precisely walking distance to anything. It's not the most pleasant block; *however,* this area is ripe for transition, so take advantage of the charm and prices while you can still afford them.

7025 Franklin Ave. (between La Brea and Highland Aves.). ☎ ***800-741-4915*** *or 323-851-0800. Fax: 323-581-4926. Internet:* www.magiccastlehotel.com. *Rack rates: $59–$159. AE, DC, DISC, JCB, MC, V.*

Maison 140
$$ Beverly Hills

Once upon a time, Maison 140 was a boardinghouse owned by silent-screen star Lillian Gish. Now, it's the sexiest, most decadently decorated hotel in the greater Los Angeles area. From the all-black lobby with the most minimal touches of white and red to the smallish but luxe rooms stocked with Frette linens, chinoiserie furnishings, and Philosophy-brand bath products (most rooms have showers only; you can request one with a tub), this boutique hotel swathes you in glamorous, sybaritic elegance. The hotel's sitting area serves continental breakfast in the morning and then shifts into a full bar at cocktail hour. Twenty-four-hour room service is provided by an off-site kitchen, there's a small fitness center with clean new machines, and you're within walking distance of all of Beverly Hills. Oh, this place is gorgeous! (And so is its glittering clientele.)

140 S. Lasky Dr. (just south of Wilshire Blvd.). ☎ ***800-432-5444*** *or 310-281-4000. Fax: 310-281-4001. Internet:* www.maison140.com. *Rack rates: $119–$179 (Internet discounts available). AE, DC, MC, V.*

Downtown Accommodations and Dining

ACCOMMODATIONS ■

Hotel Figueroa **11**

Millennium Biltmore **6**

Westin Bonaventure **8**

Wyndham Checkers **5**

DINING ◆

Ciudad **9**

Grand Central Market **4**

Nick & Stef's **7**

The Original Pantry Cafe **10**

Philippe The Original **2**

Sushi Gen **3**

Yang Chow **1**

Legend

Information ⓘ

Parking 🅿

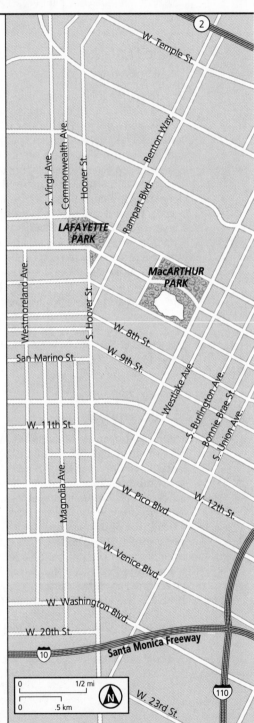

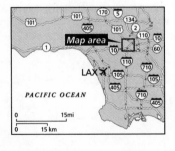

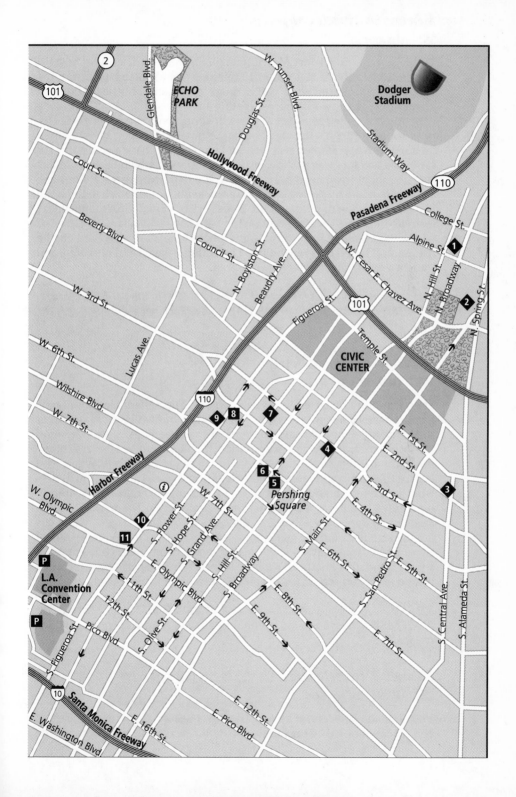

Marriott Los Angeles Airport

$$ Airport

The Los Angeles Airport Marriott is just 5 minutes from Los Angeles International Airport (LAX) and 10 minutes from Venice beach, and the friendly, helpful concierge can arrange tours and shuttles to tourist attractions. With two bars, two restaurants, a car rental outlet, handicapped-accessible rooms, an ATM, a gift shop, room service, a pool, a fitness room, a Kinko's business center, a notary public, a beauty shop, laundry and dry-cleaning services, and complimentary transportation to LAX, this is a fine way station or base camp from which to explore Los Angeles should you need to be close to the departure gates. Rooms can be hard to come by during Labor Day weekend, however, when the hotel is packed solid with guests of the Sweet & Hot Foundation's annual jazz festival; the hotel's warm relationship with the festival is demonstrated on the Jazz Walk of Fame around the pool. Rooms are nice (and can be discounted based on availability). The staff is relaxed and outgoing, and there's a calm, efficient vibe throughout.

5855 W. Century Blvd. (at the airport). ☎ *800-228-9290 or 310-641-5700. Fax: 310-337-5358. Internet:* www.marriothotels.com. *Rack rates: $194–$425. AE, DC, DISC, MC, V.*

Millennium Biltmore Hotel

$$$ Downtown

They just don't make 'em like this anymore. The Millennium Biltmore is a near masterpiece of a glorious old hotel — but while we swoon over the heavenly details (would you *look* at those ceilings?!), keep in mind the "old" part. If you require pristine high-concept whatevers, move down the listings to the Standard and let us get on with it. Would you look at that tile in and around the indoor pool? All right, we'll stop. Here's what you need to know: This full-service hotel is centrally located in downtown L.A. It has a good, Art Deco health club. The rooms (French Regency in appearance) vary in size (07s are usually largest, while 40s are the smallest, and the nicest rooms overlook Pershing Square), but all accommodations have windows that open, firm beds (but scratchy sheets), and dinky baths. It's a little frilly for the business traveler and a bit too staid and sedate for families. But we'd be thrilled to stay here.

506 S. Grand Ave. (between 5th and 6th Sts.). ☎ *800-245-8673 or 213-624-1011. Fax: 213-612-1545. Internet:* www.millennium-hotels.com. *Rack rates: $194 and up (double).*

Ramada West Hollywood

$$$ West Hollywood

This Ramada goes out of its way to show guests a good time. It offers a 10% discount on cars from Enterprise Rental next door, and the concierge works very hard at hooking guests up with tickets to the Key Club and House of Blues, along with other club attractions. And litigants from the Judge Judy and Judge Joe Brown television shows stay here, so you can often hear them discussing the wacky points of their cases in the elevator. The hotel is very gay-friendly, and the hotel gets booked up early for summer, especially during the Gay Pride celebration (the second to last weekend in June) and Halloween, which also features a major parade. Room service comes from **Du Par's** restaurant on-site; there's Nintendo, wireless WebTV, and plenty of nightlife just outside the door. The pool is huge, and long-term guests are welcome. Just mention *Los Angeles & Disneyland For Dummies* and receive 25% off the rack rate!

8585 Santa Monica Blvd. (near Sunset and La Cienega Blvds.). ☎ *800-845-8585 or 310-652-6400. Fax: 310-652-4207. Internet:* www.ramada-wh.com. *Rack rates: $165–$275. AE, DC, DISC, MC, V.*

Renaissance Hollywood Hotel
$$$ Hollywood

A former dumpy Holiday Inn has been turned into the stylish neighbor of the new Hollywood-Highland Complex. "Midcentury modern" is the motto here; "too clever by half" is our response. The restaurant is called **Twist** "because it's a twist on things." (The menus are metal, that's all we noticed.) What do you expect from what is essentially the Marriott chain's response to the hip, neat, cool, and groovy W hotels (the hot, hip happening hotels popping up all over the United States)? But still, we dig the cool Biedermeyer furniture in the rooms and the "good luck" bamboo in the bathrooms (to improve a room's feng shui and just generally promote good luck). Plus, all digs have Nintendo, WebTV, and CD players; higher-up rooms have their own Siamese fighting fish; and rooms facing north have lovely views of the Hollywood Hills. Shhh . . . it's totally booked up for the Oscars, probably by stars getting their hair done steps away from the red carpet.

1755 N. Highland Ave. (in the Hollywood-Highland Complex). ☎ *323-856-1200. Fax: 323-856-1205. Internet:* www.renaissancehollywood.com. *Rack rates: $249 double. AE, CB, DC, DISC, JCB, MC, V.*

Sea Shore Motel
$$ Santa Monica

This family-owned and -operated establishment admittedly looks a little dumpy on the outside, but rooms are better than that, though inexplicably Southwestern in theme (inspired, possibly, by the California Heritage Museum across the street), some with tile floors, and most with oddly roomy, very clean bathrooms. No room service is offered, but the beach is just a couple of blocks west, and free parking is provided in an area where spots are impossible to come by. Unless you absolutely need a posh place to rest your head, this is a fine bargain.

2637 Main St. (just south of Ocean Park Blvd.). ☎ **310-392-2787.** *Fax: 310-392-5167. Internet:* www.seashoremotel.com. *Rack rates: $75–$130 double (be sure to ask about discounts). AE, DISC, MC, V.*

The Standard
$$$ West Hollywood

This high-style, high-concept, 1970s designer retro motor lodge comes complete with Warhol print fabrics, beanbag chairs in the rooms, and blue synthetic turf around the pool. This is hip hostelry at its most extreme. The barbershop can schedule a tattooist for you, and every night, models writhe in the green glow of a glass booth behind the front desk. The not-cheap 24-hour coffee shop ($40 with tip for a two-person breakfast, yikes!) is a hot spot for clubgoers, and the lobby seethes with the sleek and chic. Or stay in your room and enjoy the round-the-clock room service. There's no health club, but your room key entitles you to half-price day rates at nearby Crunch Gym, where Leonardo DiCaprio and slews of other stars get sweaty. Rooms that face the Strip are less expensive and noisier than those in the back, and all rooms come with CDs, WebTV, Nintendo, and T-1 lines, plus heaps of cool bath products. Pets of all sizes are welcome but require a $100 nonrefundable fee.

8300 Sunset Blvd. (east of La Cienege Blvd.). ☎ **323-650-9090.** *Fax: 323-650-2820. Internet:* www.standardhotel.com. *Rack rates: $160–$650 (double). AE, DC, DISC, JCB, MC, V.*

Venice Beach House
$$ Venice

A nine-room bed-and-breakfast in an old Craftsman beach house on the National Register of Historic Places, this is the kind of detailed-to-a-fare-thee-well, antiques-filled, soft-focus romantic getaway that seems to flourish in towns like San Francisco but is oddly in short supply in L.A. Each room has its own theme — from the tiny Tramps' Quarters (the smallest room) to the luxurious Pier Suite (with a fireplace and sitting room) — and delights (like the wool plaid upholstered walls in the Abbot Kinney room and the fireplace in the James Peasgood room), as well as its own drawbacks (size varies, and four rooms share two bathrooms between them). So it's a good idea to check out the photos on its Web site. Breakfast is continental, parking is free, and the beach is across the street. The good parts of Main Street are a serious hike away, and never mind the delights of Santa Monica, so plan on having a car (though there are restaurants within walking distance).

15 30th Ave. (at Speedway). ☎ **310-823-1966.** *Internet:* www.venicebeach house.com. *Rack rates: $125–$190 (AAA discounts available). AE, MC, V.*

Westin Bonaventure
$$$ Downtown

When this five-cylinder-shaped glass tower went up in downtown L.A. in 1976, some people found it appallingly hideous, while others thought it rather remarkable. It became an instant landmark, nonetheless. It's still a cheap thrill to take one of the fast-paced glass elevators to a room (not a good idea for folks with vertigo), all of which are shaped like wedges of pie, making the somewhat small bathrooms more navigable than their size indicates. The largest hotel in Los Angeles (1,354 units), it's a mini-city, with bustling shops and restaurants galore, a boon for families or anyone craving anonymity. The best rooms have the Westin's famed Heavenly Beds (top-of-the-line everything) or at least views (on clear days) of the Hollywood Hills, though every unit has floor-to-ceiling windows. The large outdoor pool can be quite the scene on warm days, and you get $10 passes to the handsome YWCA across the street.

404 S. Figueroa St. (between 4th and 5th Sts.). ☎ *213-624-1000. Fax: 213-612-4800. Internet:* www.westin.com. *Rack rates: $259 double.*

Wilshire Crest Inn
$ Near Beverly Hills

Wilshire Boulevard is a major artery for Los Angeles, moving from downtown to the beach, past museums and shopping areas with regular, swift public transportation along its busy lanes. And the owner-operated Wilshire Crest Inn (which is actually right off Wilshire on a side street), a reasonably priced, attractive hotel, is perfectly situated to take advantage of all that the boulevard offers. Rooms are good-sized and pale pink and green; the lobby/parlor is large, with couches and chairs; and you can relax on an outdoor courtyard and patio. Complimentary pastries, bagels, coffee, and tea offered in the lobby in the morning draw visiting staff from the nearby consulates and guest speakers and curators from the many museums down the road.

6301 Orange St. (off Wilshire Blvd.). ☎ *800-654-9951 or 323-936-5131. Fax: 323-936-2013. Internet:* www.wilshirecrestinn.com. *Rack rates: $82 for one; $92 for two people. Senior citizen discounts available. AE, DC, DISC, MC, V.*

Wyndham Checkers
$$ Downtown

This stylish 1927 hotel has elegant, old-timey public spaces and rooms that are currently undergoing a total redecoration, from a mock Regency style to something more businesslike (at press time, no one at the hotel knew precisely how it would all look). Note that rooms ending in 02 are big enough to swing a cat, but only just, while 07s are the largest. Bathrooms, however, are surprisingly roomy. A tiny rooftop lap pool offers fantastic views of the downtown cityscape, which is visible from rooms on the 8th floor up; otherwise, guests are treated to views of office-building windows. You get high-speed Internet access in your room, 24-hour room service, and complimentary downtown shuttle service from 7 a.m. to 9 p.m. Plus, the lovely restaurant serves one of the nicest after-noon teas in town.

535 S. Grand Ave. (between 5th and 6th Sts.). ☎ *213-624-0000. Fax: 213-626-9906. Internet:* www.checkershotel.com/. *Rack rates: $189 weekdays; $99 week-ends (double). AE, DISC, MC, V.*

Los Angeles Runner-Up Hotels

If you find that the lodging selections in the preceding section are booked solid at the time you want to visit, the following accommodations are perfectly acceptable options.

The Beverly Hills Hotel
$$$$ Beverly Hills

It's that enormous, pink (well, faded a touch) landmark on Sunset Boulevard. You've seen its spires on the cover of the Eagles' *Hotel California* album. You've heard tales of the **Polo Lounge** and those fabulous bungalows. You've heard of endless celebs who have stayed there. Should you? Probably not, we hate to say. Although it has had a major upgrade, the hotel is terribly pricey, and you likely won't get your money's worth. Unless you run into Liz or Mick — can you put a price on that?

9641 Sunset Blvd. (at Rodeo Dr.). ☎ *800-283-8885 or 310-276-2251. Fax: 310-281-2905. Internet:* www.beverlyhillshotel.com. *Rack rates: $375–$445 double. AE, DC, MC, V.*

Doubletree Guest Suites Santa Monica
$$$$ Santa Monica

Don't be scared off by the rack rates at this hotel; Doubletree's Web site offers discounts of 40% or so, plus other specials. The location is prime, four blocks from both the beach and Santa Monica's Main Street. Plus, this is where all the heavyweights in the O.J. Simpson civil trial stayed.

1707 4th St. (4 blocks from the beach). ☎ *800-222-TREE (800-222-8733) or 310-395-3332. Fax: 310-452-7399. Internet:* www.doubletree.com. *Rack rates: $395–$1,200. AE, DC, DISC, MC, V.*

The Grafton on Sunset
$$$ West Hollywood

A hotel designed with feng shui principles to give guests a delightful stay — it's just *so* L.A. You get round-the-clock room service and a beautiful city view from the pool. Best of all, the hotel's courtesy car is a lime-green PT Cruiser. The hip minimalist steakhouse **Balboa** is located on-site.

8462 Sunset Blvd. (near Beverly Hills). ☎ *800-821-3660 or 323-654-4600. Fax: 323-654-5918. Internet: www.graftononsunset.com. Rack rates: $179–$500 (double). AE, DC, DISC, MC, V.*

Hilton Universal City & Towers/Sheraton Universal Hotel
$$ Universal City

The only real reason to stay at these big, bland corporate hotels is that they're across the street from Universal Studios, CityWalk, and Amphitheatre. Granted, these are perfectly decent upscale hotels, with all the amenities — including large, nicely decorated rooms, room service, in-room safes, coffeemakers, minibars, valet parking, fitness rooms, and pools — but you can find more centrally located hotels at the same or lower rates that feature way more personality, with no need to traverse the freeways to get around. Both hotels have efficient, professional staffs and not-cheap restaurants. (The Hilton features huge, pricey buffets daily for every meal.) Sure, it may be fun to say that you stayed at the same hotel where "guests of this show stayed" (that would be the Sheraton), and many rooms *do* have spectacular views of the city, but the only real pluses are the Universal tour packages and the sense of rich reliability offered by these hotels; both have huge two-bedroom suites available for similarly huge amounts of money. Fans of Beelzebub may want to request room number 666, available at both hotels, if only to say that they did.

Hilton Universal City & Towers: 555 Universal Terrace Parkway. ☎ **800-445-8667** or 818-506-2500. Fax: 818-509-2058. Internet: www.universalcity.hilton.com. Rack rates: $150–$1400 per night. AX, Disc, Diners, MC, V. Sheraton Universal Hotel: 333 Universal Hollywood Dr. ☎ **888-625-5144** or 818-980-1212. Fax: 818-985-4980. Internet: www.sheraton.com. Rack rates: $159–$1,000 per night.

Hotel Bel Air
$$$$ Bel Air

A "runner-up?" Are we nuts? Nope. It's just that this fabulous, 12-acre lush hideaway — preferred by the well-heeled who love its discretion and creature comforts — is too expensive for the likes of us. (Tom Cruise and Nicole Kidman *lived here,* if that tells you anything.) But if you can afford it, go there for us, okay?

701 Stone Canyon Rd. (north of Sunset Blvd.). ☎ *800-648-4097 or 310-472-1211. Fax: 310-476-5890. Internet: www.hotelbelair.com. Rack rates: $385–$525 double. AE, DC, JCB, MC, V.*

Wyndham Summerfield Suites
$$$ West Hollywood

Located in the heart of West Hollywood, walking distance from Santa Monica Boulevard and the Sunset Strip, this Wyndham offers all-suites rooms, most with fireplaces and some with kitchenettes. You get a complimentary breakfast buffet and grocery shopping, plus a rooftop pool and Bath & Bodyworks toiletries.

1000 Westmount Dr. (1 block west of La Cienega Blvd.). ☎ *877-999-3223 or 310-657-7400. Fax: 310-854-6744. Internet:* www.summerfieldsuites.com. *Rack rates: $279 double. AE, DC, DISC, MC, V.*

Wyndham Bel Age
$$$$ West Hollywood

Another Wyndham property, this hotel may be a favorite with pop stars and actors, but it still maintains a regal, luxurious elegance. Enjoy live jazz in **Club Brasserie,** California bistro cuisine in **La Brasserie,** and fine Russian dining at **Diaghilev,** plus a gift shop, a pool, a florist, an art gallery, and handicapped-accessible rooms. You may remember this hotel from the *Beverly Hills 90210* prom night and Backstreet Boyz episodes. Deep discounts are available online.

1020 N. San Vincent Blvd. (between Sunset and Santa Monica Blvds.). ☎ *877-999-3223 or 310-854-1111. Fax: 310-854-0926. Internet:* www.summerfield suites.com. *Rack rates: $300–$640. AE, DC, DISC, MC, V.*

Index of Accommodations by Location

Santa Monica
Best Western Ocean View Hotel ($$)
Doubletree Guest Suites Santa Monica
  ($$$$)
The Georgian ($$$)
Hotel Carmel ($$)
Hotel Shangri-La ($$$)
Sea Shore Motel ($$)

Universal City
Hilton Universal City & Towers ($$)
Sheraton Universal Hotel ($$)

Venice
Cadillac Hotel ($)
Venice Beach House ($$)

West Hollywood
Alta Cienega Motel ($)
Argyle ($$$$)
Beverly Laurel Motor Hotel ($)
Beverly Plaza Hotel ($$$)
Chateau Marmont ($$$$)
Elan Hotel Modern ($$)
The Grafton on Sunset ($$$)
Hyatt West Hollywood ($$$)
Le Montrose ($$$)
Le Rêve ($$)
Ramada West Hollywood ($$$)
The Standard ($$$)
Wyndham Bel Age ($$$$)
Wyndham Summerfield Suites ($$$)

Index of Accommodations by Price

$$$$
Argyle Hotel (West Hollywood)
Beverly Hills Hotel (Beverly Hills)
Chateau Marmont (Hollywood/West
  Hollywood)
Doubletree Guest Suites Santa Monica
  (Santa Monica)
Hotel Bel Air (Bel Air)
Wyndham Bel Age (West Hollywood)

$$$
Avalon Hotel (Beverly Hills)
Beverly Hills Inn (Beverly Hills)
Beverly Plaza Hotel (West Hollywood)
Crowne Plaza Hotel (Airport)
The Georgian (Santa Monica)
The Grafton on Sunset (West
  Hollywood)
Hollywood Roosevelt Hotel
  (Hollywood)
Hotel Shangri-La (Santa Monica)
Hyatt West Hollywood (West
  Hollywood)
Millennium Biltmore Hotel
  (Downtown)
Le Montrose (West Hollywood)
Ramada West Hollywood (West
  Hollywood)

Renaissance Hollywood Hotel
  (Hollywood)
The Standard (West Hollywood)
Westin Bonaventure (Downtown)
Wyndham Summerfield Suites (West
  Hollywood)

$$
Best Western Hollywood Hills Hotel
  (Hollywood)
Best Western Ocean View Hotel (Santa
  Monica)
Beverly Crescent Hotel (Beverly Hills)
Beverly Terrace Hotel (Beverly Hills)
Elan Hotel Modern (West Hollywood)
Hilton Universal City & Towers
  (Universal City)
Hotel Carmel (Santa Monica)
Hotel Figueroa (Downtown)
Le Rêve (West Hollywood)
Marriott Los Angeles Airport (Airport)
Magic Castle Hotel (Hollywood)
Maison 140 (Beverly Hills)
Sea Shore Motel (Santa Monica)
Sheraton Universal Hotel (Universal
  City)
Venice Beach House (Venice)
Wyndham Checkers (Downtown)

$

Alta Cienega Motel (West Hollywood)

Beverly Hills Reeves Hotel (Beverly Hills)

Beverly Laurel Motor Hotel (West Hollywood)

Bevonshire Lodge (Hollywood)

Cadillac Hotel (Venice)

Celebrity Hotel (Hollywood)

Hollywood Bungalows (Hollywood)

Wilshire Crest Inn (near Beverly Hills)

Chapter 9

Tying Up the Loose Ends

● ●

In This Chapter

▶ Getting the lowdown on rental cars and travel insurance

▶ Staying healthy on your trip

▶ Finding out about upcoming attractions and events

▶ Deciding what and how to pack

● ●

*Y*ou've purchased your ticket, reserved your hotel room, and even plotted out a day-to-day itinerary for your trip to Los Angeles. Now is the time to attend to the little details of your trip, from renting a car to reserving a table at a hot restaurant to deciding what clothes, shoes, assorted gear, and bare necessities to pack.

Renting a Car: Weighing Your Options

Here we have a true paradox. Los Angeles is miserable to drive in, through, even around. Car culture here is second only to Detroit's. It's bad to drive here. Oh, not Manhattan-at-rush-hour bad, but bad.

And yet, you have to drive for two related reasons:

✔ Los Angeles is a sprawling locale; it's the largest city, in terms of land mass and sheer geographical dimensions, in the United States — and that's not taking into account the cities attached to it, such as Pasadena, or cities just to the south of it, such as Anaheim (home to a little place called Disneyland) — all places that you, the visitor, will surely want to visit.

✔ The size and the ring of interrelated cities would lead you to assume that L.A. must have a fabulous public transportation system, right? Pardon us while we fall to the floor, clutching our stomachs and wheezing with laughter. Then we collect ourselves and say, "Oh, yes, there is a bus system — *snort* — and a subway — *bwa ha ha ha ha ha.*" Unfortunately, neither of these options really figures into matters. You can find more details about getting around the city in Chapter 11, but for now, just accept that you're going to be part of the traffic problem in L.A. Unless, of course, you plan to be here only for a couple of days and stay in some highly central location (like Downtown or Hollywood, near that laughable, but occasionally useful, subway system, or at the beach, and all you want to do is lie on the sand), and you don't plan to leave that neighborhood much, if at all.

With that in mind, you may indeed decide to rent a car during your stay in Los Angeles. Doing so is a snap. All major car-rental agencies have offices in the city; many can be found at the airport or in major hotels. For a complete listing of **major car-rental agencies,** with phone numbers and Web sites, go to the Quick Concierge appendix at the back of the book.

In general, car-rental rates in Los Angeles are more reasonable than those found in other U.S. markets. Still, you'll find that prices can vary greatly, depending on the size of the car, the length of time you keep it, where and when you pick it up and drop it off, where you take it, and a host of other factors.

Asking a few key questions can save you hundreds of dollars. For example, weekend rates may be lower than weekday rates. Ask if the rate is the same for pickup Friday morning as it is Thursday night. If you're keeping the car five or more days, a weekly rate is often cheaper than the daily rate. Some companies may assess a drop-off charge if you don't return the car to the same renting location; others, notably National, do not. Ask if the rate is cheaper if you pick up the car at the airport or a location in town. If you see an advertised price in your local newspaper, be sure to ask for that specific rate; otherwise you may be charged the standard (higher) rate. Don't forget to mention membership in AAA, AARP, frequent-flier programs, and trade unions. These memberships usually entitle you to discounts ranging from 5% to 30%. Ask your travel agent to check any and all of these rates.

Most car rentals are worth at least 500 miles on your frequent-flier account!

On top of the standard rental prices, other optional charges apply to most car rentals. The **Collision Damage Waiver** (CDW), which requires you to pay for damage to the car in a collision, is covered by many credit-card companies. Check with your credit-card company before you go so you can avoid paying this hefty fee (as much as $15 per day).

The car-rental companies also offer additional **liability insurance** (in the event that you harm others in an accident), **personal accident insurance** (in case you harm yourself or your passengers), and **personal effects insurance** (if your luggage is stolen from your car). If you have insurance on your car at home, it probably covers you in most of these scenarios. If your own insurance doesn't cover you for rentals, or if you don't have auto insurance, consider paying for additional coverage. (The car-rental companies are liable for certain base amounts, depending on the state.) But weigh the likelihood of getting into an accident or losing your luggage against the cost of these coverages (as much as $20 per day combined), which can significantly add to the price of your rental.

Some companies also offer **refueling packages,** in which you pay for an entire tank of gas up front. The price is usually fairly competitive with local gas prices, but you don't get credit for any gas remaining in the tank. If you reject this option, you pay only for the gas you use, but you have to return it with a full tank or face charges of $3 to $4 a gallon for any shortfall. If a stop at a gas station on the way to the airport will make you miss your plane, by all means, take advantage of the fuel purchase option. Otherwise, skip it.

For tips on driving in Los Angeles, turn to Chapter 11.

Buying Travel Insurance: Do You Need It?

Before you buy travel insurance to cover trip cancellation, lost luggage, or medical expenses, check your existing homeowner's and health insurance policies. You're likely to have partial or complete coverage. But if you need some insurance, ask your travel agent about a comprehensive package. The cost of travel insurance varies widely, depending on the cost and length of your trip, your age and overall health, and the type of trip you're taking. Insurance for extreme sports or adventure travel, for example, costs more than coverage for a cruise. Some insurers provide packages for specialty vacations, such as skiing or backpacking. More dangerous activities may be excluded from basic policies.

And keep in mind that in the aftermath of the World Trade Center attacks, a number of airlines, cruise lines, and tour operators are no longer covered by insurers. The bottom line: Always, always check the fine print before you sign on; more and more policies have built-in exclusions and restrictions that may leave you out in the cold if something goes awry.

For information, contact one of the following popular insurers:

- ✔ **Access America** (☎ 800-284-8300; Internet: www.access america.com/)
- ✔ **Travel Guard International** (☎ 800-826-1300; Internet: www.travelguard.com)

> ✔ **Travel Insured International** (☎ 800-243-3174; Internet: www.travelinsured.com)
>
> ✔ **Travelex Insurance Services** (☎ 800-228-9792; Internet: www.travelex-insurance.com)

Trip-cancellation insurance (TCI)

There are three major types of trip-cancellation insurance that cover specific circumstances:

> ✔ When you prepay for a cruise or tour that gets cancelled, and you can't get your money back
>
> ✔ When you or someone in your family gets sick or dies, and you can't travel (but beware that you may not be covered for a pre-existing condition)
>
> ✔ When bad weather makes travel impossible

Some insurers provide coverage for events like jury duty, natural disasters close to home (such as floods or fire), and even the loss of a job. A few companies have added provisions for cancellations due to terrorist activities. Always check the fine print before signing on, and don't buy trip-cancellation insurance from the tour operator that may be responsible for the cancellation; buy it only from a reputable travel insurance agency. Don't overbuy. You won't be reimbursed for more than the cost of your trip.

Medical insurance

Most health insurance policies cover you if you get sick away from home — but check, particularly if you're insured by an HMO. Members of **Blue Cross/Blue Shield** (☎ 800-810-BLUE; Internet: www.bluecares.com) can now use their cards at select hospitals in most major cities worldwide.

Some credit cards (American Express and certain gold and platinum Visa and MasterCards, for example) offer automatic flight insurance against death or dismemberment in case of an airplane crash if you charged the cost of your ticket.

If you require additional insurance, try one of the following companies:

> ✔ **MEDEX International** (9515 Deereco Rd., Timonium, MD 21093-5375; ☎ 888-MEDEX-00 or 410-453-6300; Fax: 410-453-6301; Internet: www.medexassist.com).

> ✔ **Travel Assistance International** (9200 Keystone Crossing, Suite 300, Indianapolis, IN 46240; ☎ **800-821-2828;** Internet: www. travelassistance.com). For general information on services, call the company's Worldwide Assistance Services, Inc., at ☎ **800-777-8710.**

The cost of travel medical insurance varies widely. Check your existing policies before you buy additional coverage. Also, check to see if your medical insurance covers you for emergency medical evacuation: If you have to buy a one-way, same-day ticket home and forfeit your non-refundable roundtrip ticket, you may be out big bucks.

Lost-luggage insurance

On domestic flights, checked baggage is covered up to $2,500 per ticketed passenger. On international flights (including U.S. portions of international trips), baggage is limited to approximately $9.07 per pound, up to approximately $635 per checked bag. If you plan to check items more valuable than the standard liability, you may purchase "excess valuation" coverage from the airline, up to $5,000. Be sure to take any valuables or irreplaceable items with you in your carry-on luggage. If you file a lost-luggage claim, be prepared to answer detailed questions about the contents of your baggage, and be sure to file a claim immediately, as most airlines enforce a 21-day deadline. Before you leave home, compile an inventory of all packed items and a rough estimate of the total value to ensure that you're properly compensated if your luggage is lost. You'll be reimbursed only for what you lost, no more. After you file a complaint, persist in securing your reimbursement; there are no laws governing the length of time it takes for a carrier to reimburse you. If you arrive at a destination without your bags, ask the airline to forward them to your hotel or to your next destination; it'll usually comply. If your bag is delayed or lost, the airline may reimburse you for reasonable expenses, such as a toothbrush or a set of clothes, but the airline is under no legal obligation to do so.

Lost luggage may also be covered by your homeowner's or renter's policy. Many platinum and gold credit cards cover you, as well. If you choose to purchase additional lost-luggage insurance, be sure not to buy more than you need. Buy in advance from the insurer or a trusted agent (because prices are much higher at the airport).

Ensuring a Healthy Trip

If you're concerned about getting sick away from home, consider purchasing **medical travel insurance,** and carry your ID card in your purse or wallet. In most cases, your existing health plan will provide the coverage you need. See the "Medical insurance" section earlier in this chapter for more information.

If you suffer from a chronic illness, consult your doctor before your departure. For conditions like epilepsy, diabetes, or heart problems, wear a **Medic Alert Identification Tag** (☎ 800-825-3785; Internet: www.medicalert.org), which will immediately alert doctors to your condition and give them access to your records through Medic Alert's 24-hour hotline.

Pack **prescription medications** in your carry-on luggage, and carry prescription medications in their original containers. Also bring along copies of your prescriptions in case you lose your pills or run out.

In L.A., the sun shines most of the time. Limit your **exposure to the sun,** especially during the first few days of your trip and, thereafter, from 11 a.m. to 2 p.m. Use a sunscreen with a high protection factor and apply it liberally. Remember that children need more protection than adults do.

And don't leave home without **sunglasses** and an extra pair of **contact lenses** or **prescription glasses.**

Making Reservations and Buying Tickets in Advance

Plan on spending a little time online before you come to L.A. to find out what (or who) will be where when you come to town. **Ticketmaster** is your best resource for purchasing advance tickets to concerts or special events. You can reach Ticketmaster online at www.ticketmaster.com or by calling ☎ 213-480-3232. Keep in mind that if you purchase tickets through this site, you can expect to pay an extra premium per ticket (anywhere from $2 to $20). **Laweekly.com** and **newtimesla.com** have calendar listings for a week or so in advance, along with suggestions for best bets for various live performances around the city.

If our listing of a **restaurant** mentions the word "popular" (or "expensive" or "trendy"), plan on making reservations as far in advance as you can (though you can always get in to a place if you just show up around 6 p.m. or 10 p.m., when the crowds are thinnest).

The only **museum** you need to worry about in advance is the Getty, which has limited parking. The museum requires parking reservations (except on Thursday nights), and the lot can fill up in advance. You can walk there, but because the walk is up a hill, and it takes some navigation via various public transports, taking a car is simplest. For **theater listings,** ticket information, and upcoming calendars, check **Theatre LA,** an alliance of performing arts organizations throughout the city. Check online at www.theatrela.org or call ☎ 213-614-0556.

Packing Smart

The simplest and best advice we ever got about packing came from our dad: "Before you go, spread out everything you plan to take. Then pack half the clothes and twice the money." Indeed, rare is the trip where someone says wistfully, "I wish I had packed more stuff."

There are stores here, with clothes, and cosmetics, and toiletries. You can get pretty much anything you need. So while you do need to pack the absolutely required and hard-to-replace items, such as prescription drugs, glasses, and contact lenses, keep the rest to a minimum.

Los Angeles is a clotheshorse town, but a casual one. Jeans and T-shirts are the norm. Sure, the leggy gal next to you is wearing jeans that cost $100 and a T-shirt that cost even more, but can you compete with that? No, you can't. Your chain-store jeans and shirt will do just fine. People don't even dress up here to go to the theater; a nice dress or pair of pants will do. Clubgoers wear even *more* expensive jeans and T-shirts, sometimes with glitter on them. Frankly, a pair of black pants and a black shirt will take you, male or female, anywhere. Toss in a scarf or some beads, or buy some glitter, and you have all your bases covered.

What to take

Our recommendations for what to pack for a 5- to 7-day trip, other than undergarments, socks, something to sleep in, toiletries, and this book, are

- ✔ **Two pairs of pants:** Yes, two pairs. One pair of jeans, one pair of black pants. Or maybe just two pairs of black pants.

- ✔ **A pair of shorts:** If it's hot.

- ✔ **Three short-sleeve shirts:** Maybe two short-sleeve shirts and one sleeveless.

- ✔ **Two long-sleeve shirts:** One of which is black and nice, maybe silk or with ruffles or nice trim.

- ✔ **A good pair of walking shoes:** Again, if it's hot, a pair of sandals.

- ✔ **A few lightweight accessories:** To dress up your black shirt and pants. A thin belt, for example, or a scarf or dangly earrings.

- ✔ **A skirt or a dress:** Especially if it's lightweight. On hot days, a simple cotton dress or skirt is nice to stroll around in. Pair a long gypsy-style skirt with a black top, and you're comfy and stylin'.

- ✔ **Bathing suits:** A requirement, regardless of what you think the weather is, because L.A. is known to have sudden hot days just about any month, and you'd hate to get caught unprepared for the pool or beach.

✔ **A wide-brimmed hat:** A good idea, but you can buy sunglasses or sunscreen while you're here.

Your reward for having a suitcase that isn't overstuffed: You'll have room for the clothes (and other doodads) that you're going to buy!

How to pack it

When choosing which shirts, pants, and the like to pack, go for the items that are **all cotton;** even though cotton wrinkles, it's more comfortable in the heat. Rayon isn't quite as breathable, but the wrinkles shake out more readily. Think also **loose-fitting clothes,** even though the fashionistas of L.A. are all about tight and body conscious. But take it from us: You'll be far more comfortable in the heat if your clothes are loose. Of course, if you have a model body, by all means, flaunt it. You won't be alone.

Roll things, rather than fold them, and they wrinkle less. Try separating items into **plastic baggies** (themselves handy items to toss in a suitcase, for they can hold anything from leaking toiletries to leftovers to wet bathing suits) — underwear in one, T-shirts in another, and so on, for more organized packing.

Carry on any valuables if you're flying. Don't take chances by packing your favorite heirloom jewelry and the like in checked luggage.

Part III
Settling in to Los Angeles

The 5th Wave   By Rich Tennant

Don't yell at <u>me</u>! You're the one who wanted a map to the stars when we got to LA.

In this part . . .

*T*his section helps you orient yourself in the city, whether you arrive by plane, train, bus, or car. We tell you the best ways to get to your hotel from the airport — by taxi, shuttle, rental or hired car, and public transportation. When you're settled in, we tell you the best ways to get around, with invaluable driving and parking tips for those travelers with cars, and advise you on the best neighborhoods for taking a stroll. Finally, we deal with money matters, telling you where you can get cash when you need it, what to do if your wallet is stolen, and what to expect in the way of tacked-on taxes.

Chapter 10

Arriving and Getting Oriented

• •

In This Chapter

▶ Getting there by plane, train, or automobile

▶ Getting from the airport to your hotel

▶ Discovering L.A. neighborhoods

• •

*Y*ou've arrived, in the most literal sense, in a sprawling, steaming caldron of light and energy. What, pray tell, do you do next? In this chapter, we tell you how to get to your hotel with ease and confidence, as well as give you a concise orientation of Los Angeles neighborhoods.

Arriving by Plane

Los Angeles International Airport — more familiarly known as LAX — is the third busiest airport in, sigh, the world (☎ **310-646-5252**; Internet: www.lawa.org). But you don't need to sit down and sob. The airport got a fine redesign for the 1984 Olympics, one that put departing traffic on an upper level and arriving traffic on a lower level, so that helped with traffic in and out. Signage is good; arriving travelers are clearly directed to baggage claim, taxis, and so forth. One bit of confusion is directly outside, where there are a number of shuttle stops for shuttles to hotels, airport parking lots (for long-term parking), the city, and so on. Read the signs on the shuttles carefully, or just ask someone. The airport is 9½ miles from Santa Monica and 16 miles from Hollywood. From the airport, it's approximately a half-hour drive to Downtown, and a 40-minute drive to West Hollywood, depending on the traffic.

You may arrive at the small but busy **Burbank-Glendale-Pasadena Airport**, some 8 miles northeast of Hollywood (☎ 800-U-FLY-BUR; Internet: www.burbankairport.com). It has only two terminals and is easy to get around — everyone is filtered to the same stretch of a few-yards-long sidewalk. From the airport, it's about a 25-minute drive to Downtown, and a 20-minute drive to West Hollywood, depending on the traffic.

Getting to your hotel by taxi

The easiest way to get to your hotel is probably by **cab.** Taxis can be found curbside on the Lower/Arrival Level islands in front of each terminal at LAX under the yellow sign indicating "Taxis." You'll be presented with a ticket stating typical fares to major destinations. Only authorized taxis with an official seal issued by the City of Los Angeles Department of Transportation are permitted in the airport. Cabs charge an airport fee of $2.50, in addition to a $2 pickup fee, and $2 per mile, plus additional charges when you get stuck in traffic, a common occurrence. Tipping your cab driver 10% to 15% is customary. Expect to pay between $31 and $40 (plus tip), depending on your destination. Taxis can accommodate up to five passengers.

At Burbank, you find cab racks on the island in front of each terminal, with clearly marked signs and a cab coordinator. Only authorized taxis with an official seal issued by the City of Burbank and the airport are permitted in the airport. Taxi fare will depend on your final destination, but expect to pay between $20 and $30 to Hollywood.

Getting to your hotel by rental car

All the major car-rental agencies have branches at the airport (for a listing of agencies with phone numbers and Web sites, go to the appendix in the back of the book). Each company provides shuttle service between the terminals and their off-site lot.

For tips on getting the best car-rental rates and information on car-rental insurance options, see Chapter 9. For information on renting a car in L.A. without a credit card, see Chapter 11.

Getting to your hotel by public transportation

You can also take the **Metropolitan Transit Authority** (**MTA**) Metro Rail public transportation from the airport; a combination **light rail/bus system** runs to and from an outer parking lot at LAX. Free shuttle service is provided from the airport to the MTA Aviation Station; wait for the shuttle under the LAX Shuttle & Airline Connections sign on the Lower/Arrival level island in front of each terminal, and board the G shuttle to the Aviation Station to board a light rail.

It's a long and tedious but cheap journey — less than $2 ($1.35 plus 25¢ for transfers) — and it involves transferring buses in fairly marginal, sort-of-dicey neighborhoods. It's not for the faint of heart, either, because one portion of the light rail trip involves standing on a platform right next to the fast-moving freeway, with only a cement barrier and chain-link fence between you and a slew of BMWs and big rigs.

For details, call ☎ **800-COMMUTE** (or 808-266-6883) or go to the MTA Web site at www.mta.net, which provides a handy click-through trip planner with directions on planning your commute by public transport.

The **Metro Green Line** also goes *to* the airport; you catch it by transferring from the Hollywood Red Line westbound to the Green Line. But relying on public transport to get you to the airport when you depart the City of Angels is fraught with the possibility of missing your flight if there are delays, missed connections, or other manmade disasters.

Burbank Airport is serviced by Metro Rail Monday through Friday and MTA buses daily. The Burbank Airport Web site (www.burbank airport.com) offers links to Metro schedules.

Getting to your hotel by shuttle or van

If you're traveling alone, **Prime Time Shuttle** or **Super Shuttle** may be the right choice, because prices are on a per-person basis. From either LAX or Burbank, claim your bags, then step out to the clearly marked shuttle-stop island and contact the Shuttle Guest Service Representative.

With shuttles, you travel with others who are going to the same approximate area, so if the van is crowded, it may take a while to get to your location. Also, you must wait until a van going to your destination comes around.

Schedule return trips at least 24 hours in advance, and be sure to call to confirm. The agent will tell you what time you'll be picked up, usually several hours before your flight.

Typical approximate fares from LAX are $18 to Santa Monica, and $22 to Beverly Hills or Hollywood. Rates are the same for returns to the airport. Tipping the driver $2 is customary. (**Super Shuttle** ☎ **800-258-3826** or 323-775-6600 in Los Angeles; **Prime Time Shuttle** ☎ **888-905-0000,** which is usually the cheaper of the two.)

Getting to your hotel by car service

For groups of two or more, a **car service** may be the most pleasant and reasonable alternative. Make reservations with your credit card. After you land, get your luggage, and once you arrive curbside, call the 800 number from a pay phone or from your cellphone, giving your location and description. A Lincoln Towncar, which seats up to four passengers, will appear shortly and take you to your destination.

Los Angeles Freeway

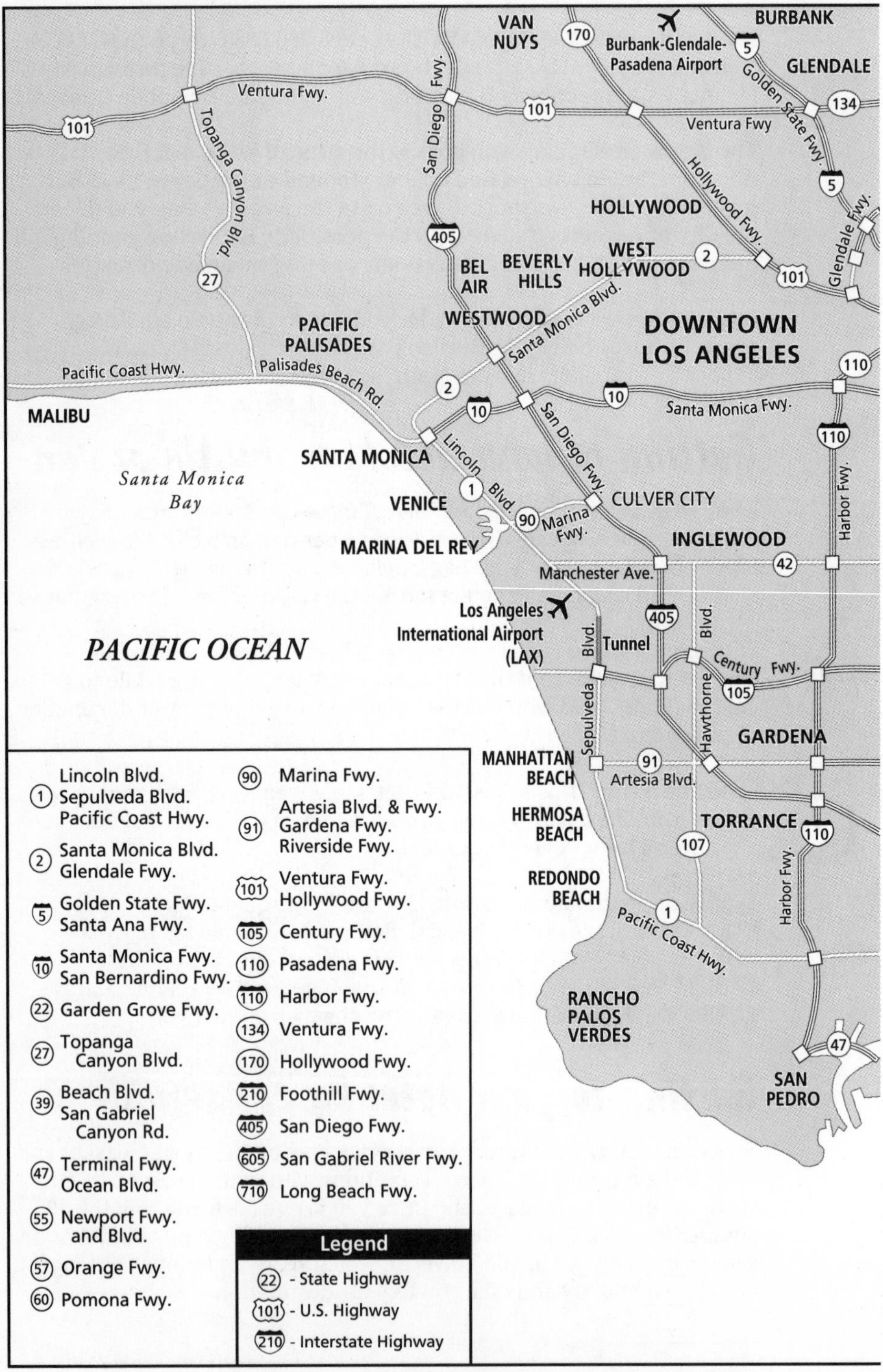
VAN NUYS
BURBANK
Burbank-Glendale-Pasadena Airport
GLENDALE
Ventura Fwy.
San Diego Fwy.
Ventura Fwy
Golden State Fwy.
Hollywood Fwy.
Glendale Fwy.
Topanga Canyon Blvd.
HOLLYWOOD
BEL AIR
BEVERLY HILLS
WEST HOLLYWOOD
WESTWOOD
Santa Monica Blvd.
DOWNTOWN LOS ANGELES
PACIFIC PALISADES
Pacific Coast Hwy.
Palisades Beach Rd.
MALIBU
Santa Monica Fwy.
SANTA MONICA
Lincoln Blvd.
San Diego Fwy.
Harbor Fwy.
Santa Monica Bay
VENICE
Marina Fwy.
CULVER CITY
MARINA DEL REY
INGLEWOOD
Manchester Ave.
Los Angeles International Airport (LAX)
PACIFIC OCEAN
Sepulveda Blvd.
Tunnel
Hawthorne Blvd.
Century Fwy.
GARDENA
MANHATTAN BEACH
Artesia Blvd.
HERMOSA BEACH
TORRANCE
REDONDO BEACH
Pacific Coast Hwy.
Harbor Fwy.
RANCHO PALOS VERDES
SAN PEDRO
1 Lincoln Blvd. Sepulveda Blvd. Pacific Coast Hwy.
2 Santa Monica Blvd. Glendale Fwy.
5 Golden State Fwy. Santa Ana Fwy.
10 Santa Monica Fwy. San Bernardino Fwy.
22 Garden Grove Fwy.
27 Topanga Canyon Blvd.
39 Beach Blvd. San Gabriel Canyon Rd.
47 Terminal Fwy. Ocean Blvd.
55 Newport Fwy. and Blvd.
57 Orange Fwy.
60 Pomona Fwy.
90 Marina Fwy.
91 Artesia Blvd. & Fwy. Gardena Fwy. Riverside Fwy.
101 Ventura Fwy. Hollywood Fwy.
105 Century Fwy.
110 Pasadena Fwy.
110 Harbor Fwy.
134 Ventura Fwy.
170 Hollywood Fwy.
210 Foothill Fwy.
405 San Diego Fwy.
605 San Gabriel River Fwy.
710 Long Beach Fwy.
Legend
22 - State Highway
101 - U.S. Highway
210 - Interstate Highway

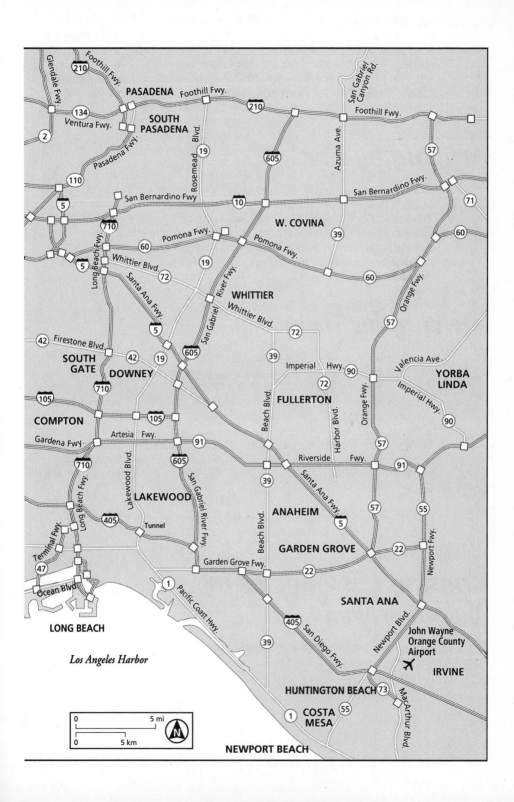

Typical fares from LAX are $38.50 to Santa Monica, $40.50 to Beverly Hills, and $45.50 to Hollywood, which includes the $1.50 airport pickup fee. For an additional $15, you'll be met in the baggage-carousel arrival section, with your name on a placard. Tipping 15% to 20% is customary. The rates are the same for returns to the airport. For car service, call **SkyRide Limo Service** (☎ 800-358-1800) or **ExecuCar** (☎ 800-413-4020).

Arriving by Car

As you may expect from the unofficial "car capital of the world," Los Angeles is accessible via a variety of freeways. From the north, take either the **101 Freeway** or **Interstate 5** into Los Angeles. **Interstate 15** connects you from Nevada, Utah, and points northeast. If you're coming from the southeast (Texas and Arizona), you can get into Los Angeles via **Interstate 10.** Arriving from the south? Enter the city via **Interstate 5.**

Arriving by Train

Los Angeles is a major destination for many Amtrak routes, and fares fluctuate depending on seasonal and special promotions. Trains arrive at **Union Station,** 800 N. Alameda St. (☎ 213-624-0171), on the northern edge of downtown just north of U.S. 101. From here, you can take one of the taxis that line up outside.

Among Amtrak's regular routes, the ***Sunset Limited*** travels from Orlando, Florida, to L.A. with stops in New Orleans and San Antonio, and the ***Coast Starlight*** travels along the Pacific Coast between Seattle and L.A.

Call ahead to make sure that services are available (Amtrak: ☎ 800-**USA-RAIL** or 800-872-7245; Internet: www.amtrak.com).

Cruising Los Angeles by Neighborhood

As we have said and will continue to say, L.A. is a really large city that spreads wantonly out over 465 square miles. Plus, a number of incorporated cities are buried within L.A. or attached to it, which makes it all the more complicated. Here we give you a brief overview.

The Westside

This area is actually several neighborhoods: **Brentwood, Bel Air, Pacific Palisades,** and **Venice,** which are part of L.A.; **Santa Monica, Malibu,** and **Beverly Hills,** which are their own cities. Santa Monica is right on the ocean. Pacific Palisades is just north of Santa Monica, Malibu north of that, and Venice to Santa Monica's immediate south. Brentwood is to the east, and then comes Bel Air and Beverly Hills.

These neighborhoods are the most upscale (collectively) parts of L.A. — the well-to-do naturally flock to the prettiest areas, and what could be more scenic than the ocean? Plus, the sea breezes keep the Westside as much as 20 degrees cooler than the rest of L.A.

The Westside begins at the Pacific Ocean and heads west until Doheny Drive, north to the mountains (once you hit the top, you begin to descend into the Valley), and south to Pico Boulevard (except for Venice, which keeps going).

You will want to spend time here because it's pretty — gorgeous houses, palm trees — and because it has temperate weather, the best walking in the city, the beach, Rodeo Drive, and the cachet of saying, "Why, yes, we were in Beverly Hills."

West Hollywood

West Hollywood is an interesting mix. It's inhabited in part by Orthodox and Conservative Jews, for which this has been a longtime central location, in a neighborhood that stretches into the area immediately south of Beverly Hills, along Pico Boulevard.

But that identity has long since been eclipsed by its "Christopher Street West" nickname; this is the heart of L.A. gay life, especially around Santa Monica Boulevard east of La Cienega Boulevard. South of here (through 6th Street) is a healthy dose of shops and cafes, catering to the beautiful but less-stodgy, more-hip people.

Hollywood

Let's clear up any misconceptions: There are no studios, and few movie stars, in Hollywood. Sure, Sony Pictures has a branch at Sunset Boulevard and Gower Street, but otherwise, the movie-making business has long since retreated from Hollywood proper. Now, it's just a name, but a name with such drawing power that the city has spent a great deal of money trying to clean up Hollywood Boulevard (long ago deteriorated into a bunch of junky shops and derelict buildings), mostly in the form of the brand-new Hollywood-Highland shopping and entertainment complex.

Hollywood begins more or less at La Brea Avenue to the west and ends around Vermont Avenue (when the hip Los Feliz and Silverlake neighborhoods take over, unless you just consider those East Hollywood, and you may) to the east, the Hollywood Hills to the north, and Melrose Avenue to the south.

You, the tourist, want to come here because it's Hollywood, darn it, even if the sights have less substance than myth attached to them.

Downtown

L.A. is too spread out to have a real urban center, but this is the de facto one, because it has the most skyscraper-type buildings, plus City Hall.

The subject of a revitalization effort, Downtown is a mixed bag, with staid offices and executives, immigrants, cheap clothing (the garment district is here), pricey restaurants, several fine museums, ethnic food, hustle and bustle of both the uniquely American sort and the type you might find in a big Third World city, and, unfortunately, a lot of homeless people.

You'll have several sights down here to see (including MOCA, the modern art museum, and the Music Center, for theater and symphony), but you probably just want to visit (because it's only pleasant to walk around during the day; it's quiet and a bit creepy at night) rather than stay — even though there are some incredible hotel bargains to be found here.

The San Fernando Valley

Although we don't list many hotels or attractions in the Valley, we would be remiss if we didn't mention the ancestral home of Valley girls everywhere. Any true Angelino knows that there are "locals" (those who live within a mile or so of the beach) and "Vals" (the intruders from over the hill), and never the twain shall meet, even if some locals had to move to the Valley because the housing is cheaper.

If you go north over the Santa Monica Mountains, you hit the Valley, and you can tell; strip malls and other generic wastelands abound, and it's really, really hot. The only part you may be going to is Burbank, because Warner Brothers and Universal Studios are there. (There are some nice pockets, for sure, but few you'll be exploring on this visit, probably.)

Pasadena

This jewel of a city lies just to the east of Los Angeles. It has gorgeous homes (thanks to old money), lovely wide streets, and the Rose Parade (see Chapter 2 for info) — all at the foot of the San Gabriel Mountains. It may be too far away for a brief L.A. visit (only half-hour or so on the freeway, but still). It does offer several major sights, however, including the Rose Bowl, the Huntington Library, and the Norton Simon Museum.

Getting the Lowdown at Visitor Centers

For more information and local maps, head to the **Los Angeles Convention & Visitors Bureau's walk-in visitor centers** at one of two locations: **Downtown** (685 S. Figueroa St.) or **Hollywood** (at the historic Janes House, 6541 Hollywood Blvd.). Or contact the LACVB directly (☎ **800-366-6116;** Events Hotline ☎ **213-689-8822;** Internet: www.lacvb.com) before you arrive, and it'll send you a free visitor kit.

Chapter 11

Getting Around Los Angeles

● ●

In This Chapter

▶ Driving in L.A.

▶ Taking the bus

▶ Catching a ride on the subway

▶ Hailing a taxi

▶ Hoofing it

● ●

*G*etting around in L.A. is really about driving. Here, people live in their cars — it's sorta like a big purse on wheels — eating, chatting (car phones are, needless to say, ubiquitous), and putting on makeup. In this chapter, you find out about other ways of getting around L.A., rather than by car, but most of those other ways have, shall we say, limitations. So for now, rev up the motor, slide in a CD, and join the masses swimming along the rivers of concrete.

By Car

The L.A. car fetish. Learn to love it, or at least deal with it. Los Angeles is hooked on cars, and you have little choice in the matter. Angelinos think nothing of a 30-minute commute; some think nothing of a 2-hour commute. Traffic is usually bad, except when it's horrendous.

But as we continue to stress, you do have options — in the form of public transportation. Unfortunately, they aren't that desirable (though whenever you can take public transportation, please do so, if for no other reason than it makes traffic easier on the permanent residents!).

Driving in L.A. is like driving in any other major city; at times, it can be a dream, but much of the time, it's an ongoing frustration. Because L.A. is so spread out, you want to take the freeway as often as surface streets to get more efficiently from Point A to Point B, because Point B may be miles away (hence, Angelinos often refer to places as "freeway close").

But keep in mind that if you're on the freeways during the evening rush hour (or in the morning on a lovely weekend day and want to head to the beach), you'll have much company. Still, if it's a nice day, driving can be pleasant, and you often have views of hills and mountains and palm trees. Ditto driving within the city; maybe the hills aren't so visible (though the palm trees are), and the buildings aren't as lovely as, say, those in San Francisco. But overall, the topography is less urban than such an urban place warrants. Just keep your cool, and build in enough time to get to your destination. Better to get somewhere early than miss out on valuable time by spending it in the car.

In theory, we simplify matters for you by suggesting hotels and restaurants more or less in all the same areas you'll be heading to anyway, for sightseeing or whatever. (Of course, we make exceptions for really special hotels or, more to the point, places where you just gotta eat.)

A basic map of L.A. demonstrates the easiest, if not most travel-time-efficient, way of getting to your destination. However, it never hurts to ask your concierge or to call the place in question; most institutes have an automated tape with directions, whereas any local hotel, concierge or no, probably has an opinion on the best way to get somewhere. You can also load up on maps at your local AAA before you come, and use MapQuest.com (Internet: www.mapquest.com) to do some pre-trip route planning.

Following the rules and making exceptions

Getting around in Los Angeles is pretty easy once you memorize a couple of basic rules and their huge exceptions.

- ✔ The mountains are always to the east and the north *unless* you're in the Valley, where they're everywhere. That's one reason many people avoid going to the 818 (the area code), as the vast parcel of suburban sprawl is called.

- ✔ Freeways with odd numbers (5, 405, 101) run north/south; even-numbered freeways run east/west, *except* the 110, which used to be the 11, and thus is a north/south with an extra zero at the end.

- ✔ The major east/west streets in Hollywood are **Sunset Boulevard, Santa Monica Boulevard, Melrose Avenue,** and **Beverly Boulevard.**

  After you hit Beverly Hills, **Wilshire Boulevard** begins to run north of **Santa Monica Boulevard,** other streets squish into a parallel northwards direction, and **Beverly Boulevard** dissolves into **Santa Monica Boulevard;** thus your main east/west routes become **Sunset, Wilshire, Santa Monica,** and **Olympic Boulevards.**

- ✔ Major north/south streets on the east side running to the west are **Vermont Avenue, Western Boulevard, Vine Street, Cahuenga**

Boulevard, Highland Avenue, La Brea Boulevard, Fairfax Avenue, Crescent Heights Boulevard, La Cienega Boulevard, Robertson Boulevard, and Doheny Drive.

Doheny Drive forms the dividing line into Beverly Hills. Once past Doheny, the major landmark streets are **Rexford Drive, Beverly Glen Boulevard, Veteran Avenue, the 405 Freeway, Barrington Avenue, 26th Street,** and **Lincoln Avenue.** The latter is eight blocks from the end of the road.

Like Atlanta, which has something like 14 streets named Peachtree, Los Angeles has a few streets that share the same name, with little else in common. This can be crucial and confusing. For example, L.A. has two Third Streets, one in Santa Monica and the other in West Hollywood, and we can tell you from firsthand experience that if you're not sure which one you're going to, you may be very late, ahem, for dinner. Another duplicate is San Vincente Boulevard; one is on the Westside, and the other is in West Hollywood. Also make sure not to confuse Beverly Drive (in Beverly Hills) with Beverly Boulevard (in West Hollywood).

Great gridlock! Avoiding the slow, the snarling, and the stationary

We want you to see the sights with a minimum of fuss, so here are some specific tips on driving the streets of L.A.

✔ To get from the east side of Hollywood to West Hollywood during the afternoon, take **Melrose Avenue,** which has no left turn from 4 p.m. to 7 p.m. **Olympic Boulevard** provides a quick zip anytime from Beverly Hills to Santa Monica. **Sunset Boulevard** is always lovely (if frequently slow), but **Santa Monica Boulevard** is just plain pokey, no matter what time of day, especially through Beverly Hills, where every street has a stoplight.

✔ **Vermont Avenue** is a particularly slow north-south street and should be avoided when commuting if possible — though you'll almost certainly have to take it if you're going north of Sunset Boulevard to get to Griffith Park, the Greek Theatre, and the Observatory.

✔ **Western Boulevard** is also notoriously bad, especially at the intersection of **Santa Monica Boulevard,** which can be so slow at times, it's actually in your best interest to go around it by making a series of left or right turns, forming a giant square. Better still, plan your travel west or east so that you are on **Fountain Avenue,** which is parallel to Santa Monica to the north.

✔ Avoid **Highland Avenue,** the major artery from Hollywood to Universal City/Burbank, on summer nights, unless you know for sure that the Hollywood Bowl is dark and empty. Otherwise, you can get caught in massive traffic tie-ups.

✔ **Hope and Grand Streets,** downtown, can be tricky; they are elevated, so they are only accessible at their starts (around First Street) and ends (around Eighth Street) — all other streets pass under them. This can be a pain if you're trying to get to the Museum of Contemporary Art, which is on Grand, so read signs carefully.

Parking the car

Parking in L.A. is both an ease and a bother. Parking is relatively plentiful, both on the street and in paid lots. Parking enforcers are vigilant and merciless, however.

A survival guide to driving L.A.

The longer your stay in L.A., the more driving yourself around is worth the grief. So how can you make it a little easier? We give you a few tricks on driving L.A. that will keep your road frustration to a minimum.

✔ **Don't drive from around 7:00 to 9:30 a.m., when the morning rush hour is at its most intense.**

✔ **Don't drive from 5 to 7 p.m., when the evening rush hour is at its thickest.**

✔ **Make sure that you build in about 40 minutes to get anywhere, just in case.**

✔ **Avoid the freeway, except in the middle of the day, and the 405 as much as you possibly can.** There was a time when the 405 was a fast thruway, but now, we swear it's crowded even at 3 a.m.

✔ **Avoid the High Occupancy Vehicle (HOV) lanes unless you have enough people in the car to qualify.** Fines are steep. Many L.A. freeways have designated carpool lanes, also known as HOV lanes. Some require two passengers; others three.

✔ **When the light turns yellow, put a brake on it.** A number of L.A. intersections (such as the one at the corner of Fairfax and Fountain Avenues) have cameras that flash right when the light turns red to catch people running through it. So you may think that you got away scot-free, only to find a big fat ticket waiting in the mail. (Yes, they even trace rental-car license plates.)

✔ **Be like all natives and make sure that KWB News Radio (980 AM) is on your car radio.** The station has traffic updates (listened to religiously by everyone) every 10 minutes, on the "ones" — 3:01, 3:11, and so on.

✔ **Above all, drive defensively!** Figure that the person next to you is not paying attention, because he's talking on his cellphone or engaging in some other vehicular-inappropriate activity. (Yet, he will be angry if you cut him off, and remember that the term "road rage" was coined here.)

Parking restrictions vary from neighborhood to neighborhood and from city to city. *Remember:* In one block, you can leave L.A. and be in Beverly Hills or, worse, in West Hollywood, where much of the street parking is restricted to residents with permits.

In L.A., you may be able to park on the street (meter or free) most of the time, except during street cleaning and rush hour — from, say, 4 to 7 p.m. Monday to Friday, or Wednesday from 10 a.m. to noon — posted signs tell you what the restrictions are.

The moral of this story: *Read the street signs carefully.* Also, check your meter to see how much time is allowed; some offer only an hour, others much, much more. And prices vary; a quarter can buy you a measly 8 minutes on the UCLA campus and an hour in other parts of the Westside. Have lots of change handy; merchants aren't always help-ful in making change.

During rush hour, many major streets, including La Cienega, La Brea, and Wilshire Boulevards, have strict no-parking/tow-away signs. If you don't read them, you will weep! If you're in doubt trying to translate "Two Hour Parking M–F 8 a.m.–6 p.m. No Parking without Permit" — park somewhere with a more user-friendly description. It's worth an extra block's walk to avoid a hefty fine or having your car towed!

Parking is probably worst in Downtown, where street parking is rare, and lots can cost quite a bit. The farther from the center of Downtown action, the cheaper the lots, though some lots offer early-bird, all-day rates. If you don't have endless parking funds, or if you don't feel like keeping your eyes open for street parking, your best bet, probably, is to take the Metro Rail into Downtown and get around with the DASH (see the section "By Bus," later in this chapter).

West Hollywood at night, when the local streets go into resident-only parking, is the second worst; you may want to consider parking in lots wherever and as often as you can, or just taking taxis.

The restaurant-shuttle–
Music Center connection

Many downtown restaurants are on a free shuttle route that transfers patrons to the Music Center, making it relatively inexpensive to park your car at a restaurant, pay the minimal parking fee, take the shuttle to your play/opera/symphony, and then return by shuttle to your car. It's a very nice service; among the restaurants on the route are Cuidad, Cafe Pinot, and Nick & Stef's. Call to see whether you can catch a ride from the restaurant of your choice.

Renting a car

Okay, so we talked you into renting a car. Here's help in doing so. All the major car-rental agencies have offices in L.A., particularly at the airport and in major hotels; for a listing of agencies with phone numbers and Web sites, go to the appendix in the back of the book. For tips on getting the best car-rental rates and information on car-rental insurance options, see Chapter 9.

Internet sites for travel and car-rental agencies often offer specials and discounts. Another ongoing discount can be found at the Enterprise agency at the Ramada West Hollywood, which offers a 10% discount on rentals for guests at the hotel.

If you want to rent a car but lack a credit card, don't despair; check out these agencies:

- ✔ **Dollar Rent A Car** (☎ **800-800-4000**), which has a location at Los Angeles Airport as well as at the Bonaventure Hotel in downtown Los Angeles, will rent you a car on your debit card, provided the piece of plastic comes with a Visa or MasterCard logo. They take a deposit for the cost of the rental, plus 15% (or $250, whichever is higher), and, of course, you must have a valid driver's license.

- ✔ At **Cash Car Rent,** also known as **Hollywood Car Rental** (1600 La Brea Blvd.; ☎ **323-464-1657** or 323-464-4147), you can rent a car for a $300-per-week deposit — no plastic required. Return the car sooner, and you get a refund, based on approximately $35-a-day rental. You must be over 21, with a valid driver's license and proof of where you're staying while in town; a return ticket also helps.

- ✔ **AA'A Rent A Car** (8820 Sepulveda #111; ☎ **310-348-1111;** Internet: www.aa-arentacar.com), located 3 minutes from LAX (with a shuttle to take you to the rental lots), requires a return ticket. Rentals start at $29 per day, and a $450 deposit is required, along with a valid license and a return ticket. California residents may also want to bring a copy of a utility bill from home to assuage the rental agent.

By Bus

Ah, the MTA (that's Metropolitan Transit Authority): the bane of the carless, the joke of the smug and fully automobiled. We love L.A., we really do, but for pity's sake, it's the only major bustling industrialized city we can think of with such a lousy public transportation system. The buses are slowpokes, and they hardly seem to go where you want to go. We discuss the subway later on — after we stop giggling.

To be fair, plenty of people take the bus in L.A., and some even do so by choice rather than necessity. You can, too, though you must be patient and flexible. Some bus lines really do go (more or less) where you want to go, and when they do, it's a great pleasure. But the same traffic that an L.A. driver must contend with is also a hindrance for the buses, and buses are even slower going, because they have to stop every couple of blocks or so. No wonder few in L.A. want the hassle.

Still and all, you can check the MTA Web site (Internet: www.mta.net), which is, we have to admit, nicely and helpfully laid out, and see whether any of the routes cover your needs, for it certainly is nice to occasionally pretend that L.A. is like other cities where residents aren't so dependant on cars. Plus, the bus only costs $1.35 one way.

Also note that Santa Monica is serviced by the somewhat less laughable **Big Blue Buses** (Internet: www.bigbluebus.com), which are swifter, cleaner, and more reliable than the MTA buses. Downtown has the **DASH** (Internet: www.ladottransit.com), a commuter bus that runs at frequent intervals throughout Downtown and costs just 25¢ one way. The latter is a particularly fine way to get around Downtown, which has miserable parking. We highly recommend it.

By Subway

Oh, dear, it still makes us laugh — *giggle* — to refer to this 2-mile-long, four-stop wonder as a subway. No, really, the **Metro Rail** is longer than that, though it hardly seems it. A multibillion-dollar public scandal years in the making and days in the discarding, it's big, clean, and bright, and it goes almost no place useful (it seems). At times, you may be the only person standing in one of the big, clean, bright terminals. And if that doesn't give you one of those "last standing after the Apocalypse" feelings, nothing will.

Joking aside, the Metro Rail has some truly handy uses, and locals are gradually taking advantage of it. The rail travels tidily between the center of Hollywood and Universal Studios (the Red Line), and somewhat less tidily between Hollywood and Downtown (parts of Downtown require a transfer from the Red Line to the Blue Line). A trip from Hollywood and Vine to Staples Center, even with the transfer, is about 20 minutes, which beats the heck out of driving and saves you some serious parking costs.

We encourage you, in all seriousness, to use the itty-bitty "subway" as much as possible, because it can make sightseeing a bit easier. It costs $1.35 one way, and one transfer is free. You buy your tickets from service machines in each station, though some people skip this part. You probably shouldn't; plainclothes agents wait at some stations and may demand to see your (up-to-date, so don't try to use an old one) ticket. Get caught without it, and pay a hefty ($250) fine. A weekly pass is $11. The Web site (Internet: www.mta.net) and toll-free number (☎ **800-COMMUTE/266-6883**) provide trip planning; give your departure and desired arrival point, and the services will tell you how to best get to where you want to go.

By Taxi

The cab alternative isn't a bad one — you don't have traffic or parking hassles — the cabs in Los Angeles don't have cabstands, except at the airport and outside Santa Monica Place Mall and the Beverly Center. Plus, they don't drive by with the same frequency you find in other major cities.

To hire a cab, get your hotel to call one for you, or use one of the main cab services in the city (which we list in this section).

Cabs charge a $2 pickup fee and then $2 per mile, plus additional charges when you get stuck in traffic, a common occurrence. Tipping your cab driver 10% to 15% is customary.

 A word of warning: Pirate cabbies sometimes try to intercept your ride, and you may find yourself being transported in an unlicensed cab and paying way too much for a ride. We know; it once happened to us. Make sure that before you get in, the cab has license stickers displayed and that the color and name of the cab matches the one you called.

With that in mind, here are a few of the cab companies that run the streets (and ones we've actually used), all of which are licensed:

- ✔ **Yellow Cab** (☎ 800-200-1085): Yes, they're yellow

- ✔ **United Independent** (☎ 800-411-0303): Green and white cabs

- ✔ **Independent Taxi** (☎ 800-521-8294): White, with red and blue lettering

- ✔ **Checker Cabs** (☎ 800-300-5007): Yellow and blue, with yellow and blue checkerboard trim

On Foot

It's not true that nobody walks in L.A., but heavens, it feels like it at times. The best areas of town to walk in are Santa Monica and Beverly Hills: They're both flat, pretty neighborhoods, with lots of scenic stuff (both commercial and residential), palm trees, and, in the case of Santa Monica, the ocean.

Downtown and Hollywood are walkable areas, but sights and such are sporadically placed; for every few good blocks, there are a few icky ones to get through before the next set. Melrose and Third Street in West Hollywood are fun to meander down, thanks to a plethora of shops and cafes.

Chapter 12

Managing Your Money

• •

• •

*B*y now, you should have a good idea of exactly how much money you plan to spend on your trip to Los Angeles. (If not, see Chapter 3 for tips on planning your budget.) All that's left to do now is to find out where in the city to go to get more cash, what to do if something happens to your wallet, and what to expect in the way of tacked-on taxes.

Where to Get Cash in Los Angeles

ATMs are linked to a network that most likely includes your bank at home. **Cirrus** (☎ 800-424-7787; Internet: www.mastercard.com) and **Plus** (☎ 800-843-7587; Internet: www.visa.com) are the two most popular networks in the United States; call or check online for ATM locations at your destination. **Be sure to find out your daily withdrawal limit before you leave home.** You can also get cash advances on your credit card at ATMs. Keep in mind that some credit-card companies try to protect themselves from theft by limiting the funds customers can withdraw when they're away from home. It's therefore best to call your credit-card company before you leave and let someone know where you're going and how much you plan to spend.

Most banks impose a withdrawal fee every time a card is used at an ATM in a bank that is different from your own — and the fee varies, from $1 to $2 per withdrawal. On top of this, the bank from which you withdraw cash may charge a fee; call before you leave home to find out.

Los Angeles is lousy with ATMs. Banks like **Wells Fargo** (☎ 800-225-5935; Internet: www.wellsfargo.com), **Bank of America** (Internet: www.bankof america.com), and **Washington Mutual** (Internet: www.wamu.com) are everywhere, mostly linked by Cirrus, Star, and Maestro, as well as bank links. Malls and convenience marts like 7-11 have ATMs and charge a fee for their use.

And for the safest ATM in town, especially in the wee hours of the morning, drop in on the friendly folks at the **Hollywood Division of the Los Angeles Police Department** (1358 N. Wilcox Ave.). You will be charged unless you're a member of Co-Op Network, but it's open 24/7 and has plenty of free parking.

What to Do If Your Wallet Is Stolen

Almost every credit-card company has an emergency toll-free number you can call if your wallet or purse is stolen. The credit-card company may be able to wire you a cash advance off your credit card immediately; in many places, you can get an emergency credit card within a day or two. Be sure to block charges against your account the minute you discover that your card has been lost or stolen. Then be sure to file a police report.

The issuing bank's toll-free number is usually on the back of the credit card, but that won't help you much if the card was stolen. Copy the number on the back of your card onto another piece of paper before you leave, and keep it in a safe place, just in case.

Citicorp Visa's U.S. emergency number is ☎ **800-645-6556. American Express** cardholders and traveler's check holders should call ☎ **800-221-7282** for all money emergencies. **MasterCard** holders should call ☎ **800-307-7309.**

If you opt to carry **traveler's checks,** be sure to keep a record of their serial numbers so that you're prepared if they're lost or stolen — and keep the list in a safe and separate place, so that you're ensured a refund if the checks are lost or stolen. Also, dual checks are available for traveling couples, and either person can sign for them.

Odds are that you won't recover your lost or stolen wallet. However, it's still worth informing the authorities. Your credit-card company or insurer may require a police-report number or record of the theft.

If you need emergency cash over the weekend, when all banks and American Express offices are closed, you can have money wired to you via **Western Union** (☎ **800-325-6000;** Internet: www.westernunion.com/). You must present a valid ID to pick up the cash at the Western Union office.

Taxing Matters

The sales tax on most commonly purchased items (except for snack foods) is 8.25% in all of Los Angeles County. For hotels, the tax is 14%; for rental cars, 8.25% plus $1.25 per day.

Part IV
Dining Los Angeles Style

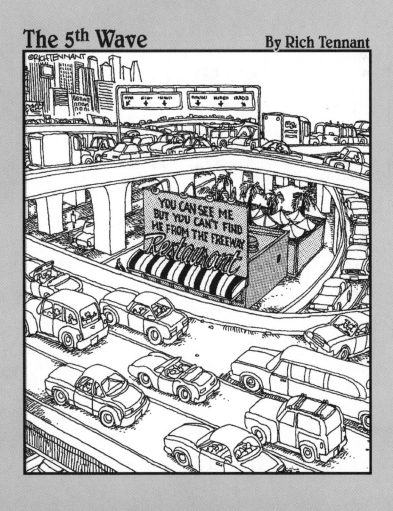

The 5th Wave   By Rich Tennant

YOU CAN SEE ME
BUT YOU CAN'T FIND
ME FROM THE FREEWAY
Restaurant

In this part . . .

Part IV may be the tastiest part of the book. Here we describe the current dining scene in Los Angeles — the latest trends, the hottest chefs, and the celebrity hangouts. For those of you on a budget, we give you smart cost-cutting tips on how to save money on food. Then we describe our favorite restaurants in the city, from sleek new hot spots to old-school classics to off-the-beaten-path ethnic eateries. We also tell you where you can find quick snacks and cheap meals that are guaranteed delicious.

Chapter 13

The Lowdown on the Los Angeles Dining Scene

In This Chapter

▶ Spotting the trends and trendsetters in L.A. dining

▶ Discovering the top neighborhoods for dining

▶ Eating where the locals do

▶ Finding ways to cut food costs in L.A.

▶ Making reservations, dressing up or down, and displaying good manners

*L*os Angeles may not have the reputation for big-time dining that certain other cities claim (hello, New York), but we think that is entirely unfair. This is the city, after all, that gave the world chef **Wolfgang Puck and his high-wattage culinary shrine, Spago,** and, ubiquitous or not, Nouveau and California Cuisine followed in his wake.

As good as the city's three- and four-star restaurants are (and they are indeed worthy of your attention), it's the **hole-in-the-wall ethnic spots** that L.A. does best. Because it's such a melting pot of cultures, blessed with an extraordinarily diverse number of immigrants from all over the world, Los Angeles has a vast number of unprepossessing eateries, often found in ugly strip malls or in the farther reaches of the metropolis, in which you can pay a ridiculously small amount of money and dine on food the gods themselves would envy. There are Thai, Vietnamese, Russian, Armenian, Romanian, and Mexican restaurants — that's just a starter sampler, and from a measly 1-mile stretch of Hollywood Boulevard, to boot.

In this chapter, we give the lowdown on the latest culinary trends, the hottest neighborhoods, and the star chefs on the scene — plus tips on cutting costs, making reservations, and what to wear.

What's New, What's Hot, and Who's in the Kitchen

These days (at least, as we write this), it's all about **braising.** Everywhere, it seems, haute-cuisine chefs are taking previously-sniffed-at cuts of beef, from pot roast to short ribs to veal cheeks, and cooking them with loving care for hours and hours until the meat falls apart at the slightest touch.

The return of meat is further evident in the **rise in steakhouses** — no lesser slabs of beef here, thank you. You'll only find premium cuts at premium prices. Everywhere, too, is **comfort food,** from mac and cheese and potpies to the homemade butterscotch pudding of your childhood. Small, precious plates of food seem to be out, with **generous portions** currently in favor. But don't be surprised to find high-end restaurants reviving the whole **"a la carte" concept,** cheerfully charging you for anything beyond the barest herbal topping for your entree.

And who's in the kitchen these days? Los Angeles has chefs who would shine in even the most hardcore restaurant scene: **Jochaim Splichal** of the Patina Group consortium of restaurants, including Patina, Nick & Stef's, and the Pinot Bistro; **Susan Fennister** and **Mary Sue Milliken** of Border Grill and Cuidad (to say nothing of their popular Food Network show, "Two Hot Tamales"); and **Mark Peel** and **Nancy Silverton** of Campanille and La Brea Bakery, to name but a few. L.A. has 'em all, and even a few more.

New and noteworthy restaurants include Mark Peel's **Jar,** a lovely steak-house with a pot roast that is causing near riots of gastronomic delight, and **Alex,** a restaurant whose chef was previously associated with the highly touted and even more highly priced Saddlepeak Lodge in Malibu. Then there's **the house,** in Hollywood, which serves highfalutin twists on comfort food, and **Angelina Osteria,** in West Hollywood, for perfect Italian food. All of these restaurants are reviewed in Chapter 14.

Although we didn't have space for them, **Zax,** in West Los Angeles, and **Mastro's Steakhouse,** in Beverly Hills, are getting raves — the former for its nouveau cuisine and the latter for its generous portions and well-chosen cuts of beef. By the time you read this, the Patina Group will have two new downtown restaurants, with one right at the Music Center.

The Top Neighborhoods to Dine

Just as L.A. has no one main neighborhood, it also has no main dining area. Obviously, you find a greater number of seafood places closer to the ocean, but in this day of modern transportation and refrigeration, a few lousy miles is not going to stop anyone from serving up sole.

We focus on the same three areas featured in the hotels chapter; the **Westside** (especially Santa Monica and Beverly Hills), **West Hollywood/ Hollywood,** and **Downtown.** Admittedly, the crowds change according to the neighborhood, but more often they change according to price range. Old money (pearls and suits) can generally be found in Beverly Hills, the hip-and-happening crowd is often seen in West Hollywood, and the funky-and-fun types gravitate to Hollywood.

Downtown sees business folks during the day, and theatergoers and business travelers at night. Fox and Sony Studios are in the Westside, and Paramount is in Hollywood, so you're likely to see movie industry types — don't get excited, we are generally (though hardly exclusively) talking executives and agents here — in those neighborhoods during lunch.

If you're willing to travel a bit for outstanding ethnic food, head to the **San Gabriel Valley** (the towns of Alhambra, San Gabriel, and Rosemead), where the Chinese food will blow your mind, or **East L.A.,** where you find not just authentic Mexican, but Cuban, El Salvadoran, and Honduran, as well.

For ethnic delights a tad closer to Los Angeles, there's **Little Tokyo** (the southeastern part of Downtown) — we are systematically working our way through every sushi bar we can find there. And although the official **Chinatown** (northeastern Downtown) doesn't have nearly the breadth and range of what's found in San Gabriel, it is considerably closer.

But don't stop at Chinatown for Asian food; the area south of Hollywood (Wilshire Boulevard to Olympic Boulevard north and south, and Crenshaw Boulevard to Vermont Avenue on the west-east borders) is called **Koreatown.** And don't forget **Thai Town** (Hollywood Boulevard, starting around Western Avenue to around Vermont Avenue) and **Little Armenia** (which overlaps a bit with Thai Town, beginning at Hollywood, Sunset, and Santa Monica Boulevards at Wilton Drive and heading east until at least Virgil Avenue).

While we focus on certain neighborhoods for most of our restaurant choices (neighborhoods you are most likely to either stay in or visit), there are other areas to keep in mind. **Melrose Avenue** (from Fairfax to LaBrea Avenues) and **Third Street** (LaCienga Boulevard to Fairfax Avenue) both fairly jump with small cafes, as does the bohemian-trendy **Los Feliz/Silverlake** area just east of Hollywood (Sunset Boulevard east of Virgil Avenue, all the way down to where it becomes Caesar Chavez Boulevard).

Travel to **Vermont and Hillhurst Avenues,** between Sunset and Los Feliz Boulevards, where the food is likely to be cheaper and the clientele terrifyingly hip and cutting edge rather than forbiddingly chic.

Where the Locals Meet to Eat

The well-heeled and timid are found in the Westside and the fine-dining establishments; everyone else is found everywhere else. If there is one place to consistently find locals, it's probably Starbucks. We shall ignore that, and say, instead, that to consistently find locals you must seek out the ethnic places we mention in the previous section. Do not fear modest, unprepossessing storefronts and interiors lacking any kind of taste or ambience. If the crowd is there, the food is likely to be a treat. Frankly, once the word is out, many an Angelino will be seen chowing down inthose places the locals have cheekily dubbed "roach coaches" (especially in Hollywood, East L.A., and Koreatown) — for they know that some of the best tacos and such are found within.

If you're interested in seeking out curious cuisines, down-home diners, or cool cafes, we are going to urge two essential books on you:

✔ *Hungry? A Guide to LA's Greatest Diners, Dives, Cafeterias and Coffee Shops* (edited by Kristin L. Petersen, published by Really Great Books). This bright green volume more or less takes over where the Zagat Guide leaves off. It's opinionated and full of tips, such as how to avoid the crush, where the punks eat, and how to find the best parking space. No late-night spot or cheap meal deal goes undisclosed. It's essential for the budget-minded, and well worth it for anyone who wants to find the real and the surreal in L.A. dining.

✔ *Counter Intelligence* by Jonathan Gold (published by LA Weekly Books for St. Martin's Press, Inc.) is just slightly less essential (and only because it covers fewer establishments, but in much, much greater detail). Gold, the long-time guru of goat stew and anything else you never knew you wanted to eat until he described it, has a talent for sniffing out obscure culinary outposts and hole-in-the-wall establishments that feature sublime concoctions of often alarming ingredients. It's a talent that has earned him, via his regular "Counter Intelligence" column in the *L.A. Weekly* (one of two free weekly papers in L.A.) and his monthly column in *Gourmet* magazine, a rapid following of foodies who dote on his regular reports on where to find the best Thai dish, or who does the most with frog. But don't fear: Gold covers less adventurous dining, too. Every time we've followed his lead to some locale and ordered what he recommended, we've been thrilled. His taste is to be trusted.

You can also trust the taste of Meredith Brody, food critic for the *New Times* (the other free weekly paper). Brody writes not just of food, but of life around it. A check of her recent forays is a must before coming to L.A. Go to www.newtimesla.com, click on Dish, and see where she says you ought to eat. And then go there.

But admit it: What you really care about is **star spotting.** Where do *they* eat? Well, you can find them preening and posing in any high-end restaurant, for sure, but keep your eyes peeled on the midrange restaurants, as well. You may be able to find celebrities in spots like Beverly Hills (more likely to be "old school" actors) and WeHo/Hollywood (anyone from Brad and Jen to WB stars). Again, if you patronize a restaurant in a neighborhood near the studios, you have a greater chance of spotting some bigwig being wooed by a studio head — though it is much more likely that such charm is being laid on in the relative privacy of a studio dining room. We will try, in appropriate reviews, to tip you off to the places where you will be most likely to spot a star (look for the Star Spotting icon), but, of course, it's hit and miss — sometimes *miss* if only because some of these folks, darn it, don't dress the part. See that pretty girl, with messy hair and no makeup, wearing blue jeans or sweats? Look carefully, for she may be Drew or Cameron.

Don't Lose Your Shirt: Tips for Cutting Costs

Okay, so you've made up your mind to patronize primarily those places that fall into the "cheap" category, and you may even get one of the books we talk about in the previous section, because they're full of even more affordable places. But, doggone it, you want to have a couple of fancy meals. What can you do?

Well, first, when possible, **visit the high-end places for lunch.** Many of these restaurants offer a cheaper menu at midday. The lunch menus may have several of the same items as the dinner menus, or they may even have something special that you can't get at dinnertime (as is the case at Angelini Osteria).

You can also save money at fancy restaurants by **ordering judiciously.** Skip wine — it can really drive up a bill — or dessert if you can; go to a good coffeehouse or bakery early in the day and buy a treat for later. (We provide a list of delightful delicacies in Chapter 15.) You may also want to consider ordering just appetizers; a couple can make a meal by dining on appetizers alone, sometimes enjoying more interesting fare than the entrees offer.

Take advantage of the continental breakfast if your hotel offers one. If you have kids in tow, keep in mind that they may be perfectly happy with a bowl of cereal and milk rather than some big, expensive breakfast out.

Eat one of your daily meals on the cheap. Enjoy a hearty, full-course ethnic meal for peanuts, or grab a specialty sandwich for a picnic meal (see Chapter 15 for information on both).

How to Make Reservations

You should assume that you'll need to have a reservation for any high-end restaurant ($$$$ to $$$$$ in this guide). Make your reservations as far in advance as you can. If you can be flexible with your time, however, you stand a better chance of securing a reservation. Don't eat lunch between 1 and 2 p.m., for that is when movie industry folks tend to deal over meals, and avoid the popular dinner hours between 7:30 and 9:00 p.m. Weekends, naturally, are more crowded than weekdays.

Dress to Dine, Los Angeles Style

L.A. is a pretty informal town, so you will not need to pack gowns and pearls. Basic black always works, but even some of the nicest restaurants tolerate blue jeans (assuming, often correctly, that those blue jeans cost at least $100 a pair).

Etiquette Tips: Lighting Up and Using Your Cellphone

It is entirely illegal to smoke in restaurants in Los Angeles. This restriction does have a few bonuses: For nonsmokers, it means clothes that don't reek; for smokers, many restaurants offer pretty patio dining where smoking is allowed, and who knows what other famous nicotine addict you may end up standing with outside the restaurant, having a quick puff?

Cellphones aren't illegal, but they may as well be for the number of restaurants that ask you, with varying degrees of politeness, to please keep yours turned off. It's just as well; after you sit in a crowd of movie industry heavyweights or fanciers who are dripping with self-importance and talking loudly on their little toy phones, you'll applaud the movement to silence their noisy illusions of grandeur.

Chapter 14

The Best Places to Dine in Los Angeles

In This Chapter

▶ Los Angeles restaurants by price, location, and cuisine

▶ Los Angeles restaurants from A to Z

▶ Dining out, the old-school way

*W*hether you're springing for a glitzy four-star extravaganza or checking out the brilliant hole-in-the-wall ethnic spots, you can eat very well in Los Angeles. In this chapter, we give you our favorite places to dine in the City of Angels. In fact, you may discover dishes here that are found nowhere else — many of the local restaurants take advantage of the region's glorious seasonal offerings, and there's no telling what flights of whimsy the city's innovative chefs will engage in when the farmers' markets start to burst with veggies, from heirloom tomatoes to curious greens to delicate squash blossoms.

Note: When we give the price range for a restaurant, that range is often out of whack, because the most expensive dish on the menu may be several dollars higher than everything else. The reality is probably closer to the middle of the range. So don't be intimidated by a place that seems to top out at, say, $40. That could easily be for lobster, and everything else could be in the upper twenties. Make a call and ask.

We also index restaurants by location, so you can find a spot that's convenient for you by price, so you can stay within your budget, and by cuisine, so you'll know exactly where to find the food that most appeals to you (check the end of the chapter).

For restaurants with locations in Hollywood, go to the Hollywood Accommodations & Dining map in Chapter 8. For restaurants with locations Downtown, go to the Downtown Accommodations & Dining map in Chapter 8.

What the $ Symbols Mean

Each listing in this chapter includes a main-course price range and a dollar-sign icon. Prices per person include standard entrees, along with appetizer, dessert, beverage, and tip (from 15% to 20% of the total check). Here's a breakdown of the symbols:

$	Under $20
$$	$20–$30
$$$	$30–$40
$$$$	$40–$50
$$$$$	Over $50

Los Angeles Restaurants from A to Z

The Abbey

$$ West Hollywood   AMERICAN

Noted mostly for its scene, which is very, very gay — and we don't mean cheerful, though it's that, too — this semi-gothic coffeehouse/bar is included here because it serves affordable, quite tasty food. Sandwiches, pastas, and salads are all made to order, so don't be in a big rush. But you don't want to hurry, no siree, because there is much people-watching to be had here (oh, the psychodramas you are likely to witness) — especially at night, and even more so on weekend nights. Plus, with a full, full dessert case (which flaunts the Tuxedo Cake, a confection containing more amounts of white and chocolate frosting than any one piece of cake ought to have; we are so in favor of it), you need the time to work through it all. Grab a seat on the patio, if the weather permits, as it usually does (and space heaters are there when it doesn't), or inside the gloomy interior, and enjoy yourself.

692 N. Robertson Blvd. (near Santa Monica Blvd.). ☎ 310-289-8410. Main courses: $7.95–$12.95. Open: Daily 8 a.m.–2 a.m. AE, DC, DISC, MC, V.

Alex

$$$$ Hollywood   MODERN EUROPEAN

This brand-new restaurant is a delight from start to finish, served up in a romantic Arts and Crafts–with-a-twist setting. Chef Alex Scrimgeour made his name at the highly regarded (and highly priced) Saddlepeak Lounge in Malibu. Speaking of pricing, we love the prices here: At dinner, all first

Dining in Santa Monica & Beaches

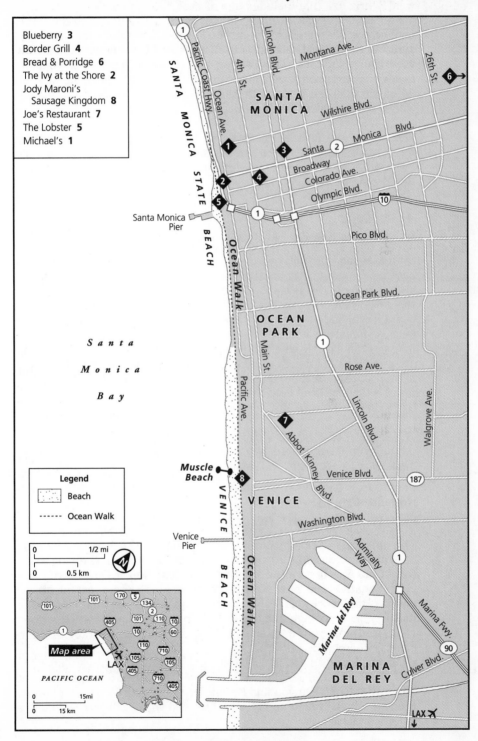

Blueberry **3**
Border Grill **4**
Bread & Porridge **6**
The Ivy at the Shore **2**
Jody Maroni's
  Sausage Kingdom **8**
Joe's Restaurant **7**
The Lobster **5**
Michael's **1**

Legend
:::: Beach
----- Ocean Walk

0   1/2 mi
0   0.5 km

PACIFIC OCEAN

0   15mi
0   15 km

Map area

LAX ✈

courses are $15, all middles $12, and all mains $29. No muss, no fuss. But wait! A prix fixe that includes one of everything, plus dessert ($9 normally), is $58 (or $29 for three courses at lunch)! Go for it, oh do — this may be one of the meals of your life. Portions are dainty and pretty, for sure, but the *flavors!* Alex uses only a real wood-burning grill, and the flavors of anything cooked on it simply pop — from a heavenly langoustine to sea bass wrapped in pancetta. To say nothing of the goat cheese soufflé on caramelized pears with bits of thick bacon — every ingredient stands out and yet melds together.

6703 Melrose Ave. (west of Highland Ave.). ☎ *323-933-5233. Reservations highly recommended. Lunch main courses: $18 ($29 three-course prix fixe). Dinner main courses: $29 ($58 four-course prix fixe). Open: Tues–Fri noon to 2 p.m., Tues–Sat 6–10 p.m. AE, DC, DISC, MC, V.*

Angeli Caffe
$$ West Hollywood   RUSTIC REGIONAL ITALIAN

Evan Kleiman, the chef/owner of this much-beloved near-institution, is known for haunting the local farmers' markets to ensure that her menu always reflects the seasons. Curious experiments with produce aside, this restaurant offers dedicatedly authentic Italian; the pizza is thin, the pasta fresh, and you can bet that if something has tomatoes in it, it's because tomatoes are in season, and they're ripe and perfect. *Note:* This may seem like a chic cafe, but it's quite child friendly; kids who come in are given a ball of dough to mash and shape as they please. The dough is then cooked in the oven and presented to them when it's done, a process that can keep even the most wriggly kid entertained long enough for parents to enjoy a nice meal.

7274 Melrose Ave. (near Alta Vista Blvd.). ☎ *323-936-9086. Internet:* www.angeli caffe.com. *Reservations highly recommended. Main courses: $8–$17. Open: Mon–Thurs noon to 10 p.m., Fri–Sat noon to 11 p.m., Sun 4–10 p.m. AE, DISC, MC, V.*

Angelini Osteria
$$$ West Hollywood   HOME-STYLE ITALIAN

The operators of this instantly likable restaurant (everyone seems so darn pleased you came in) are long-time fixtures on the L.A. dining scene (chef Gino Angelini cooked for the now-defunct Rex in Downtown L.A.); consequently, their new establishment was an almost instant hit. Of course, that success is also due to the quality of the food — genuine Italian cooking, lovingly and thoughtfully prepared. Try the whole striped bass (*banzino*) roasted in sea salt, if only for the dramatic tableside ceremony, wherein the salt crust is cracked open, and the fish is carefully removed piece by piece. It just barely tops the drama of the carving of the veal shank when *stinco di vitello* is ordered. All the pastas are heavenly, but only at lunch can you find Nonna Elvira's (that's Gino's mom) green lasagna, which is light and airy and topped with flash-fried spinach, a favorite at Rex.

7313 Beverly Blvd. (near Martell Ave.). ☎ *323-297-0070. Reservations recommended. Lunch main courses: $7–$16.50. Dinner main courses: $7–$30. Open: Daily 11:30 a.m.–11:00 p.m. AE, MC, V.*

Authentic Cafe
$$ Hollywood   SOUTHWESTERN/CARIBBEAN

No longer the hot spot that had lines out the door nearly all the time (and created a desperate need for expansion), the Authentic Cafe is still a pleasant place to dine on Southwestern and Caribbean-influenced dishes. It's also vegetarian friendly, thanks to tamales and other blue-corn-emphasis items. Try the jerk chicken, or the Brie poblano-chile papaya quesadilla, or the seared albacore-tuna salad.

7605 Beverly Blvd. (at Curson Ave.). ☎ *323-939-4626. Reservations accepted only for parties of 8 or more. Main courses: $10–$19.75. Open: Mon–Thurs 11:30 a.m.–10:00 p.m., Fri 11:30 a.m.–11:00 p.m., Sat 10:30 a.m.–11:00 p.m., Sun 10:30 a.m.–10:00 p.m. AE, MC, V.*

Blueberry
$ Santa Monica   CAFE/BREAKFAST

They bring blueberry muffins to your table as soon as you sit down, and you can keep 'em coming as long as you want, you greedy goose. This cute cafe on the Westside is maybe not as strong foodwise as Bread & Porridge, its almost neighbor, but its service is well-meaning, if not always swift and sure, and the pancakes are good (multigrain, especially, but how can you resist the blueberry?), and so are the salads. And then there are the muffins. Bring the little ones; Blueberry has a casual, kid-friendly ambience. *Note:* As this book was being written, plans were in the works for the cafe to stay open in the evenings (midnight or even as late as 3 a.m.) with dinner specials.

510 Santa Monica Blvd. (at Fifth St.). ☎ *310-394-7766. Everything under $10. Open: Daily 8 a.m.–3 p.m. (call for new dinner hours). AE, MC, V.*

Border Grill
$$$ Santa Monica   MEXICAN

Mary Sue Milliken and Susan Fenniger have been a serious presence on the L.A. food scene for a number of years, thanks to their first restaurants — the now defunct City on La Brea Avenue and the original Border Grill on Melrose. Now the nation knows them as "Two Hot Tamales," from their Food Network series and from several cookbooks. They made their rep by bringing real Mexican home cooking into the southern California mainstream. Although purists may legitimately grumble that the Tamales have backed away from some of their more adventurous offerings (like pig's foot tacos!), those who know Mexican food only from (blech) chains are in for some bemusement when faced with a Border Grill menu. The tacos, for example, are beautifully stuffed with fresh ingredients, from fish to marinated pork, with heaps of herbs and veggies thrown in, all on homemade tortillas. Ropa vieja is a big, stewy mess that will have your eyes spinning, and the chicken *chilaquiles* (a casserole layered with tortillas, chicken, salsa, *cotija* cheese, and more) is worth trying, though we find the lauded fish dishes often rather bland. If creamy Mexican chocolate pie is available, be sure to get some. It's a loud, hectic, wildly colored place; you should make a reservation, because it's justly popular.

1445 4th St. (between Broadway and Santa Monica Blvd.). ☎ *310-451-1655 (also: 260 E. Colorado, Pasedena.* ☎ *626-844-8988). Internet:* www.millikenand feniger.com. *Reservations recommended; online reservations (for 4 people and under) require 48-hour notice. Lunch main courses: $8–$14. Dinner main courses: $15–$26. Open: Sun–Thurs 11:30 a.m.–10:00 p.m., Fri–Sat 11:30 a.m.–11 p.m. AE, DC, MC, V.*

Bread & Porridge
$ Santa Monica   AMERICAN

This adorable little cafe is most notable for breakfast, though lunch is worthwhile, as well. Omelets are huge affairs (the vegetarian has three eggs, spinach, mushroom, tomato, cheddar cheese, and onion, garnished with red potatoes and fruit), and the fluffy, well-constructed pancakes aren't much smaller. (We admit to having a great fondness for the chocolate chip pancakes, oozing melted chocolatey goodness.) In short, all of the meals are portioned to share. Hardcore bacon snobs say the applewood smoked version here is not quite up to snuff, but breakfast fans will revel in the aforementioned goodies plus gourmet sausages (try the chicken tequila or spicy Portuguese) and individual coffee pots ready for pressing. Lunch offerings include generously portioned fresh salads and sandwiches. *Note:* It's a popular place (with plenty of kid-friendly dishes), and on the small side, so you may want to time your meal for off-hours.

2315 Wilshire Blvd. (near 26th St.). ☎ *310-453-4941. Breakfast main courses: $3.95–$8.55. Lunch main courses: $6.25–$9.95. Open: Daily 7 a.m.–2 p.m.*

Cadillac Cafe
$$ West Hollywood   ECLECTIC

Garish and hilarious, this is the reincarnation of a much-beloved '80s eatery. It's notable for its eccentric interior, clever salads (available in a tri-plate that allows you to sample several at a pop), "picnic plates" that offer combos that can include deviled eggs with caviar and crab salad, hilarious entrees like the "turkey sundae" (layers of turkey, dressing, and cranberry sauce), or just delightful ones like the black-and-white angel-hair pasta with shrimp. It also holds silly events, such as the Dali Week, wherein it offers choices from the Salvador Dali Cookbook (yeah, there is such a thing!). A local treasure.

359 N. La Cienega Blvd. (north of Beverly Blvd.). ☎ *310-657-6591. Internet:* www.cadillaccafe.com. *Reservations recommended. Lunch main courses: $6.95–$12. Dinner main courses: $7.50–$17. Open: Mon–Fri 11 a.m.–11 p.m., Sat 11 a.m. to midnight, Sun 11 a.m.–10 p.m. AE, DC, DISC, MC, V.*

Campanile

$$$$ West Hollywood   CALIFORNIA/MEDITERRANEAN

It's one of two restaurants most likely to be the answer to the question, "What's the best restaurant in LA?" (the other is Patina), and it remains to be seen whether Campanile can live up to the hype (though to be fair, what could?), but we can say that it's someplace special. Housed in an old building originally built by Charlie Chaplin as office space, it's all gracious, indoor courtyard, replete with Mexican tile and splashing fountains. Chef/owner **Mark Peel** is a great talent, and his wife, **Nancy Silverton**, is the genius behind La Brea Bakery (you've eaten their bread, no doubt, which is served all over the city), the original of which is next door. Come for dinner, where you can eat the likes of rosemary-charred baby lamb, cedar-smoked Tasmanian salmon, pulled-pork ravioli, or roasted beets and blood-orange salad; or for brunch, considered the best in town; or for Thursday night, when they try gourmet twists on the humble grilled cheese sandwich. And always save room for dessert; the pastry chef is renowned.

624 S. La Brea Ave. (north of Wilshire Blvd.). ☎ *323-938-1447. Internet:* www.campanilerestaurant.com. *Reservations recommended. Main courses: $23–$33. Open: Mon–Fri 11:30 a.m.–2:00 p.m., Mon–Thurs 6–10 p.m., Sat–Sun 9:30 a.m.–1:30 p.m., Fri–Sat 6–11 p.m. AE, MC, V.*

Canter's Deli

$$ West Hollywood   DELICATESSEN

We just love Canter's. It's the whole package: classic old deli, open 24 hours, full of both elderly Jewish couples and young hipsters drawn to the large menu, and solidly good food. Okay, the musicians come because they can get soup at 3 a.m. and because two good clubs are across the street; plus, Canter's own **Kibbitz Room** still hosts its own music shows (for years, Jakob Dylan, before he was anyone other than his father's son, played there regularly). Local DJ legend Rodney Bigenhiemer eats here nearly every day, so they put up a plaque at his booth. We've eaten more than our share of Canter's brisket (the Brooklyn: brisket, Russian dressing, slaw on a roll) when we aren't eating a bagel liberally covered with lox. Be nice to the waitresses, many of whom have been there since Hector's grandfather was a pup.

419 N. Fairfax Ave. (just north of Beverly Blvd.). ☎ *323-651-2030. Sandwiches: $3.60–$10.25. Entrees: $8.50–$14.95. Open: Daily 24 hours. AE, MC, V.*

Diner pies, BLTs, and movie stars

A West Hollywood landmark since the Depression, the **Farmer's Market** is not to be confused with those weekly farm stands all over town; instead, this is a series of buildings — a somewhat maze-like complex — nominally outdoors but with a roof over much of it, featuring everything from tacky souvenirs to pets to various dining options to, yes, even produce (and meat counters!).

It's on the brink of revitalization or extinction, depending on how a new adjacent development goes. You should be interested, for there are a number of fun places to grab anything from a nosh to a full meal.

Choose among **Kokomo's,** the trendy breakfast and lunch place (it used to have the best BLT in town); **Dupar's,** the classic old diner (noted for its pies); **Bob's Donuts** (noted for its doughnuts!); the **Gumbo Pot,** serving the closest this area has to authentic Cajun cuisine; not to mention delis, soft-serve ice cream, Asian food, and more.

Look carefully, for this is a favorite hangout of up-and-coming, and already arrived actors, writers (they are the grumpy ones with laptops), and other celebrated sorts, along with the many plain old folks who've made this a gathering spot for decades. You may have to elbow your way through the market crowds (if you see tour buses in the parking lot, run), so it's a good idea to have breakfast or lunch during off-hours. Prices vary, and most places prefer cash. Parking is currently free, though that may change as the development progresses. (6333 W. 3rd St.; ☎ 323-933-9211. Open: Mon–Sat 9 a.m–7 p.m., Sun 10 a.m.–6 p.m.).

Caroussel

$$ Hollywood   ARMENIAN

Our hands-down favorite Armenian restaurant, which is not to say the hands-down best in town, but it's mighty darn close. Located in the eastern part of Hollywood, at the back corner of a dingy strip mall, it's actually a jumping joint, full of locals celebrating, well, life. If you have at least three in your party, we strongly urge that you get one of the sampler specials — about $20 each can produce an array of choices from the menu, blanketing the table with one of about every appetizer, from hummus, which you expect, to a walnut/red-bell-pepper paste, which you may not expect, plus stuffed grape leaves, beef tartare, and sausages, and on it goes. And then come the entrees, which you completely forgot about, at which point you may cry uncle. But carry on; we know you can.

5112 Hollywood Blvd. (near N. Normadie Ave.). ☎ 323-660-8060. Lunch entrees: $7–$12. Dinner entrees: $10–$15. Open: Daily 11 a.m.–9 p.m. MC, V.

Chao Praya

$ Hollywood   THAI

It's a more upscale Thai than the others listed here — you know, table-cloths, actual decor, heck, it looks like an actual restaurant, rather than just a hole in the wall — but it's still good nonetheless, and well-situated if you are staying (or just touring) in Hollywood. (And it's often full of executives from very nearby Capital Records.) Consequently, we aren't going to steer you toward anything adventurous — this may be the right place for you to try Thai food if you never have before. You'll get fine, fine coconut soup, very good Pad Thai, and pleasurable chicken stir-fried with garlic.

6307 Yucca St. (near Vine St.). ☎ *323-466-6704. $5.95–$11.95. Open: Mon–Fri 11:30 a.m.–10:30 p.m. (closed 4 p.m.–5 p.m.), Sat–Sun noon to 10:30 p.m. AE, DC, DISC, MC, V.*

Clementine's

$ West Los Angeles   HOMEMADE SEASONAL FOOD

A small, charming cafe on a side street near Century City, Clementine's has quickly become a local favorite. The menu changes according to season, so only the most current, fresh ingredients are used in its sand-wiches and salads. But here are some things we know that you can get at all times: tiny ham biscuits, hot chocolate with homemade marshmallows, perfect deviled eggs. Among the dishes we ate recently, and happily, was an autumn chicken salad with apples, grapes, and celery root on pecan raisin bread. Plus, it has a charming kid's menu. It's lovely. Come here.

1751 Ensley Ave. (near Santa Monica Blvd.). ☎ *310-552-1080. Everything under $10. Open: Mon–Fri 7 a.m.–7 p.m., Sat 8 a.m.–5 p.m. AE, MC, V.*

Ciudad

$$$ Downtown   LATIN

The "Two Hot Tamales," Mary Sue Milliken and Susan Fenniger, the hard-working chefs behind Border Grill, branched out a bit with this Downtown location. Instead of just focusing on regional Mexican cook-ing, here they get to flex their muscles by utilizing any and all Latin-influ-enced cuisines: a little Spanish tapas, a little Argentine steak, a little Cuban fried bananas, and so much more, all of it housed in a noisy, cheer-ful space that continues to show the Tamales' love for all things bright and wild. The menu changes regularly, but you can sample some tapas (goat-cheese-and-avocado-stuffed piquillo peppers, for example, or Morcilla sausage), try a couple different kinds of cerviche, order the but-ternut squash empanadas, and save room for dessert.

445 S. Figueroa St., Suite 100 (at 5th St.). ☎ *213-486-5171. Internet:* www. millikenandfeniger.com. *Reservations recommended; online reservations* *(for 4 people and under) require 48-hour notice. Lunch main courses: $7.75–$18.50. Dinner main courses: $16–$27. Open: Mon–Thurs 11:30 a.m.–9:00 p.m., Fri 11:30 a.m.–10:00 p.m., Sat–Sun 5–10 p.m. AE, DC, DISC, MC, V.*

El Cholo

$$ Hollywood/Santa Monica   MEXICAN

Okay, so you want to try real Mexican food. We could make a case for dining at Border Grill (because the chef-owners learned everything from actual home cooks in Mexico) or, better still, for heading to certain remote parts of East L.A. But that's probably not what you have in mind when you imagine "real." You want burritos and tacos, you want the familiar, but you want it good, not gloppy and bland — well, maybe a little gloppy — and you like bean sauce, and cheese, and maybe even mole. And so we bring you over to El Cholo, an L.A. institution (the Hollywood location has been around since 1927) that serves authentic Southern California Mexican food, in all its glory. It's noisy, crowded, and entirely fun. Be sure to try the guacamole.

1121 S. Western Ave. (south of Olympic Blvd.). ☎ 323-734-2773 (also: 1025 Wilshire Blvd. ☎ 310-899-1106). Reservations recommended at dinner. Main courses: $8–$16. Open: Mon–Thurs 11 a.m.–10 p.m., Fri–Sat 11 a.m.–11 p.m., Sun 11 a.m.–9 p.m. AE, DC, DISC, MC, V.

The Fabiolus Cafe

$$ Hollywood   ITALIAN

Sure, this often overlooked Italian restaurant isn't as innovative as some, but it isn't just spaghetti and meatballs. Portions are generous (we've rarely finished one), prices are reasonable, everything is cooked fresh and well, the servers put bowls of olive oil dipping sauce on the table with the bread, it's got three locations, and each one is colorful and pleasant. What more can you want? (Well, avoid the Melrose locations at lunchtime, for both are located near Paramount and tend to fill up with studio folks, so it can get crowded.)

6270 W. Sunset Blvd. (near Argyle Ave.). ☎ 323-467-2882 (also: 5750 Melrose Ave. ☎ 323-461-1549; 5255 Melrose Ave. ☎ 323-464-5857). Reservations always recommended. Main courses: $5.75–$18.75. Open: Daily 11:30 a.m.–10:00 p.m. AE, DC, DISC, MC, V.

Fred 62

$$ Hollywood   ECLECTIC DINER

Okay, it tries *waaaay* too hard to be hip. You can tell, because it's a very loud shade of green. And one may ask, legitimately, why wannabe hipsters come here, to a prefab old-fashioned diner, instead of to the House of Pies, a *real* diner, right across the street. But come they do, partly for the ambience (hip, remember; your waitperson probably has many tattoos and a hair color not found in nature) and partly for the food — big burgers, like the Juicy Lucy, or French fries delivered in cunning little boxes of twisted brown paper. Or maybe it's the toasters on the tables or a menu that lets you build your own sandwich (our current fave combines toasted rye bread with smoked salmon and avocado) and offers Asian noodle dishes in very large portions, just right for budget-minded folks.

1850 N. Vermont Ave. (in Los Feliz). ☎ *323-667-0062. Main courses: $3–$15. Open: Daily 24 hours. AE, DC, DISC, MC, V.*

Grand Central Market
$ Downtown   VARIOUS

Operating since 1914, the Grand Central Market is precisely the sort of chaotic market place (open sides, but with a roof overhead) you'd find in, say, Turkey or Asia but not in Los Angeles. Stall after stall offers fresh produce, spices, meats (check out the cow tongues!), and junky toys and kitsch, and in between all that is stall after stall selling some of the best and most affordable Mexican food in town — when they aren't hawking Thai, Chinese, or deli fare. Try a monster burrito, a Mexican sandwich stuffed with pork and topped with fresh cilantro, or a bowl full of Chinese soup. Sample a little of this and some of that, grab some fruit (pay for it, of course) from a nearby stall so that you can tell your mom you're eating a balanced meal, and then sit at a table and watch the Mariachis play amid the bustle, while you try to figure out what to try next.

317 S. Broadway (near 3rd St.). ☎ *213-624-2378. Prices vary (but nothing over $10). Open: Mon–Sat 9 a.m.–6 p.m., Sun 9 a.m.–5 p.m. Cash only.*

The house restaurant
$$$$ Hollywood   AMERICAN

Yes, it's in a house all right, an old Craftsman, to be precise, and that just adds to the charm of this spot (which also has a lovely patio) — that, and the fact that the chef/owner's name is Scooter. It's a fun place, which is reflected in the food; again, the menu changes seasonally, but you should try Scooter's take on mac and cheese, as well as cookies and milk for dessert, for she believes in comfort food. But she also believes in intriguing items like duck sloppy joe, wild mushroom pot au feu, sea bream with pearl risotto and carrot broth, and a heavenly baked hot chocolate (which is actually a soufflé). Scooter doesn't seem to believe in huge portions, but we can nearly forgive her that. It's not her fault, or maybe it is, that we want more.

5750 Melrose Ave. (at N. Lucerne Blvd.). ☎ *323-462-4687. Internet:* www.thehouse restaurant.com. *Reservations suggested. Main courses: $19–$28. Open: Tues–Sat 6:00–10:30 p.m., Sun 5–9 p.m. AE, MC, V.*

Jar

$$$$ West Hollywood STEAKHOUSE

A new restaurant from Mark Peel and Suzanne Tracht (he brought us Campanile, considered one of the best restaurants in town; she cooked with him there), this instantly likable space (modern, clean, just a step or two above cozy) is meant to be a more modest outing — food more familiar, prices less dear. Hence, a steakhouse, and one that is, while hardly burger-stand cheap, certainly more affordable than its peers around town. Even so, who could have predicted the single most popular dish would be pot roast? Braised with care, cooked for hours until it falls apart at a touch, it's what Mom would make if she were a gourmet cook. The steaks are just fine, but oh, that pot roast. If the savory pork belly appetizer is on the menu, get it; otherwise, indulge yourself in a lobster cocktail, the sweet meat still warm from the shell. Dinners are à la carte, but sides, such as creamed spinach, are big enough to share.

8225 Beverly Blvd. (corner of Harper Ave., between La Cienega and Fairfax Blvds.). ☎ *323-655-6566. Internet:* www.thejar.com. *Reservations recommended. Main courses: $18–$29. Open: Lunch: Mon–Fri 11:30 a.m.–2:30 p.m. Dinner: Sun–Mon 5:30–10:00 p.m., Tues–Sat 5:30–10:30 p.m. AE, DC, MC, V.*

Jerry's Famous Deli

$$ Los Angeles DELICATESSEN

With its many locations and colossal menu, to say nothing of round-the-clock hours, Jerry's fits many a bill and budget. Although it is officially a deli and has all the usual suspects, its mile-long menu also has pastas, veggie dishes, Mexican entrees, oh, heck, we can't even keep up (14 kinds of chicken breast sandwich! Fajitas! Greek pasta salad! Meat loaf! Romanian skirt steak!). Plus, breakfast is served all day long. The odd thing is that they manage to do credible versions of it all, belying the conventional wisdom that trying to do too much means you do nothing well. Families with differing tastes (one dieter, one vegetarian, and one ravenous but unadventurous teenager) will find it a godsend. And for those on a budget, note that sandwiches are piled precariously high and can easily feed two.

8020 Beverly Blvd., West Hollywood. ☎ *310-289-1811 (also: 10925 Westwood Blvd, Westwood.* ☎ *310-208-3354; 12655 Ventura Blvd, Studio City.* ☎ *818-980-4245; Universal City Walk, Universal City.* ☎ *818-622-3354; and several other locations). Internet:* www.jerrysdeli.com. *Main courses: $6–$12.95. Hours vary depending on location; some 24 hours. AE, MC, V.*

Joan's on Third

$ West Hollywood TUSCAN/MEDITERRANEAN

It's just a tiny little cafe, better known for takeout (though it does have a few tables), but it's an absolute treasure. From the lovely sandwiches (ham and brie with mustard caper sauce or turkey meatloaf) on fresh, terrific bread (the baguettes, especially) to daily specials (pesto-crusted salmon or grilled maple-rosemary chicken breast), salads of all sorts, and finally, but most importantly, the desserts (coconut cupcakes; chocolate roulade — flourless chocolate cake rolled up with whipped cream; and the traditional and oh-so-sweet-and-frosting-heavy chocolate layer cake), everything is a delight. It also has a small but well-chosen cheese counter. Skip some fancy place for dinner and get Joan's for takeout to eat in your hotel room or in some nearby park.

8350 W. Third St. (near Beverly Blvd.). ☎ *323-655-2285. Everything under $10. Open: Mon–Sat 10 a.m.–8 p.m., Sun 11 a.m.–6 p.m. AE, MC, V.*

Joe's Restaurant
$$$$ Venice   CALIFORNIA

One expects funky beach cafes in this part of town, but this little gourmet spot is not only surprisingly elegant, it's also affordable ($48 for a high falutin' prix fixe with four courses!), with a most doable price for lunch (cost includes soup or salad). Portions for the latter are the right size for a midday meal (larger than spa-size but not enough to destabilize your pants size), and it's all tasty and lovely. Butternut squash soup is astonishingly rich for having no cream. The most popular dish is California sand dabs (flatfish) with avocado and sweet shrimp, but we prefer the grilled sea scallops on tomato couscous with a veggie confit. Dessert includes an amazing chocolate crunch cake.

1023 Abbot Kinney Blvd., in the Venice Place Building. ☎ *310-399-5811. Internet:* www.joesrestaurant.com. *Reservations highly recommended. Brunch main courses: $7–$13. Lunch main courses: $10–$13. Dinner prix fixe: $38 or $48. Open: Tues–Fri 11:30 a.m.–2:30 p.m.; Sun, Tues, Wed, and Thurs 6–10 p.m.; Fri and Sat 6–11 p.m.; Sat and Sun brunch 11 a.m.–2:30 p.m.; AE, DC, MC, V.*

John O'Groats
$$ West Los Angeles   AMERICAN

You'd never believe that hidden behind this modest front is one of the hot breakfast spots for the movers and shakers of Hollywood, on weekdays at least, because of its proximity to Fox Studios. But it's also a very family-friendly place, so on weekends, there's a line by 9 a.m. (when they put coffee out). Everyone is lured by the famous biscuits, tall and fluffy, but also by some of the best pancakes in town, as well as dishes like its version of huevos rancheros, which comes on biscuit dough instead of a tortilla. But the biscuits are served at night, too, along with tender pork entrees (smoked pork chop with apple pecan sauce) and moist fish dishes, one of the best meatloafs in town, large salads, and fish and chips.

10516 W. Pico Blvd. (near Overland Ave.). ☎ *310-204-0692. Breakfast main courses: $5–$12. Lunch main courses: $5–$13. Dinner main courses: $9–$16. Open: Mon–Fri 7 a.m.–3 p.m., Sat–Sun 7 a.m.–2 p.m., Sat–Wed 6–9 p.m. AE, DC, MC, V.*

Kate Mantilini

$$$ Beverly Hills   AMERICAN

Kate Mantilini's is the place that made meatloaf chic. This upscale restaurant with dark wood, steel sculptures, and crisp white linens was featured briefly in the movie *Heat*. It's also where you can find agents, couples on dates, Beverly Hills families, wealthy senior citizens, actors, and successful writers — in other words, anyone willing to spend almost $15 for macaroni and cheese. The sand dabs are delightful, the steaks are tender; the icebox lemon pie is nicely tart, and the sourdough bread is (dare we say?) better than Musso & Frank's, to which Kate Mantilini's menu and decor owes a stylistic debt — it's a younger, modern version. The famous meatloaf is not all beef (we suspect there's turkey rather than pork in the mix) and is made with carrots, herbs, and green onions. It comes with superlative garlicky kale and very mashed potatoes and okay gravy. We especially like that they don't seat women dining alone or in pairs out in Siberia by the kitchen; we've gotten booths every time!

9101 Wilshire Blvd. (at Doheny Dr.). ☎ *310-278-3699. Reservations accepted for 6 or more. $13.95–$30. Open: Mon–Thurs 7:30 a.m.–1:00 a.m., Fri 7:30 a.m.–2:00 a.m., Sat 11 a.m.–2 a.m., Sun 10 a.m. to midnight. AE, MC, V.*

Lawry's The Prime Rib

$$$$$ Beverly Hills   PRIME RIB

Okay, by rights, perhaps this should go in the "old school" section — it's been around long enough. But darn it, Lawry's is good — as long as you like prime rib. Otherwise, it's not so good. Time was when Lawry's had only the one dish — the prime rib — though now they've added chicken and fish. Don't bother. Come instead for a ritual shared by generations of Angelenos, one unchanged by time. A waitress comes up and asks if you want any side dishes (creamed corn, creamed spinach, baked potato) and then does the famous spinning salad bowl, a preparation production number to rival Busby Berkley's. After that, she comes back with plates of Yorkshire pudding, and a man in a tall chef's hat wheels up a cow-sized steel cart and asks how big you want your cut of meat and at what degree of doneness you'd like it cooked. (That would be the prime rib we keep mentioning.) You tell him. Then you eat one heck of a good cut of prime rib, possibly as good as you've ever had. You may also want dessert. And that is all. And that is enough.

100 N. La Cienega Blvd. (just north of Wilshire Blvd.). ☎ *310-652-2827. Reservations recommended. Main courses: $24–$40. Open: Mon–Thurs 5–10 p.m., Fri 5–11 p.m., Sat 4:30–11:00 p.m., Sun 4–10 p.m. AE, DC, DISC, MC, V.*

The Lobster

$$$$ Santa Monica   SEAFOOD

A former rundown fishermen's shack right smack at the start of the Santa Monica Pier, The Lobster is now a gleaming restaurant, thanks to a total renovation. Thanks to high prices, but also undeniably stunning views (floor-to-ceiling windows wrap nearly the entire exterior and look out on beach, pier, and sea), this is definitely a special-occasion place (or a place to impress your busty, blonde girlfriend, judging from a recent late-night crowd). As you may guess, it serves lobster — good-sized steamed Maine and smaller grilled Pacific spiny (the grilled helps the flavor of the latter, but we prefer the classic perfection of the former) — but also other local fresh fish dishes. Get the crabcakes, plump and dabbed with chili citrus sour cream, as a smaller portioned appetizer (you have to ask), and do also try the spicy snow crab soup. Enjoy the view and hold hands, and remember that you are worth it.

1602 Ocean Ave. (at Colorado Blvd.). ☎ *310-458-9294. Reservations recommended. Main courses: $16–$32 (lobster priced $25–$28 per pound). Open: Sun–Thurs 11:30 a.m.–10:00 p.m., Fri–Sat 11:30 a.m.–11 p.m. AE, DC, DISC, JCB, MC, V.*

Lucques

$$$ West Hollywood   CALIFORNIA

A new star in the L.A. foodie firmament, Lucques (say "Luke" — it's a kind of olive, and one that is placed on your table, along with salt, sweet butter, and wonderful bread) features California cuisine with French and Mediterranean influences. It's in a pretty room, simple, with a fireplace that is often roaring away. The menu changes seasonally; a recent lunch menu found duck confit with celery root remoulade, and a grilled pork burger with chipotle aioli. Dinner features items like grilled snapper with winter vegetables, Portuguese pork and clams with chorizo, and Lucques' (quickly growing famous) braised short ribs. Desserts may feature bittersweet chocolate pot de crème. *Tip:* Lucques offers a late-night menu until midnight. Also, those on a budget can always come in for a drink at the bar, or in front of that fireplace, and still enjoy the olives and bread.

8474 Melrose Ave. (east of La Cienega Blvd.). ☎ *323-655-6277. Internet:* www. lucques.com. *Reservations recommended. Main courses: $18–$25. Sun 3-course prix fixe dinner: $30. Open: Tues–Sat noon to 2:30 p.m., 6–11 p.m.; Sun 5:30– 10:00 p.m. AE, DC, MC, V.*

Newsroom Cafe

$$ West Hollywood   ECLECTIC

So-called for its bank of TVs set to CNN and the rack of periodicals in the front, the Newsroom is a happening spot, both the West Hollywood location (where we have never yet gone and not seen a celebrity) and the Santa Monica location. It's also heaven-sent for vegetarians and anyone trying to eat a bit healthy. With a focus on low-fat (if not low-carb, but that, too) and meatless dishes (like vegan burgers, vegetarian Caesars, and lots of fun with tofu, including tofu scrambles), not to mention an array of juices and smoothies, it attracts the young and healthy crowd, who wants to stay that way. Fear not, however: There is meat to be found here, and all the portions are generous.

120 N. Robertson Blvd. (near 3rd St.). ☎ *310-652-4444 (also: 530 Wilshire Blvd, Santa Monica.* ☎ *310-319-9100). Breakfast main courses: $5–$9. Lunch and dinner main courses: $5–$13. Open: Mon–Thurs 8 a.m.–9 p.m., Fri 8 a.m.–10 p.m., Sat 9 a.m.–10 p.m., Sun 9 a.m.–9 p.m. AE, MC, V.*

Nick & Stef's

$$$$ Downtown   STEAKHOUSE

Joachim Splichal (the man behind Patina, considered one of the best restaurants in L.A., and its numerous spinoffs) has created a lovely, modern steakhouse in downtown L.A. Check out the windows full of beef, properly aging. Then order a slab. Share, we think, because too much beef, even this good, may not be good for you, and besides, that gives you more opportunity to order some of the incredible sides like Caesar salad made tableside, heavenly spinach, and 12 kinds of potatoes. (Vegetarians can get a fine meal off the sides.) Sadly, everything is à la carte. *Note:* They make one wonderful burger (using their own prime beef), which is served only at lunch and during happy hour (3 to 7 p.m. weekdays) in the sleek bar. The burger is pretty pricey for lunch ($12!),

Help! My money is burning a hole in my pocket . . .

And I really want to spend some of it on expensive food! Okay. Start with **Matsuhisa** (129 N. La Cienega Blvd., Beverly Hills; ☎ 310-659-9639) and tell the master sushi chefs that you are putting yourself in their hands. They will place concoctions before you that will cause your eyes to spin with aesthetic delight, your mouth to buzz, and your heart to stop when you see the bill.

The Ivy (133 N. Robertson Blvd., West Hollywood; ☎ 310-274-8303) has a famous Cajun blackened prime rib, along with other high-priced entrees, but you may not notice the bill, because you'll be too busy ogling the famous face sitting next to you. (**The Ivy At the Shore** is its west-side version: 1541 Ocean Ave., Santa Monica; ☎ 310-393-3113.)

L'Orangerie (903 N. La Cienega Blvd., West Hollywood; ☎ 310- 652-9770) is staggeringly French and terrifyingly self-important. Many awards have been lavished upon its cuisine, but we worry that we don't dress well enough, nor speak with the right inflection, to eat here.

The chef at **Michael's** (1147 3rd St., Santa Monica; ☎ 310-451-0843), along with Alice Waters at Berkeley's Chez Panisse, was one of the pioneers of California cuisine, and this has been a beloved restaurant since 1979. But anything that has been around a length of time runs the risk of ups and downs in quality, and Michael's has gone through its own. Currently, the food is marvelous (anything with fresh fish is a must), though service can be spotty. The room is romantic, and one can dine inside or out. But it will set you back a fair amount (entrees run close to $40 a pop) for this privilege.

but at happy hour, it drops to $5 — a good budget saver but also useful for a pre-theater meal (if you're going to the nearby Music Center).

330 S. Hope St. (near 4th St.). ☎ *213-680-0330. Internet:* www.patinagroup.com. *Reservations recommended. Main courses: $19–$32. Mon–Fri 11:30 a.m.–2:30 p.m., 5:00–9:30 p.m.; Fri–Sat 5–10 p.m.; Sun 5–9 p.m. AE, MC, V.*

Off Vine

$$ Hollywood   AMERICAN

A charming restaurant in an old Craftsman house, Off Vine doesn't have the high profile it used to, and that's a shame, for we've never not enjoyed a meal here, both for taste and ambience. We've had lunches of veggie-intensive chopped salads and mango-avocado combos, and dinners of thick lamb chops, sweet crab cakes (with paprika lime sauce), and penne with turkey sausage in a spicy marinara sauce. Nothing, truth be told, is shockingly innovative, but you aren't going to feel cheated, for the food is interesting enough and done well, and the prices are reasonable. The room is pretty, as is the plant-filled courtyard. It's romantic but not intimidating, and nicely situated for the Hollywood area.

6263 Leland Way., off Vine St. ☎ *323-962-1900. Reservations accepted. Lunch main courses: $8.95–$14.95. Dinner main courses: $10.95–$17.95. Open: Mon–Fri 11:30 a.m.–2:30 p.m., Sat–Sun 10:30 a.m.–2:30 p.m., Mon–Thurs 5:30–10:00 p.m., Fri 5:30–11:30 p.m., Sat 5:00–11:30 p.m., Sun 4–10 p.m. AE, DC, DISC, MC, V.*

101 Coffee Shop

$$ Hollywood   DINER

A landmark restaurant, kinda, in that it is housed in the Best Western Hollywood Hills Hotel, the side of which carries a large sign informing the freeway-bound that it's the "Last Cappuccino Stop until the 101," a sign that has turned up in various movies, including *The Brady Bunch*. However, the coffee shop the sign used to signal has now moved to Vermont and lost considerable gusto; the 101 has taken its place, and nicely. Check out the hours ("Why even close at all?" wonders one loyal patron), check out the patrons in the booth next to you (you've probably seen them in the latest movie or TV show), and check out the menu: the thick, hearty soups, the honest tuna melts, the more-exotic salmon and the grilled skirt steak, the wonderful banana shakes, and the honest-to-gosh breakfasts (served all day). It's an essential, you bet.

6145 Franklin Ave. (in the Best Western Hollywood Hills Hotel). ☎ *323-467-1175. Main courses: $6.25–$12.95. Open: Daily 7 a.m.–3 a.m. AE, MC, V.*

Patina

$$$$$ Hollywood   FRENCH-CALIFORNIAN

The Patina is the other restaurant (besides Campanile) considered by most, and justly, to be L.A.'s finest, and the first by Joachim Splichal, whose name (and restaurant conglomerate, the Patina Group) pops up a great deal more here. With a fresh facelift that made the room even more attractive, this is a holy temple to gastronomy, and maybe just a tiny bit intimidating. But heavens, it's good. Look at this recent sampling (the menu changes regularly) and tell us if it doesn't read like food pornography: foie gras and sweetbread strudel; pavé of salmon baked en croûte; roasted lobster tail with hand-rolled fettuccine and lobster bolognese; and desserts like chocolate-caramel truffled beignets with cardamom ice cream. Nightly tasting menus are often designed around a theme. Lunch is served on Fridays only.

5955 Melrose Ave. (near Cahuenga Blvd.). ☎ *323-467-1108. Reservations a must. Lunch main courses: $12–$19. Dinner main courses: $29–$35 (tasting menus higher). Open: Fri noon to 2:30 p.m., Sun–Thurs 6:00–9:30 p.m., Fri 6:00–10:30 p.m., Sat 5:30–10:30 p.m. AE, DC, DISC, MC, V.*

Philippe the Original
$ Downtown AMERICAN/SANDWICHES

Believe it or not, there are people in L.A. who have never heard of Philippe's, which completely bemuses those who consider it an essential component of life in this city. Founded in 1918 — right there, reason enough to come — Philippe's claims that one day its owner dropped part of a sandwich roll in the juices of a roast beef and gave it to a customer who raved. Voila!, the French dip was invented. Curiously, Cole's P.E. Buffet, on the other side of Downtown, makes a similar claim. We don't care. We prefer the concoction here. Not only is it a heck of a fine sandwich, especially if you add its tangy mustard to it, but it's cheap (around $4), and coffee is but 10¢ a cup. The restaurant has many a little side and upstairs rooms, all with sawdust on the floor and long tables for customers to share, customers who range from businesspeople at lunch and breakfast and formally dressed folks on the way to the theater to punk rockers on a break and skid-row types. All that, and mysterious purple pickled eggs in glass jars.

1001 N. Alameda St. (at Ord St.). ☎ *213-628-3781. Internet:* www.philippes.com. *Everything under $10. Open: Daily 6 a.m.–10 p.m. Cash only.*

Pig 'N Whistle
$$$ Hollywood AMERICAN/ITALIAN

They don't make 'em like this anymore, and we are so grateful that the owners went to the loving care to resuscitate an old Hollywood establishment. It's conveniently located right on Hollywood Boulevard adjacent to all the new development. We just wish the food was an eensy bit better. Pastas are basic pestos and creams and roasted tomatoes; dinner entrees are grilled steaks and roasted chickens. Lunchtime offers solidly good sandwiches and salads. The French fries are heaven, and the scene at the bar is choice at night. You may even see some New Hollywood faces here.

6714 Hollywood Blvd., near Highland Ave. ☎ 323-463-0000. Lunch main courses: $8–$15. Dinner main courses: $12–$23. Open: Daily 11:30 a.m.–11:00 p.m. AE, DISC, MC, V.

Pink's
$ West Hollywood   HOT DOG STAND

A dumpy little hot-dog stand, you might think, except there *is* that line of people standing outside at all hours of the day or night. Hmmm. Do they know something you don't? You bet — except, of course, we are letting you in on the secret. They know Pink's has divine hot dogs, juicy, with a casing that has the right amount of snap, available with chili or Chicago-dog style, or just plain. Or you can get a Polish dog, or chili fries. Or even, horrors, a hamburger, except nobody ever does. And you can sit down in what is basically a dumpy little shack, which has been around since the 1930s (Mr. Pink died not too long ago), and notice that you're sitting next to a face you saw on a magazine cover. They know, too. And now, so do you.

709 N. La Brea Ave. (at Melrose Ave.). ☎ 323-931-4223. Everything under $5. Open: Sun–Thurs 9:30 a.m.–2:00 a.m., Fri–Sat 9:30 a.m.–3:00 a.m. Cash only.

Pinot Hollywood
$$$ Hollywood   BISTRO

Although it would be a misnomer to think that coming here is a budget way of eating at Patina, the parent restaurant (sorta) of the Pinot chain, it is correct to think that it is a way to eat food created by the same originator of Patina. This is largely bistro food — one of the most popular dishes is a roast chicken with garlic fries — and it is less serious to eat here, though this particular Pinot hops with Hollywood heavyweights, drinking and noshing their way through deals. It's our choice for a midrange fancy, midpriced gourmet, with a number of vegetarian (like pumpkin crumble with honey-glazed cipollini onions) and diet-conscious (thyme-marinated swordfish or seared mahi mahi over parsley pearl pasta risotto) options. If the homemade Valhrona chocolate ice cream is on the menu, do get it, and think of us.

1448 N. Gower St. (at Sunset Blvd.). ☎ 323-461-8800. Reservations recommended. Lunch main courses: $12.50–$19.95. Dinner main courses: $14.50–$22.50. Open: Mon–Thurs 11:30 a.m.–10:00 p.m., Sat 5:30–11:00 p.m., closed Sun. AE, DC, DISC, MC, V.

Royal Star Seafood Restaurant
$$ West Los Angeles   CHINESE

Westside dim sum lovers no longer need despair over the long drive to Chinatown and points farther. Royal Star Seafood Restaurant, on the border of Santa Monica and Los Angeles, offers the cheap, filling, and tasty morsels 7 days a week, 365 days a year from 11:00 a.m. to 2:30 p.m., with regular — and excellent — traditional Chinese food served, as well, until closing. We like Royal Star as a relaxing alternative to holiday brunches! The baked honey pork bun (baked *bao*) is a decadent version of a Southern barbecue sandwich; steamed shrimp dumplings with cilantro are delicately flavored and satisfyingly shrimp-filled. As the carts of dim sum delicacies circle the room, brave souls can order chicken feet, while culinary chickens can just stick to the basics, like egg rolls or fried pork dumplings — or order off the menu. Dim sum brunch gets very crowded on weekends, so going on weekdays or getting there early on Saturday or Sunday is a good idea.

3001 Wilshire Blvd. (near Santa Monica Blvd.). ☎ *310-828-8812. Dim sum: $3 and up. Entrees: $6–$15. Open: Daily 11 a.m.–10 p.m. AE, MC, V.*

Sanamluang Cafe
$ Hollywood   THAI

We call it "Samalangadingdong," because we can never remember how to pronounce it, but this carelessness does not reflect our real feelings for this utterly unprepossessing cafe. It's the first place we think of when we want to eat Thai food. Sanamluang is famous for its noodle dishes (General's Noodles, full of garlic, pork, duck, and spices; a bowlfull feeds several and can cure the common cold), and you won't believe how good and cheap the food is. Some of the meat dishes (pork done several ways and barbecued duck) may be heavier on the rice accompanying it than the meat, but hey, that's filling. Skip the usual Pad Thai and go for noodle dishes you've never tried before (note that if you get them "wet" — in a broth — there is that much more to portion out), or get anything with garlic, especially the fried garlic and shrimp over rice. Or just see what looks good at a neighbor's table and get that. Open way late, it's situated in a tacky mini-mall.

5170 Hollywood Blvd. (near Winona Blvd.). ☎ *323-660-8006. Everything under $7. Open: Daily 10 a.m.–4 a.m. MC, V.*

Sepi's Giant Submarines
$ Westwood   SANDWICHES

Right at the edge of the UCLA campus, Sepi's has been a local favorite since 1970, and deservedly so. Subs (small or large, which they claim is 1 foot long, but we've measured, and it's longer) come with the usual fillings (roast beef, turkey, Italian cold cuts, you get the idea) plus shredded lettuce, tomato, onion, and oil and vinegar dressing; darn it, you can keep your famous name-brand sub chain — this is the real thing, and mighty good. Bring a sub to a UCLA basketball game (you won't be alone), order takeout for a picnic, or dine at this humble little store surrounded by Bruins boosterisms.

10968 Le Conte Ave. (near the San Diego Frwy). ☎ *310-208-7171. Everything under $7. Open: Daily 10 a.m.–11 p.m. AE, MC, V.*

Spago Beverly Hills

$$$$$ **Beverly Hills   CALIFORNIA**

Time was, Spago was the symbol of all that was rich and fabulous, the most high-falutin' place you could go in L.A. It was the spot where the paparazzi hung around the entrance to get photos of a veritable who's who of Hollywood. But Spago has moved from its original location to this admittedly much larger and more user-friendly spot in Beverly Hills. And its owner/creator Wolfgang Puck has such a large empire (two dozen restaurants, plus a frozen food line) that he's no longer likely to be in the kitchen. Too bad; in becoming a brand name, the reason Puck was so successful in the first place has been lost. Still, look at some of these recent menu offerings: lobster club sandwich with grilled walnut bread, sautéed calf's liver with braised leeks; agnolotti fonduta with French black truffles (Puck recently made headlines by buying a white truffle for about $20,000; it was shaved over entrees at Spago diners' requests) — and, of course, it is Spago you have to blame for the trend of putting barbecue chicken on pizza. (*Tip:* The most popular pizza is not on the menu, the "Jewish" pizza of smoked salmon and crème fraîche. Ask for it, like everyone else.) It's an experience, for sure, and perhaps one you ought to have at least once.

176 N. Canon Dr. (just north of Wilshire Blvd.). ☎ *310-385-0880. Reservations a must. Lunch main courses: $15–$28. Dinner main courses: $29–$42. Open: Mon–Fri 11:30 a.m.–2:15 p.m., 5–10 p.m.; Sat noon to 2:15 p.m., 5:30–11:00 p.m.; Sun 5:30–10:00 p.m. AE, DC, DISC, MC, V.*

Sushi Gen

$$ **Downtown   JAPANESE**

There are those who say that you can only have really good sushi in pricey locales, such as Los Angeles' Matsuhisa, and perhaps they are right — but you can come darn close for considerable less money at Sushi Gen. When you've had Sushi Gen's lovely, ultra-fresh cuts of yellowtail or toro (fatty tuna), it's hard to go back. And when you've sat back and let a skilled chef do what he wants with you, it's hard to settle for mere California rolls again. Sure, it may be a gimmick when the chefs all shout gleefully when you come in, sounding for all the world like a Japanese "Cheers," but we fall for it every time. Plus the appetizer menu features "original salted squid guts."

422 E. 2nd St. (near S. Central Ave.). ☎ *213-617-0552. Sushi: $4 and up. Open: Mon–Fri 11:15 a.m.–2:00 p.m., 5:30–10:00 p.m., Sat 5:30–10:00 p.m., Sun closed. AE, JCB, MC, V.*

Swingers

$ West Hollywood   COFFEE SHOP

It's a hip, modern — which means retro, somehow — coffee shop, so you can expect burgers (we like 'em), fries, shakes, veggie burgers, and sandwiches. That sort of thing. You don't come here for that (though again, we like the burger), you come for the scene. You come here to see stars canoodling, way before the gossip pages report it. You come to see up-and-coming WB actors. You come to see what the fashion-savvy are wearing. You can do all that just about any time of day. You get the idea.

In the Beverly Laurel Motor Hotel, 8020 Beverly Blvd. (between Fairfax Ave. and La Cienega Blvd.). ☎ *323-653-5858. (also: 802 Broadway, Santa Monica.* ☎ *310-393-9793). Everything under $10. Open: Wed–Mon 6:30 a.m.–4:00 a.m., Tues 6:30 a.m.–1:45 a.m. AE, DC, DISC, MC, V.*

Taylor's Steak House

$$$ Hollywood   STEAKHOUSE

You may notice that the other steakhouses listed here have something in common: They're expensive. You may well wonder why — are their steaks dipped in gold? At Taylor's, you can dine very well indeed on cuts of beef like the culotte steak, a baseball-sized and -shaped hunk of meat that is quite tender and, better still, affordable. This is an old-school steakhouse — red leather (or leatherette) booths, dark wood on the walls — with an old-school clientele. If you've got a hankering for meat and your budget is tight, come here, and you'll be quite happy.

3361 W. 8th St. (at Ardmore St.). ☎ *213-382-8449. Internet:* www.taylors steakhouse.com. *Main courses: $13.95–$23.95. Mon–Fri 11:30 a.m.–4:00 p.m., Mon–Sun 4–10 p.m. AE, DC, MC, V.*

Versailles

$$ Los Angeles   CUBAN

While it's not our hands-down favorite Cuban place (for that, you have travel farther afield to the east side of town), it's certainly a mighty good one with a loyal fan base — it's not uncommon to find a line at dinnertime at the Culver City location. Roast garlic chicken is the top menu item, but we are too fond of the garlicky roast pork to care. Most dishes come with sides of black beans and rice, and if they don't include plantains (bananas fried to lovely carmelization), be sure to get a side order of them.

1415 S. La Cienega Blvd. (near Pico Blvd.). ☎ *310-289-0392 (also: 10319 Venice Blvd, Culver City.* ☎ *310-558-3168). Main courses: $7.95–$18.95. Open: Daily 11 a.m.–10 p.m. AE, MC, V.*

Yang Chow

$$ Downtown   CHINESE

This Downtown Chinese is awfully good, and nowhere else can you eat Yang Chow's Slippery Shrimp, a dish that inspires devotion in countless customers and is not at all slippery; the dish features shrimp battered and deep-fried and then doused in a sweet, garlicky sauce of indefinite origin (but it came from somewhere good). They make platters and platters of this stuff daily; hardly a table is without one. After you get your own, try the moo shu pancakes, or the General Tseng's chicken, or the tofu with black bean sauce. And then have another plate of shrimp.

819 N. Broadway (at Alpine St.), Chinatown. ☎ *213-625-0811 (also: 3777 E. Colorado Blvd, Pasadena.* ☎ *626-432-6868). Internet:* www.yangchow.com. *Main courses: $5–$15. Open: Sun 11:30 a.m.–9:45 p.m., Fri–Sat 11:30 a.m.–10:45 p.m. AE, MC, V.*

Yuca's Hut

$ Hollywood   MEXICAN

Just a little shack (so don't expect much in the way of a place to sit down) in one of the hippest neighborhoods in town (that would be Los Feliz, just east of Hollywood), Yuca's serves some of the best tacos in L.A. — well, apart from those found in certain roach coaches, but we aren't going to get into *that*. It's cheap, too. Be sure to try the *cochinita pibil*, Yucatan-style marinated pork in a soft taco, and finish off with some French pastries at La Conversation up the street.

2056 Hillhurst Ave., Los Feliz. ☎ *323-662-1214. Everything under $7. Open: Mon–Sat 11 a.m.–6 p.m. Cash only.*

Zankou Chicken

$ Los Angeles   ARMENIAN/CHICKEN

The day we accidently stepped into this unprepossessing strip-mall hole-in-the-wall joint, with its dull Formica tables and utter lack of decor, is a day that will forever live in our hearts, for it is the day we discovered Zankou chicken. It's not just because when you place an order, you barely have time to read one of the many glowing reviews on the wall before said order is ready. It's not just because the roast chicken is, well, perfect — juicy and flavorful, with a crispy seasoned skin that has you forgetting all the health warnings about fat and battling your loved ones for that last piece. It's all that, and then there's the garlic sauce. Trust us when we say that when we die, the food served to us in heaven will have Zankou garlic sauce accompanying it.

5065 W. Sunset Blvd. (near N. Mariposa Ave.). ☎ *323-665-7842 (also: 5658 Sepulveda Blvd # 103, Van Nuys.* ☎ *818-781-0615; 1296 E Colorado Blvd, Pasadena.* ☎ *626-405-1502). Everything under $7. Open: Daily 11 a.m. to midnight. AE, MC, V.*

Dining in Westside & Beverly Hills

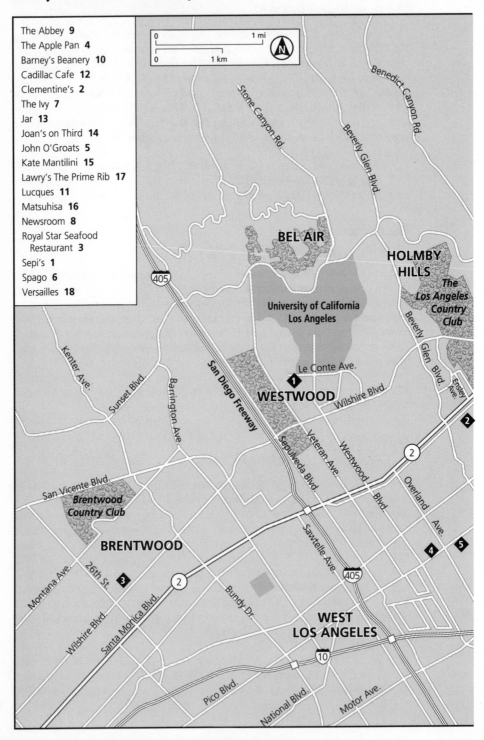

The Abbey **9**
The Apple Pan **4**
Barney's Beanery **10**
Cadillac Cafe **12**
Clementine's **2**
The Ivy **7**
Jar **13**
Joan's on Third **14**
John O'Groats **5**
Kate Mantilini **15**
Lawry's The Prime Rib **17**
Lucques **11**
Matsuhisa **16**
Newsroom **8**
Royal Star Seafood Restaurant **3**
Sepi's **1**
Spago **6**
Versailles **18**

0   1 mi
0   1 km
N

Stone Canyon Rd.
Benedict Canyon Rd.
Beverly Glen Blvd.

BEL AIR

HOLMBY HILLS

The Los Angeles Country Club

University of California Los Angeles

405

Kenter Ave.
Sunset Blvd.
Barrington Ave.
San Diego Freeway

Le Conte Ave.
WESTWOOD 1
Wilshire Blvd.
Veteran Ave.
Sepulveda Blvd.
Westwood Blvd.
Beverly Glen Blvd.
Ensley Ave.
2
2
Overland Ave.

San Vicente Blvd.
Brentwood Country Club

BRENTWOOD

Montana Ave.
26th St.
3
2
Wilshire Blvd.
Santa Monica Blvd.
Bundy Dr.
Sawtelle Ave.
405
4
5

WEST LOS ANGELES

10
Pico Blvd.
National Blvd.
Motor Ave.

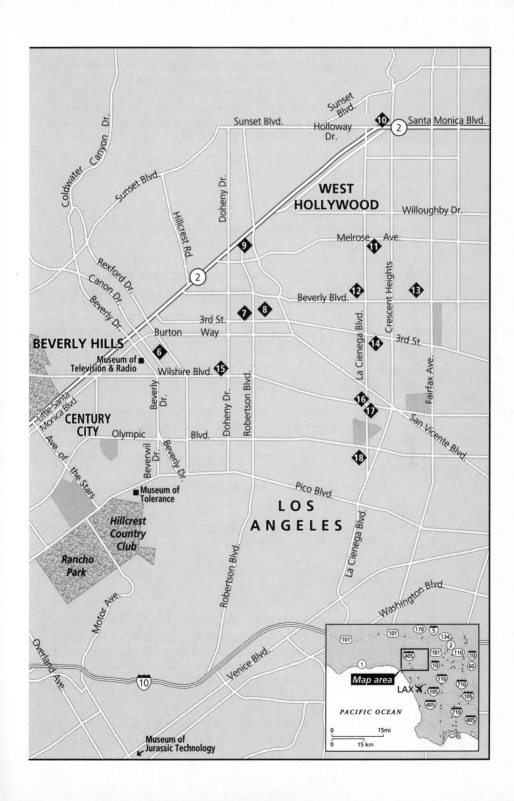

Old-School Dining

This section includes the "restaurants we so want to love because they are institutions and have been around a long time in a town where that is unusual, but we really can't say that the food is any better than average." In other words, go to these places for the experience, and you may dine well, but then again, you may only dine okay, but you probably won't care, because the experience will be so thoroughly enjoyable.

Barney's Beanery

$ West Hollywood AMERICAN

Anywhere else, this would be a down-and-dirty biker bar, but Barney's lies in the heart of West Hollywood, and boy, did they endear themselves to their gay neighbors with their "No Faggots Allowed" sign. (That's gone now.) Rockers love it — Jim Morrison would eat here, and we've sat next to Bono and the Edge. It's all about burgers, barbecue, fries, sawdust on the floor, much beer quaffed at the bar, and a very loud jukebox.

8447 Santa Monica Blvd. (east of La Cienega Blvd.). ☎ *323-654-2287. Main courses: $5–$13. Open: Daily 11 a.m.–2 a.m. AE, DC, DISC, MC, V.*

El Coyote

$ West Hollywood MEXICAN

This very old-school Mexican restaurant has a hardcore loyal following who will be furious to find it in this box, but let's face it, gang, we've all had better Mexican food. Still, it's such a wacky place (and Sharon Tate ate her last meal here) — the waitress dresses up in frou-frou outfits, the margaritas are huge, the atmosphere is family friendly, plus, it's the Mexican food we remember from our childhood — that customers find it hard to care.

7312 Beverly Blvd. (near Martell Ave.). ☎ *323-939-2255. Everything under $10. Open: Sun–Thurs 10 a.m.–11 p.m., Fri–Sat 11 a.m.–11 p.m. AE, MC, V.*

Musso & Frank Grill

$$$$$ Hollywood AMERICAN

This is the oldest restaurant in Hollywood (1919, which means that everybody who was anybody has eaten here), all red leather booths and dark wood-paneled walls and a menu that screams dated (red meat, and lots of it). Everything, but everything, here is à la carte — even your salad dressing costs an extra $3. People love the chops, the flannel cakes (thin, and slightly vanilla-tasting), and the martinis at the bar.

6667 Hollywood Blvd. (at Cherokee Ave.). ☎ *323-467-5123. Reservations recommended. Main courses: $12–$30 (à la carte). Open: Tues–Sat 11 a.m.–11 p.m. AE, MC, V.*

Original Pantry Cafe
$ Downtown STEAKHOUSE

This 24-hour joint's rep is built largely on the fact that in decades of business, it's never been closed. Never. Even when it switched locations; patrons just picked up their plates, walked down to the new place, and kept eating. The front door doesn't even have a lock on it. The waiters are all crusty and bad-tempered, but that's part of the fun (plus, they tell you if what you order isn't worthwhile), as is the sourdough bread and coleslaw they plunk down in front of you shortly after you're seated.

877 S. Figueroa St. (at E. 9th St.). ☎ *213-972-9279. Dinner main courses: $5.75–$13.75; all other meals, everything under $10. Open: Daily 24 hours. Cash only (ATM on site).*

Index of Restaurants by Location

Beverly Hills
Kate Mantilini (American, $$$)
Lawry's The Prime Rib (Prime Rib, $$$$$)
Matsuhisa (Japanese/Sushi, $$$$$)
Spago Beverly Hills (California, $$$$$)

Downtown
Cuidad (Latin, $$$)
Grand Central Market (Various, $)
Nick & Stef's (Steakhouse, $$$$)
Original Pantry Cafe (Steakhouse, $)
Philippe the Original (Sandwiches, $)
Sushi Gen (Japanese/Sushi, $$)
Yang Chow (Chinese, $$)

Hollywood
Alex (Modern European, $$$$)
Authentic Cafe (Southwestern/ Caribbean, $$)
Caroussel (Armenian, $$)
Chao Praya (Thai, $)
El Cholo (Hollywood/Santa Monica) (Mexican, $$)
The Fabiolus Café (Italian, $$)
Fred 62 (Eclectic Diner, $$)
The house restaurant (American, $$$$)
Musso & Frank Grill (American, $$$$$)
Off Vine (American, $$)
101 Coffee Shop (Diner, $$)

Patina (French-Californian, $$$$$)
Pig 'N Whistle (American, $$$)
Pinot Hollywood (Bistro, $$$)
Sanamluang Cafe (Thai, $)
Taylor's Steak House (Steakhouse, $$$)
Yuca's Hut (Mexican, $)

Los Angeles
Jerry's Famous Deli (Delicatessen, $$)
Versailles (Cuban, $$)
Zankou Chicken (Armenian, $)

Santa Monica
Blueberry (Cafe/Breakfast, $)
Border Grill (Mexican, $$$)
Bread & Porridge (American, $)
El Cholo (Hollywood/Santa Monica) (Mexican, $$)
The Ivy at the Shore (American, $$$$$)
The Lobster (Seafood, $$$$)
Michael's (California, $$$$$)

Venice
Joe's Restaurant (California, $$$$)

West Hollywood
The Abbey (American, $$)
Angeli Caffe (Italian, $$)
Angelini Osteria (Italian, $$$)
Barney's Beanery (American, $)

Campanile (California/Mediterranean,
   $$$$)
Canter's Deli (Delicatessen, $$)
Cadillac Cafe (Eclectic, $$)
El Coyote (Mexican, $)
Farmer's Market (Various, $)
The Ivy (American, $$$$$)
Jar (Steakhouse, $$$$)
Joan's on Third (Tuscan/
   Mediterranean, $)
L'Orangerie (French, $$$$$)
Lucques (California, $$$)

Newsroom Cafe (Eclectic, $$)
Pink's (Hot Dog Stand, $)
Swingers (Coffee Shop, $)

West Los Angeles

Clementine's (Homemade Seasonal, $)
John O'Groats (American, $$)
Royal Star Seafood Restaurant
   (Chinese, $$)

Westwood

Sepi's Giant Submarines (Sandwiches, $)

Index of Restaurants by Cuisine

American

The Abbey (West Hollywood, $$)
Barney's Beanery (West Hollywood, $)
Bread & Porridge (Santa Monica, $)
The house restaurant (Hollywood,
   $$$$)
The Ivy (West Hollywood, $$$$$)
The Ivy at the Shore (Santa Monica,
   $$$$$)
John O'Groats (West Los Angeles, $$)
Kate Mantilini (Beverly Hills, $$$)
Musso & Frank Grill (Hollywood,
   $$$$$)
Off Vine (American, $$)
Philippe the Original (Downtown, $)
Pig 'N Whistle (Hollywood, $$$)

Armenian

Caroussel (Hollywood, $$)
Zankou Chicken (Los Angeles, $)

Bistro

Pinot Hollywood (Hollywood, $$$)

California

Joe's Restaurant (Venice, $$$$)
Lucques (West Hollywood, $$$)
Michael's (Santa Monica, $$$$$)
Spago Beverly Hills (Beverly Hills,
   $$$$$)

California/Mediterranean

Campanile (West Hollywood, $$$$)

Cafe/Breakfast

Blueberry (Santa Monica, $)

Chinese

Royal Star Seafood Restaurant (West
   Los Angeles, $$)
Yang Chow (Downtown, $$)

Coffee Shop

Swingers (West Hollywood, $)

Cuban

Versailles (Los Angeles, $$)

Delicatessen

Canter's Deli (West Hollywood, $$)
Jerry's Famous Deli (Los Angeles, $$)

Diner

101 Coffee Shop (Hollywood, $$)

Eclectic

Cadillac Cafe (West Hollywood, $$)
Newsroom Cafe (West Hollywood, $$)

Eclectic Diner
Fred 62 (Hollywood, $$)

French
L'Orangerie (West Hollywood, $$$$$)

French-Californian
Patina (Hollywood, $$$$$)

Homemade Seasonal
Clementine's (West Los Angeles, $)

Hot Dog Stand
Pink's (West Hollywood, $)

Italian
Angeli Caffe (West Hollywood, $$)
Angelini Osteria (West Hollywood, $$$)
The Fabiolus Café (Hollywood, $$)
Pig 'N Whistle (Hollywood, $$$)

Japanese/Sushi
Matsuhisa (Beverly Hills, $$$$$)
Sushi Gen (Downtown, $$)

Latin
Cuidad (Downtown, $$$)

Mexican
Border Grill (Santa Monica, $$$)
El Coyote (West Hollywood, $)
El Cholo (Hollywood, $$)
Yuca's Hut (Hollywood, $)

Modern European
Alex (Hollywood, $$$$)

Prime Rib
Lawry's The Prime Rib (Beverly Hills, $$$$$)

Sandwiches
Philippe the Original (Downtown, $)
Sepi's Giant Submarines (Westwood, $)

Seafood
The Lobster (Santa Monica, $$$$)

Southwestern/Caribbean
Authentic Cafe (Hollywood, $$)

Steakhouse
Jar (West Hollywood, $$$$)
Nick & Stef's (Downtown, $$$$)
Original Pantry Cafe (Downtown, $)
Taylor's Steak House (Hollywood, $$$)

Thai
Chao Praya (Hollywood, $)
Sanamluang Cafe (Hollywood, $)

Tuscan/Mediterranean
Joan's on Third (West Hollywood, $)

Various
Farmer's Market (West Hollywood, $)
Grand Central Market (Downtown, $)

Index of Restaurants by Price

$$$$$
The Ivy (American, West Hollywood)
The Ivy at the Shore (American, Santa Monica)
Lawry's The Prime Rib (Prime Rib, Beverly Hills)
L'Orangerie (French, West Hollywood)
Matsuhisa (Japanese/Sushi, Beverly Hills)
Michael's (California, Santa Monica)

Musso & Frank Grill (American, Hollywood)
Patina (French/Californian, Hollywood)
Spago Beverly Hills (California, Beverly Hills)

$$$$
Alex (Modern European, Hollywood)
Campanile (California/Mediterranean, West Hollywood)

The house restaurant (American, Hollywood)
Jar (Steakhouse, West Hollywood)
Joe's Restaurant (California, Venice)
The Lobster (Seafood, Santa Monica)
Nick & Stef's (Steakhouse, Downtown)

$$$

Angelini Osteria (Italian, West Hollywood)
Border Grill (Mexican, Santa Monica)
Cuidad (Latin, Downtown)
Kate Mantilini (American, Beverly Hills)
Lucques (California, West Hollywood)
Pig 'N Whistle (American, Hollywood)
Pinot Hollywood (Bistro, Hollywood)
Taylor's Steak House (Steakhouse, Hollywood)

$$

The Abbey (American, West Hollywood)
Angeli Caffe (Italian, West Hollywood)
Authentic Cafe (Southwestern/Caribbean, Hollywood)
Canter's Deli (Delicatessen, West Hollywood)
Cadillac Cafe (Eclectic, West Hollywood)
Carousel (Armenian, Hollywood)
El Cholo (Mexican, Hollywood)
The Fabiolus Cafe (Italian, Hollywood)
Fred 62 (Eclectic Diner, Hollywood)
Jerry's Famous Deli (Delicatessan, Los Angeles)
John O'Groats (American, West Los Angeles)
Newsroom Cafe (Eclectic, West Hollywood)

Off Vine (American, Hollywood)
101 Coffee Shop (Diner, Hollywood)
Royal Star Seafood Restaurant (Chinese, West Los Angeles)
Sushi Gen (Japanese/Sushi, Downtown)
Versailles (Cuban, Los Angeles)
Yang Chow (Chinese, Downtown)

$

Barney's Beanery (American, West Hollywood)
Blueberry (Cafe/Breakfast, Santa Monica)
Bread & Porridge (American, Santa Monica)
Chao Praya (Thai, Hollywood)
Clementine's (Homemade Seasonal, West Los Angeles)
El Coyote (Mexican, West Hollywood)
Farmer's Market (Various, West Hollywood)
Grand Central Market (Various, Downtown)
Joan's on Third (Tuscan/Mediterranean, West Hollywood)
Original Pantry Cafe (Steakhouse, Downtown)
Philippe the Original (Sandwiches, Downtown)
Pink's (Hot Dog Stand, West Hollywood)
Sanamluang Cafe (Thai, Hollywood)
Sepi's Giant Submarines (Sandwiches, Westwood)
Swingers (Coffee Shop, West Hollywood)
Yuca's Hut (Mexican, Hollywood)
Zankou Chicken (Armenian, Los Angeles)

Chapter 15

On the Lighter Side: Top Picks for Cheap Eats and Snacks to Go

. . . .

In This Chapter

▶ Eating ethnic

▶ Grabbing a great sandwich

▶ Satisfying a sweet tooth

▶ Finding the city's best coffee, burgers, bagels, and gourmet sausages

. . . .

*I*t is our contention that some of the best food in Los Angeles is often found in funky down-home dives or unprepossessing ethnic spots in less-than-swanky neighborhoods — and, as you can see in this chapter, you'll have your pick of some good ones.

For those of you who find yourselves busily racing from one L.A. attraction to another, have no fear: You can enjoy some deliciously fine snacks and meals on the run — wherever you happen to be. Or maybe you are just itching for a good cuppa joe, need a quick sugar fix, want to wrap your hands around a greasy burger, or crave a hot, chewy bagel. Look no further: Here are our favorite spots for all.

Great, Cheap Ethnic Eats

We natter on about the delights of ethnic food in Los Angeles, and even include some of our favorites, in Chapter 14. But now is our chance to tip you off to a few more terrific choices. (Most of them missed the first cut, because they are just a bit off to the left of "Centrally Located.")

At good, affordable, and reliable **Al Wazir** (6051 Hollywood Blvd.; ☎ 323-856-0660), about $6 gets you a combo plate of juicy Armenian chicken kebobs (or lamb or beef kebobs), hummus, rice, salad, and pita. It even delivers within a certain mile radius (call and ask). Or try the Lebanese versions over at **Marouch** (4905 Santa Monica Blvd.; ☎ 323-662-9325), a more plush (though still located in a strip mall) restaurant, where the happy owner will be thrilled to guide you through the choices — try its garlic *labneh* (tart sour-cream dip), some of its fat, dry, or spicy sausages, or the stuffed turnovers called *borek*. Note that it also offers many animal-free salads — happy news for vegetarians.

Vegetarians should also be pleased at **Electric Lotus** (4656 Franklin Ave.; ☎ 323-953-0040), a well-priced and quite pretty Indian restaurant that is full of come-with-me-to-the-kasbah ambience. It's fairly vegan friendly — it doesn't use ghee (the butter base that many Indian dishes are normally cooked in), and it's happy to make substitutions in other dishes that use cream and the like. Weekday lunch specials range from $6 to $10 and deliver a prodigious, and shareable, amount of food. To continue servicing the needs of vegetarians, we direct you to Fairfax Avenue, just south of Olympic Boulevard and north of Pico Boulevard, where a number of Ethiopian restaurants have propagated. Each one has its fan base, especially **Nyala** (1076 S. Fairfax Ave.; ☎ 323-936-5918) and **Rosalind's** (1044 S. Fairfax Ave.; ☎ 323-936-2486).

Not the least bit vegetarian friendly but delicious nonetheless is the Hungarian **Czardas** (5820 Melrose Ave.; ☎ 323-962-6434) Here we order *porkolt* (stew with sour cream) and goulash, and, if available, the multi-layered *dobos* torte cake.

Switching cultures again, we head to the **L.A. Food Court at Thailand Plaza** (5321 Hollywood Blvd.; ☎ 323-993-9000), where a strip mall has been blown up to department store size with a grand palace of a Thai food court that once boasted eight different eateries. Although the kitchens have consolidated, and the food is no longer quite as magnificent (originally, you could find Thai food here that was as good as it was anywhere else in the Southland), it's still a hoot to visit. Thumb through the gaudy menu, with its photos of potential dishes (we direct you to the fried rice, the beef dish known as "crying tiger," and the pig-parts-intensive *nam sod kao tod*). Pray also that the phenomena known as the "Thai Elvis" is performing while you are there.

If your Asian food tastes stray more toward Chinese, head downtown (Broadway and Hill Streets) and take your pick of the Chinese restaurants — just follow your nose. Our top choices include **Empress Pavilion** (988 N. Hill St., 2nd floor; ☎ 213-617-9898) for dim sum or Dungeness crab covered in blankets of snowy garlic (The Empress Pavilion is crowded on weekends, so expect to take a number and wait a long time.), and the **Hong Kong Low Deli** (408 Bamboo Lane; ☎ 213-680-9827). Located on an alley that cuts between the two main streets of Chinatown, the Hong Kong Low Deli is overseen by a despotic Asian woman, the Chinese equivalent of the "Soup Nazi" from the television show *Seinfeld*. You better have your order ready as she barks, "What you want? And what else? And what else?" or she is likely to pass you up and go on to the next customer. But she can be a softy in her own way; come late in the day, and she is likely to force something on you, "6 for $1!" Even without such discounts, you can feed a hungry family of four for about $10, as you load up on shrimp dumplings and flaky curry beef pies. In theory, this stuff ought to be taken home and heated for maximum effect; but we wouldn't know, for we've always consumed it all right on the spot, in the car, or by the Wishing Well in the heart of Chinatown.

The Earls (and Kings) of Sandwich

A sandwich is the perfect portable food, and oh so right for a picnic in Griffith or Will Rogers Park, or a beach lunch, or dinner at the Hollywood Bowl, or the "I'm tired and staying in tonight" munchies on the hotel bed.

It's just as well that the following joints are takeout, for most are humble establishments and not the most attractive of dining spots; some are even situated in less than aesthetically pleasing locations.

We do so love our Italian groceries, especially in Italy, but we live near the Venice of the West Coast. Luckily, **Bay Cities Italian Deli & Bakery** (1517 Lincoln Blvd., Santa Monica; ☎ 310-395-8279) helps fill those Tuscan Sun cravings. We've been eating dry salami on good Italian rolls (with just a touch of mustard, thank you) since we were bambinos. The bread is notable, but so is the array of cold cuts. You can stuff your bread with these cold cuts yourself, or you can let the employees fill it for you. Sandwiches cost under $10.

A claimant to the "inventor of the French Dip sandwich" title, **Cole's PE Buffet** (118 E. 6th St., Downtown; ☎ 213-622-4090) has been here since 1908. There are those who prefer Cole's to Philippe the Original (see Chapter 14). We are not among them, though we do note that the sandwiches are bigger, and the rolls are crustier. Cole's PE Buffet is a funky (and sometimes, truth be told, a tad too _Barfly_) bar and buffet, where you can find good mac and cheese, and nothing on the menu is priced over $10.

The usual winner of the "best pastrami in town" contest, which is sadly often overlooked by folks afraid to venture to this once fashionable, now rather seedy, part of town, is **Langer's Deli** (704 S. Alvarado St., Downtown; ☎ 213-483-8051). But here's the thing: It's right off a Metro Line stop, _and_ you can call and place your order in advance, give them your ETA and let them know whether you're coming by car or on foot and what kind of cash you are bringing, and someone will meet you outside, at the curb, with a bag of food at the ready and exact change — no muss, no fuss, no parking, and no waiting. Just perfect pastrami (and other deli delights, but why bother?), and away you go.

It's greasy, it's fatty, it's fried — get in line for the latest L.A. street snack

The latest junk food making inroads on L.A. waistlines is the **bacon-wrapped hot dog**. Judging by the vendors most likely to carry it, it seems to be a Hispanic community contribution, and we thank them profusely. A strip of bacon is wrapped diagonally around a large (and well-chosen) hot dog, and then the whole shebang is fried up (which allows the hot dog to get warm and permeated with the grease from the bacon), then placed on a warmed bun along with all sorts of goodies (particularly onions and peppers, which are fried along with the dog). We recommend that you get yours loaded with everything, especially if that includes mayo, which puts the whole concoction even more over the top of the fat scale. So wrong, as they say, it has to be right. Bacon-wrapped dogs are turning up at various street festivals, but they can regularly be found at any number of independent curbside vendors outside Staples Center whenever there is an event therein. Skip the pricey food inside and take advantage of the outside vendors. Sure, these guys are health department regulated, but we doubt that there is much of a hygiene problem to worry about in the first place. Certainly, such fears have never stopped us from glorying in the results.

Basturma is an Armenian cold cut that's sort of a cross between salami and pastrami (that's not really accurate, but it will do); it's dry, but it packs a wallop of spices. At **Sahag's Basturma** (5183 Hollywood Blvd., Hollywood; ☎ 323-661-5311), basturma is served on toasted French bread, complete with some garlic sauce, tomatoes, and pickles. You can also try two kinds of Armenian sausage: one spicy, and one milder. If in doubt, ask Sahag, the welcoming owner who is usually behind the counter. He is always tickled when customers like you come by. He will happily offer samples and advice that only a fool, which you are not, would ignore.

Way on the outskirts of Hollywood, east of where you may well be spending most of your time, but right in the heart of Bohemian Central, is the **Tropical Cafe** (2900 W. Sunset Blvd., Silverlake; ☎323-661-8391). It's essentially a coffeehouse, but with a Cuban twist, which means, in this case, marvelous Cuban sandwiches. You take ham, roast pork, cheese, pickles, and mustard, put it on French bread, and stick it in a grill that mashes the whole concoction down flat while heating it all the way through. The sandwiches are crusty, sticky, and good. You can get a version on a sweet roll, or you can substitute straight roast pork. Top it off with a guava pastry, and you have a true L.A. experience.

Let 'em Eat Cake (And Candy, and Ice Cream, and All Things Sweet)

Yes, even in a town where a size six can seem stocky, especially at a sample sale, there are desserts. Start by trying the West Coast boxed-candy favorite **See's** (various locations; Internet: www.sees.com), a longtime local tradition that devotees believe is superior even to Belgium chocolates like Godiva.

See's most popular candy flavors are the slightly maple Bordeaux, the creamy chocolate butters, and all of the truffles. *Tip:* They liberally hand out a piece of candy as a "sample," even if you're just buying a single piece.

Next, we move on to baked goods, starting with the humble doughnut. Except the goodies found at Westwood's beloved **Stan's Corner Donut Shoppe** (10948 Weyburn Ave.; ☎ 310-208-8660) are anything but unassuming. For 35 years, UCLA students have feasted on the infamous Peanut Butter Pocket (creamy peanut butter stuffed in a raised dough, then coated in chocolate frosting and chocolate chips; sometimes they add bananas!) or the chocolate pretzel-shaped number that is larger than a softball and faintly flavored with cinnamon. There are many good reasons why this corner counter in a larger shop has outlasted dozens of others that have tried to take hold in the rest of the store — and most of the reasons feature glaze.

Just up the street from Stan's is **Diddy Reese Cookies** (926 Broxton Ave.; ☎ 310-208-0448), a more youthful institution that has been an instant hit since it showed up in the mid-'80s. All your favorite cookies, such as chocolate chip, peanut butter, and macadamia nut, are here, but each one costs a mere — *get this* — 25¢ each.

Okay, if pressed, we would have to grudgingly admit that the cookies at Diddy Reese Cookies are perhaps just a tad below Mrs. Field's (to name a comparable rival) as far as quality is concerned, but they are about one-fifth the price, so who cares? One dollar gets you three cookies and a container of milk, *or* two cookies with a blob of good ice cream smushed between 'em. The same dang prices they've had since they opened. No wonder there are lines out the door.

Moving eastward, we come to the Jewish **Beverlywood Bakery** (9128 W. Pico Blvd.; ☎ 310-278-0122), where you can find black-and-white cookies gooey with frosting, sterling chocolate chip Danishes, *hamantaschen* (tri-cornered filled cookies), and our favorite, a checkerboard cake (yellow and chocolate cake in squares, happily mingling with chocolate frosting). The immigrant ladies who run it are brisk but thorough; the shop is closed on the Sabbath and High Holy Days.

The first, the original, and still champeen **La Brea Bakery** (624 S. La Brea Ave.; ☎ 323-939-6813; Internet: www.labreabakery.com) is a must-stop on any L.A. visitor's list. The owner, Nancy Silverton, is one of the world's great pastry chefs, and here you can find her creations. Cookies, tarts, pies, muffins, scones, and fruit crisps sound so simple, but if they really were, could she have built such an empire? (Oh, yeah, and they also have bread.)

Beware of the lines at La Brea Bakery on weekend mornings, when Los Angelinos get their brunch fixins.

The fluffy, glossy, multi-layered treats at **Sweet Lady Jane** (8360 Melrose Ave.; ☎ 323-653-7145) have made many a fashion-conscious local say "to hell with it," which is why this tiny (and pricey) cafe is always crowded. Most notable are the cakes and cheesecakes; famous folk love getting their birthday cakes here.

But we cannot live by cake alone, and so this brings us to the fabulously named **Mashti Malone's** (1525 N. La Brea Ave.; ☎ 323-874-6168), where homemade ice cream rules the day. The moniker comes from the Middle Eastern proprietor who took over the old-fashioned ice cream parlor. And aren't we glad! Not only do they still make their flavors right there on the spot, but they added, alongside superb cookies 'n cream and chocolate brownie, the less mainstream rosewater (it's like a flowery vanilla, only better — smooth and creamy, and an absolute must-have).

Speaking of cookies 'n cream, the first place we ever tasted this ice-cream flavor was at **Eiger Ice Cream** (124 S. Barrington Place; ☎ 310-471-6955). Although they have since switched locations and no longer use Double Stuf Oreos in their cookies 'n cream, they still have a loyal following, which includes us. Try their peanut butter fudge flavor — you can tell they use all-natural ingredients.

Eye Openers

Coffeehouses are no longer the rage they were in L.A. a few years ago, but they are still places to see, be seen, and, for poets and singer-song-writers, be heard. Sure, there are ample chain places — and we must admit, the **Coffee Bean and Tea Leaf** at Sunset Plaza (also at Larchmont Boulevard) are reliable star-sighting spots — but why would you go there when you can get far superior coffee and far superior visuals at independents around town?

The **Bourgeois Pig** (5931 Franklin Ave.; ☎ 323-962-6366) is so very, very dark that you may not be able to discern the red cloth pool table through the gloom. It has its own fame as the long-time employer of the real-life Gunther on *Friends* — James Michael Tyler, the actor who plays Rachel's peroxided and unrequited swain who runs Central Perk, worked here for years, even after he got his regular sitcom gig.

The Coffee House (8226 Sunset Blvd.; ☎ **323-848-7007**) is so fashionable and trendy that it can get by with a generic name. It's open 24 hours a day, and thus is a superb spot for night owls. **Nova Express** (426 N. Fairfax Ave.; ☎ **323-658-7533**) is a sci-fi, rave-dazed themed spot open only at night, but it stays open until the wee wee hours of the morning. **Highland Grounds** (742 N. Highland Ave.; ☎ **323-466-1507**) is still the place for performers to strut their stuff. Smokers love it because it has an outdoor patio. You may like it because it serves a fine breakfast. Finally, relax after shopping or check out the late-night scene at **Stir Crazy** (6917 Melrose Ave.; ☎ **323-934-4656**). And for those of you who prefer tea for two instead of coffee for . . . oh, forget it, there is the **Chado Tea Room** (8422½ W. 3rd St.; ☎ **323-655-2056**), where the varieties of tea are mind-boggling (and tend toward Eastern-style teas, rather than your basic English breakfast teas). The Chado Tea Room also has lovely sandwiches for lunch and afternoon tea.

Burger Joints

We are working our way through all the burger joints in the city — it's our job, after all — and we anticipate that this extensive research project will take, oh, years. But here are our findings so far: The **101 Coffeeshop** (see Chapter 13) has a thick hamburger patty that spits juice at you. The **Apple Pan** (10801 W. Pico Blvd; ☎ **310-475-3585**) has been serving what is considered the best burger on the Westside for 55 years. **Original Tommy's** (several locations, but most notable at 5873 Hollywood Blvd., ☎ **323-467-3792**, which has a drive-thru, and 2575 W. Beverly Blvd., ☎ **213-389-9060;** Internet: www.originaltommys.com) is not to be confused with Tommie's, Tomy's, or even Tony's. These are all wannabe imitators who hope to sucker folks into thinking that they are Original Tommy's — the place where generations of Angelino youths have wound up at 3 a.m., or even 3 p.m. (a 24-hour business, don't you know), inhaling drippy chili burgers, iridescent with sauce that will perfume any car interior for days. The Beverly location is the original Original Tommy's. It's just a shack in a seedy neighborhood, so you may be more inclined to head to Hollywood Boulevard, where the location is more convenient, if less atmospheric and less of a scene, offering tidy indoor dining and, better still, a drive-thru.

Competing chili burgers can be found at the 50-plus-year-old shack **Jay's Jayburgers** (somewhat southeast, at 4481 Santa Monica Blvd.; ☎ **323-666-5204**), which is not open 24 hours, but so close as to make no difference. And **In-N-Out** (various locations; Internet: www.in-n-out.com) is the fast-food joint that devotees swear by. You should see those expat residents return to town, demanding their Double Double (double patty, double cheese) before their plane has barely touched the tarmac.

Bagel Baby

The chain **Noah's Bagels** (various locations) can be found throughout the city, and it is good, we grudgingly admit — after all, it is from Brooklyn. But in our opinion, the best bagels in the city can be found at **Bagel Broker** (7825 Beverly Blvd.; ☎ 323-931-1258). We are not alone in loving the crusty, chewy jobs found here. We especially enjoy how it lavishly layers its lox.

Haut Dog

From its humble beginnings as a stand along the Venice boardwalk, **Jodi Maroni's Sausage Kingdom** (2011 Ocean Front Walk, Venice; also look for them at Universal City Walk and Century City Shopping Plaza; ☎ 310-822-5639), "Home of the Haut Dog," has indeed become a kingdom; everything is under $8, and you can get their inventive sausages (Moroccan lamb, apple maple pork, Toulouse garlic, or tequila chicken, just for starters), made with all-natural ingredients, in a number of Southland locales (and elsewhere in the country). They are served at Dodger Stadium and Staples Center, as well. But the original stand remains, still beckoning passersby with offers of sample bites. The buns are soft, the condiments a nice complement, and the sausages divine. Despite their increased prevalence around the city, we never leave the boardwalk without having one.

Part V
Exploring Los Angeles

In this part . . .

This part takes you straight to the top attractions the city has to offer. We offer you the lowdown on the city's famed beaches, the wealth of museums, the theme parks and studio tours, and the strange and fascinating charms of Hollywood. We recommend places to go with kids, where to enjoy the city's natural beauty, where to see big-time sports events, and where to see stellar architecture. Here, too, are the top shopping neighborhoods, and our favorite spots to shop, whether you're searching for antiques, books, music, or clothing. Finally, we include five fun-filled itineraries that are uniquely L.A.

Chapter 16

The Top Sights in Los Angeles

- -

- -

*O*ne of the major frustrations that comes with guiding folks around Los Angeles is that a great deal of what you point out will be prefaced by "and that parking lot/strip mall/empty lot used to be . . ." Alas, far too much of L.A.'s architectural history has been hit with the wrecking ball, and the amount of time we take using the past tense when showing folks around makes us sheepish.

Which isn't to say that there's not still plenty to see and do. Heck, just come for the beach or the all-around welcoming weather. We won't get too worked up if all you do is sit and think "Gee, it's pretty here. And warm." Though that brings us to the second most common guiding-people-around frustration; from the mountains to the sea, much of the best of L.A. scenery may be obscured by smog or haze. The solution is simple; come in December, January, or February. It may be cold (although you may not think so), but the sky will be clearer than it is in the warmer months.

Of course, the average visitor wants to see *Hollywood*, by which they mean "movies" or, better still, "movie stars," neither of which are often found in Hollywood proper. In the next chapter, we discuss how to tour studios (not nearly as thrilling as it sounds), and in the Part of Tens, we tell all about star spotting (tricky business, that, since movie stars tend not to sit still for very long, being the rare, attention-deficit birds that they are).

The following is a list of the more or less absolute must-do sights and attractions in L.A. There are still quite a lot more, and those can be found in the next chapter. In each case, we try to tell you just *why* you ought to consider an attraction — and only occasionally get bossy and *insist* that you do so.

The Beaches

Tell the truth: You don't care about anything other than warm water, nice sand, and girls in bikinis. To say nothing of wry surfer boys. Fine. It's easy enough to get all that — just drive west and stop when you hit water. Actually, you don't even have to worry about that; most of the L.A. beaches are separated from the road by A) another road, B) a grassy parklike area, or C) a parking lot. Which brings us to the problem with going to the beach — you almost always have to pay. You can't park along the **Pacific Coast Highway,** which runs parallel to the ocean. The closer the parking lot (say, right next to the sand), the higher the price to park.

When you get to the sand, one beach is pretty much like another, except when it's not. The **Santa Monica** and **Venice** beaches are the most popular, because they're closest to business areas. (For details on Venice Beach's famous boardwalk, check out "Venice Ocean Front Walk," later in this chapter.)

The farther up the coastline you go, into **Pacific Palisades** and **Malibu,** the "purer" the beach experience: fewer tourists, more locals, and more surfers. The waves get bigger, the beaches seem less touched by man (an illusion; this whole coastline is developed in one way or another), and the water quality is better. The Santa Monica Bay has struggled with bacteria and other contamination problems for some time, and the problem is often most acute at beaches beside piers or near storm drains. Heal the Bay, a nonprofit environmental group, has done a wonderful job helping to clean up the coastal waters, but beaches may still be closed for swimming from time to time. Signs will tell you when to avoid the water. As you get into Malibu, residences start popping up (full of really rich folks, by and large), and the beaches aren't precisely public. No one has fences all the way into the water, but residents do glare at you as you cruise along in front of their pricey property. *Note:* The high-tide line is where private property officially begins. Respect this property line, for you are essentially walking in someone's backyard. **Zuma,** the beach farthest north, is also by far the nicest, though the water is colder than at the southern beaches.

If you visit the beach in the winter, you probably won't be doing much swimming (unless you come equipped with a wetsuit or a really good constitution), although some splashing around can be done on all but the most inclement days. During the summer, as temperatures soar so do the crowds; the hottest weekend days will find nary an extra towel space on the sand.

Few experiences fuel the appetite like a day at the beach. Fortunately, many area beaches offer food and drink concessions. Concessions are available at **Dockweiler Beach, Manhattan Beach, Redondo Beach, Torrance County Beach, Zuma Beach County Park, Will Rogers State Park,** and **Hermosa Beach.** For full-blown restaurant dining, as well as shopping and entertainment options, you'll have plenty of choices at the **Santa Monica beaches, Venice Beach,** and **Redondo Beach.**

Los Angeles Beaches

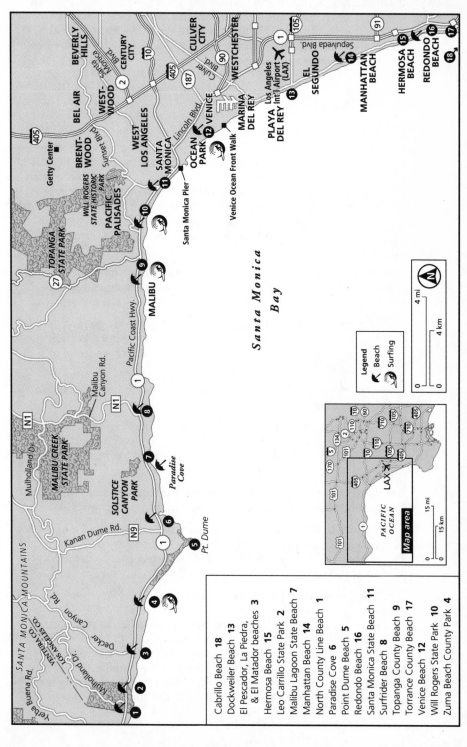

Cabrillo Beach **18**
Dockweiler Beach **13**
El Pescador, La Piedra,
 & El Matador beaches **3**
Hermosa Beach **15**
Leo Carrillo State Park **2**
Malibu Lagoon State Beach **7**
Manhattan Beach **14**
North County Line Beach **1**
Paradise Cove **6**
Point Dume Beach **5**
Redondo Beach **16**
Santa Monica State Beach **11**
Surfrider Beach **8**
Topanga County Beach **9**
Torrance County Beach **17**
Venice Beach **12**
Will Rogers State Park **10**
Zuma Beach County Park **4**

Many Los Angeles County beaches are well-equipped for travelers with disabilities, with ramps and boardwalks leading to the beach. Beach wheelchairs are available at **Zuma Beach County Park, Topanga County Beach, Venice, Will Rogers State Park, Dockweiler Beach, Manhattan Beach,** and **Torrance County Beach.** Check with the lifeguard headquarters at each beach.

Here are some tips to keep in mind when planning a day at a Los Angeles County beach:

- ✔ For **general information**, contact the Los Angeles County Department of Beaches & Harbors, which operates many of the beaches along the county's 72 miles of coastline (☎ **310-305-9503;** Internet: http://beaches.co.la.ca.us/). County beaches that are run by the California state parks system include **Dockweiler Beach, Leo Carillo State Park, Point Dume, Will Rogers State Park,** and **Santa Monica State Beach** (Internet: http://cal-parks. ca.gov). For recorded surf conditions and weather forecasts up and down the Los Angeles area coast, call ☎ **310-457-9701.**

- ✔ Plan to **arrive early** during the summer and on most weekends; otherwise, expect to have trouble finding parking and a place to sit.

- ✔ Seniors can get a permit for **free weekday parking** at any county beach lot staffed by an attendant. All you have to do is show proof of age (62 and older). The permit is not valid for weekend or holiday parking.

- ✔ Keep in mind that **alcohol** and **pets** are prohibited on all county-run beaches.

- ✔ **Campfires** are prohibited on every L.A. County beach *except* Dockweiler Beach (at the end of the 105 Freeway/Imperial Boulevard) and Cabrillo Beach (in San Pedro), which have fire rings and special hours for evening picnics.

- ✔ Most county and state beaches provide restrooms or chemical toilets. Many provide outdoor showers and picnic facilities.

- ✔ Be sure to **bring sunscreen** (and a wide-brim hat) and reapply it frequently, especially when you come out of the water — you *will* sunburn otherwise, and it can ruin your trip (not to mention your complexion).

- ✔ **Bring and drink plenty of water,** as well.

Naturally, the amount of time you spend at the beach depends on personal preference. You may want to walk up to, or at least near, the water and say the appropriate things — "hmm . . . Awe-inspiring. Magnificent. Big. Wet." — then wander off to do something else. You may want to take a nice long stroll along the shore. Or you may want to spend an entire day (even two!) basking in the sun and playing in the surf. The Pacific is happy to accommodate any and all. Here are the best beaches to

✔ Take the family:

- **Dockweiler Beach:** It's the only L.A. beach with an RV park, plus you can light a campfire at night.
- **Leo Carrillo State Beach:** It has camping, good windsurfing, sea lion sightings, and lots of neat coves and sea caves.
- **Redondo Beach:** It's got the beach, volleyball courts, and an arcade and shopping on the Redondo Beach Pier.

✔ Surf till you drop:

- **Malibu's Surfrider Beach:** It's the classic surfing beach, of Frankie and Annette fame.
- **Topanga County Beach:** The waves roll deep into the bay, giving surfers long, satisfying rides.
- **Torrance County Beach:** Longboarders love it, and so will you, if you're looking for a quiet haven from the crowds.
- **Zuma Beach County Park:** The largest, nicest beach in Los Angeles offers big, strong waves.

✔ Pretend you're a Beach Boy:

- **Manhattan Beach:** Hang out with the surfers and boogie boarders at one of the gestation points for California beach music. Manhattan Beach is where surfer boy Dennis Wilson hit upon the theme that catapulted the Beach Boys to *Billboard* stardom.

Surfing etiquette 101

Rule number one: If you don't know what you are doing, at least do one thing; stay out of the way of those who do. The hardcore surf rats may have no qualms about mowing over some inept tourist. Not only is staying out of the way generally good manners — and safer all around — but there remain some vestiges of the fierce regionalism that characterized the surfing scene in the mid-'70s, when "Locals Only" was the rallying cry, along with "Death to Vals" (referring to the kids from the Valley who dared to venture into the holy waters).

Besides, surfing is not something you can suddenly just up and do. Arrange for surfing lessons at **Malibu Ocean Sports** (22935 Pacific Coast Hwy., Malibu; ☎ 310-456-6302); hang with them, and you'll be much the wiser.

And finally, keep the following in mind for a happy, healthy dip in the ocean: If you are a boogie boarder, stay away from the surfers, and if you're body surfing, stay away from the boogie boarders *and* the surfers.

Hollywood Area Attractions

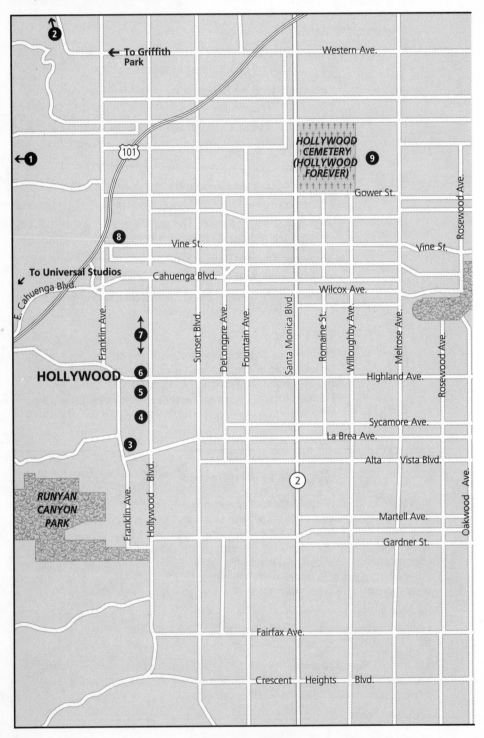

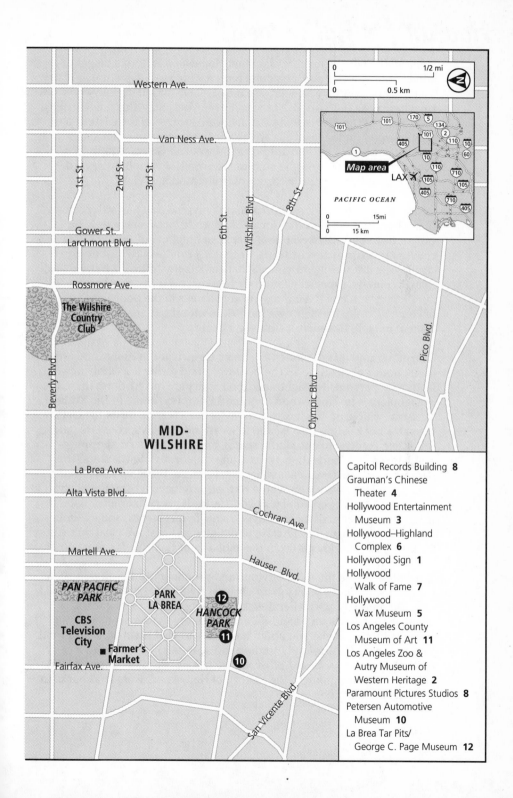

Western Ave.

Van Ness Ave.

1st St.

2nd St.

3rd St.

Gower St.
Larchmont Blvd.

Rossmore Ave.

6th St.

Wilshire Blvd.

8th St.

The Wilshire
Country
Club

Beverly Blvd.

Pico Blvd.

Olympic Blvd.

0   1/2 mi
0   0.5 km

170
101   101   5   134
101   2
405   101   110   10
1   10   60
Map area   10
110
LAX ✈   105
PACIFIC OCEAN   405   710   105
710   405
0   15mi
0   15 km

**MID-
WILSHIRE**

La Brea Ave.

Alta Vista Blvd.

Cochran Ave.

Martell Ave.

Hauser Blvd.

PAN PACIFIC
PARK

PARK
LA BREA   12

CBS
Television
City   ■ Farmer's
Market   HANCOCK
PARK   11

Fairfax Ave.   10

San Vicente Blvd.

Capitol Records Building **8**
Grauman's Chinese
  Theater **4**
Hollywood Entertainment
  Museum **3**
Hollywood–Highland
  Complex **6**
Hollywood Sign **1**
Hollywood
  Walk of Fame **7**
Hollywood
  Wax Museum **5**
Los Angeles County
  Museum of Art **11**
Los Angeles Zoo &
  Autry Museum of
  Western Heritage **2**
Paramount Pictures Studios **8**
Petersen Automotive
  Museum **10**
La Brea Tar Pits/
  George C. Page Museum **12**

Hooray for Hollywood!

Right off the bat, we must explain that Hollywood is both a neighborhood in Los Angeles and a catchall term for the motion-picture industry, which is not, contrary to what you may believe, based in Hollywood. Or anywhere near Hollywood. Nor was it ever. Well, okay, that's not strictly true. Many of the silent-movie studios were located in the eastern part of Hollywood (in the Los Feliz and Silver Lake neighborhoods), and Columbia, which once had studios at Sunset and Gower, still shoots TV shows there. But none of the studios were on Hollywood Boulevard, much less at the legendary corner of Hollywood and Vine.

Of course, the reality doesn't explain the mythos that has arisen around that name, that term, or that locale. And while locals may rarely be caught dead on **Hollywood Boulevard,** sniffing that it's either full of clueless tourists or tourist traps, or that it's rundown (true, but expensive efforts are seeking to change that) or kitschy (ditto), we stand firm that all tourists, especially first-time tourists, need to come here to puzzle over some of the unrecognizable names in the boulevard's **Walk of Fame** or compare their own footprints with those enshrined in cement outside **Grauman's Chinese Theater.**

Enormous amounts of money are being thrown at the Hollywood area in the hopes of cleaning up the boulevard and giving it a whole new legitimate personality. Right now, the results are mixed. Sure, there is the fabulous new **Hollywood-Highland Complex,** home to the **Kodak Theatre** (which, on the fourth Sunday of each March, hosts the Oscars; when it's not hosting the Oscars, folks attending plays, concerts, and other live entertainment fill the seats), and many generic **shopping-mall stores**, not to mention several fine glamorous **old theaters** (the Pantages for live theatrical events; the Chinese, the Egyptian, and the El Capitan for movies) renovated to their original over-the-top glory. But the neighborhood still lacks good, affordable restaurants. Instead, it retains an excess of tacky souvenir and T-shirt stores, and a number of shops selling naughty lingerie and high heels that are clearly meant for strippers. Sparkly glitter in the asphalt only goes so far, you know.

The following are the most obvious and prominent Hollywood locales. Don't be snooty; it's your job as a tourist to go see these places at least once (and frankly, we rather delight in having out-of-town guests, because then we have a legitimate opportunity to make return visits ourselves). It will take you about half a day to visit them all. If you want to tour the *real* Hollywood (studios and scandals), get yourself a copy of Ken Schessler's *This is Hollywood* (Ken Schessler Publishing; $5.95), a comprehensive guide to the history of Hollywood, from landmarks to murders and suicides.

Grauman's Chinese Theater
Hollywood

Normally, this is when we haul out phrases like "newly restored to its former glory." Although it is true that Sid Grauman's fabulous movie palace, which was built in 1927 and designed to look like a Chinese temple, has been given a massive facelift, the restoration removed some of the 1950s glitz — usually a good thing, but in this case, it turned what was a riot of Oriental stylings into a rather dull, gray concrete structure. Authentic is not always best, we note. Heck, even the neon dragons are gone! But at least the Mann chain (which bought the theater some years ago) officially returned the name Grauman (locals never did cave in and call it *Mann's* Chinese Theater), and the interior remains a classic example of glorious movie-theater pomp, with deep reds, gilt, fanciful curlicues, and one giant screen. And of course, there are the footprints immortalized in concrete outside the theater. It began as a publicity stunt — oh, heck, it's *still* a publicity stunt, but thank heavens for it, because how else could we see that Mary Pickford had such itty bitty feet? How else could there have been one of the best *I Love Lucy* shows of all time, when Lucy "borrowed" John Wayne's bootprints as a souvenir? (The Duke's bootprints are still here.) Yes, the stars of yesteryear, and some of today, have enshrined their shoeprints and handprints, and in some cases noseprints (Jimmy Durante) and legprints (Betty Grable), in concrete to last beyond their ruin. Go ahead, compare your appendages to theirs; you know you want to. And when you're done, you can see a movie here (as long as it's on the big screen), even some cheap action piece of junk, because it's what the movie-going experience ought to be.

6925 Hollywood Blvd. ☎ *323-464-MANN/6266 or 323-461-3331. Showtimes vary. Call for movie ticket prices.*

Hollywood Entertainment Museum
Hollywood

Even though we are utterly jaded about the dubious value, artistic or otherwise, of the relics of movies or television, this museum isn't quite as schlocky as it seems. We will allow you to go here if you promise — solemnly vow — that you will never visit a Planet Hollywood. See, it's a bunch of Hollywood memorabilia — really good stuff, like an entire "Star Trek" set, to say nothing of the by-gosh *original* bar set from "Cheers" (everybody yell "NORRRRRRRMMMMM!!!"). It even has all the old fixings from the defunct (and lamented) Max Factor Museum (check out the "beauty calibrator" gizmo that looks like a futuristic torture device), plus costumes and the like. Not in and of itself an essential sight, it is right there along Hollywood Boulevard, so why not stop in and check it out?

7021 Hollywood Blvd. ☎ *323-465-7900. Internet:* www.hollywoodmuseum.com. *Admission: $8.75 adults, $5.50 seniors, $4.50 students, $4 children 5–12, children under 5 free. Open: Labor Day–Memorial Day, Thurs–Tues 11 a.m.–6 p.m. Memorial Day–Labor Day, daily 11 a.m.–6 p.m.*

Seeing the movies in style

If you, like us, prefer to see movies the way God, or at least Cecil B. DeMille, intended, not only should you catch a flick at Grauman's, but you should also try the nearby **El Capitan** (6838 Hollywood Blvd.; ☎ 323-467-7674). Restored to full gilded glory, thanks to Disney (consequently, only their movies are shown here), each summer's animation headliner gets its premiere at this location. The theater is complete with ushers in uniforms and the frequent prescreening of live shows (another touch from the early days of cinema).

The American Cinematheque restored the 1922 **Egyptian Theatre** (another Sid Grauman special). The theater's pharaoh-style decor is mostly confined to the outside areas; inside is what appears to be a state-of-the-art modern theater. Film buffs have made a number of complaints about the theater's updated design (sight-lines, noise, you name it).

The **Cinematheque** does regular wonderful screenings (special programs, revivals, new works, and documentaries); be sure to check out its offerings during your visit (6712 Hollywood Blvd.; ☎ 323-466-3456; Internet: www.egpytiantheatre.com).

And finally, the humbler but still noteworthy **Vista** (first-run movies) is another Egyptian-revival house that has gotten a facelift plus new seats that leave enough legroom between rows to allow for strolling elephants (4473 W. Sunset Blvd.; ☎ 323-660-6639).

Hollywood-Highland Complex
Hollywood

The Hollywood-Highland Complex is a little bit *nightlife,* a little bit *attraction,* and a whole lot *shopping* — but we're sticking it here because it's in Hollywood, right in the middle of everything else you're going to be seeing and doing. Plus, it is the spiffy new centerpiece of what the city desperately hopes will be a major rejuvenation of Hollywood Boulevard. But basically, when you get right down to it, it's a shopping mall. A grand shopping mall, to be sure; we glory in the detailing that includes quotes in mosaic from anonymous actors and others about their epic struggles to "Make It," the way the staircase entrance is designed to frame the Hollywood sign, the courtyard full of stands and umbrellas and cafe tables, and, best of all, the **Babylon Court,** which pays homage to D.W. Griffith's fantastic Babylon set for his movie *Intolerance*. Scheduled for completion by the time you read this book, the complex includes the **Hollywood Motion Picture Museum** (featuring Debbie Reynold's own extensive memorabilia collection, which includes Dorothy's gingham *Wizard of Oz* dress, Marilyn's breezy *Seven Year Itch* subway grate dress, many more costumes, props, and even some whole sets). The **Kodak Theatre** was built specifically as a permanent home for the annual Academy Awards, although it also hosts concerts and theater road companies throughout the year. And there are **two nightclubs,** including **One**

Seven, a club designed to give those under 21 and without fake IDs a place to party. The complex also offers **movie theaters, restaurants,** and a **self-guided audio tour of the Walk of Fame.** They did a fine job with the design, we have to admit — for a shopping mall.

Northwest corner of Hollywood and Highland. Internet: www.hollywoodand highland.com. *Hours: 10 a.m.–10 p.m. (some establishments may be open later).*

The Hollywood Sign
Hollywood

Icon. What else would you call those nine 50-foot-tall white letters perched high up in the Hollywood hills? They constitute one of the most instantly recognizable sights in the world. The sign dates back to 1923, and it originally read "Hollywoodland," the name of the development it was drawing attention to. (The last four letters came down in the '40s.) Struggling actors, despairing of ever getting their big break, were rumored to have made it a favorite suicide spot. But the only person confirmed to have actually done so was actress Peg Entwhistle, who jumped off the letter H in 1932, the poor despondent dear. You can't drive up to the sign, nor can you walk right up to it, but you can hike up from Durand Avenue off of Beachwood Canyon. You can get a good picture of it from Sunset Boulevard at Gower and also at Bronson, but otherwise, you may have drive up Beachwood until it gets closer and closer and you get the shot you want.

At the top of Beachwood Canyon.

Hollywood Walk of Fame
Hollywood

All together now: *"You can see all the stars as you walk along Hollywood Boulevard/some that you recognize, some that you've hardly even heard of"* (it's a song by the British rock band the Kinks). Granite stars rimmed in brass are implanted in the sidewalk along Hollywood Boulevard (and down Vine Street towards Sunset Boulevard). They feature names of the Greats and the once Greats (and those who had really good publicists and some pocket change) of film, radio, television, and the recording arts. We hate to shatter any illusions, but the stars *pay* for their stars; pretty much anyone, with a rather minimal level of success, can get nominated. The Hollywood Chamber of Commerce makes sure that they can cough up the money, and then they give out a star. But so what? Walk along Hollywood Boulevard and see how many of those names you still recognize (to say nothing of seeing what strange accidental neighbors the juxtaposition of names creates). It's something you should do at least once.

Hollywood Blvd., between Gower St. and La Brea Ave., and Vine St. between Hollywood Blvd. and Sunset. ☎ *323-469-8311. Call for information such as who is where and who may be getting a star while you are in town.*

Etiquette tips for celebrity encounters

"Oh, my god," you shriek (to yourself, we hope), "it's *him!*" Or her. Or them. Anyway, you've spotted one: There they are, a star, a celeb, a famous face, or whatever, sitting right next to you at In 'N' Out Burger. What to do? Act like a local, we say, and ignore 'em. Although, you may want to take note of what they're wearing through a discreet glance out of the corner of your eye so that you can tell your friends. Remember, even if they do look better than us, they're simply real people out having a burger or going to a movie.

You will not be the first, nor the tenth, person to run up to the them and say, "I hate to bother you, but I just love your movies and can I have your autograph?" If you must, you must. But don't blame us if your target is less than polite, even if you're the soul of charm, as we don't doubt you will be — especially if said celebrity is, at the very moment you make your request, chomping down on a greasy chili burger. Here are some tips on how to handle the encounter.

✔ **Don't** ask them why their album and/or movie didn't do as well as their last one, even if *you* thought it was great. Believe me, *they* know.

✔ **Don't** ask, "Hey, aren't you married?" if you happen to see them out with a giggling blonde or buxom redhead, or . . . you get the idea.

✔ If you've met a celebrity before, you **don't** need to remind him. ("We met at the book signing at Borders a couple of years ago, remember? I had on a navy sweater. . . .")

✔ **Don't** ask them if they ever think of "retiring" like Demi Moore did.

✔ **Don't** tell them you have an old yearbook of theirs, and "gosh, it says you graduated in 1980, not 1987 — what gives?"

✔ **Do** smile and keep it brief. Trust us, they aren't really listening to you.

✔ **Don't** think that because you won an MTV contest or a backstage pass from a radio station, they're thrilled to finally meet you too! Sure they're pleased, but remember that they are working . . . do you like it when the intern or office temp gazes dreamily at you when you have a deadline?

✔ **Do** have a pen if you want an autograph and feel that it's an okay time to ask. "Oh, can I have your autograph, and oh, by the way, do you happen to have a pen with you, man?" is pushing the limit. Hey, the UPS guys offer a pen; why can't you?

(Special thanks to the studio tour guides at Universal Studios Hollywood who came up with the idea — we simply ran with it.)

J. Paul Getty Museum at the Getty Center
Brentwood

Once upon a time, there was an oilman named J. Paul Getty. He made a great deal of money. Buckets of it. He left it to his heirs, who then made tabloid history . . . but that's another story. He also amassed a great deal of art. He then created a trust to oversee and add to the collection after his death. This trust has to spend a certain sum every year, and that sum is more money than God has in His own checking account, which is why the Getty frequently outbids other institutions for great works of art. In the 1960s, J. Paul Getty built a re-creation of a first-century Roman villa on grounds located high above Pacific Coast Highway, specifically to house his collection of antiquities. It was opened to the public in 1974. The collection quickly outgrew the space, and the villa was closed to the public in 1997, when the new, billion-dollar Getty Center opened high above the 405 Freeway in Brentwood. This latter museum was designed by Richard Meier (and took 12 years to build) and houses scholarly facilities as well as the art galleries. (The villa is undergoing restoration and will be reopened to the public some time in the future.) The museum specializes in Greek and Roman antiquities, European paintings, and photographs. It's an impressive collection, but can we say, without too many cries of heresy, that it's a little boring? That it's kind of underwhelming for all the hype? That it's more interesting that they paid $53.9 million to acquire Van Gogh's *Irises,* and that a couple of times they spent a ton of money acquiring art that proved to be forgeries? But all of that applies strictly to the collection.

The structure itself is extraordinary, a feat of modern design that dominates the hill it's perched on. The building offers a view of L.A. (to the sea) that's worth the visit alone. Come here in the early evening with a picnic and enjoy the views, the warm air, and the generally good-natured crowds. Some consider it a true, albeit uniquely L.A., urban experience (people! outside! mingling! doing cultural things!). Either way, the experience is a treat. Also, you can't beat the prices — admission is free! (You have to pay for parking, which often calls for reservations, or public transportation.) The tram ride up from the parking lot is a bonus hoot. The Getty has a special series of evening concerts, often musical gems that you simply can't see elsewhere. We strongly encourage you to find out what is playing and take advantage of these concerts.

1200 Getty Center Dr. ☎ *310-440-7330. Internet:* www.Getty.edu. *Admission: Free. Parking: $5. Open: Tues–Thurs 10 a.m.–6 p.m., Fri–Sat 10 a.m.–9 p.m., Sun 10 a.m.–6 p.m. Closed major holidays. No parking reservations needed on Sat and Sun or after 4 p.m. on weekdays. College students with current school ID and visitors arriving by public transportation, motorcycle, or bicycle can visit at any time without parking reservations. Reservations are required for weekday parking (before 4 p.m., event seating, and groups of 15 or more; no parking reservations are needed on Saturday and Sunday or after 4 p.m. on weekdays. Parking reservations for RVs and other oversized vehicles required at all times. Parking on surrounding streets is restricted. Visitors to the Getty Center may now use a free parking and shuttle service available during public hours from a nearby lot on Sepulveda Blvd. and Constitution Ave. (located just north of Wilshire Blvd.). This shuttle is offered, in addition to on-site parking, as a service to Getty visitors and does not require reservations. The bus lines serving the Getty Center are the MTA Bus 561 and the Santa Monica Bus 14. Passenger drop-offs are permitted from vehicles of 15 passengers or less.*

La Brea Tar Pits/George C. Page Museum
Los Angeles

It's goopy, it's smelly, it's oozing, and it's wonderful . . . it's the La Brea Tar Pits. It's a gruesome story, so let's repeat it. Millions of years ago (okay, 40,000; *whatever*), unsuspecting prehistoric critters (wooly mammoths, saber-toothed tigers, and so on) would wander over to an attractive pool of water and wade into it, only to discover that the water was floating on top of tar in which they would then be permanently stuck. Death would follow (through starvation or suffocation). Their bodies would sink down into the muck (sometimes additionally condemning a predator who had hopped on thinking it was getting an easy meal by preying on a trapped beastie — sucker!), and there they stayed, until the world discovered archaeologists. The archaeologists found that if you dredge those pits, you can find whole, beautifully preserved skeletons. And so they dig around in the tar pits and put what they find on display. And amazingly, all this is located right along Wilshire Boulevard, one of the busiest streets in L.A. In fact, all the buildings in this complex (including the Los Angeles County Museum of Art, the LACMA, next door) are built to float, more or less, on the tar, which remains in full forceful presence. (And it's still sticky, even if you are just picking up a little bit to give to someone as a souvenir — not that we know from personal experience or anything.) Kids love it, not the least for the pathos-ridden life-size-critter sculptures that adorn some of the bubbling pools (the doomed pacyderm, with its sad baby calling from the banks is a perennial fave). During the late summer, the pits are open to the viewing public, so you can see the scientists at work as they try to excavate more bones. The museum is less enjoyable than the pits — the bones aren't quite as interesting after they are all cleaned up. *Fun fact:* La Brea means "the tar." So, yes, these are the Tar Tar Pits.

5801 Wilshire Blvd. ☎ *323-934-7243. Internet:* www.tarpits.org. *Admission: $6 adults, $3.50 students & seniors, $2 children 5–10, under 5 free. Open: Mon–Fri 9:30 a.m.–5:00 p.m., Sat–Sun 10 a.m.–5 p.m.*

Los Angeles County Museum of Art
Los Angeles

Though for many years the Los Angeles County Museum of Art (LACMA) was *the* museum of the city, it is now much overlooked in favor of the splashy (and wealthy) Getty, which is probably why it recently announced plans for a massive redesign, one that may well replace the long-time buildings with new construction. (Said redesign is still probably some considerable time off. If you read this any later than, say, late 2003, you may want to call to make sure that nothing has begun closing in anticipation.) But can we go out on a limb and say that, as local museums go, we prefer this to the Getty? Frankly, going to LACMA doesn't seem like such an event, and that may well be why we prefer it; it's more user friendly. You don't find any of the "can we get parking reservations?" that you find at the Getty. Just drive, park, visit whatever parts you want, and leave without feeling guilty that you didn't put in more time, because, after all, it was less of an investment of effort. The collections run the gamut from antiquities to masterpieces (Rembrandt, Degas, and Cézanne) to contemporary art (including Magritte's *Ceci n'est pas une pipe*). The institution is housed in several buildings, so it is easy to focus a visit on sampling your particular interests. Further, it is shockingly uncrowded during the nonsummer months, when not even all that many groups of schoolchildren are running about. Note that street parking is cheaper than the LACMA lots and that the meter readers are notoriously vigilante.

5905 Wilshire Blvd. ☎ *323-857-6000 (for general information). Internet:* www. lacma.org. *Admission: $7 adults, $5 seniors and adult students with ID, $1children 6–17, children under 6 free. Open: Mon, Tues, Thurs noon to 8 p.m., Fri noon to 9 p.m., Sat–Sun 11 a.m.–8 p.m., closed Wed.*

Museum of Contemporary Art/MOCA at the Geffen Contemporary
Downtown

See, first they decided to build L.A. a contemporary art museum, but they needed to start the museum before the real building was in place, so they used a warehouse-like building near Little Tokyo. It was dubbed the Temporary Contemporary. The real building (a geometric structure that promptly won architectural awards) opened on Grand Street near the Music Center, but by then, everyone loved the Temporary Contemporary so much (for one thing, it's fun to say!) that it was made permanent. Then David Geffen gave a great deal of money (as he is wont to do) to the institution, and the Temporary became the Geffen Contemporary, except many of us don't call it that, for it's not as euphonious. Anyway, the upshot is one museum, two locations. All mediums are represented, from abstract to pop art to emerging new artists. The Geffen (Temporary, whatever) is more likely to have conceptual or installation art simply because the shape of the facility is conducive to such exhibits. Free gallery tours, offered by most-knowledgeable docents, are offered several times during most days — we highly encourage you to plan a visit around these tours, as they are one of the best deals in L.A. (Having said that, take the latest tour you can; the museums tend to be the most busy until around 1:30 p.m.) Admission covers both buildings, and a shuttle runs regularly between the two buildings.

250 S. Grand Ave. & 152 N. Central Ave. ☎ *213-626-6222. Internet:* www.moca.org. *Admission: $8 adults, $5 seniors and students with ID, children under 12 free. Open: Tues–Wed and Fri–Sun 11 a.m.–5 p.m., Thurs 11 a.m.–8 p.m., closed Mon.*

Olvera Street
Downtown

Olvera Street is the oldest remaining street in Los Angeles. It is made up of what may be the original cobblestones, or at least ones that date back to the 1930s, when this monument to old L.A. was erected. Its official name is El Pueblo de Los Angeles Historic Monument, but no one refers to it by this name. Several 19th-century adobe buildings remain standing alongside this street (one is the oldest existing building in L.A.). The rest of the structures are newer, but it feels like a bustling marketplace in Mexico. It's both a festive tourist trap and an utterly authentic South-of-the-Border experience; some wonderful Mexican food can be had here, and the stalls that clutter the streets are full of cheap trinkets (to say nothing of Mexican sweets). You can easily run through here in well under an hour, unless you shop and snack.

Entrance is located near Alameda St. across from Union Station. ☎ *213-628-1274.*

Universal Studios Hollywood
Burbank

Out-of-town visitors put this attraction at the top of their must-see list, while the rest of us, quite frankly, tend to forget it exists. The magic of moviemaking is revealed — sort of — at this combination studio back lot/theme park. The latter features 11 rides/attractions (six of which have height restrictions and/or which may be too intense for young children; pregnant women are advised to avoid several rides, including, oddly, the incredibly popular Studio Tour, no doubt because there are bumps and jostles along the collapsing bridge). Universal offers visitors a chance to see and experience how movies are made. For the price of admission, you get a full day of things to do.

The real attraction at Universal Studios has always been the tram tour, which is guided by a real human, with help from videotaped comments by the likes of Ron Howard. In order to really see what's on the video screens, sit at least two rows back from the front of each car. Most of the action on the tour takes place on the left side of the bus, although the shark leaps up on the right. Director's Pass holders (more on that in the sidebar, "Rating the rides at Universal") and V.I.P. Tours members (they pay $125 per ticket; do you really want to do that?) sit in the first two cars of the tram. The tour (still just a touch creaky and dated) is in itself as artificial as the movie sets visitors get to peer at (real moviemaking will remain out of the sight of gawkers), but it does offer some interesting sights, such as the Munsters house, which, amusingly, is on the same block in Studio Land as Beaver Cleaver's suburban home and the residences of Nancy Drew and the Hardy Boys. You can also travel through effects-laden soundstages (which are really fun and exciting), find out how movie rain is made, experience a shark attack, and watch union crew members eat donuts. After the tour is done, kids will want to race off to the rides (see the "Rating the rides at Universal" sidebar in this section). Aside from the tour, a big reason Universal is such a popular theme park is that they serve beer, and lots of it. There are also margaritas next to the Jurassic Park ride, so you can get soused after just getting drenched. Food is readily available, but it's of the costly junk-food sort. Your best bet may be to leave the park (ins-and-outs are allowed) and stroll over to the CityWalk (see Chapter 18 for details) for slightly more nutritious, if not more reasonably priced, food options. Even without crowds, we spent 5 hours seeing shows and riding rides. With a summer crowd, expect to spend at least 3 hours longer because of lines. Get there when the park opens to maximize your time!

Note: At this writing, Universal is offering one of the best tour packages in Los Angeles; for $10 over regular admission, guests receive one-time-use tickets (good for 30 days) for **Starline Tours, the Petersen Automotive Museum, the Museum of Radio and Television, American Cinematheque, the Hollywood Entertainment Museum,** and the **Gene Autry Museum of Western Heritage.**

Universal Studios Hollywood, 100 Universal City Plaza, Universal City. ☎ *800-864-8377. Internet:* www.universalstudioshollywood.com. *Admission: Adults $49, children 3–9 $33, seniors $44. Director's Pass: $69 per person. V.I.P.: $125 per person, no children under 5 permitted on V.I.P. tour. Open: Hours can vary, so call ahead. At times, special savings coupons are passed out upon admission to the park. Please check Universal's Web site for updates, changes, and additional specials, as well as changes in shows and attractions.*

Rating the rides at Universal

Here's what to expect on your tour of the latest rides at Universal Studios Hollywood:

✔ Expect the most jostling from **Back to the Future,** which left us longing for a massage, or at least a vibrating chair. The ride's conceit is that some evil guy in an ugly Hawaiian shirt has stolen a time-traveling DeLorean (wasn't this funnier in the 1980s?), and you're along for the ride.

✔ You will get very, very wet on **Jurassic Park.** We paid $1 for a disposable plastic poncho, and we seriously suggest you buy two, one for your upper body and one for your lower body.

✔ **The Mummy Returns: Chamber of Doom** is a walk-through haunted house that's about as scary as the one put on by any local chamber of commerce for Halloween. The first part, as you wait in line to shuffle through the actual attraction, is all about promoting the *Mummy* franchise, including the new animated cartoon based on the movie. Some of the props displayed in cases are pretty dang cool, though; and oh we wish they were offered as souvenirs in one of the many shops that fill the theme park. The actual Chamber of Doom is sort of dull.

✔ On the **E.T. Adventure** ride, you get to help E.T. get back to his planet by riding a bicycle over the heads of policemen. And then, because you're so darn nice, E.T. takes you on a brief tour of his planet, which features talking mushrooms, smiling flowers, and lots of black light.

✔ **Terminator 2 3-D** is a live-action show mixed with 3-D filmmaking effects. It is based on plot points of the first two *Terminator* movies.

The wait can be long (interminable actually) for these attractions, which brings us to the Director's Pass. With it, you get to cut to the head of the line on all attractions. Is this a good idea? Well, you pay $69 per person, including children, and you won't be the only person with one.

Venice Ocean Front Walk
Venice

This several-mile stretch of beach is hemmed by a sidewalk, which is itself lined with shops, cafes, stalls selling clothes, sunglasses, and ear-piercings, street performers, and what used to be called bums. Every day is a scene — it's one of the best people-watching places in the city. Truth be told, this one-time epicenter of bohemia (you know, when it was new) and then hippiedom (Jim and Ray created The Doors on the beaches here!) got swallowed up a long time ago by the tourists who wanted to gawk at the bohos and hippies. Not that counterculture isn't still a major presence, but geez, kids in tie dye and long dreads aren't new anymore. **Muscle Beach,** the famed weightlifters' spot, still features young "Ahnuld-wannabes," although they preen for the voyeurs more than they work on their physiques. Every first-time visitor needs to walk down the boardwalk at least once, buy a pair of cheap sunglasses, get a henna tattoo — unless those, too, are outlawed by the time you read this — have a sausage at Jodi Maroni's original stall (where they still hand out free bite-sized samples of all their wares), rent a bike or in-line skates for some speedy travel and exercise, and maybe even stick his or her toes in the water. It's less crowded on weekdays, although parking is always in short supply.

Between Venice Ave. and Rose Ave. Parking in paid lots at Rose and Windward Aves.

The Sensational, Star-Studded, Scandalous Sunset Boulevard Tour

It's been called the most famous street in America. It inspired a TV show, and a movie, which in turn spawned a Broadway musical hit.

"Sunset *BOOO-LA-VAHD!*" bellows whoever is playing the musical Norma Desmond these days. It may be kitsch, it may be hokey, it may more often than not be seedy, but for better or worse, Sunset Boulevard is *the* artery for Los Angeles. It's not the fastest way to get around, but if you have only a few hours in which to try to get a sense of this sprawling, schizophrenic town, the legendary Sunset Boulevard is the way to do it.

Think about it. Sunset begins at Olvera Street, the oldest street in L.A., dating back to when the city was El Pueblo de Nuestra Senora, La Reigna de Los Angeles ("City of Our Lady, Queen of the Angels"). From there it winds its way through a fabulous cross section of everything Los Angeles has to offer, from the good, to the bad, to the ugly, to the glamorous, until it ends smack at the Pacific Ocean. Sunset Boulevard has it all: movie stars and moguls; immigrants, nouveau riche, and old money; sushi bars and strip joints; punks, parks, and prostitutes. And then some.

When you drive Sunset, you can get a taste of every flavor of L.A., from conventional tourist sights to a bit of the history of the city (both early and movie) to the sordid and sensational. You can see beautiful old buildings, garish homes, and decrepit structures. You can gawk at the spots where John Belushi and River Phoenix shuffled off their mortal coils. You get a spectacular view of the Hollywood sign and a glimpse of the stars on the sidewalks.

This tour is designed to be driven westward, beginning at Olvera Street, passing through such famous neighborhoods as Hollywood, the Sunset Strip, Beverly Hills, Bel Air, and Brentwood, and ending at the Pacific, but you can do it backwards if you are more of a deconstructionist than a dreamer. Just reverse the directions where appropriate (east becomes west, right becomes left, and so forth). Plan on setting aside about 3 hours if you stick strictly to Sunset (this allows for some photo op stops), though it will take longer, depending on the traffic or if you take in some of the suggested side trips. A whole day can easily be devoted to this tour, but it's a day well spent.

Naturally, the optimum mode of travel is a convertible, preferably a '02 T-Bird. But your style-free rental car will get the job done, as long as it has a stereo — soundtrack suggestions are provided.

Note the sidebars that alert you to special side trips along the route. Side trips are those serendipitous little detours off Sunset Boulevard where we've found something truly delicious for you to see. Of course, for time's sake, you may choose to stay firmly on the route.

Ready? Let's cruise. . . .

Get your kicks on old Route 66

We begin at ❶ **Olvera Street** (400–500 N. Main). Los Angeles was founded in 1781, and this is traditionally considered the oldest street. (If you need to fuel up before the tour, there are plenty of opportunities for Mexican food here, and for Chinese a few blocks away in Chinatown.) Sunset originally began a block above at Spring Street. Over the last couple years, the first few blocks have been renamed Cesar Chavez Boulevard. Start at the original Spring Street beginning, anyway, for history's sake, though it's the 900 block where Sunset now officially begins.

Now crank up your stereo with "Route 66" by Bobby Troupe. Yes, this portion of Sunset was part of the late, lamented, and much-celebrated American Drive.

Sunset Boulevard Tour

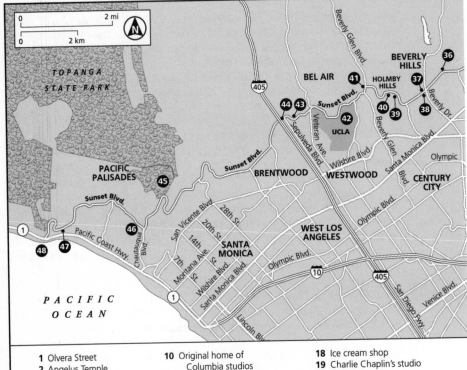

1 Olvera Street	10 Original home of	18 Ice cream shop
2 Angelus Temple	Columbia studios	19 Charlie Chaplin's studio
3 1712 Glendale	11 Hollywood Palladium	20 Ralph's
4 KCET	12 Earl Carroll Theater	21 English Disco
5 Vista Theater	13 Corner of Hollywood	22 Virgin Megastore
6 Vons Market	and Vine	23 Garden of Allah apartments
7 Scientology Center	14 Cinerama Dome Theater	24 Pandora's Box
8 William Fox's studio	15 Hollywood Athletic Club	25 Chateau Marmont
9 Original Warner	16 Crossroads of the World	26 Dudley Do-Right Emporium
Brothers studios	17 Hollywood High	27 Source Restaurant

Now put on some mariachi music as you hit the Hispanic part of Sunset; it's a little rundown, a mix of sagging apartments and some older, funkier architecture, but it has a warm community feel. Or you can play "Take Me Out to the Ballgame" — you'll see the signs on the right directing you to the pride of the O'Malleys, Dodger Stadium, just to the east of Sunset.

Turn left at the corner of Glendale Boulevard and Sunset. On the left is the Deco/Moderne ❷ **Angelus Temple,** built by the evangelist Aimee Semple McPherson, whose ministry and good works were overshadowed by scandal; McPherson was at the height of her fame when she disappeared for a month in 1926. She was presumed drowned. When she turned up, she insisted that she had been kidnapped. Her fake story quickly fell apart, and the truth came out — she had rendezvoused with her married lover. McPherson's ministry never recovered from the scandal, and she eventually committed suicide in 1944.

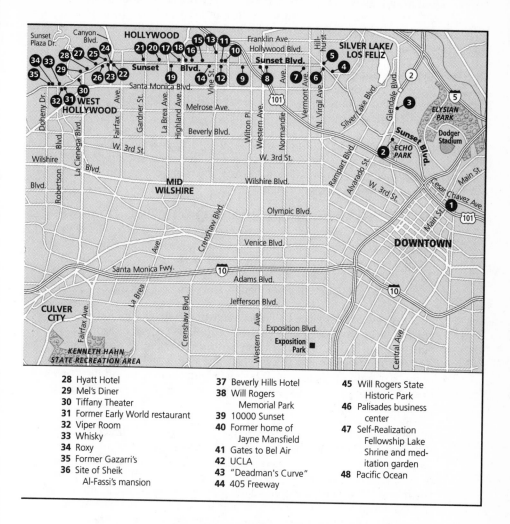

28 Hyatt Hotel	37 Beverly Hills Hotel	45 Will Rogers State
29 Mel's Diner	38 Will Rogers	Historic Park
30 Tiffany Theater	Memorial Park	46 Palisades business
31 Former Early World restaurant	39 10000 Sunset	center
32 Viper Room	40 Former home of	47 Self-Realization
33 Whisky	Jayne Mansfield	Fellowship Lake
34 Roxy	41 Gates to Bel Air	Shrine and med-
35 Former Gazarri's	42 UCLA	itation garden
36 Site of Sheik	43 "Deadman's Curve"	48 Pacific Ocean
Al-Fassi's mansion	44 405 Freeway	

Cross Sunset to ❸ **1712 Glendale.** It's the former site of Mack Sennett's Keystone Studio, where Charlie Chaplin, Fatty Arbuckle, Gloria Swanson, and the Keystone Cops got their starts. Then return to Sunset Boulevard, traveling west.

Silver Lake and Los Feliz: Of bungalows and haciendas

As you cross Coronado Street, you enter Silver Lake, a remarkable multicultural, eclectic community of arty bohemians and homosexuals, young yuppies in love, budding Sammy Glick types burning to climb the Hollywood ladder by whatever means possible, immigrants, and older couples who have been residents for decades. Notice that the architecture, much left over from the early days of L.A., begins to improve — observe Hollywood bungalows (many built to house silent-screen actors) and Spanish haciendas.

If you're feeling hungry, stop at **Café Tropical** (2900 W. Sunset Blvd., corner of Parkman Avenue; ☎ **323-661-8391**), where many Silver Lake residents hang out, to load up on coffee, fruit shakes, guava pastries, and Cuban sandwiches.

As you keep driving, if the weather gods are kind, you should get a great view of the Hollywood hills straight ahead. As you cross the little bridge past the corner of Myra Avenue and Sunset, you can see the hills of Silver Lake on your right.

Just past Fountain Avenue on the right is ❹ **KCET,** the Los Angeles PBS affiliate. This lot was built as a movie studio in 1912 and has been in continuous use ever since, changing hands several times (the East Side Kids/Bowery Boys made their movies here). Next door is the **Tiki Ti Room** (☎ **323-669-9381**), a bar shack that says it invented the tropical drink. Judge for yourself, if you can — the owner keeps his own hours.

You are now entering the Los Feliz neighborhood. On the northeast corner of the three-way intersection of Hillhurst Avenue (as it crosses Sunset going south, it changes names to Virgil Avenue), Sunset, and Hollywood boulevards is the ❺ **Vista Theater,** which was built in the early '20s and now boasts an interior facelift that shows off its Deco/Egyptian roots. It's a small but prime example of an early movie palace.

Diagonally across from the Vista to the left is a ❻ Vons Market. Big deal. But wait. In 1916, D. W. Griffith filmed his classic epic *Intolerance* at his **studio backlot,** which occupied the block on Virgil between Fountain and Sunset. He built the largest outdoor set ever for the "Babylon" segment of the movie. Afterward, the opulent set just sat there, decaying. It towered in the background over the increasingly growing skyline of Los Angeles. It was this sight that inspired Kenneth Anger's now-iconic phrase, "Hollywood Babylon." So go stand in the parking lot of Vons Market; you are actually right smack dab in the middle of a metaphor for an era.

A taste of Victorian L.A.

Turn left off of Sunset onto Marion Avenue, right on Edgeware Road, and then left on Carroll Drive to an area known as Angelino Heights. This long block of perfectly restored **Victorian homes,** brave with much gingerbread trim, is all that remains of fashionable 1800s Los Angeles — proof that this city once had as much character as San Francisco, thank you very much. (There are more homes one block over on the less impressive Kellam Street.)

Stan and Ollie's famous staircase

Just past Silverlake Boulevard and Parkman Avenue, turn left on Vendome Street. Down on the right between 923 and 927 Vendome is a very steep, very long **staircase** (it's sometimes overgrown with vegetation, so it can look deceptively short). Imagine carrying a piano up it. Laurel and Hardy did, in their classic short *The Music Box*, and a nearby plaque honors the film.

Sunset veers to the left at the three-way corner. If you continue straight, you end up on Hollywood Boulevard.

Keep going until you reach the intersection of Berendo Street and Sunset. On the left is the massive, blue ❼ **Scientology Center,** which actually takes up the whole block in all directions. The cult — oops, religion — owns most of the property around here. Right next door is a branch of the **Self Realization Fellowship** (the bigger version is in the Palisades — see "Pacific Palisades: Sun, sand, and sea," later in this chapter).

Hollywood or bust

As you cross Vermont Avenue, you enter Hollywood proper, and it ain't pretty. A little dingy, with quite a few businesses, it's hardly the glamorous place of lore. But then, it never was. Play X's "Los Angeles" is the soundtrack for this stretch.

Both sides of the south corner of Sunset and Western Avenue used to be ❽ **William Fox's studio** (he eventually merged and became Twentieth Century Fox). Not only did Western movie star Tom Mix shoot bad guys here, but this is also the place where John Wayne got his start.

On the left on Sunset Boulevard, ❾ 5858 is local station KTLA, Channel 5, owned by Gene Autry. The station used to be the **original Warner Brothers studios**, where Al Jolson helped sink many of his silent-film colleagues' careers by making the first talking movie, *The Jazz Singer*. Pop on some Glen Miller or Artie Shaw for that nostalgic feel.

At the southeast corner of Sunset and Gower Street is the ❿ **original home of Columbia Studios** (founded in 1921). Now mostly TV shows are filmed there. Across the street is "Gower Gulch," where Western players would wait, hoping for a shot in a cowboy picture. It was also the site of the movie studio where bit player Virginia Rappe was working when she achieved her own level of fame by dying — Fatty Arbuckle, then the most famous actor in Hollywood, was accused (and eventually acquitted) of her "murder" (it's not clear why she died of a ruptured spleen following a raucous Hollywood party).

Where Mickey Mouse was born

Make a right from Sunset onto Fountain Avenue and note the white triangle-shaped building a few yards down, on the right. It was built in 1916 for silent film comedienne Mabel Normand, as her own studio. Normand, a gifted comic and film pioneer, was best known as Fatty Arbuckle's sidekick and was probably the first female star to direct her own movies.

Follow Fountain east as it curves to the left and becomes Hyperion Avenue. Go left on Griffith Park Boulevard (1.3 miles from the turn onto Fountain). At the corner is a Mayfair Market food store, which was **Walt Disney's first official studio,** where he made the first Mickey Mouse cartoon and *Snow White and the Seven Dwarfs.*

A half-block up on the right are a **set of bungalows** that local legend swears were built by Disney or, at least, served as inspiration for the animators for his first movie classic. They certainly look like cottages for Sneezy, Dopey, Doc, and the gang.

Turn your head to the right at the Gower stoplight (and the next couple thereafter). Look up at the hills. There's the **Hollywood sign.** Built in 1923 and refurbished in the 1980s, it used to read "Hollywoodland," the name of the development below it.

One block west, on the right, is the ⑪ **Hollywood Palladium.** It was the site of the studio that made the first feature-length movie (Cecil .B. DeMille's *The Squaw Man*), and the spot where Rudolph Valentino made most of his movies. At one time it was the place to hear the big bands (Lawrence Welk played there for years), and it now hosts regular concerts. Across the street was the ⑫ **Earl Carroll Theater,** where the "most beautiful girls in the world" appeared. (A "gateway to Hollywood" at the corner of Hollywood and LaBrea pays stylistic tribute to Carroll's girls.) It went through several incarnations after Carroll's plane-crash death in 1948, including a recent mortifying stint as the Chevy Chase Theater, when it was tarted up for Chase's short-lived talk show.

At the next signal is Vine Street. Look to the right on Vine, at the sidewalk. You should be seeing stars — for this is part of the famous **Walk of Fame.** Take a right turn at Vine. The ⑬ **corner of Hollywood and Vine** is one of the most famous places in the world. It's said that if you stand here long enough, you will see everyone pass by. (You may have to wait longer these days.) The **Brown Derby,** the legendary hat-shaped restaurant where all the stars dined and where Gable proposed to Lombard, was at the northwest corner (it's now a pawn shop). Farther north on Vine, on the right, is the round **Capital Records building** (squint and it looks like a stack of records with a spindle on top).

Return to Sunset Boulevard. A block and a half to the corner of Ivar Avenue and Sunset, on the left, is the ⑭ **Cinerama Dome Theater,** the largest regular (not IMAX) movie screen in the nation. It's currently undergoing a massive expansion and renovation. (Try to see a movie there. It's an experience.)

At the northeast corner of Hudson Avenue and Sunset is the ⑮ **Hollywood Athletic Club,** which was recently nicely refurbished. It's the place where John Wayne and John Barrymore would drink, Valentino would hide from angry wives, and Roman Navarro would tryst. Tyrone Power, Sr., died there in the arms of Jr.

The ⑯ **Crossroads of the World,** the world's first planned outdoor shopping mall, is at 6671 Sunset (on the right). It opened in 1936, and yes, it looks like a ship.

At the northwest corner of Sunset and Highland Avenue is ⑰ **Hollywood High,** where Lana Turner, Carol Burnett, and both David and Ricky Nelson went to school. Elvis Costello recorded a famous concert here in 1979. Across the street on Highland stood the ⑱ **ice cream shop** where someone once asked then teenaged Turner if she wanted to be in movies. She said she had to ask her mother.

Keep driving until you reach the stoplight at LaBrea Avenue. Just south of Sunset, on the left at 1418, is a series of Tudor-style buildings. This compound was ⑲ **Charlie Chaplin's own studio** (1918). It's now the home of Jim Henson Productions, as you perhaps can tell from the giant Kermit (dressed like Chaplin's Little Tramp character) standing on the top of the building.

Welcome to Guitar Alley

Just past La Brea Avenue, Sunset starts to turn into Guitar Alley — note all the music stores (including Guitar Central and their "Rock Walk" of musicians' handprints). Crank up Guns N' Roses "Welcome To The Jungle" — or if you feel more goofball, some Van Halen.

The ⑳ **Ralph's** on the right, at the corner of Poinsettia, is *the* place to see rock stars and wannabes buying red meat, sugar, and alcohol at 3 a.m. The ㉑ early 1970s home of local DJ and ancient scenester Rodney Bingenhiemer's **English Disco,** where sex and drugs and rock 'n' roll was a lifestyle, was at 7561 Sunset Boulevard.

Say farewell to Bela Lugosi

One block past Western Avenue, turn right at St. Andrew's Place, and then turn left a block later onto Harold Way. Number **5620**, on the left, is where Bela Lugosi, one of filmdom's creepiest Count Draculas, died in 1956 at the age of 73. He was reportedly buried in his Dracula cape.

If you were Hugh Grant, the corner of Sunset and Courtney Avenue would be a good place (or perhaps not so good) to pick up a prostitute.

At the southeast corner of Crescent Heights Boulevard and Sunset, you now have to resort to being discovered at the ㉒ **Virgin Megastore** — the famous Schwab's Drugstore is no more. Oh sure, no one *really* got discovered there, but Harold Arlen stopped in to write down a melody that struck him while driving, and "Somewhere Over the Rainbow" was born. Across the street, on the southwest corner, was silent film star Alla Nazimova's fabulous ㉓ **Garden of Allah apartments.** The apartments were home to dozens of celebrities and such Manhattan artistic refugees as Dorothy Parker, Robert Benchley, Harpo Marx, and a struggling-to-stay-sober F. Scott Fitzgerald. It was a wild and yet arty place, immortalized in songs written by musicians as diverse as Don Henley and L.A's own Ringling Sisters. Right in the middle of Crescent Heights (the triangular cement patch) is the former site of ㉔ **Pandora's Box.** In the '60s, when the club was closed to make this part of Sunset wider, a hippie protest against the action turned into a riot. The Buffalo Springfield song "For What It's Worth" is about this event.

You can go north on Crescent Heights and into Laurel Canyon for a glimpse at the **golden landscape** that was home and nirvana to so many rock musicians and hippies of the late '60s/early '70s.

About half a block down, looming over Sunset, is the ㉕ **Chateau Marmont.** A magnificent, stately old hotel, which has been favored by celebrities (from Garbo to Keanu) for decades, it's now most famous for being the spot where John Belushi had one speedball too many in Bungalow #2. The grounds are striking, and the Art Deco rooms are straight out of *Barton Fink.* Next door is the Hollywood hangout Bar Marmont.

James Dean's last meal, Oz's abode, and the Dahlia's roots

Turn right at Highland off of Sunset if you want to check out **Hollywood Boulevard.** Continue north on Highland to Yucca Street; then take a right. At 6735, on the left, stood the **Villa Capri restaurant** (now Luther Vandross Studios), where James Dean had dinner the night before he headed down the highway and never came back.

Continue east on Yucca, turn right on Las Palmas, then left on Hollywood, and then left on Cherokee. L. Frank Baum used his earnings from his beloved *Wizard of Oz* books to build **Ozcot,** his dream house, here in 1909 (1749 on the left — it's now a vacant lot). And it was here he "crossed the shifting sands" in 1919.

Elizabeth Short lived at 1842 Cherokee (on the right) four months before she achieved fame in 1946 as the **Black Dahlia.** Of course, she had to be murdered and dismembered to gain her fame.

Across Sunset is the ㉖ **Dudley Doo-Right Emporium,** where cartoonist Jay Ward's widow still sells Bullwinkle and Nastasha tchotchkes. (A Bullwinkle statue is a little farther west, in front of a psychic's shop.)

Get your kicks on Sunset Strip

Like Melrose Place, Sunset Strip became legendary thanks to a TV show, *77 Sunset Strip*, which showcased the Strip in all its early-'60s-cool (T-birds! Beatnik jive! Kooky sidekicks!) glory. Put on the Doors' "L.A. Woman" now — this is the beginning of the Sunset Strip, so the song fits. (Besides, the first billboard to advertise an album on the Strip was for the first Doors record.)

L.A.'s industry is entertainment, and every part of its cultural development has been reflected along these next couple miles. The street was once filled with glamorous nightclubs. Then, in the '60s and '70s, the sidewalks teamed with teenagers in bell bottoms and spandex, respectively. Now it's home to upscale rock 'n' roll clubs — and weekend evenings are likely to find the Strip jammed with cars — so you may want to avoid it during those times.

At the corner of Sweetzer Avenue and Sunset (on the right) is the site of the former ㉗ **Source Restaurant,** where Woody Allen and Diane Keaton had their last meal in *Annie Hall*.

The corner of King's Road brings you to the ㉘ **Hyatt Hotel** — also known as the "Riot House" because of the many rock bands who turned hotel staying into performance art (the TV-tossing capers of such guests as Led Zeppelin are rock 'n' roll legend). This corner is also home to the modern-day theme restaurants **Thunder Roadhouse** (owned in part by Dwight Yoakum and Peter Fonda) and the **House of Blues.** The corrugated tin on the outside of the House of Blues came from a building that stood at the famous crossroads where bluesman Robert Johnson made his mythical pact with the devil.

Just past La Cienega Boulevard, on the right, is ㉙ **Mel's Diner.** In the '60s, it was Ben Frank's 24-hour coffee shop and the hip place for rock-and-rollers to nosh (Arthur Lee and Bryan MacLean conceived of the band Love there, and when auditions were held to cast *The Monkees*, the notices asked for "Ben Frank's types"). It remains a good place for gawking.

On the other side of Sunset is the ㉚ **Tiffany Theater,** which is now surrounded by a mall. To its left was the site of **Dino's,** Dean Martin's nightclub, used as the stand-in for *77 Sunset Strip*. To the right stood the **Trocadero** and the **Mocambo,** fabulous nightclubs of the Hollywood glamour years.

At the corner of Holloway, on the left, is a ㉛ **restaurant** (it keeps changing hands) that used to be called the Early World. It's where Diner's

Club founder/Reagan kitchen cabinet member Alfred Bloomingdale met Vicki Morgan and started a bizarre adulterous relationship that ended in palimony, allegations of S&M sex with powerful men, and murder.

The next light is Larabee Street. On the left-hand corner is ㉜ **The Viper Room.** It's gone through many incarnations as a rock club (the London Fog, Filthy McNasty's, the Central), but it's as Johnny Depp's prize that it became notorious. River Phoenix tossed away a beautiful life and career on the sidewalk outside the Larabee Street entrance.

The next light is Clark Street, and on the right is the ㉝ **Whisky a Go-Go,** where many a famous L.A. rock band, like The Doors, found fame. At the corner of Hammond, on the right, is ㉞ **The Roxy,** another landmark rock club. Next door is the **Rainbow Bar & Grill**. Under another name, it was where Vincente Minelli proposed to Judy Garland, and where Marilyn Monroe met Joe DiMaggio on a blind date. Later, bands such as Led Zeppelin made the Rainbow their favorite place for debauched behavior. Big-haired rock dudes of varying degrees of fame still hang there. Two blocks down, also on the right, is the former ㉟ **Gazarri's** (now the Key Club), where such heavy-metal bands as Van Halen and Guns N' Roses got their starts. It's been a club since the '30s.

The big, the brassy: Beverly Hills

Beverly Hills begins at Doheny Drive and Sunset. Suddenly, the landscape becomes considerably more upscale (indeed, from here on out, no house you see will sell for much less than a million bucks.) The transition is so abrupt that it almost causes a mental car crash. Beverly Hills is green and manicured within an inch of its life. And everything is big. Really big.

Drive one more block, and on the right you'll find a ㊱ **huge vacant lot.** Sheik Al-Fassi bought this once-gorgeous mansion in 1978, and horrified his neighbors by painting the statues with anatomical correctness and adding other tacky elements. (For glimpses of the Sheik's interior-decorating skills, rent Steve Martin's *The Jerk*. The mansion scenes later in the movie were shot at the Sheik's home, which was untouched by set decorator hands.) The house burned down in 1980 and was leveled a few years later. The lot is for sale, in case you have some loose change.

Drive two more blocks; on the right is the landmark ㊲ **Beverly Hills Hotel.** The hotel just got a facelift, turning its famous hot pink façade into more of a peach tone. Play the Eagles' *Hotel California* while admiring the hotel's inspiration; the top of the three towers is the shot on the cover of the album.

Across the street is the dainty and pretty ㊳ **Will Rogers Memorial Park** (not to be confused with the Will Rogers State Historic Park). Apparently ascribing to Rogers' motto ("I never met a man I didn't like"), singer George Michael was arrested in the men's room here for committing a solo lewd act. (In an unrelated incident, Rod Stewart proposed to his last wife, Rachel Hunter, here.)

Check out ❸❾ **10000 Sunset,** on the left. Nope, that's not a crowd of people milling about on a stranger's lawn — they're statues. The almost certainly eccentric folks who live here have been adding figures to their lawn for some years.

Sunset now takes a long, hard curve (one of two referred to as the famous "Deadman's Curve" — put on the Jan and Dean song and try not to cut your trip short by wiping out), and on the left (corner of Carolwood Drive) is a ❹⓿ **very large, very pink house.** It was Jayne Mansfield's — pink was her favorite color. Singer Englebert Humperdinck owns it now.

Old money Bel Air

Bel Air, which starts at Beverly Glen Boulevard, feels somewhat older and warmer than Beverly Hills. Notice how the trees stand taller and wilder; everything is considerably less landscaped and ostentatious — symbolizing, perhaps, the difference between old money and nouveau riche. Notice the ❹❶ **gates to Bel Air** at Beverly Glen Boulevard (and later intersections) on the right. They have been closed only once — during the 1962 Bel Air fire (though closure was threatened again during the 1992 riots).

Looking up Lupe, Lana, Clara, and Bugsy

Go south on Rodeo Drive, which comes off Sunset at the same point as Benedict Canyon. One block down, **732** on the left, is the home where "Mexican Spitfire" Lupe Velez, despondent over a fading career and an unplanned pregnancy, took an overdose of pills. Scandal lore has it she dressed herself in all white, hoping to leave a gorgeous, picturesque corpse. Instead, nauseous from the pills, she stumbled to the toilet and drowned. It's too good not to be true.

Go back up to Lomitas Avenue; make a left. Two blocks down, on the corner of Bedford Drive, on the left **(730)** is the house where Lana Turner's daughter Cheryl stabbed her mother's mobster boyfriend to death.

Go left on Bedford, 2½ long blocks down, to **512** (on the left); that's where "It Girl" Clara Bow, according to legend, "entertained" the entire USC football team, including Marion "John Wayne" Morrison.

Go back up to Lomitas, turn left again, and then go right on Linden Drive. **810**, on the right, is the house where mobster Benjamin "Don't call me Bugsy" Siegel was murdered. (Shots went through the windows on the right.)

④② **UCLA** begins as Hilgard Avenue, and the left-hand side continues to be UCLA until Veteran Avenue. The next big curve you encounter is the other so-called **④③** "Deadman's Curve."

The freeway you cross is the legendary **④④** San Diego **405 Freeway,** bane of all L.A. drivers. This is also the beginning of **Brentwood;** despite its Peyton Place reputation of the last couple years (courtesy of O.J. and company), it used to be a wealthy, low-profile, family-oriented community.

Pacific Palisades: Sun, sand, and sea

Mandeville Canyon marks the beginning of **Pacific Palisades.** (Notice how the temperature has dropped as much as 20 degrees since the beginning of the tour at Olvera Street. Thank the ocean breeze.) Put on the Beach Boys' "California Girls," and admire how open, sunny, and, well, California-y it all gets.

About a mile down the road on the right is the sprawling **④⑤** **Will Rogers State Historic Park**, which is built around the humorist's home. It's a fine place for a picnic and hiking, and polo matches are frequently held in the field.

A mile later, you hit the **④⑥** business center of the Palisades.

About a mile and a half after that, you should have your **first ocean sighting.** Put on Randy Newman's "I Love L.A." (yes, it's more than a little sarcastic and ironic, but somehow it's also just right) as you round the home stretch. (Of course, you've now gone from the east side to the west side. The song sings about going in the opposite direction, so don't get confused.)

The final, and perhaps most unexpected, stop on the Sunset tour is the **④⑦** **Self-Realization Fellowship Lake Shrine and meditation garden** (watch carefully, or you may miss the entrance) at 17190 Sunset Blvd. It was dedicated in 1950 by the Fellowship's founder, guru Paramahansa Yogananda. (It's the bigger sibling of the one in East Hollywood.) This impossibly calm and lovely parklike shrine, complete with lake, is dedicated to meditation and harmony among all religions. It's a surprising find along busy Sunset and well worth taking a walk through. But the best part of the garden may be the marble sarcophagus containing the only entombed ashes of Mohandas Gandhi. The rest of Gandhi's ashes were scattered in India — but a portion was sent here as a gift, a most unlikely addition to Los Angeles.

And now, just keep driving. See the water? That's the **④⑧** **Pacific Ocean.** Don't forget to hit the brakes.

Fittingly, this is the literal end of Western Civilization — and don't think that we don't know it or aren't proud. From here out, it's the mysteries of the Far East.

Chapter 17

More Cool Things to See and Do

*T*here are those who say that although Los Angeles is a fine place to live, it's not so fine a place to visit, mostly because L.A.'s charms, while many, are not as easily apparent as those of, say, London or other major tourist-attracting cities. We don't disagree (although we can and do sniff about people who need *obvious* sights, you know, all the tourist goods in the sightseeing window — frankly, this city is simply more subtle and requires more finesse), but then again, you have us to point you in the right direction.

Museums Galore

L.A. may not have museums on the level, recognition-wise, of the Louvre, but that doesn't mean that the city lacks for museums of which it can be justly proud. Although we include the highlights in the preceding chapter (the **Getty**, for example, and the **Los Angeles County Museum of Art/LACMA**), the following all have their merits, be it the strength of their collections, the breadth of their vision, or simply their entertainment value. There is enough variety here, in fact, that we divide them further within this section, so that you, our handsome and charming reader, can pick the ones best suited to your own taste or curiosity.

Los Angeles Museums, Parks & Other Attractions

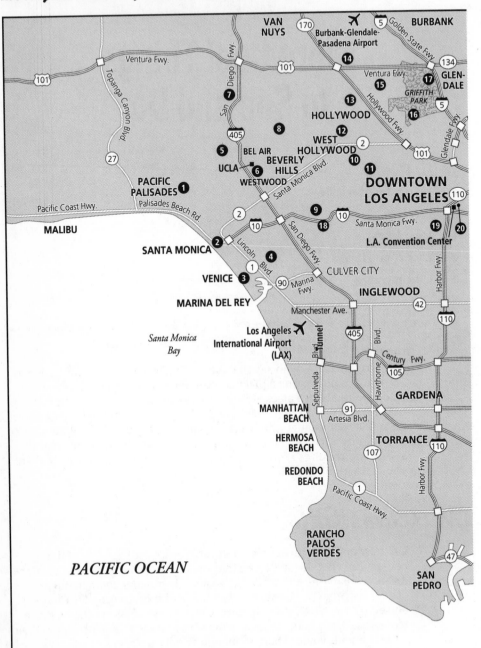

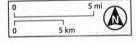

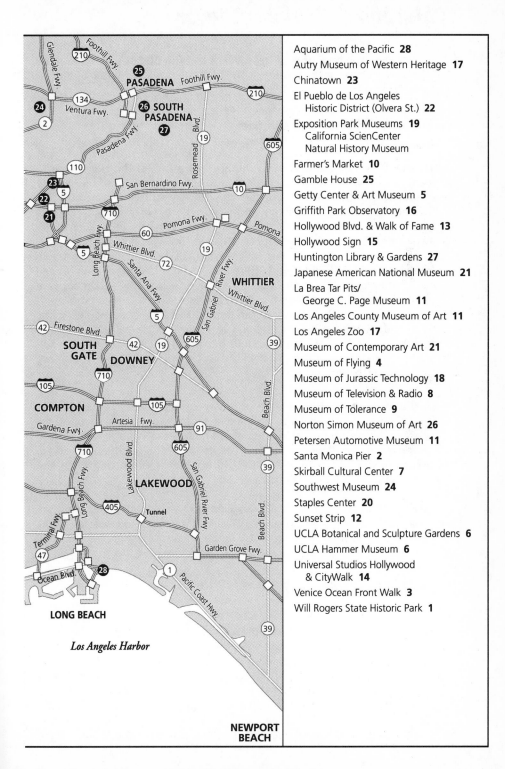

Aquarium of the Pacific **28**
Autry Museum of Western Heritage **17**
Chinatown **23**
El Pueblo de Los Angeles
  Historic District (Olvera St.) **22**
Exposition Park Museums **19**
  California ScienCenter
  Natural History Museum
Farmer's Market **10**
Gamble House **25**
Getty Center & Art Museum **5**
Griffith Park Observatory **16**
Hollywood Blvd. & Walk of Fame **13**
Hollywood Sign **15**
Huntington Library & Gardens **27**
Japanese American National Museum **21**
La Brea Tar Pits/
  George C. Page Museum **11**
Los Angeles County Museum of Art **11**
Los Angeles Zoo **17**
Museum of Contemporary Art **21**
Museum of Flying **4**
Museum of Jurassic Technology **18**
Museum of Television & Radio **8**
Museum of Tolerance **9**
Norton Simon Museum of Art **26**
Petersen Automotive Museum **11**
Santa Monica Pier **2**
Skirball Cultural Center **7**
Southwest Museum **24**
Staples Center **20**
Sunset Strip **12**
UCLA Botanical and Sculpture Gardens **6**
UCLA Hammer Museum **6**
Universal Studios Hollywood
  & CityWalk **14**
Venice Ocean Front Walk **3**
Will Rogers State Historic Park **1**

Museums for the art lover

You don't have to go to Italy or Spain to see masterpieces of art. After you exhaust the treasures of the LACMA and the Getty — and that may take several trips, right there — you still have many more museums to look forward to.

Huntington Library and Gardens
Pasadena

This is a true treasure of L.A., though one a bit off the beaten path, located as it is in one of the oldest and richest sections of old-money Pasadena. Huntington was a turn-of-the-century railroad baron, and this was his home — yes, that mansion over there, with the art, was his house, and that lawn lined with classical statues (surely we've seen many an early rock video shot there?) was his side lawn. This place has something for nearly everyone. Art lovers will thrill to the famous portraits fondly known as "Pinkie" and "Blue Boy," which had no connection to each other until they were displayed here in the '20s — Pinkie was painted by Thomas Lawrence 25 years after Thomas Gainsborough painted Blue Boy. By the way, Sarah Barrett Moulton, the real-life Pinkie, who died a few months after being the subject of the painting, was the paternal great-aunt of poet Elizabeth Barrett Browning. The library collection here is one of the finest in the world and includes a Gutenberg Bible and a Chaucer manuscript.

Horticulturists will thrill to the expansive gardens (200 acres' worth), from rolling English lawns to a Japanese fantasy tea garden to an otherworldly 12-acre section of succulents (which recently got a lot of attention when a rare "corpse flower" bloomed — one of the few times a corpse flower has bloomed in the United States — putting forth the putrid smell that gives it its name).

1151 Oxford Rd., San Marino. ☎ *626-405-2100. Internet:* www.huntington.org. *Admission: $10 adults, $8.50 seniors, $7 students with ID and children 12–18, children under 12 free. Open: Sept–May Tues–Fri noon to 4:30 p.m., Sat–Sun 10:30 a.m.–4:30 p.m., closed Mon; June–Aug Tues–Sat 10:30 a.m.–4:30 p.m.*

Norton Simon Museum of Art
Pasadena

This is one of the world's foremost art collections, with an emphasis on old masters and Impressionists. We put it here instead of in the "must sees" partly because it's not in L.A. proper, and so it's a bit of a distance from where you may expect to find the average tourist. For art lovers, it certainly can't be missed. Here's just a sample of what you can expect — Picasso (*Girl with Guitar*), Rembrandt, Degas, Monet, Manet, Cézanne, Kandinsky, and Rodin. The museum houses a copy of Rodin's iconic *The Thinker*, plus one of the world's great collections of South Asian sculpture. But despite an architectural facelift by the ever-amusing Frank Gehry, this museum always struck us as the kind you go to because it's good for you, and because it's important. Our view of the musuem is doubtless doing it a disservice, and with the patient help of art students and scholars, we could come to see the error of our ways.

411 W. Colorado Blvd., Pasadena. ☎ **626-449-6840.** *Internet:* www.nortonsimon. org. *Admission: $6 adults, $3 seniors, children under 17 and students with valid ID free. Open: Wed–Thurs and Sat–Mon noon to 6 p.m., Fri noon to 9 p.m.*

UCLA Hammer Museum
Westwood

So much has been written about billionaire (except he really wasn't a billionaire) art lover (except he really wasn't an art lover) Armand Hammer (much of it by his own self), that it's hard to separate the publicity, scandals, and whatnot from the true value of this institution. There is too much history to go into here (darn the luck, because it's a hoot). Suffice it to say that UCLA had to take over the art museum. Although the true significance or value of its permanent collection is debatable (it focuses primarily on collections with such recognizable names as van Gogh, Monet, and Cassett), the frequent special exhibitions are truly noteworthy. Check and see what will be exhibited during your stay.

10899 Wilshire Blvd. (at Westwood Blvd.). ☎ **310-443-7000.** *Internet:* www. hammer.ucla.edu. *Admission: $4.50 adults, $3 seniors and UCLA alumni with ID, children 17 and under free (accompanied by an adult). Thurs is free for all visitors. Open: Tues–Wed and Fri–Sat 11 a.m.–7 p.m., Thurs 11 a.m.–9 p.m., 11 a.m.–7 p.m., Thurs 11 a.m.–9 p.m., Sun 11 a.m.–5 p.m.*

A museum that's also an art project

Believe us when we say that we tried to justify putting the Museum of Jurassic Technology under "must-see," but we had to admit that not everyone will get it, even though everyone should. Find out why below.

Museum of Jurassic Technology
Culver City

You will spot this little storefront along a nondescript street in an unremarkable part of town and wonder why we sent you here. You will probably be greeted at the door by a slightly distracted, amiable, elfish man, who happens to be the proprietor. You will begin to wander through the deliberately arcane exhibits, all of which seem dusty, even if they actually aren't. You will learn about bats, and stink ants, and how one man can carve images into a single strand of hair. You may or may not realize that some of what you see is entirely made up. This wholly remarkable museum — there is nothing like it in the world — is one giant art project, all of it springing from the incredibly fertile mind of its owner, David Wilson, who is already the subject of a book (*Mr. Wilson's Cabinet of Wonder*, by Lawrence Weschler, published by Vintage Books) and the recipient of a 2002 MacArthur Genius Grant. And this is his homage to wonder, to creativity, and to the imagination.

9341 Venice Blvd. (four blocks west of Robertston Blvd.). ☎ *310-836-6131. Internet:* www.mjt.org. *Admission: Adults $4, children 12–21, students with ID, seniors, and unemployed $2.50, disabled or active military in uniform $1.50, children under 12 free. Open: Thurs 2 p.m.–8 p.m., Fri–Sun noon to 6 p.m.*

Museums for those who like to play Cowboys and Indians

Anyone interested in the heritage of the Wild West, the land of six shooters, white hats, horses, and, unfortunately, a great deal of social injustice, should check out the following Los Angeles museums.

Autry Museum of Western Heritage
Los Angeles

Gene Autry was the "Singing Cowboy;" he loved the Wild West and the money it made him. This museum was his gift to Southern California. It's mostly a romanticized view of the Old West, with an emphasis on the romance of the cowboy. The uninformed could easily come away from a visit to the museum believing that nothing really bad happened during the country's relentless pursuit of Manifest Destiny, and that what did take place in the Old West was all for the good of America. (You know, as in, it's kind of too bad we killed the buffalo, but wasn't it fun to shoot them from trains?) Still, even though it's more or less Hollywood pop culture, the museum is most entertaining, and popular with the kids, who love the part where they get to dress up in period clothes and enter dioramas depicting L.A. and Chinatown in the 1930s. A terrific gift shop features everything from cornbread mix to videotapes.

7400 Western Heritage Way (at Curson Ave.). ☎ *323-667-2000. Internet:* www.Autry-museum.org. *Admission: $7.50. Open: Tues–Sun 10 a.m.–5 p.m., Thurs 10 a.m.–8 p.m. Free parking.*

Southwest Museum
Highland Park

Opened in 1907, this was the first museum in Southern California. Exhibits focus on the grim flip side of the Old West myth presented by the Autry Museum (see above). This very serious and very well done museum outlines different aspects of American Indian life by covering the Western tribes. There are three ways to enter this Mission-style building; you can journey through a tunnel lined with very good dioramas of

American Indians, you can walk up the "Hopi Trail," which is very steep and landscaped, or you can bypass it all and drive up to the tippy-top. Local educators prefer the Southwest Museum (politically correct, sensitive, and enlightened, not to mention educational) to the Autry Museum of Western Heritage (rip-roaring, cowboy fun). We don't disagree with their preference. Nonetheless, if you have to pick only one, do you want to learn or do you want to have a really good, goofy time?

234 Museum Dr. (in the Highland Park District). ☎ 323-221-2164. Internet: www.southwestmuseum.org. *Admission: $6 adults, $4 students and seniors, $3 youths 7–18, children under 6 free. Open: Tues–Sun 10 a.m.–5 p.m.*

Museums that teach

For a city supposedly populated with clueless airheads, Los Angeles has some pretty thought-provoking — and smartly developed — museums. The following institutions are well worth your time.

Japanese American National Museum
Downtown

This small and often neglected gem is easy to visit if you're already in Downtown checking out the Geffen Contemporary, for it's virtually right next door. In addition to art exhibits and a moving reconstruction of an actual building from a relocation camp (that term is never used; here, they are rightly called concentration camps), this museum explores the Japanese-immigrant experience in America, which, of course, began primarily on the West Coast. Displays show artifacts such as a set of typical belongings brought over by an immigrant, the schoolbooks children once used here in America. They all lead up to a heartbreaking display about the camps and the Japanese-American war experience. (Our favorite exhibit is the display that features 100 small birds, all carved and painted by hand as a way of passing the time in the camps.)

369 E. First St. (at Central Ave.). ☎ 213-625-0414. Internet: www.janm.org. *Admission: $6 adults, $5 seniors, $3 students and children 6–17, children under 5 free. Open: Tues–Wed and Fri–Sun 10 a.m.–5 p.m., Thurs 10 a.m.–8 p.m. Closed Mon.*

Museum of Tolerance
West Los Angeles

One can make the argument that tolerance, or rather, a lack thereof, is at the base of many of the most pressing issues of our day. This isn't to say that everyone has to like each other; they just have to *tolerate* each other by learning to understand each other and allowing for differences in appearance, religious worship, and cultural mores. The Holocaust is the most obvious example of the tragedies and horrors that occur when this sort of understanding fails to manifest. This excellent facility naturally focuses much attention on that event. Located in the Simon Weisenthal

Center, the museum covers many more related areas — in other words, this isn't just a Holocaust museum. It's designed to topple many of your preconceived notions at the very beginning of your visit, when you have a choice of starting your tour through one of two doors — "prejudiced" and "not prejudiced." Guess which one simply doesn't open at all? Note that the museum is laid out so that you follow a mandatory route, which can take upwards of 3 hours to complete. Note, too, that kids who have been convicted of hate crimes are often sentenced to do community service here.

9786 W. Pico Blvd. (at Roxbury Dr.). ☎ *310-553-8403. Internet:* www.wiesenthal. com/mot/. *Admission: $9 adults, $7 seniors, $5.50 students and children 3–10. Open: Mon–Thurs 11:30 a.m.–6:00 p.m., Fri 11:30 a.m.–3:00 p.m. Nov–Mar and 11:30 a.m.–5:00 p.m. Apr–Oct, Sun 11:00 a.m.–7:30 p.m. Closed Sat.*

Skirball Cultural Center
Los Angeles

This institution is devoted to all aspects of Jewish life and history, both in Europe and in America, from historical beginnings to immigration to political involvement to artistic achievements. Obviously, the Holocaust figures prominently, but it does not overshadow the rest of the exhibits; there is so much more to a people than even the greatest catastrophe. It's a lovely facility (with both permanent and traveling exhibits; examples of the latter include an exhibit on a Colonial-era Jewish silversmith), noted for its frequent cultural offerings. It features everything from the obvious (klezmer concerts, lectures on religious archaeology) to the not so (a conversation between sex columnist Dan Savage and actor Andy Dick). It's easy to miss, because it's located in the shadow of the great big Getty.

2701 N. Sepulveda Blvd. (at Mulholland Dr.). ☎ *310-440-4500. Internet:* www. skirball.org. *Admission: $8 adults, $6 seniors and students, children under 12 free. Open: Tues–Sat noon to 5 p.m., Sun 11 a.m.–5 p.m. Closed Mon.*

A museum perfect for Los Angeles

The following museum is located right where it should be, smack dab in television land — even if the original is in New York City.

Museum of Television & Radio
Beverly Hills

Ah, the timeless family vacation dilemma; Junior is whining about having to visit some dusty old art exhibit because he feels that it would really be a lot more fun to watch TV. Voilà — the solution: a contemporary museum (a branch of the institution located in New York City) where the idiot box is enshrined and treated like the cultural touchstone it really is. From Muhammad Ali to the Muppets, Ed Sullivan to Ed Norton, Walter

Cronkite to Bill Cosby, it's all viewable here (in private cubicles). Request a favorite program, re-experience a special TV moment, or rediscover the glories of radio. Finally, you won't have to justify your *Three Stooges* habit; you're watching in a museum! It's educational! ***Note:*** The Museum's William S. Paley Television Festival is an annual event of great local popularity, and nearly every event sells out, and fast, so start checking the museum Web site around January (events generally start toward the end of February and run into March) for info on tickets.

465 N. Beverly Dr. (at Santa Monica Blvd.). ☎ *310-786-1000. Internet:* www. mtr.org. *Admission: $6 adults, $4 students and seniors, $3 children under 13. Open: Wed and Fri–Sun noon to 5 p.m., Thurs noon to 9 p.m.*

Museums that kids love

We consider ourselves big kids, by the way, and you may as well, too. So that's why we find ourselves making regular forays to those museums whose child-friendly offerings bring out the kid in all of us.

Natural History Museum of Los Angeles County
Los Angeles

We are most fond of this place, although we have to admit that a great deal of that fondness is attributable to nostalgia. Many a local child, ourselves included, has passed through these Beaux Arts halls (so beautiful, they're often booked for fancy parties), admiring the dioramas of taxidermied animals (likely the same dusty critters throughout the generations), exclaiming over the gem collection (one of the finest in the country), and cooing over the dinosaur skeletons (especially the *Tyrannosaurus rex* and triceratops, locked in mortal combat). That said, we have to admit that this is not the most up-to-the-minute museum (though it does often host important traveling exhibits, such as *T. rex* Sue, the largest and most complete *Tyrannosaurus rex* skeleton ever found). The hands-on explorer room, featuring all kinds of touchy-feely stuff, is such low-tech fun that kids won't even know that they are getting an education.

900 Exposition Blvd. (Exposition Park). ☎ 213-763-DINO. Internet: www.nhm.org. Admission: $8 adults, $5.50 seniors and students, $2 children 5–12, children under 5 free. Open: Mon–Fri 9:30 a.m.–5:00 p.m., Sat–Sun 10 a.m.–5 p.m.

California ScienCenter
Downtown

This highly enjoyable institution, a long-term staple of L.A. childhood formerly known as the Museum of Science and Industry, got a complete makeover, which helped bring it as up to date as a museum that focuses on the wonders of science and industry ought to be. Learn about the human body thanks to Tess, the 50-foot visible woman, build miniature structures and see how earthquake-proof they are, or ride a bike on a cable three stories above ground (it's safe, but there's an extra charge). There is plenty of hands-on, interactive fun — again, the sort of fun that probably thrills adults for its cleverness more than it does kids, who are often more interested in the bright lights and loud noises than they are in learning. But that's okay, you're both on vacation, and a little education is bound to sink in anyway, even by accident. It's hugely popular with school field trips, so take that into consideration when you plan your own visit.

700 State Dr. (Exposition Park). ☎ *323-724-3623. Internet:* www.casciencectr. org. *Admission: Free. Open: Daily 10 a.m.–5 p.m. Parking: $6 per vehicle (lot at 39th and Figueroa).*

Museums for guys

Not that we approve of gender-stereotyping, but Y chromosomes do seem more attracted to the following museums.

Museum of Flying
Santa Monica

The aerospace industry was once hugely prominent here in Los Angeles — second only (and perhaps not even second) to the movie industry. So it seems fitting that this museum is located on the site of the old Douglas plant, birthplace of the DC3, possibly the finest plane ever built and certainly a major breakthrough in the transportation of both people and cargo. This museum is all about planes — vintage WWII fighter planes, primarily. Buffs shouldn't miss it; the rest of us can. The museum is sometimes closed for special events, so call ahead to confirm that it's open to the public.

2772 Donald Douglas Loop N. (at the Santa Monica Airport). ☎ *310-392-8822. Internet:* www.museumofflying.com. *Admission: $8 adults, $6 seniors and students, $3 children ages 3–16. Open: Sat–Sun 10 a.m.–5 p.m.*

Petersen Automotive Museum
Los Angeles

The Miracle Mile, as the strip along Wilshire Boulevard between Fairfax and La Brea is known, was built in the 1920s as the world's first linear shopping district (that's architectural lingo for "strip mall") designed specifically for drive-by viewing. So it's fitting that the Petersen Automotive Museum — with a changing display of over 150 cars, motorcycles, and trucks — sits at the corner of Wilshire and Fairfax in what was once Orhbach's department store. Even people who aren't obsessed with cars (like us) enjoy the super-friendly layout and displays. The first-floor dioramas allow visitors to move through and around the displays, which include a re-creation of a highway crash, a pretty effective reminder to stay at the speed limit. On the second floor, theme exhibits — featuring celebrity-owned cars, movie cars, custom cars, hot rods, and motorcycles — demonstrate automobiles as objects of art and desire. Occasionally we find ourselves lusting for a flame-painted woody or the Batmobile, both of which have been on display. The third-floor Discovery Center provides interactive fun geared toward kids, including the opportunity to dress up in vintage clothes and pose on a Model T.

6060 Wilshire Blvd. (at Fairfax Ave.). ☎ *323-930-2277. Internet:* www.petersen. org. *Admission: $7 adults, $3 children 5–12, $5 seniors, children under 5 free. Open: Tues–Sun 10 a.m.–5 p.m. Closed Mon and some major holidays.*

Los Angeles Especially for Kids

The following sights are for kids. This, by no means, implies that you, the more grown-up reader, will not have a blast at any of these attractions.

Aquarium of the Pacific
Long Beach

Our only complaint about this state-of-the-art fishy facility is that it is in Long Beach instead of Los Angeles, and so a (doable, certainly) drive is required whenever we need a fish fix. It is so worth it. The aquarium features 12,000 (give or take) critters from the planet's largest body of water, which is mere yards away. Because the Pacific covers icy northern waters and tropical reefs, the range of finny bodies is remarkable. Some of the aquarium's recent highlights included, in terms of science, the first successful breeding of weedy sea dragons. In terms of sheer delight, you can't beat the Lorikeet exhibit, a walk-in aviary full of colorful birdies who enjoy sitting on visitors, especially if the visitor has thoughtfully prepurchased a cup of nectar for a feathered friend to drink. (Purchase the nectar or just wear something sparkling — and sturdy, because it will get pecked at — and you may well end up covered in birds; don't forget the camera to prove it later.) Kids, needless to say, love the place — especially the younger, unjaded ones. Be sure to pick up a "fish spotting" map on the way in (see if you can find an Oriental Sweetlips or, our personal favorite, a Sarcastic Fringehead). Ask about the "sleep with the fishes" kids' slumber parties and the behind-the-scenes tours (they cost extra). *Note:* Consider taking a combo MetroRail Blue Line and bus, which is a not unreasonable alternative to driving, to the aquarium.

100 Aquarium Way, Long Beach. ☎ *562-590-3100. Admission: $16.95 adults, $13.95 seniors, $9.95 children 3–11. Open: Daily 9 a.m.–6 p.m.*

Downtown Attractions

Bradbury Building **10**
California ScienCenter **14**
Central Library **12**
Chinatown **2**
City Hall **8**
El Pueblo de Los Angeles
  Historic District **3**
Geffen Contemporary at MOCA **5**
Grand Central Market **11**
Japanese American National Museum **6**
Little Tokyo **7**
Natural History Museum
  of Los Angeles County **15**
The Los Angeles Times Building **9**
The Southwest Museum **1**
Staples Center **13**
Union Station **4**
University of
  Southern California (USC) **16**

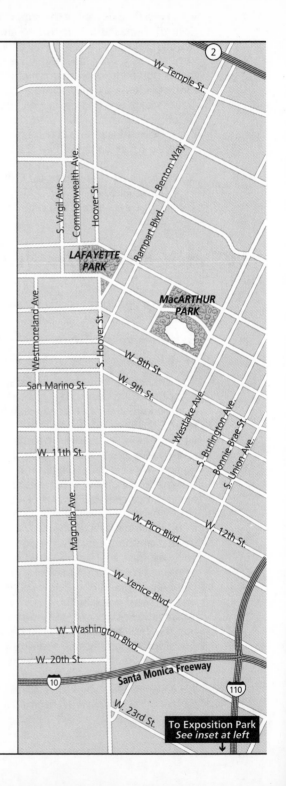

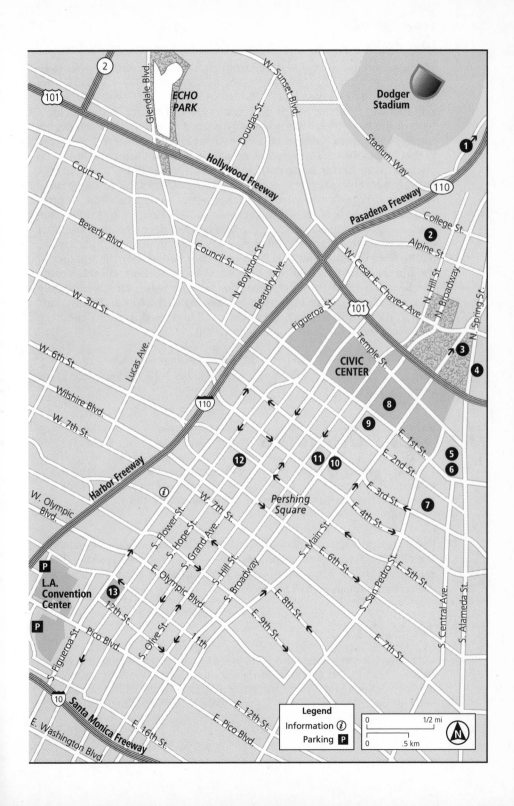

Los Angeles Zoo
Los Angeles

The L.A. Zoo has always suffered from an inferiority complex, thanks to the huge recognition factor enjoyed by its compatriot down in San Diego. The inferiority complex is a bit unjustified, for sure. Certainly, the L.A. Zoo has had its share of ups and downs over the years, experiencing a high in the late 1980s after it not only hosted a panda exhibition during the 1984 Olympics but opened a permanent koala exhibit (well designed in that it exhibits these nocturnal animals in twilight during zoo hours, so visitors have better odds catching the rather sluggish, if admittedly entirely adorable, creatures doing something other than snoozing) and a fabulous children's zoo area, full of interactive playful exhibits. At present, the L.A. Zoo is not in the top echelon of zoos (following various management and fiscal scandals in the '90s), but it does continue to boost attractive natural habitats, including a new chimp exhibit. Kids love it; adults need to remember that it gets very hot here during the summer — the phrase "dumb animal" is a canard, as most animals will rest during the heat of the day. So come early or late, or figure on spotting only snoozing beasts. *Note:* The single busiest day at the zoo is Thanksgiving Day; apparently, it's a way to get kids and noncooking adults out from underfoot while the feast is being prepared.

5333 Zoo Dr. (Griffith Park). ☎ *323-644-6400. Internet:* www.lazoo.org. *Admission: $8.25 adults, $5.25 seniors, $3.25 children 2–12, children under 2 free. Open: Daily 10 a.m.–5 p.m.*

The Great Outdoors

It doesn't matter whether you're an exercise fiend who is determined to work up a sweat or a confirmed couch potato who just wants to partake of the city's fresh-air attractions; everyone can enjoy L.A.'s many outdoor pleasures.

Regardless of what you do and where you do it, remember that even in the cloudy days of "June gloom" or the overcast moments during the rest of the year, the sun shines strongly in SoCal, so apply a sunblock with a minimum SPF of 15 accordingly.

No sweat

Certainly, the very image of L.A. is one of healthy people jogging, in-line skating, hiking, and generally sweating up a storm. Good for them. But if you just want to stroll around and enjoy the warm California sun without intentionally exercising, you have a number of options; you

can stroll around the neighborhoods best suited for walk'
to shop if you want (particularly at the Third Street Prome..
Venice Main Street, both listed in Chapter 18, or the Venice Boaru~.
discussed in Chapter 16), or you can make a trip to one of the following
outdoor attractions.

UCLA Botanical and Sculpture Gardens
Westwood

A trip to this outdoor museum operated by the UCLA Hammer Museum
is also a good opportunity to explore the lovely UCLA campus. The
Franklin D. Murphy Sculpture Garden is 5 acres of some of the finest
outdoor sculptures in the country, including works by Matisse, Moore,
Rodin, and Calder. It's only enhanced by the many good-looking college
students studying beneath and against the statues — what a pleasure to
see art out in the open, incorporated into daily life! If you prefer life in
your inanimate objects, you can walk over to the **Botanical Gardens,**
7 acres worth of highly significant plant life. And then you can skip
around the campus, which is so attractive that it ends up standing in for
many a typical gorgeous college in various TV and movie sets.

*405 Hilgard Ave; UCLA is bordered by Sunset and Le Conte to the south and north,
and Hilgard and Veteran to the east and west. The sculpture garden is in the
northeast part of the campus, while the botanical garden is in the southeast. area
of campus.* ☎ *310-825-4321. Open: Sculpture garden is always open, botanical
garden is open Mon–Fri 8 a.m.–5 p.m. (8 a.m.–4 p.m. during winter months), Sat–Sun
8 a.m.–4 p.m. Closed university holidays.* **Note:** *The Garden may close without
notice because of bad weather or hazardous conditions.*

The Farmer's Market
Hollywood

A collection of buildings dating back to the Great Depression (and surrounding an adobe house, one of the older buildings in L.A.), the Farmer's
Market is a local favorite, but tourists may wonder what all the hype is
about. Many stalls and shops sell tacky souvenirs, as well as all kinds of
food (donuts to deli, sushi to sweets), but the produce tends to get over-
whelmed in the bustle. Still, it's a regular hangout for many a Hollywood
writer wannabe and already-is, retired folks, and lots and lots of tourists.
The locals' fondness for the place is probably due to sentiment more than
anything else, but it's well-placed sentiment. The market is potentially
endangered, thanks to a brand-spanking-new development going up next
door that may economically threaten many of the mom-and-pop businesses here.

6333 W. 3rd St. (corner of Fairfax Ave.). ☎ *323-933-9211. Open: Mon–Sat 9 a.m.–
7 p.m., Sun 10 a.m.–6 p.m.*

Santa Monica Pier
Santa Monica

Part tourist cheesiness, part genuine pleasure, this longtime L.A. institution (it's been around since 1909!) is worth at least one stroll. It's free, so you can walk down and look at the motley collection of souvenir shops, people gamely fishing, the Pacific Park's carnival rides (including one scary roller coaster), various undistinguished restaurants, and best of all, a genuine all-wood, 1930s-era merry-go-round, which may seem familiar to you — it played a large role in the movie *The Sting*. It costs something like a quarter for a turn, and we've seen even nihilistic punk rockers burst into grins riding it, so what are you waiting for?

Ocean Ave. (at the end of Colorado Blvd.). ☎ 310-458-8900.

Sweat city

The following recreational opportunities just scratch the surface of all that L.A. has to offer. Remember, you can always join in with all the runners, in-line skaters, and surfers going about their merry way all over the city. Runners take note: One of the most popular spots for jogging is along the coral trees that run down the meridian of San Vicente in Brentwood (not to be confused with the San Vicente in West Hollywood). For general info on the area beaches, go to Chapter 16.

Hiking

If you like to hike, the Los Angeles area offers some lovely trails. Keep in mind that you should always bring a nice big bottle of water and wear sunblock when hiking, even in the city. **Will Rogers State Historic Park** (1501 Will Rogers State Park Rd.; ☎ 310-454-8212), off of Sunset Boulevard in Pacific Palisades, is the former home of the man who never met a man he didn't like. It's a sweet little spot, with convenient trails through the Santa Monica Mountains. Covering 4,000 acres in Los Feliz, **Griffith Park** (4730 Crystal Springs Dr.; ☎ 323-664-2255) is America's largest park in a municipal area. The park was a donation from the double-barreled-named Colonel Griffith J. Griffith, who was trying to get on the city's good side after a messy courtroom drama involving the attempted murder of his wife, seek tax relief, and remove a curse put upon him by his first wife (bad luck with women), a Spanish heiress, after he stole much of the property from her. Located in the hills above Los Feliz, it is home to the Griffith Observatory, the Greek Theater, the L.A. Zoo, the Gene Autry Museum, a fine golf course, a merry-go-round, and Travel Town. Thus, it's popular with a strong cross section of L.A., from families at play to picnicking bohos to the healthy and health-seeking, who march up and down trails that range from easy to challenging. The Bronson Canyon Trail goes past the Bat Cave entrance from the old *Batman* TV series. **Runyon Canyon** (Franklin Avenue at Fuller Boulevard) is part of the old Errol Flynn estate, and the trails are easy, with astounding views. But they can be crowded. If you don't like dogs (many of which are off leash), you may want to avoid this place, especially daily after 4 p.m. and on weekends. You may be missing out, however: Anytime you go, you run the chance of passing actors and other famous faces catching fresh air alone, with their dogs, or with their trainers.

When hiking in the spring and summer, please be aware that there are snakes, specifically rattlesnakes, in the brush, and that they can be very cranky if disturbed. Wear light-colored clothes and appropriate shoes, stay on the trails, and don't try to pick up anything that looks like a stick.

Golf

Los Angeles boasts acres and acres of golf courses; many of the city's courses are municipal, open-to-the-public courses. **Rancho Park** (10460 W. Pico Blvd.; ☎ **310-838-7373**) is gorgeous and challenging — Arnold Palmer once took 12 strokes to finish the 18th hole. The **Armand Hammer Pitch-n-Putt** (601 Club View Dr.; ☎ **310-276-1604**) is located in Tony Holmby Hills. **Griffith Park**'s courses include the 9-hole Roosevelt (2650 N. Vermont Ave.; ☎ **323-665-2011**) and the 18-hole Wilson and Harding courses (4730 Crystal Springs Dr.; ☎ **323-663-2555**). The courses were built in the 1920s. All are tournament quality, and all provide golf-club rental. For a complete listing of municipal courses, go to www.laparks.org/dos/golf/golf.htm.

Tennis

In Los Angeles, you can find convenient courts in Westwood (1350 Sepulveda Blvd.; ☎ **310-575-8299**), West Los Angeles (2551 Motor Ave.; ☎ **310-836-8879**), and Los Feliz (2715 Vermont Canyon; ☎ **323-664-3521**). For more information, go to www.laparks.com/dos/tennis/tennis.htm#pay. West Hollywood and Beverly Hills also offer public courts at La Cienega Park (325 S. La Cienega Blvd., Beverly Hills; ☎ **310-550-4765**) and Roxbury Park (471 S. Roxbury Dr., Beverly Hills; ☎ **310-550-4979**).

West Hollywood's courts at Plummer Park (1200 N. Vista St.; ☎ **323-876-8180**; Internet: www.weho.org/hsd/recreation/index.cfm) are popular and packed.

Spectator Sports

If you're a sports fan, you can have a very good time, indeed, in L.A. The five major professional sports teams, the **Lakers** (NBA basketball), the **Clippers** (NBA basketball), the **Sparks** (WNBA basketball), the **Dodgers** (MLB baseball), and the **Kings** (NHL hockey), are big draws and receive national coverage.

For some time, L.A. has been without a **professional football team** (down from a high of two!); this is something that only occasionally seems to bother anyone. But there is **college football,** in the form of a decades-long fierce rivalry between **UCLA** and **USC.** The University of California Los Angeles (UCLA) plays at the Rose Bowl in Pasadena; the University of Southern California (USC) uses the Coliseum near Downtown. Football tickets, with very few exceptions, are easy to get for both UCLA and USC home games. Occasionally, one of these teams plays a top-name team, and then it's harder to find tickets (even these games rarely sell out).

Tickets are difficult to get for **college basketball games** at UCLA, because season ticket holders have held all the prime locations for about 37 years now. Some individual games don't sell out (all the big ones do), so you may be able to walk up and buy one for one-third to one-half of the games, perhaps more. But that wasn't the case until recent years. The USC basketball ticket is the easiest to get, because they've been trying to build their own arena for over 30 years. During the time the Trojans have left to play in the 40-year-old Sports Arena (pending construction of a new arena), they will have thousands of tickets available for almost every game (the only one you may have difficulty getting a ticket for is the UCLA/USC game).

For ticket information for **UCLA** football and basketball games, contact the UCLA General Ticket Office at ☎ **310-825-2101,** or go online (Internet: http://uclabruins.fansonly.com/tickets/ucla-tickets.html). For ticket information for **USC** football and basketball games, contact the USC ticket office at ☎ **213-740-4672,** or go online (Internet: http://usctrojans.fansonly.com/marketplace/tickets/tickets-body.html).

World champs: Los Angeles Lakers

With back-to-back-to-back world championships (2000, 2001, and 2002) as well as two of the most well-known players in basketball — Shaquille O'Neal and Kobe Bryant — the Lakers are the most dominant franchise in basketball. Mere mortals can't really get tickets, thanks to the popularity of this powerhouse team and the buckets of money spent on the Lakers' still relatively new home, the Staples Center (☎ **877-673-6799;** Internet: www.staplescenter.com), a state-of-the-art arena in Downtown L.A. In other words, you can give up dreams of just strolling in and buying tickets to sit courtside next to Jack Nicholson and Dyan Cannon. But don't despair: Although season ticket holders have snatched up all the seats by the time you read this for, well, just about every season until the end of time, you may still be able to buy tickets either through local ticket brokers (expect to pay a premium) or on eBay (because season ticket holders do unload single game tickets there). Otherwise, tickets are officially only available through Ticketmaster or at Ticketmaster outlets around the city (Tower Records, The Wherehouse, and Robinsons-May stores). Hey, you never know — some of those limited cheap seats

($22, the least expensive) *waaaay* up in the rafters may still be available (check the team's Web site at www.nba.com/lakers/ or www.staplescenter.com). For ticket info only, write to: **Los Angeles Lakers,** 555 N. Nash St., El Segundo, CA 90245. Note that parking is fiendishly expensive, and traffic is nasty on game nights. You may want to use the MetroRail subway, which has an outlet right near the Staples Center.

Up-and-comers: Los Angeles Clippers

Not so long ago, it was considered acceptable, if not expected, to roll your eyes and snicker whenever the Clippers came up in conversation. Such was the lowly opinion held by sports-loving Angelinos of its second-tier NBA team. Sure, the Clippers remain a young, frisky bunch, but they've become a team to be reckoned with of late, with the addition of wise-beyond-his-years Elton Brand and a handful of talented guys who have the legs to play all night. This may be the time to see them for yourselves. The Clippers also play in the Staples Center in Downtown L.A. (see the previous blurb on the Lakers for the location and ticket information). For Clippers information, call ☎ **213-745-0400** or go to www.nba.com/clippers.

Belles of the basketball: Los Angeles Sparks

While the NBA men hibernate through the summer, the women come out to play. The WNBA Sparks play at the Staples Center from May through August (see the preceding section on the Lakers for the location and ticket information). For Sparks information, call ☎ **310-330-2434** or go to www.wnba.com/sparks.

Former Bums of Brooklyn: Los Angeles Dodgers

The Dodgers were once the "Bums of Brooklyn," where an entire borough's hopes and dreams rested on their rise and fall. They broke the hearts of countless fans by moving to L.A. in 1958. (By then, they had already made history by signing Jackie Robinson, the first African-American major league ball player.) Overall, Dodger Stadium is one the most attractive parks in the country, thanks to a graceful shape and a picturesque setting (the audience gazes out over the field to foothills with palm trees dotting the horizon). Naturally, there are frequent rumblings that it needs to be torn down and made more fancy.

Season ticket holders have snapped up the good seats, but you can still get tickets for these prime spots. Not only do season ticket holders dump their seats through eBay and ticket brokers, they also hand them off to scalpers who can be found waving extra tickets on the roads leading up to the ballpark. Or you can get really sneaky by buying the cheap seats, which generally do remain available up to game time for many dates (so just getting inside isn't that hard, and it's rather cost-effective if you sit in the upper levels), and moving closer (from the foul lines inward to home plate) during the game when you see that a number of those season ticket snots haven't shown up, and their seats are empty and begging for someone to sit in them. Just be discreet and move if the rightful owner does show. And if you really want to do like the natives, show up around the third inning and leave right after the seventh-inning stretch, regardless of the score. Maybe L.A. doesn't deserve a team like the Brooklyn Dodgers.

Tickets can be purchased at the box office (1000 Elysian Park Ave.; Monday through Saturday 9 a.m.–5 p.m., and during games), online (www.dodgers.mlb.com), or over the phone (☎ 323-224-1-HIT). Tickets are $6 to $21 for adults, and $4 for kids under 12 (the latter available 1½ hours before game time on day of game only). There is ample parking at the stadium, but it does get slow and crowded, so consider arriving early. Also, unless you arrange for handicapped parking, there is a very long walk from the parking lot to the stadium, and there are many, many stairs to climb inside the stadium (there are elevators, but they're small and limited to those who really need them).

L.A. on ice: The Los Angeles Kings

The Los Angeles Kings play hockey in the Staples Center (see the preceding section on the Lakers), thanks to Jack Kent Cooke, who founded the team in the late 1960s on the premise that many Canadians had moved to Southern California. Unfortunately, Mr. Cooke discovered that the reason they had moved was because they hated hockey. Nonetheless, the team has at times been exciting enough to draw a solid following, although they've never won the championship. Thus, tickets, which are priced from $19 to $325, are scarce but not as pricey as those for the Lakers. You can order tickets online (www.lakings.com) or over the phone (☎ 888-KINGS-LA).

And speaking of hockey, the Los Angeles area is also home to the **Mighty Ducks.** They're located in Anaheim and owned by Disney. And they're called "The Mighty Ducks," for cryin' out loud. Oh, all right, for ticket information, check out the team's Web site (www.mightyducks.com) or call ☎ 877-WILDWING.

Structural L.A.

Okay, L.A. is not, we admit, the most impressive-looking of cities, at least to the naked eye. It lacks the *fin de siècle* romance of Rome, Paris, and London. It lacks the impressive skyline of Manhattan. It lacks the Victorian aesthetic of San Francisco.

But L.A. used to have some of those impressive features — well, the Victoriana, at least — in fact, it had more than its share of gingerbread Victorian buildings back in the day (see "A taste of Victorian L.A." in Chapter 16). But earthquakes and fires took their toll, and, more to the point, so did development and lack of hind- or foresight. (After all, this is the city where your humble travel-book writer keeps pointing out parking lots and strip malls, mumbling things like, "and that used to be the Brown Derby.")

However, L.A. still has its architectural landmarks: Some are significant, some are historical, and some are just plain wacky. From Frank Lloyd Wright, Rudolph Schindler, and Richard Neutra to hot dog stands shaped like hot dogs to, yes, a sprinkling of Victorians, we've got a list of L.A. landmarks well worth checking out. Don't want to do it for yourself? **Architecture Tours LA** (P.O. Box 93134, Los Angeles, CA 90093; ☎ **323-464-7868;** E-mail: info@architecturetoursla.com) offers several 2-hour tours, ranging from overviews and highlights of L.A. architecture to specific programs designed around various neighborhoods and their own special look (the Pasadena tour might specialize in Greene & Greene, for example, while the Silver Lake tour gives you plenty of Neutra and Schindler). Customized tours are also available. The owner has a master's in architecture history, and she conducts most of the tours herself in a 1962 vintage Caddie.

Buildings you can just drive by and look at

Capitol Records Building
Hollywood

It looks like a stack of records, it does, complete with stylus (remember those?) on top. They claim that's a coincidence. We doubt it. Elvis once said his great ambition was to play on the roof.

1750 Vine St.

Griffith Observatory
Los Angeles

This gleaming white jewel crowning a Griffith Park hillside will be closed during the lifetime of this book, but it's worth noting nonetheless. It will open again (probably in 2005) with a brand-new facelift, a fine new theater, and updated exhibits to aid visitors in better understanding what they see as they gaze toward the heavens. (A fundraiser for the renovation included a hefty donation by Leonard Nimoy, who seems to have accepted that he is indeed Spock.) This glorious Art Deco structure (you can see it in the climatic scene in *Rebel Without A Cause* — there is even a bust of James Dean at the observatory) has one of the best views in all of L.A. See if you can drive up fairly close to take advantage of the view (which, of course, can vary depending on the weather and smog level).

2800 E. Observatory Rd. (in Griffith Park at the end of Vermont Ave.). ☎ *323-664-1191.*

Former Charlie Chaplin Studios
Hollywood

It's a bird, it's a plane, it's a . . . frog? Dressed like . . . Charlie Chaplin? What gives? It's simple enough; in 1918, Charlie Chaplin built his own studio (back when the road was just dirt) in this charming English Tudor style. It later became the long-time home of A&M Records. In 2000, the studio was bought by the Jim Henson Company. The new owners understood the importance of acknowledging one's roots, so they put a giant statue of Kermit, dressed as the Little Tramp tipping his hat to Charlie, on the roof. Go by and wave hi.

1416 La Brea Ave. (at Sunset Blvd.).

Tail O' the Pup
West Hollywood

It's a hot-dog stand shaped like a hot dog in a bun. So simple. So sublime. So utterly ridiculous. (We miss representational architecture. We really do.)

San Vincente Blvd. (between Beverly Blvd. and Melrose Ave.). ☎ *310-652-4517.*

Buildings you can — and should — tour

Bradbury Building
Downtown

The Bradbury Building is an unbelievably fabulous bit of turn-of-the-20th-century architecture. Don't think of it as Victorian, for this office building (which still has commercial tenants) was way ahead of its time. (You can argue that the results are noir in a Raymond-Chandler kind of way, but even that doesn't do it justice.) Five floors surround an indoor courtyard. The courtyard is an airy atrium that combines tile, brick, wrought iron, marble, oak, and glass, and bedazzles as a result.

304 N. Broadway (at 3rd St.). ☎ *213-626-1893.*

Gamble House
Pasadena

Arts and Crafts fans should not miss this building, which is perhaps the high point of the career of the famous architect team of Greene & Greene.

The two-story home, built in 1908, has Mission detailing (everything from windows to light switches to wood grooves) done to a fair-thee-well, and all is lovingly maintained. You can see it by tour only (which lasts an hour). Don't miss the bookshop, which has helped many a preservationist, or just enthusiast, re-create period touches for their own homes; it's run by knowledgeable clerks, eager to help you find that piece of Batchelder-inspired tile.

4 Westmoreland Pl. ☎ *626-793-3334. Admission: $8 general admission, $5 seniors and students, children under 12 free. Hours: Thurs–Sun noon to 3 p.m. (Arrive early, because they sometimes sell out.)*

Downtown delights

L.A. may not have a traditional city center, but it does have some jewels. **Central Library** (recently renamed for former L.A. Mayor Richard Rhiordan; 630 W. 5th St.; ☎ 213-228-7000) was built in the 1920s around a fabulous Egyptian-revival motif (which explains some of the statues and rotundas, but it doesn't explain certain ceilings adorned with huge rafters, or those medieval murals). Badly damaged in an arson fire in 1986, it was gloriously restored, including a splendid (if not, to our mind, organic to the whole) atrium. **Union Station** (Alameda St. at Cesar Chavez Ave.) is an increasingly archaic, but no less delightful, tribute to the glory days of railroad travel. It was constructed as part of the WPA projects. Today, the railroad station contains several public art installations thanks to the Blue Line MetroRail, which runs through here. Many parts are no longer used, though some of them can be rented out for parties. While the 1927 **City Hall** is no longer the tallest building in L.A. (it hasn't been since the 1950s), it's still one of the most distinctive structures in the city; it stood in for the Daily Planet office in the *Superman* TV series (200 N. Spring St.; ☎ 213-473-5870). Because parking Downtown can be atrocious, take the MetroRail instead and use the DASH to get around between stops.

Legacies of the giants of architecture

Some of the giants of architecture, particularly within the area of residence-design, worked in Los Angeles, and each left a lasting legacy. Although Spanish-influenced homes (thanks in large part to **Wallace Neff,** who favored old-world styles) and Arts and Crafts–style housing (in large part drawn from the inspired work of architects **Greene & Greene**, whose "ultimate bungalows" are still found around Southern California) immediately evoke quintessential early Los Angeles, it was arguably the advent of the great **Frank Lloyd Wright** that changed California forever. Not only did he leave behind a number of extraordinary buildings, but it was thanks to him that **Rudolph Schindler** came to town. Schindler started working with the master in 1920 and eventually became the first to design buildings that took true advantage of California's unique climate. From 1922 to his death in 1953, he designed houses and commercial buildings that are considered landmarks in the modern architectural movement. Then came **Richard Neutra,** a former schoolmate of Schindler's, who worked with him for a few years and became, in his own right, one of the most important modern architects in Los Angeles. Schindler and Neutra were essentially responsible for creating the California look; indeed, it was Schindler who designed the "California House" — a one-story dwelling with an open floor plan and a flat roof, which opened to the garden through sliding doors while turning its back to the street — which became a staple of post-war housing.

In the following sections, we introduce and detail a few of the key houses for each of the architects, although there are plenty more to be seen.

Schindler House

Schindler's own home and studio served as what was perhaps one of the first New Age hippie communes; it was an experiment in artistic and healthy living, full of nuts, berries, natural fibers, and few rules for kids. It's also a highly influential structure, known for its simplicity and integration of both outdoor and indoor space. It currently houses the MAK center for Art and Architecture in Los Angeles (835 N. Kings Rd.; ☎ 323-651-1510; Admission: $5, free Fri 4–6 p.m. and on Sept 10, Schindler's birthday; Open: Wed through Sun 11 a.m.–6 p.m.).

Works from Frank Lloyd Wright

The legendary architect Frank Lloyd Wright left a number of his works behind him in L.A.; here are three that are regularly open to the public. Hours vary, so please call in advance to find out the latest hours and the tours they offer.

Freeman House was built by Frank Lloyd Wright as an experiment in affordable mass-produced housing. The textile block structure is what sets it apart from any tract house you may have seen (1962 Glencoe Way; ☎ 323-851-0671). Having said that, the **Ennis-Brown House** really has to be seen to be believed. The house, patterned after a Mayan temple, was built in 1924. It is located in the Los Feliz hills near Griffith Park. It's a breathtaking piece of work, perhaps the most extraordinary private residence in the United States. Trust us when we say that this is one of the (alas, not too well-known) highlights of L.A., and think of us as you gasp when you step into the living room. Regular tours and special packages are offered (2655 Glendower Ave.; ☎ 323-660-0607; Internet: www.ennisbrownhouse.org).

Hollyhock House was built between 1919 and 1921 for an oil baroness who, a few years later, donated it and the 60-plus-acre hillside it rested on to the city of L.A. It is now part of **Barnsdall Art Park** (where affordable art classes are offered for adults and children, along with rotating exhibitions), an oasis of calm and trees in a surprising urban setting (a decidedly unglamorous stretch of Hollywood Boulevard). The house and park were undergoing extensive renovations and were closed as this book was going to press, but the plans (and hope) were that both would reopen by late 2002 (4800 Hollywood Blvd.; ☎ 213-473-8434).

Applause, Please: Touring Studios and Going to a TV Taping

This is Tinseltown, so of course you want to see Hollywood in action. Note that, as of this writing, in reaction to September 11, many of the television and movie studios have cut or at least severely curtailed their tour offerings. The tour schedules are likely to have changed by the time you read this, but we urge you to call in advance.

Studio tours

NBC Studios
Burbank

This 70-minute behind-the-scenes walking tour lets you check out the sets of *The Tonight Show with Jay Leno,* wardrobe, makeup, special effects and sound effects sets, and set construction demonstrations. You should call at least 2 weeks in advance for tickets.

3000 W. Alameda, Burbank. ☎ *818-840-3538. Admission: $7 adults, $6.25 seniors, $3.75 children 5–12, and children under 5 free. Open: Mon–Fri 9 a.m.–3 p.m. on first-come basis.*

Paramount Studios
Hollywood

This 2-hour narrative walking tour features a historical and informative overview of the renowned movie and television lot. Highlights include a working soundstage (when available), a brief movie clip, an Oscar show-case, and photos taken at the *Forrest Gump* bench.

5555 Melrose Ave., Hollywood. ☎ *323-956-4552. Admission: $15 Adults and children 10 and over, no one under 10 admitted. Open: Mon–Fri (call for hours).*

Sony Pictures Studios
Culver City

This 2-hour walking tour guides visitors through the facets of a real working studio (home to Columbia Pictures and Columbia TriStar Television).

Visit the archival museum, watch movie clips in a private screening room, sneak a peek at artists painting scenic backdrops, and visit the stage sets of current television shows.

10202 W. Washington Blvd., Culver City. ☎ 323-520-TOUR. Admission: $20 adults and children 12 and over, no one under 12 admitted. Open: Mon–Fri (call for hours).

Universal Studios Hollywood
Universal City

Enjoy a behind-the-scenes tour of the world's biggest motion picture and TV studio. Attractions include the new The Mummy Returns: Chamber of Doom, as well as Terminator 2 3-D, Back to the Future, and Jurassic Park The Ride. Nickelodeon Blast Zone and Animal Planet Live! are geared toward families.

100 Universal City Plaza, Universal City. ☎ 818-508-9600. Admission: $39 adults and children 12 and older, $34 seniors, $29 children 3–11, free for children under 3. Call for hours.

Warner Brothers Studio Tour
Burbank

Visitors to this working movie and TV studio observe filming whenever possible. The 2-hour tour includes a film collage (Errol Flynn to Denzel Washington), the Warner Bros. Museum, historic backlots, cavernous soundstages, and what they bill as "the world's most extensive costume department."

Gate 4, Hollywood Way and Olive Ave., Burbank. ☎ 818-972-TOUR. Admission: $30. Open: Mon–Fri 9 a.m.–3 p.m.

TV tapings

For tickets to live tapings of TV shows, contact **Audiences Unlimited** at ☎ 818-753-3470, or go to their Web site (www.tvtickets.com). They provide audiences for over two dozen shows, and their schedule is updated daily, listing available shows up to 30 days in advance. Your best chance of getting tickets is to request shows that are new or aren't big hits. The highest-rated comedies sell out months in advance, so don't plan a special trip on the off chance that you'll get tickets to your favorite show.

Audiences Unlimited also has a booth inside Universal Studios, near the tour departure area, that provides tickets for shows taping that day. They often provide bus transportation from Universal Studios to the set of the show. For details on show requirements (some talk shows include shots of the audience, for example, and may require a dress code for some tapings), go to Audiences Unlimited's Web site or voice mailbox.

Universal City & Nearby Studios

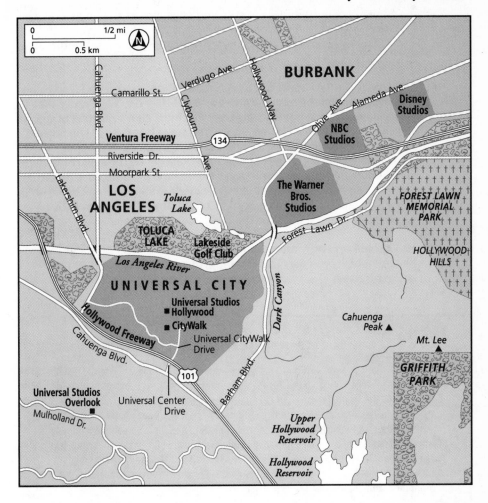

Note: **Paramount Studios** offer the opportunity to be an audience member at shows taped on the Paramount lot. Call ☎ **323-956-1777** for tickets and information. Tickets are released five business days prior to a taping; you can call and ask what shows have seats available. A show that tapes on a Thursday will release tickets the previous Wednesday.

Some general rules and tips for attending a TV taping:

✔ All TV shows begin taping in the early evening, and audience members are requested to line up an hour in advance.

✔ You must be over 18 to attend. Photo ID is a must.

✔ No backpacks or large bags are permitted. Security is very tight at studios in the aftermath of 9/11.

✔ No photos can be taken during the taping.

✔ There are potty breaks for the audience, because tapings usually take 4 hours, but audience members will not be fed. Some studios do allow discreet snacking; bring non-noisy foods, be unobtrusive, and pick up after yourself.

TV tapings can be a thrill and an economical way to have a real show-biz experience to tell the folks back home. What they don't tell you is that you will be sitting for a very long time. For most shows, seating begins in the late afternoon. A warm-up act will tell some jokes to get you relaxed, and then the taping begins. TV show scenes are often shot out of sequence, especially if there is more than one set on the stage or if there are children in the show. (Producers like to tape the little ones first to stay in compliance with labor laws.) Scenes are shot multiple times to allow for different camera angles — and yes, they think it would be nice if you laugh every single time the stars offer up the same joke.

You should probably attend a TV taping at least once. Although, after having done it, you may understand why natives get jaded and rarely go themselves.

The art of the card

As you wander L.A., you will often be approached by someone offering tickets to a free movie screening. These are test screenings of early cuts of upcoming features. At the end of the movie screening, you will be asked to fill out a card rating the movie. It's no small deal — important and lasting decisions are often made based on these cards. A famous example is *The Big Chill,* which originally ended with a shot of the whole gang, including the character who committed suicide, alive and well, back during their college heydays. The audience hated it, and that's why the only visible parts of Kevin Costner, who played the character who committed suicide, are his wrists in the opening scene.

The practice is derided by moviemakers and critics alike, but it's also here to stay. Art's loss is your gain; you can see some high-profile flicks way in advance. Lie like crazy if you have any connection at all to the entertainment business; otherwise they won't want you at the screening. Tickets are free, but screenings are sometimes held at inconvenient times. They always tell you the title and stars of the movie so that you can decide whether it's worth your time or not.

Chapter 18

A Shopper's Guide to Los Angeles

. . . .

In This Chapter

▶ The skinny on shopping L.A.

▶ The big boys (and girls) of retailing

▶ Shopping by neighborhood

▶ A mall primer

▶ Where to find that special something

. . . .

*L*os Angeles may lack for ancient monuments, but it doesn't want for ways to lighten your wallet. None too surprisingly, the City of Disposable Income offers much in the way of fine shopping, from the very best of designer clothing to some of the most curious and wacky stores anywhere. Shopping is a major activity in this city, and though we admit that it may not be as mentally stimulating as a couple of hours in, say, the Getty Museum, browsing is a perfectly legitimate cultural pastime. Plus, think of the people-watching possibilities. Come up with your own justifications; for us, shopping is just plain fun. Herewith is the nitty-gritty on shopping L.A.

Making the Shopping Scene

You can buy just about anything you want in L.A., in a variety of price ranges. If you're looking for ultra-high-end stores, head to legendary **Rodeo Drive** (where we, frankly, can't even afford the oxygen). For all things trendy, try **Melrose Avenue** (where punk rock first went mainstream). For the cheap stuff, keep reading. You can give your wardrobe a facelift, refurnish your house, or just buy a little something for the folks back home. And keep your eyes open: There's nothing a TV star making $1 million an episode likes better than spending some of that hard cash, and he or she could easily be doing so *right next to you.*

Where the sales are

The major department stores and malls tend to have sales during most holiday weekends (Labor Day, President's Day, Memorial Day, and so on), to say nothing of their half-price, let's-get-rid-of-stuff sales right after Christmas and their back-to-school events beginning around mid-August. Right before these events begin, the *Los Angeles Times* is crammed with full-page ads, which often have coupons that promise still more discounts.

Open and shut

In the greater Los Angeles area, most stores open at 10 a.m., Monday through Saturday, and close between 6 and 7 p.m. On Sunday, most stores open at 11 a.m. *Exceptions:* Some bookstores and record stores stay open late every night, some mall shops stay open until 8 or 9 p.m., and some stores in Beverly Hills decline to open at all on Sundays. It's always best to call ahead.

Divine inspiration

The biggest shopping event of the year is probably the **Divine Design sale,** held the first week in December. Hundreds of clothing, housewares, and accessory designers donate extra goods and samples, which are then offered to the public at steep discounts that decline sharply each day. Nervy shoppers try to stick it out as long as they can, watching the prices plummet to 75% off by the last day. Crowds are big, bargains are bigger, and every penny goes to Project Angel Food, which supplies hot meals to the ill and otherwise housebound. In other words, you can do good while indulging yourself — what a deal! The most recent event was held at the Barker Hanger of the Santa Monica Air Center, and it's likely to be held there again; call ☎ **323-845-1800** or go to www.angelfood.org for more information.

Checking Out the Big Names

You won't want for basic department stores in Los Angeles. The nicest of the mainstream ones are **Macy's** (Downtown: 750 W. 7th St., ☎ **213-628-9311;** Beverly Center: 8500 Beverly Blvd., ☎ **310-854-6655**), **Robinsons-May** (Downtown: Citicorp Plaza, 920 7th St., ☎ **213-683-1144;** Beverly Hills: 9900 Wilshire Blvd., ☎ **310-275-5464**), and **Nordstrom** (Westside Pavilion: 10830 West Pico Blvd., ☎ **310-470-6155;** Howard Hughes Center: 6081 Center Dr., ☎ **310-641-4046**). **J.C. Penney** and **Mervyn's** (various locations) are a little more, oh, let's try not to be snobbish and say, um, *economical.* These are the spots to do basic shopping, where you can expect to find typical brand-name goods.

Then you have those stores with real star-spotting potential. If you have the figure and the financial wherewithal, head over to **Barneys New York** (9570 Wilshire Blvd., Beverly Hills; ☎ **310-276-4400**), the only local branch of the fabled fashionista New York department store. It helps to be well-heeled and well-shaped, as you'll find little here that costs under three digits and comes larger than a size 6 — but oh, the filmy lingerie, the Vera Wang dresses, and *the shoes*. It also has some of the best makeup selections in town, including one of the few places to find Kiehl's products. The store is five levels of chic heaven.

You may also want to visit **Fred Segal** (8100 Melrose Ave.; ☎ **323-651-4129** and 500 Broadway, Santa Monica; ☎ **310-458-9940**). If Carrie Bradshaw from *Sex and the City* lived in L.A., she would be here every single day. As it is, Gwyneth Paltrow makes up for her. Actually, to heck with the clothes (hip), the shoes (flimsy and gorgeous), and the accessories (trendy) — the star spotting is so good here that one wag quipped that celeb hounds may just as well set up a lawn chair and a cooler in the parking lot and make a day of it. Although it looks like a bunch of different stores or stalls cobbled together under one roof, it's really just one store. The salespeople appear terrifying (perhaps they are), but they seem to care about their jobs, so don't be intimidated.

Taking It to the Street

Sure, the big names, the sprawling malls, and the steel-and glass behemoths of commerce are at your disposal. But come on: Did you really come to Los Angeles to sift through the same old stuff at the same old places you can patronize in your own backyard? Here are some shopping venues, street markets, and thrift shops where you are likely to chance upon that truly unique gewgaw or thoroughly L.A. memento.

Vintage and resale

In a glamour capital like Los Angeles, it makes sense that people would recycle their clothes with more regularity than they recycle their bottles and cans. And, in a town where dressing to impress can mean sporting a pair of 40-year-old Levi's with a $4,000 leather jacket, it's important to know where to go to get your goods. Only a few folks can actually afford $4,000 for a coat, however, so it's also important to know the tricks of dressing well for less.

Vintage designer clothes have been made popular by actresses like Winona Ryder, Chloe Sevigny, and Julia Roberts. **Paper Bag Princess** (8700 Santa Monica Blvd., West Hollywood; ☎ **310-358-1985**) and **Decades** (8214 Melrose Ave., West Hollywood; ☎ **323-655-0223**) both offer vintage wear from the likes of Halston, Chanel, and Pucci. Be prepared to drop some heavy cash for highly collectible names. You can find basic vintage clothes at dozens of outlets. **Aardvarks** (7579 Melrose Ave.; ☎ 323-655-6769), **Squaresville** (1800 Vermont Ave.; ☎ 323-669-8464 and 7312 Melrose Ave.; ☎ 323-525-1425), **Jet Rag** (825 N. La Brea Ave.; ☎ 323-939-0528), and **Muskrat** (1248 Third Street Promenade, Santa Monica; ☎ 310-394-1713) are some of the best, with wide selections and price ranges. **American Rag** (150 S. La Brea Ave.; ☎ 323-935-3154) and **Wasteland** (7428 Melrose Ave.; ☎ 323-653-3028) charge more for vintage designer pieces than they do for the racks of plain vintage clothes lining their stores. You may find that certain types of used jeans and tennis shoes are worth hundreds of dollars!

When women (and some men) tire of their pricey designer duds, they often resell them to **consignment shops,** such as the **Address Boutique** (1116 Wilshire Blvd., Santa Monica; ☎ 310-394-1406), **Monopoly** (8421 W. 3rd St.; ☎ 323-655-8480), or **P.J. London** (11661 San Vincente Blvd.; ☎ 310-826-4649). With consignment shops, prices are 20% or more below retail, the clothes are usually only a season or so old, and you can find a wide array of sizes.

Thrift shops can often be a source of cool clothes, but the previously listed vintage stores regularly raid them to flesh out their own stock. **Out of the Closet,** a store that benefits the AIDS Healthcare Foundation, has a dozen locations in the greater Los Angeles area. The Fairfax (360 N. Fairfax Blvd.; ☎ 323 934-1956) and Hollywood (1408 Vine St., Hollywood; ☎ 323-467-6811) locations are home to two of the largest Out of the Closet stores. The Santa Monica branch of the **Salvation Army** (1665 10th St., Santa Monica; ☎ 310-450-7235) is huge, and so is the Hollywood-area **Goodwill** (4575 Hollywood Blvd.; ☎ 323-644-1517).

Flea markets

Flea markets are major scenes in L.A.; many locals attend them religiously. Flea market addicts know to arrive as soon as the doors open; otherwise, you can kiss the true bargains and finds good-bye. Still, these are the places to pick up one-of-a-kind souvenirs, articles of clothing, and unique furniture, household goods, and accessories. Wear sunblock and comfy shoes, bring cash in small bills, and prepare to haggle. Buy only what you love, and leave the rest for someone else.

Churches and schools hold **swap meets** as fundraisers; these giant rummage/tag sales are often not worth the time.

Those big buildings you see with "Swap Meet" painted on the side are simply mini-malls stocked with cheap T-shirts, off-brand tennis shoes, and strange plastic utensils.

The **Melrose Trading Post** (Fairfax High School, 7859 Melrose Ave.), held every Sunday from 9 a.m. to 4 p.m., is packed with vendors selling all types of clothes, antiques, and knickknacks — it's a huge garage sale/party with plenty of bargains and a $2 admission fee.

Not your local thrift shop

When film, television, and video productions need to dump wardrobes after they've served their purpose, **It's A Wrap** (3315 West Magnolia Blvd., Burbank; ☎ **818-567-7366**) is happy to provide an outlet. This is a great place to pick up a soap-opera-fan souvenir, such as a T-shirt worn by a favorite hero or villain. Clothes, shoes, and accessories are labeled with the name of the show or film they are from and the name of the actor who wore them. Prices range from $10 to thousands of dollars, with the latter being the price for a specific costume worn by, say, Arnold Schwarzenegger in a major film. Keep in mind that many actresses are teeny-tiny (size 4 or under), so you may not find the dress of your dreams to fit, but you'll certainly find some bargains and unique gifts.

Plan to get to the second-Sunday-of-the-month **Pasadena Rose Bowl Flea Market** (1001 Rose Bowl Dr., Pasadena; ☎ **323-560-7469**; Admission: $6 from 9 a.m. to 3 p.m., $10 from 7:30 a.m. to 9:00 a.m., $15 from 6:00 a.m. to 7:30 a.m., and free for children age 12 and under) early, by say 8 a.m. Although, in the latter part of the day, vendors are willing to make a deal on whatever dregs are left at their stands. You'll find more than 2,000 stalls, which hold everything from old lunchboxes and LPs to ashtrays and fur coats. The **Pasadena City College Flea Market** (1570 E. Colorado Blvd., Pasadena; ☎ **626-585-7906**) is held on the first Sunday of each month. It's not as overwhelmingly large, but it's still full of cool stuff. The flea market is open from 8 a.m. to 3 p.m., and admission is free.

Farmers markets

Not to be confused with the permanent buildings on Fairfax known as the Farmers Market (although produce is naturally in abundance there on a daily basis), L.A.'s farmers markets are weekly neighborhood events where vendors from various parts of the Southland gather to hawk their wares. Local chefs, both professional and home-based, shop at the markets, because they know that the best cooking is dictated by the season. Naturally, the joints jump more during spring and summer, when produce productivity is at its highest, and choices run amok. Organic produce has a high profile — this is L.A., after all — but the offerings are not exclusively organic. Many of the stands feature wonderful fresh breads, prepared foods, and even clothing.

The two largest and most popular farmers markets are **Santa Monica** (Arizona Ave. between 2nd St. and 3rd St.; ☎ **323-661-4380**; Open: Wednesday from 9 a.m. to 2 p.m. and Saturday from 8:30 a.m. to 1:00 p.m.) and **Hollywood** (Ivar St. and Selma St. between Sunset and Hollywood Blvds.; ☎ **323-463-3171**; Open: Sunday from 8 a.m. to 1 p.m.).

The Best Shopping Neighborhoods

The many neighborhoods that make up Los Angeles are rich with shopping areas. Some neighborhoods sport giant malls, such as the **Beverly Center,** the **Glendale Galleria,** or the **Century City Mall** (see "Hitting the Shopping Malls," later in this chapter), while others — such as **Melrose, Rodeo Drive, Sunset Plaza, Main Street, Vermont,** and **Montana** — developed organically to serve the changing needs of their residents. The malls may be rife with teenagers with too much money or time on their hands, but the neighborhoods are where the hardcore really come to do their business. In each of the following neighborhoods, you get genuine pedestrian action, just like real cities!

Melrose Avenue: The ultimate scene

The ultimate scene is to be found on **Melrose Avenue** between Fairfax and La Brea Boulevards, especially on weekends, when music blasts from every storefront. Youth culture propels the street. The neighborhood also has a few retirement homes, from which senior citizens can watch punk rockers with unnaturally bright-colored hair, and tourists, who meander from shop to shop, loaded with purchases.

Melrose may no longer be the true cutting-edge mecca it was in the '80s, but it's still the place to come for clothes and style. **Retail Slut** (7308 Melrose Ave.; ☎ 323-934-1339) is one of the original retailers on Melrose, stocking shocking garb and glittery goods. **Shrine** (7574 Melrose Ave; ☎ 323-655-1485) has ghoulish gear for the Goth set. Trendy styles and retro wear line both sides of the street. You can find Doc Marten shoes (half-a-dozen stores stock them) and vintage clothes at such stores as **Wasteland** (7428 Melrose Ave., ☎ 323-653-3028) and **Aardvark's** (7579 Melrose Ave., ☎ 323-655-6769). You can buy silver jewelry at **Maya** (7452 Melrose Ave.; ☎ 323-655-2708) and expensive antique jewelry at **Wanna Buy a Watch** (7366 Melrose Ave.; ☎ 323-653-0467). For the latest music, as well as new and used discs, check out **Beat Non-stop** (7262 Melrose Ave.; ☎ 323-930-2121), **Vinyl Fetish** (7305 Melrose Ave.; ☎ 323-935-1300), and **Bleecker Bob's** (7555½ Melrose Ave.; ☎ 323-951-9111).

The west end of Melrose, from Fairfax to Doheny, is the more grownup section of this busy retail district. Lined with antiques shops and clothing boutiques, this portion of Melrose offers a soothing respite from the frantic trendiness of the eastern section. Revive and relax your senses at **Spirituali** (7928 Melrose Ave.; ☎ 323-653-3471), a candle and aromatherapy boutique that provides gift baskets for celebrities and regular folks, before blowing your mind over the racy lingerie at **Agent Provocateur** (7961 Melrose Ave.; ☎ 323-653-0229) or blowing your souvenir budget on Disney collectibles at **Fantasies Come True**

(8012 Melrose Ave.; ☎ **323-655-2636**). **Ruby Mae** (7959½ Melrose Ave.; ☎ **323-651-4086**) offers romantic, frilly sundresses, while **Xin** (8064 Melrose Ave.; ☎ **323-653-2188**) delivers clean, minimalist designs for women. **Miu Miu** (8025 Melrose Ave.; ☎ **323-651-0072**), showcasing Prada's secondary line, and **Costume National** (8001 Melrose Ave.; ☎ **323-655-8160**), the Gap for the very rich, are across the street from the high-fashion haven **Fred Segal** (8118 Melrose Ave., Los Angeles; ☎ **323-651-1800;** see "Checking Out the Big Names," earlier in the chapter). And for the vintage shopper, **Decades** (8214 Melrose Ave., West Hollywood; ☎ **323-655-0223**) has plenty of high-end collectible and wearable designer clothes, many of which were once owned by celebrities.

Refreshments can be had at **Sweet Lady Jane** (8360 Melrose Ave., West Hollywood; ☎ **323-653-7145**), where luscious cakes and pastries beckon from the cases. **Urth Café** (8565 Melrose Ave., West Hollywood; ☎ **310-659-0628**) is a favorite with models, actors, agents, and others who are drawn as much to the outdoor see-and-be-seen patio as they are to the organically grown coffees and vegetarian snacks, including an egg-and-butter-free chocolate cake that, despite its lack of "normal" ingredients, is actually good. Across the street, the Zen-style garden at **Elixir** (8612 Melrose Ave., West Hollywood; ☎ **310-657-9300**) is the perfect place to relax with a sparkling tonic made in accordance with Chinese herbal principles.

Melrose West also features a fine selection of bookstores and antiques stores, as well as art galleries. **Dailey Rare Books** (8216 Melrose Ave., West Hollywood; ☎ **323-658-8515**) and **Heritage Books** (8540 Melrose Ave., West Hollywood; ☎ **310-659-3674**) have provided rare and first editions to the likes of Johnny Depp and U2. Visit the world-famous **Bodhi Tree** (8585 Melrose Ave., West Hollywood; ☎ **310-659-1733**), where actress Shirley MacLaine and other less famous folk have received enlightenment (and lightened wallets) amongst the spiritual and pop-religious books, feng shui mirrors, and statues of Egyptian gods. **Open Door** (8275 Melrose Ave., West Hollywood; ☎ **323-653-5296**) and **Grumps** (7965½ Melrose Ave.; ☎ **323-655-3564**) are just two of the antiques shops on Melrose emphasizing American and European furnishings.

From Robertson Boulevard to Doheny Drive, Melrose is lined with design studios for interior decorators and art galleries that have exhibited such familiar artists as Picasso and Maxfield Parrish, as well as rising local painters like Mark Ryden and Sandow Jones.

Melrose has street parking with meters, so bring plenty of quarters. If you decide to park on side streets, read the signs carefully; some areas are permit-parking only; other streets only allow 2-hour parking.

Rodeo Drive and Sunset Plaza: Where the stars are

The heart of the Beverly Hills shopping experience is **Rodeo Drive.** It's loaded with jewels, dripping with furs, and swathed in silk and leather. Do yourself a favor and go on a weekday, and please don't dress like a tourist. In other words, black jeans and a white T-shirt will help you blend in (you will never look as chic and thin as the regulars here, but go ahead and try if you dare), but a pair of shorts and a backpack are no-gos. Check out **Gucci** (347 N. Rodeo Dr.; ☎ 310-278-3451), the store that features the latest in stratospheric fashions, including $300 dog collars, and **Harry Winston** (371 N. Rodeo Dr.; ☎ 310-271-8554), where the stars get their award-show gems. **Tiffany & Company** (210 N. Rodeo Dr.; ☎ 310-273-8880) is located in a mall called **Paseo Rodeo,** which is designed to look like a medieval European street. To the east and west of Rodeo Drive are other Beverly Hills standards, such as **Eidelweiss Chocolates** (444 N. Canon Dr.; ☎ 310-275-0341) and **Fred Hayman** (190 N. Canon Dr.; ☎ 310-271-3100). To the south is Wilshire Boulevard, with big department stores such as **Barney's** (9570 Wilshire Blvd.; ☎ 310-276-4400), **Neiman Marcus** (9700 Wilshire Blvd.; ☎ 310-550-5900), and **Saks Fifth Avenue** (9600 Wilshire Blvd.; ☎ 310-275-4211).

The city of Beverly Hills provides 2 hours of free parking in the city lots, which are clearly marked, and then charges $1 for each additional hour. Lost tickets pay the maximum charge. If you don't park in the Beverly Hills lots, expect to pay at least $5 to park in private lots. You can also search for a parking meter.

Sunset Plaza is one of the oldest and poshest shopping districts in Los Angeles. It lines both sides of Sunset Boulevard, from 8720 Sunset to 8589 Sunset, and is anchored by the celebrity dining spot **Le Dome** (8720 Sunset Blvd.; ☎ 310-659-6919) on the southwest (James Coburn, Elton John) and the celebrity "caffeination" spot **Coffee Bean & Tea Leaf** (8591 Sunset Blvd.; ☎ 310-659-1890) on the northeast (Britney Spears, Mark Wahlburg). Sunset Plaza is also home to superstar retailer **Tracey Ross** (8595 Sunset Blvd., West Hollywood; ☎ 310-854-1996), whose clients include some of the brightest stars in Hollywood, and jeweler **Philip Press** (8601 Sunset Blvd., West Hollywood; ☎ 310-360-1180), which offers fine platinum, gemstones, and diamonds. **Armani Exchange** (8700 W. Sunset Blvd., West Hollywood; ☎ 310-659-0171), **H. Lorenzo** (8660 Sunset Blvd.; Los Angeles; ☎ 310-659-1432), **Calypso** (8635 Sunset Blvd., West Hollywood; ☎ 310-652-4454), and other boutiques beckon. With over a half-dozen restaurants offering sidewalk brunching, lunching, and dining, (expect smokers on the patios), Sunset Plaza provides a wealth of people-watching and a cosmopolitan flair.

Free parking is offered in the Sunset Plaza lots only for people who are eating and shopping at Sunset Plaza. Under no circumstances should you leave your car and go off the boundaries of Sunset Plaza. If you do so, you will be ticketed and/or towed; Sunset Plaza employs undercover security to both safeguard its clientele and ensure that the free parking is not abused. Once again, park at the Sunset Plaza lots *only while you're at Sunset Plaza.*

Third Street: Eclectic energy

Third Street in West Hollywood is very different from Santa Monica's Third Street Promenade. The latter features one chain store and fast-food outlet after another, while the former is an eclectic blend of unique boutiques, antiques shops, bookstores, and restaurants, strung along a three-block section of the city.

Located next door to each other, **Free Hand** (8413 W. 3rd St.; ☎ 323-655-2607) and **New Stone Age** (8407 W. 3rd St.; ☎ 323-658-5969) are high-end shops with handcrafted giftware and objets d'art, including glass, clothing, pottery, and jewelry. **Plastica** (8405 W. 3rd St.; ☎ 323-655-1051), which is located on the same block, celebrates plastic furniture, toys, and household goods.

Antiques at **Memory Lane** (8387 W. 3rd St.; ☎ 323-655-4571) and **Sophie's Stuff** (8377 W. 3rd St.; ☎ 323-651-4325) lean toward vintage collectibles and cool retro housewares. Vintage clothes can be found at **Polka Dots & Moonbeams** (8367 W. 3rd St.; ☎ 323-651-1746) — which also has a shop featuring modern clothes on the same block — while new styles, including handbags and Robert Clergerie shoes, are featured at **Noodle Stories** (8323 W. 3rd St.; ☎ 323-651-1782). **Paul Frank Store** (8101 W. 3rd St.; 323-653-6471) stocks the designer's signature monkey-faced tees, pajamas, and other cute things favored by Britney Spears and Drew Barrymore.

Of three shops that specialize in bathing beauty supplies, we especially like **Glow** (8358½ W. 3rd St.; ☎ 323-782-9080), with its rubber duck selection and luxury bath salts, bath bombs, and scented cocoa butter meltaways. For cute, pricey clothes and toys for babies, go to **Ga Ga** (8362 W. 3rd St.; ☎ 323-653-3388). **Room Service** (8115 W. 3rd St.; ☎ 323-653-4242) has expensive haute-moderne toys, such as metal address books for adults. **Cook's Library** (8375 W. 3rd St.; ☎ 323-655-3141) and **Traveler's Bookcase** (8373 W. 3rd St.; ☎ 323-655-0575) are excellent examples of niche marketing, both well stocked with specialty books on cooking and travel, respectively.

Food fanatics love **Joan's on Third** (8346½ W. 3rd St.; ☎ 323-655-2285), a small cafe with sandwiches, desserts, and salads (see Chapter 14 for more info). Others find respite from their busy shopping at **Chado Tea House** (8422½ W. 3rd St.; ☎ 323-655-2056). After the sun goes down, hipsters fill up on tacos and tequila at campy chic **El Carmen** (8138 W. 3rd St.; ☎ 323-852-1552).

All of Third Street, except the food, has been distilled into one shop, **Zipper** (8316 W. 3rd St.; ☎ 323-951-0620), whose motto, "Art Form +

Function," is demonstrated by the pillows, incense, bathware, toys, books, and gift items attractively displayed and lovingly collected for your viewing and buying pleasure.

Montana Avenue: Upscale boutiques

This Santa Monica beachside community was once a sleepy enclave with little more than a couple of markets, a couple of pharmacies, and some dry cleaners. Then the upscaling began, as the ritzy boutiques and decaf-nonfat-lattes unleashed their relentless assault on Montana Avenue. Even the local funeral parlor was recently torn down; a retail-residential complex will be put up in its place. Thank goodness actor Robert Redford bought the Aero Theatre so that it could not be turned into an overpriced antiques store.

Be careful driving along Montana Avenue — oblivious locals love to jaywalk as they juggle their packages, lattes, baby strollers, and golden retrievers.

Fine silk and velvet dresses with exotic prints beckon at **Harari** (1406 Montana Ave.; ☎ 310-260-1204) and **Citron** (1613 Montana Ave.; ☎ 310-458-6089), while antiques gleam from the windows at **Rosemarie McCaffrey** (1203 Montana Ave.; ☎ 310-395-7711) and **Room with a View** (1600 Montana Ave.; ☎ 310-998-5858). There's plenty of stuff for the wealthy here, including funky one-of-a-kind furnishings at **Raw Style** (1511 Montana Ave.; ☎ 310-458-7662), soul-soothing bath and body care products at **Palmetto** (1034 Montana Ave.; ☎ 310-395-6687), and hip toys and clothes for kids from **Tattle Tales** (1233 Montana Ave.; ☎ 310-899-0962). Guys can find high fashion at **Weathervane for Men** (1132 Montana Ave.; ☎ 310-395-0397) and **Trek & Travel** (1412 Montana Ave.; ☎ 310-260-2500).

Montana Avenue provides street parking with meters; bring quarters. Some parking is available on side streets. Be sure to read signs carefully for time limits.

Vermont Avenue: Boho L.A.

Vermont Avenue is the hip shopping spot for the bohemians of the Los Feliz and Silver Lake areas of Los Angeles, also known as the East Side. From peculiar knickknacks, such as the rubber skulls and tiki statues, at **Y-Que** (1770 N Vermont Ave.; ☎ 323-664-0021; pronounced ee-*kay*) and **Archaic Idiots** (1720 N. Vermont Ave.; ☎ 323-666-6354) to the fine selection of reading material at **Skylight Books** (1818 N. Vermont Ave.; ☎ 323-660-1175) and the interesting clothing boutiques, Vermont provides a quirky view of L.A. life.

Follow Vermont Avenue south to Hollywood Boulevard and turn left to find the irrepressible **Soap Plant/Wacko** (4633 Hollywood Blvd.;

☎ **323-663-0122**). It's really three stores in one (including the La Luz de Jesus Gallery), all originally located on Melrose. If you can't find a gift among the oddball books, candles, specialty soaps, goofy toys, and modern art here, you aren't trying.

Vermont Avenue offers street parking with meters; parking is available on side streets, as well. Read signs carefully for time limits and street cleaning information.

Third Street Promenade: Street shops

The Third Street Promenade, which runs between Wilshire Boulevard and Broadway Street in Santa Monica, is a pedestrian mall that gamely attempts to emulate the street scenes that have popped up organically in big European cities. Day or night, it's always packed with people. On Thursday and Saturday mornings, there's a farmers market on Arizona Street with fresh fruits, vegetables, and tasty snacks. The mall has three multi-screen movie theaters, a police station (at 1400 3rd St., in the Market Pavilion kiosk), and plenty to take in, including street vendors and musicians, who must be licensed and pay a fee to be there, and grungy street people, who exhibit their charms free from city regulations. It's both charming and kind of creepy, in that it is so carefully tended.

The promenade is grounded by Santa Monica Place Mall on the south, with **Barnes and Noble** (1201 Third Street Promenade; ☎ **310-260-9110**) and **Banana Republic** (1202 Third Street Promenade; ☎ **310-394-7740**) to the north. The flagship Banana Republic will even recharge your cellphone for you while you shop — so *very* L.A. Upscale chains like **Anthropologie** (1402 Third Street Promenade; ☎ **310-393-4763**), the **Discovery Channel Store** (301 Arizona Ave.; ☎ **310-899-9021**), and **Urban Outfitters** (1440 Third Street Promenade; ☎ **310-394-1404**) line both sides of the walkway, but there are also gems, such as **Midnight Special Books** (1318 Third St Promenade; ☎ **310-393-2923**), which specializes in social and political titles, **Hennessy & Ingalls** (1254 Third Street Promenade; ☎ **310-458-9074**), an art and architecture bookshop, and **Puzzle Zoo** (1413 Third Street Promenade; ☎ **310-393-9201**), with its unique stock of puzzles and toys.

The promenade has street parking and city lot parking; bring quarters, and read the meters carefully — some street meters are only 36 minutes! City lots on Fourth and Second Streets offer meters on the bottom floors and longer-term parking on the top levels, with hourly rates. If you lose your ticket, you will pay the maximum charge at lots that use the ticket method. You can park in the Santa Monica Place Mall on Broadway for 3 hours for free, but any longer will get you a ticket.

Universal CityWalk: Family fun

Look, ma — it's like all of Los Angeles in one place, only smaller, louder, cleaner, more crowded, and *waaaaay* more contrived. Universal CityWalk mimics the urban experience with sanitized, safe shopping and people-watching. You won't find a single local here, except for the teen and teen gangsta sets. We only come here when we are paid to do so, like when writing this book. Still, we grudgingly admit that it's good for families. Spots of humor do appear (the entrance to the **Hard Rock Cafe** is a 78-foot neon green Fender Stratocaster); the movie theaters are great (we applaud their policy of banning small children in movies rated R and PG-13), plus there's an IMAX theater; and there are plenty of ways to spend your money, whether it's surfwear from **Billabong,** skatewear from **Atomic Garage,** mass-produced punk-rock garb from **Hot Topic,** or really cool bobble heads, tops, and candy from the retro-toy shop **Sparkey's.**

But the coolest store by far is **Them,** which sells horror and sci-fi gift items and is the only place in the entire CityWalk/Universal Studio area where you can buy reproductions of vintage movie posters. Sadly, they aren't posters from classic Universal films; these veer more to the B-movie genre, but it's nice to find one CityWalk shop that appreciates the cinematic past, even if it's on the cheesy side.

Along with plenty of shops selling schlock, including a place where you can have your face digitized onto a magazine cover for $34.95 plus tax, there are two sports-gear/memorabilia shops, **UCLA Spirit** and **All Star Collectibles** (NBA Barbies, who knew?), and food — plenty of it. Really, what self-respecting mall would be complete without a food court? CityWalk provides a sumptuous bounty reflecting the finest in local fast food — and you don't have to drive all over town to get it. **Tommy's Burgers** and **Versailles** (great garlicky Cuban chicken and pork plates) are the premier examples of the food you'll find. And the balcony provides an awesome view of the giant-screen TV monitor that plays videos from Vivendi-Universal Music acts. Along with fast food — such as **Jodi Maroni's** exotically flavored sausages and our vote for best onsite food buy, **Tropic Nut**'s peanut butter and jelly sandwich, cookie, and soda combo for $5 — you'll find stuff to do, most of which costs money. You can have a psychic reading for $6 at **Wizard's,** the dining area attached to the magic store of the same name, and catch a magic show, as well — for a minimum of $20.

There's the testosterone-fueled **NASCAR** racing experience, where drivers sit in bouncing replica cars and try not to wipe out at video-induced "speeds" of up to 195 miles per hour. *A word to the wise:* If you are prone to motion sickness, avoid this ride! **Jillian's Hi-Lite** has a black-light bowling alley with a Jetsons' vibe. The more sedentary types will be relieved to discover **Upstart Crow,** a fairly decent bookstore with a cafe and a children's bookshop named **Crow's Nest.** People-watching is free, and so is running through the fountain in front of **Sam Goody's** music store.

Parking is available in the Universal City lot off Universal City Drive at a cost of $7. Make sure that you write down your location within the lot; it's easy to get confused by "Curious George Yellow Level 7" and "Curious George Blue Level 5." Or do what the locals do: Park at the meters on Cahuenga West and walk up the very steep, long hill; this area is fine if you only plan to spend a couple of hours at Universal City. A trip to see a movie there will get you a $2 parking rebate. You can also take the Metro Rail from Hollywood Boulevard to Universal City and walk up to CityWalk.

Main Street: From hippie to hip

This low-profile Westside street blends Santa Monica chic with Venice funkiness. The result? A stimulating seven-block mix of hippie (check out **One Life Market**, at 3001 Main St.; ☎ 310-392-4501) and hip (head for **Blonde**, at 2430 Main St.; ☎ 310-396-9113). The street even has its own Web site (www.mainstreetsm.com).

Vintage-fashion aficionados flock to **Paris 1900** (2703 Main St.; ☎ 310-396-0405) for lace and frills that make us want to get married again and again, just to wear the dresses it sells. **Sumiko** (3007 Main St.; ☎ 310-399-2803) — located in what was once the Vixen adult theater — has romantic modern dresses.

Aromatherapy addicts drift languidly through the doors of **Bey's Garden** (2919 Main St.; ☎ 310-399-2803) for a scent fix. Pets are not neglected at **Nature's Grooming Boutique** (3110 Main St.; ☎ 310-392-8758), with its treats, toys, themed collars, leashes, and accessories (such as sweaters and hats) for all sizes of canines.

Angel City Books (218 Pier Ave.; ☎ 310-399-8767) specializes in new and used volumes about Los Angeles. Collectors of vintage magazines, posters, and prints shop at **Santa Monica Trading Company** (2705 Main St.; ☎ 310-392-4806). Check out framed political cartoons by award-winning artists at **Impolitic** (2665 Main St., Courtyard Suite F; ☎ 310-396-2720).

For food, there's always the neighborhood taco stand, **Holy Guacamole** (2906 Main St.; ☎ 310-314-4850). Along with tacos, the stand also sells a large selection of bottles of searing hot sauces. **The Galley**, Santa Monica's oldest restaurant and bar (2442 Main St.; ☎ 310-452-1934), is open from 5 p.m. to closing, seven days a week.

The **California Heritage Museum** (2612 Main St.; ☎ 310-392-8537), located in a Craftsman-style house, lives up to its name with exhibits that have included tiles, pottery, and textiles. The heritage of designer

Charles Eames is preserved at **Eames Office Gallery** (2665 Main St; ☎ **310-396-5991**), which features originals and licensed reproductions from this seminal modernist.

Metered parking is available on Main Street and in city lots west of Main Street. All the lots have extended hours, so read signs carefully.

Hitting the Shopping Malls

Los Angeles has its fair share of mega malls, where you can spend many blissful hours roaming for shopping finds in (largely) brand-name stores and chains.

The Beverly Center
Westside

Known colloquially as the Bev Center, this mall was built on the site that once held an amusement park called Kiddie Land, and it's the only mall in the world to have a working oil well on its property (it's hidden behind a wall on the San Vincente Boulevard side of the building). The Bev Center is anchored by **Macy's** and **Bloomingdales,** with restaurants, including the country's first **Hard Rock Cafe,** on the ground floor, a food court and movie theaters at the top, and parking and plenty of shops sandwiched in between. Most of the stores at The Beverly Center are chains such as **Victoria's Secret, Restoration Hardware,** and the **Gap,** but there are high-end retailers like **Traffic** and **Shauna Stein** that feature designers such as Helmut Lang and Gaultier. **Louis Vitton, Betsy Johnson,** and **Mont Blanc** also have stores at the Bev. These high-end retailers are among the reasons the Beautiful People haunt this place, but frankly, we tend to avoid it. The multistory parking garage is a locally known horror — it gets really crowded, and it's constructed in such a way that it takes a long time to get in, find a place to park, and find your way to the mall. Then you have to do the reverse when you leave. Shudder. A **California Welcome Center** (☎ **310-854-7616**) is located on the ground floor, with the entrance on the Beverly Boulevard side of the building. The Welcome Center provides fax and Internet services, free maps, tour information, and tickets for attractions, along with free coffee and free shuttle service.

8500 Beverly Blvd., Los Angeles, with entrances on Beverly, La Cienega, and San Vicente Blvds. ☎ ***310-854-0070.*** *Internet:* www.beverlycenter.com. *Parking: First 3 hours or portion thereof $1, with each additional hour $1; parking validation not required; lost ticket pays maximum.*

Century City Shopping Mall
Century City

The Century City Shopping Mall was once part of Twentieth Century Fox Studios (the high cost of making the Elizabeth Taylor/Richard Burton movie *Cleopatra* forced the studio to sell off land to developers). This outdoor mall was also featured in the movie *Battle for the Planet of the Apes.* It holds a **Macy's** and **Bloomingdale's** (larger than the one at the Bev Center), 14 movie theaters, a food court with a Stage Deli and a good selection of ethnic and American food, and ubiquitous chains like the **Gap, Ann Taylor, Origins,** and **Crate & Barrel.** For truly unique items, check out the **Woofery** (☎ 310-553-9663), a specialty boutique with dog-themed gift items, including pillows, calendars, jewelry, and rugs featuring all breeds, or the color-therapy and aura-healing kiosk in the center of the mall by **Kenneth Cole Shoes.**

10250 Santa Monica Blvd. ☎ *310-277-3898. Parking: First 3 hours free with validation; make sure you take your ticket with you for validation; lost ticket pays maximum.*

The Glendale Galleria
Glendale

The Glendale Galleria is a huge shopping mall anchored by **Nordstrom, J.C. Penney, Robinsons-May, and Macy's.** Add in almost any conceivable chain store — plus a food court with Hawaiian barbecue, Indian, and Thai snacks, and a **Hot Dog on a Stick** with servers dressed in fetishistic striped costumes, along with the **Zone,** "a one-of-a kind multimedia and shopping experience customized for teens," on the second floor — and you have a whole downtown shopping arena under one roof. But despite its size and ambition, The Glendale Galleria is comfortable and almost cozy. Maybe that's because of the giant plastic palm trees or the carpeting, or the lack of movie theaters. No matter; this is a mall on steroids, complete with more than 50 stores devoted to women's wear (including **Bebe** and **Frederick's of Hollywood**), a **Thomas Cook Foreign Exchange** and postal center, a police substation, and, thankfully, plenty of places to sit and rest as you shop.

100 W. Colorado Blvd. ☎ *818-240-9481. Internet:* www.glendalegalleria.com. *Free parking. From Santa Monica, Beverly Hills, and Hollywood, take the I-10 east to the I-5 north and exit at Colorado, then drive east to the Galleria.*

Specialty Shopping

You may simply not have the time to waste milling about big shopping malls or stores, looking for that special something. Here, we cut to the chase and give you our favorite places to shop in L.A. for collectibles and unique goods and gifts.

Antiques

Antiques and retro furnishings abound in Los Angeles. A number of stores on Santa Monica's Montana Avenue provide vintage furnishings and accessories, including **Rosemarie McCaffrey** (1203 Montana Ave.,

☎ 310-395-7711) and **Room with a View** (1600 Montana Ave., ☎ 310-998-5858). There are a lot of stores along Robertson Boulevard that offer vintage furnishings and accessories, as well, including **Anna Hauck's Art Deco** (458 N. Robertson Blvd.; West Hollywood; ☎ 310-659-3606). The **Antique Guild** (3225 Helms Ave., Los Angeles; ☎ 310-838-3131), a renovated bakery off of Venice Boulevard, offers dozens of antiques and collectible vendors under one roof, as do **Chelsea Antique Center** (5800 W. 3rd St., Los Angeles; ☎ 323-937-2500) and **Cranberry House** (12318 Ventura Blvd., Sherman Oaks; ☎ 818-506-8945). **Sonrisa** (7609 Beverly Blvd., Los Angeles; ☎ 323-935-8438) and **Modernica** (7366 Beverly Blvd., Los Angeles; ☎ 323-933-0383) fulfill minimalist urges with sleek mid-century styles.

Books

General independent bookstores such as **Vromans**, (695 E. Colorado Blvd., Pasadena; ☎ 626-449-5320), **Duttons** (11975 San Vicente Blvd., Los Angeles; ☎ 310-476-6263), and **Book Soup** (8818 Sunset Blvd., West Hollywood; ☎ 310-659-3110) — all are top-flight shops with knowledgeable, helpful staff and a marvelous variety of books, and we urge you to patronize them — vie for business with the big chains, such as **Borders** (1360 Westwood Blvd., Los Angeles; ☎ 310-475-3444 and 1415 Third Street Promenade, Santa Monica; ☎ 310-393-9290), while other independent booksellers have carved out niches in specialty markets.

The **Bodhi Tree** (8585 Melrose Ave., West Hollywood; ☎ 310-659-1733) stocks tomes on Eastern, Western, and pop philosophies, along with incense, gifts, and candles. **Storyopolis** (116 N. Robertson Blvd., West Hollywood; ☎ 310-358-2500) entertains the youngster in all of us with a huge range of children's books, while **Midnight Special** (1318 Third Street Promenade, Santa Monica; ☎ 310-393-2923) slants toward politics and social history. **Wacko** (4633 Hollywood Blvd.; ☎ 323-663-0122) blends art and pop-culture books with toys and collectibles, and throws free art openings on the first Friday night of the month. **Hennessy & Ingalls** (1254 Third Street Promenade; ☎ 310-458-9074) focuses purely on art and architecture books. **Dailey Rare Books** (8216 Melrose Ave.; ☎ 323-658-8515) and **Heritage Books** (8540 Melrose Ave., West Hollywood; ☎ 310-659-3674) sell fine first editions and other rarities. **Mystery Pier** (8826 W. Sunset Blvd.; ☎ 310-657-5557) and **Mysterious Bookshop** (8763 Beverly Blvd., Los Angeles; ☎ 310-659-2959) solve readers' desire for crime fact and fiction. **Cook's Library** (8373 W. 3rd St., Los Angeles; ☎ 323-655-3141) is dedicated to the culinary arts (you will not believe how many cookbooks have been written throughout the years) and is a paradise for chefs. Cinema fans browse the movie posters, books, photos, and other cinema memorabilia at **Larry Edmunds Bookshop** (6644 Hollywood Blvd., Hollywood; ☎ 323-463-3273). For new and used books about Los Angeles, drop into **Angel City** (218 Pier St., Santa Monica; ☎ 310-399-8767). A vast selection of used books can be found at **Iliad** (4820 Vineland Ave., North Hollywood; ☎ 818-509-2665) and **Cosmopolitan** (7017 Melrose Ave., Los Angeles; ☎ 323-938-7119), while tiny, dusty **Aldine Books** (4663 Hollywood Blvd.; ☎ 323-666-2690) often has books (of which it has a curious selection) for sale by the pound.

Nerd alert: HiDeHo (525 Santa Monica Blvd., Santa Monica; ☎ 310-394-2820), **Golden Apple** (7711 Melrose Ave., Los Angeles; ☎ 323-658-6047), and **Meltdown** (7529 Sunset Blvd., Los Angeles; ☎ 323-851-7283) are premier comic-book shops.

For the wee ones

Kids and pets are often interchangeable for Angelinos, who love nothing better than pampering, spoiling, and cooing over little two- and four-legged creatures.

Kid stuff

Sure, you can find kids' clothes at **Old Navy** (8487 3rd St., Los Angeles; ☎ 323-658-5292 and 1232 Third Street Promenade, Santa Monica; ☎ 310-576-7787) and **Gap Kids** (1931 Wilshire Blvd., Santa Monica; ☎ 310-453-4551), as well as in department stores and malls, but why go generic when you can pick up way-out, cool, funky stuff, such as surfer-print onesies, at **Ga Ga** (8362 W. 3rd St., Los Angeles; ☎ 323-653-3388) and rock 'n' roll–themed toddler wear at **Meltdown/Baby Melt** (7529 Sunset Blvd., Los Angeles; ☎ 323-851-7283), a combination comic book and kids' clothing store?

Sophie Fox (1308 Montana Ave.; ☎ 310-656-0238) and **Tattletales** (1233 Montana Ave., Santa Monica; ☎ 310-899-0962) dress Westside wunderkinds who also find colorful clothes at **Cotton Rainbow** (1210 Montana Ave., Santa Monica; ☎ 310-393-0336). **Storyopolis** (116 N. Robertson Blvd., Los Angeles; ☎ 310-358-2500) has an amazing range of children's books, and **Puzzle Zoo** (1413 Third Street Promenade, Santa Monica; ☎ 310-393-9201) has smart, fun toys for kids of all ages.

Pet paraphernalia

Three Dog Bakery (24 Smith Alley, Pasadena; ☎ 626-440-0443) has tasty snacks for dogs, such as Pet-It Fours, Ciao Wow Cheese Pizzas, Beastro Biscotti, and Snickerpoodles made with ingredients such as whole wheat flour, carob, and lots of love. It also sells pet accessories. **Fifi & Romeo** (7282 Beverly Blvd., Los Angeles; ☎ 323-857-7215) is a special store for special pets; check out the vintage cashmere sweaters ingeniously repurposed for Rover-wear, along with pet-and-person matching outfits (go ahead; I dare you) and precious pooch carriers. The **Woofery** (10250 Santa Monica Blvd., Los Angeles; ☎ 310-553-9663) at the Century City Mall has hundreds of dog-related items for the canine-obsessed, and **Nature's Grooming & Boutique** (3110 Main St., # 104, Santa Monica; ☎ 310-392-8758) has everything from Halloween to Hanukkah and Christmas accessories for dogs and cats. It also has collars, leashes, and tasty treats.

Records and music

If you are one of the people who saw *Hi Fidelity* and wondered if those record-obsessed geeks really exist, come to super-sized **Amoeba Records** (6400 Sunset Blvd., Hollywood; ☎ 323-245-6400), and you'll realize that the movie was actually a documentary. People lined up 4 hours in advance for the grand opening of this used-music-hound's paradise (a highly anticipated branch of the northern California–based store). The record store features tens of thousands of used LPs and CDs at bargain prices, along with rarities, oddities, and cool stuff. And if the geeks aren't there, you can bet that it's because they are pouring over the bins at **Vinyl Fetish** (7305 Melrose Ave.; ☎ 323-935-1300) and **Beat Non-Stop** (7262 Melrose Ave.; ☎ 323-930-2121), which have the latest in imports and dance music, or at **Bleecker Bob's** (7555½ Melrose Ave.; ☎ 323-951-9111), **Rhino** (yes, the label was spawned from the store, 1720 Westwood Blvd., Los Angeles; ☎ 310-474-8685), and **Aron's** (1150 N Highland Ave., Hollywood; ☎ 323-469-4700) — all of which offer good deals on used records and stock a wide range of new product. If new items are more your bag, **Tower Records** (8801 W Sunset Blvd.; ☎ 310-657-7300 and 8844 W. Sunset Blvd.; ☎ 310-657-3344) and **Virgin Megastore** (8000 W. Sunset Blvd.; ☎ 323-650-8666) are giant super-stores selling hot-off-the-assembly-line records, CDs, videos, and DVDs.

Sam Ash Music (☎ 323-654-4922), located next door to the Virgin Megastore in the same West Hollywood mall at 8000 West Sunset Blvd., stocks musical equipment from amps to zithers, as does **Guitar Center** (7425 W. Sunset Blvd.; ☎ 323-874-1060), which also boasts the Rock Walk of Fame in front of the store. **McCabe's** (3101 Pico Blvd.; ☎ 310-264-9704) sells both musical equipment and music, with a focus on blues and folk.

Chapter 19

Four Great Los Angeles Itineraries

*W*e wish, oh how we do, that we all were European and therefore could enjoy weeks-long vacations. But the reality is that many of us are not European, and so we do not have the opportunity to take weeks-long vacations. If we were European, we would probably spend all those weeks in Italy, which is weird if you think about it. So if your time in Los Angeles is of the essence, here is a way to see it all, at least briefly.

But if you want to just plunk yourself down on the beach and never move, we won't say a word.

Los Angeles in Three Days

This itinerary provides a general tour of the city's highlights, giving you a taste of the beach, touching down at a museum or two, and delivering you to some of our favorite restaurants and snack spots.

Day one

Start by driving the **Sunset Boulevard Tour** (with or without the designated side trips) listed in Chapter 16. It gives you the opportunity to see a little bit of everything, from the city to the sea, with a little cinema, a little music, a little Hollywood, a little Beverly Hills, a few scandals, a few stars, and the rich and the not-so-rich thrown in for good measure.

You can modify the tour to take up an entire day, or maybe even two, depending on how often you get out of your car to look more closely at the sights listed and how long you spend looking. Because the tour ends (or begins, depending on your whims) at the ocean, you can spend part of a day at the **beach.** In truth, between Sunset and the beach, you cover some of the very best of L.A., soaking up the history and the kitsch, and getting a glimpse of the timeless and a sense of what has passed.

Or you can take a more ambitious tack. If you remembered to make reservations in advance, or if it's after 4 p.m. on Thursday, you can turn off Sunset on to Sepulveda Boulevard near the 405 Freeway and see the **Getty Museum** (for more information on the museum, see Chapter 16). But that would make for a pretty crowded day, so if you have just the one day, stick to Sunset and the water.

Do stop for lunch at **Zankou Chicken** on Sunset Boulevard, probably our hands-down favorite place to eat in L.A. (and now semi-famous thanks to a song by Beck), and have some of its roast chicken with divine garlic-paste sauce. At the end of the day, have drinks at **Shutters on the Beach** (1 Pico Blvd.; ☎ 800-334-9000; Internet: www.shutters onthebeach.com), the poshly casual Santa Monica hotel so loved by the beautiful people. Or continue those drinks over dinner at **Spago** in Beverly Hills, even if you can't precisely afford it — because perhaps you can't precisely afford *not* to if you want to claim that you "did" Beverly Hills. For more on Spago and Zankou Chicken, see Chapter 14.

Day two

Hit the beach, if you haven't already. Stroll **the Venice Ocean Front Walk** and maybe even the **Santa Monica Pier.** Sit on the sand and admire the water. Drive up Pacific Coast Highway and admire the ocean some more.

After you're done with the beach — if you ever are — go do the **Getty Museum** properly. Try to time it so that you're there at sunset, which is dramatic, of course, and tends to lead into a fragrant, balmy evening, especially in summertime.

As for food, eat whatever strikes your fancy — yesterday you had some of the best ethnic and nouveau food that L.A. has to offer, so you've covered, in just two meals (how efficient of you!), the most typical L.A. dining. If your budget is holding up, tonight you may want to head to Hollywood to try **Campanile** or **Patina,** considered by many to be the city's two best restaurants. **Jar,** in West Hollywood, the new restaurant from Campanile's owner, is somewhat more affordable. For more information, see Chapter 14.

This evening, try one of our **star-spotting** suggestions (check out Chapter 25); there are a number of bars ranging from cozy to trendy to classy, and even if a famous face fails to materialize, you will pass the time well. Or just admire the spread of twinkling lights, like jewels on black velvet, as Steve Martin said in his book *Shopgirl.* Take a vantage point like **Yamashiro,** a gorgeous Japanese restaurant situated in the Hollywood Hills, featuring average food, solid drinks, and some of the best views of L.A. around.

Day three

Today you have to make some choices. If you have kids, and you aren't going to **Disneyland,** this is the time to visit **Universal Studios.** Otherwise, head to the **Los Angeles County Museum of Art (LACMA),** perhaps the finest comprehensive museum west of Chicago. While you're there, stroll around the **La Brea Tar Pits,** and try to think of another city that has something so absurd and yet so wonderful right in the very center of it. For more on these attractions, go to Chapter 16.

These choices will leave you nicely situated for some noshing on Melrose Avenue or Beverly Boulevard, where you have a number of choices, such as delightful cafes (perhaps takeout sandwiches from **Joan's on Third** for a picnic on the LACMA or Getty grounds?) or dinner at **Campanile.** Check out Chapter 14 for more on these eateries.

If your art tastes are more toward the modern, head downtown to the **Museum of Contemporary Art (MOCA)** (see Chapter 16). While there, you can also stroll **Olvera Street,** L.A.'s oldest street and home to a rollicking Mexican-style market area. You can also experience the delightful chaos of the **Grand Central Market,** where you can grab cheap, wonderful ethnic food. MOCA is also right by Little Tokyo, so you can dine on fresh sushi at **Sushi Gen** (see Chapter 14 for more on this and Grand Central Market). If it's a summer night, grab some of those cheap seats in the **Hollywood Bowl** for a perfect L.A. evening. (And don't forget to carry a box dinner to eat up there! Any of the aforementioned places will be happy to put one together for you, but you may have to order in advance.) Check out Chapter 20 for more on the Hollywood Bowl.

A Quintessential L.A. Day

It's awesome, dude. Unless, of course, it's righteous. Totally.

This is a day in which you spend your time seeing the sights and doing the activities that can only be described as quintessentially L.A. Be sure to wake up very early, because right where Sunset Boulevard meets the Pacific Coast Highway (call it the "PCH," and you'll fit right in), there's a swell of tasty waves forming, and you won't be the only surfer waiting to ride a few of them. Want to be sure? Double-check the best spot for waves by calling the hotline, better known as **L.A. surf** and weather (☎ 310-578-0478), to get the current surf and beach conditions. As you head toward the beach on the bike you rented from **Spokes n' Stuff** (1715 Ocean Front Walk, Venice), don't forget to stop at **ZJ's Boarding House** (2619 Main St.; ☎ 310-392-5646) to rent that wetsuit (which you'll need from October through May) and, preferably, a *long* surfboard. (The wider and longer the board, the easier the ride, and thus the better chance for you to actually stand up.) Think of it as renting a colorful canoe for a few hours. Make sure to pack a high-energy snack in your backpack to get you up and running.

Conveniently, one of the best surf spots is next to **Gladstone's 4 Fish** (17300 Pacific Coast Hwy.), all the better to rinse the sand off your teeth with a few Coronas on its outdoor patio.

Whoa, dude, forgot you don't know how to surf? Bummer. You can always arrange for lessons at **Malibu Ocean Sports** (22935 Pacific Coast Hwy., Malibu; ☎ 310-456-6302; prices vary), where they happily take on beginners (perhaps only so they can enjoy a few laughs).

After the morning batch of tasty waves, you'll be in the right frame of mind to do some power yoga, but not before you have your shot of wheat-grass juice, which can be found at **Jamba Juice,** a chain that makes smoothies with fresh-squeezed juices. There's a Jamba Juice on Santa Monica Boulevard and La Cienega, which is perfect, because you won't be late for yoga class at **Body and Soul,** (8599 Santa Monica Blvd., West Hollywood; ☎ 310-659-2211), where the Asian-inspired decor and non-gym-like setting mellow you out long before you realize that the Downward Dog pose you're holding is starting to burn.

Because you've, like, *totally* expended plenty of calories already, head south in your new Zen state until you hit the greasy love shack in West Hollywood — **Tail O' the Pup** (see Chapter 17). This classic California hot dog stand is shaped like — you guessed it — a hot dog. You've seen this colorful building in a million movies; now go and enjoy the Mexican Ole chili dog at the "Tail," as the locals call it.

As your sports watch can tell you, it's almost sundown. So cruise back toward the beach for a relaxing hour to watch the dolphins and catch the sunset. Why not do it from the best seat in the house? Malibu Ocean Sports (yes, them again; see earlier in this section) rents a single kayak for around $15 an hour. While you're at it, paddle over to **Shutters on the Beach** (see "Los Angeles in Three Days," earlier in this chapter). It's the only hotel in Santa Monica that is actually *on* the beach — well, it and its hottie lil' sister spot, the **Hotel Casa Del Mar** (1910 Ocean Way, Santa Monica; ☎ 310-581-5533; Internet: www.hotelcasadelmar.com). Stop in for a coffee or drink by the fire. Those ocean breezes can get chilly, you know.

End your day at **Chez Jay's** (1657 Ocean Ave.; ☎ 310-395-1741), an old beachfront roadhouse in Santa Monica that was established in 1959. You can freely embellish your morning surf session up at the bar with the other surfers and dream about your awesome SoCal day.

Rock Star L.A.

So you want to be a rock 'n' roll star? Here's how to live like one for a rock 'n' roll L.A. day. Read on.

Start your day late by rolling out of bed, preferably one in a fleabag crash pad (or, at the very least, the **Alta Cienega Motel,** where Jim Morrison regularly slept it off). Don't wash your hair. Get your motor up and running at the **Rock N' Roll Denny's** (Sunset Boulevard and Gardner Avenue). A Grand Slam breakfast is economical, which is good, because you need to save your money for later. Of course, it may be lunchtime by now, in which case you may opt for a bacon-cheddar burger.

Head over to Melrose for some rock duds; your first stop should be the **SERIOUS store,** but if you have a bigger budget, try **Blest Boutique** (featuring many local designers). Or you can get a pair of nicely worn-in, strategically torn jeans at **Aadvark's Old Ark** (7579 Melrose Ave.; ☎ 213-655-6769) or **Wasteland** (7428 Melrose Ave.; ☎ 323-653-3028). Head to the nearest **Rite-Aid,** or other large pharmacy, to stock up on **Wet 'n' Wild** cheap makeup (as little as 99¢); girls and boys both need their black eyeliner and mascara. Grab some serious eyeshadow, red lipstick, and a can of hairspray while you're at it. Check out the stores on Hollywood Boulevard between Cahuenga Boulevard and Highland Avenue, such as **LaLa** (6440 Hollywood Blvd.; ☎ 323-957-3170), for footwear. Think excellent spike heels and platforms.

Head back to Sunset Boulevard and over to the **Guitar Center** (see Chapter 16), where metal and hard rock never, ever go out of style. You may wish you had a model girlfriend who would help you pay for that Marshall amp. Admire the handprints of famous rock stars, such as Aerosmith, and know that one day, your prints will reside alongside them.

After all that shopping, you will need some fuel to help keep up your energy. Dine on burgers and barbecue at **Barney's Beanery** (see Chapter 14), located right near the **Alta Cienega Motel** (see Chapter 8), or order the breakfast you slept through this morning at **Duke's** coffee shop (8909 Sunset Blvd.; ☎ 310-652-3100), near the main rock clubs. You can stop along the way at **Rock and Roll Ralph's grocery** (5257 Sunset Blvd.; ☎ 213-874-6333) and stock up on the three food groups of the rocker set: red meat, sugar, and alcohol.

After dinner, it's time to hit the club circuit. Start with — and heck, end with — drinks at the **Rainbow,** which is conveniently located right next to **The Roxy** and down the street from the **Whisky a Go-Go.** Gazarri's, where Van Halen and so many hair bands got their start, is now the **Key Club.** Finish up at **The Troubadour,** where, if you don't like the band, you may just want to have a drink in the bar. For more on these night spots, see Chapter 21. Speaking of drinks, it's probably been a quarter of an hour since your last one, so it's time to go bar-hopping; **Boardner's** (1652 N. Cherokee Ave.; ☎ 323-462-9621) and **Bob's Frolic Room** (6425 Hollywood Blvd.; ☎ 323-462-5890) are waiting for you. After you are finished, you can roll your way home to bed (perhaps you should have someone drive you) . . . if you can find it.

Morbid L.A.

We have many suggestions for star spotting scattered throughout this book, but we know of one tried-and-true method of getting within 6 feet of your favorite celeb. There is, however, just one catch; said celeb has to be dead. Even celebrities have to shuffle off their mortal coils some day, and when that day comes, they gotta go somewhere, unless they opt for cremation (spoilsports). And that brings us to cemeteries. Morbid, perhaps, but more efficient and reliable than those Maps of the Stars' Homes hawked on every street corner, many of which are seriously out-of-date.

A number of books give thorough details to who's buried where, including *Hollywood: Remains to Be Seen*, by Mark Masek (Cumberland House); *This is Hollywood,* by Ken Schessler (self-published); and the out-of-print but findable *Permanent Californians* (Chelsea Publishing Co.), by Judi Culbertson and Tom Randall.

For precise directions and photos of celebrity gravesites, go to www. findagrave.com. For now, here is a brief sampling. But please, wherever you go, be respectful, especially if there is a funeral going on or if there are people visibly mourning. Cemetery workers will probably help you, but not if they're busy, for these are, after all, places of business.

The cemeteries

Hollywood Forever (6000 Santa Monica Blvd.; ☎ 323-469-1181), formerly Hollywood Memorial Park, is L.A.'s most user-friendly cemetery, thanks to new owners who understand the tourist appeal of their property. Maps and guidebooks, plus little ad hoc memorials here and there, help you find the graves of **Rudolph Valentino, Alfalfa** from the *Little Rascals,* **Cecil B. DeMille, John Huston, Marion Davies, Virginia Rappe** (the woman whose death ruined silent-star Fatty Arbuckle's career), several **Chaplin family members** (but not **Charlie,** who is eternally resting in Switzerland), **Douglas Fairbanks (Sr., and Jr.),** and **Tyrone Power.** It's aesthetically appealing, culturally and historically significant, and right near the heart of Hollywood. It offers a gift shop full of the precise kinds of tchotchkes you want as mementos.

Pierce Brothers Westwood Village Memorial Park (1218 Glendon Ave.; ☎ 310-474-1579) is small and tucked behind a movie theater in the very heart of Westwood. It's so crammed full of famous people, that we don't know where to begin. Oh, wait, it's obvious: **Marilyn Monroe.** But here, too, are the gravesites of **Natalie Wood, Jack Lemmon and Walter Matthau, Truman Capote, Frank Zappa** and **Roy Orbison** (both are unmarked), **John Cassavetes, Bob "Hogan's Heroes" Crane, Will and Ariel Durant, Eva Gabor, Joseph Heller** (author of *Catch 22*), **Dean Martin, Carroll O'Conner, Donna Reed,** and **Dorothy Stratten.** The cemetery is visitor-friendly, and if workers aren't busy, they're often happy to point out the park's famous residents.

Forest Lawn, whose founder, Hubert Eaton, more or less invented the concept of the modern-day cemetery — whoops, excuse us, *memorial park* (you know, flat, park-like, grave markers flush to the ground, boring) — has for years marketed itself as a nice place to visit, with worthy burial locations and self-proclaimed "great works of art" (the Last Supper in stained glass, most notably). So you would think that they would encourage respectful visitation of their more notable residents. Wrong. They try to pretend that they have no celebrities, and asking will get you turned away. Fear not; the aforementioned books and Web site will help you find your way to the gravesites of the likes of **Buster Keaton, Bette Davis, Liberace, Andy Gibb, Lucille Ball, Freddie Prinze, Stan Laurel,** and **Ozzie, Harriet, and Rick Nelson,** in their Hollywood Hills location — which is really in **Burbank** (6300 Forest Lawn Dr.; ☎ 800-204-3131). Over in the **Glendale** location (1712 S. Glendale Ave.; ☎ 800-204-3131), which is right next to Silver Lake, you can find **Jimmy Stewart, Mary Pickford, Walt Disney, Clara Bow, George Burns and Gracie Allen, Dorothy Dandridge, Nat King Cole, Chico and Gummo Marx, Spencer Tracy,** and **Sammy Davis, Jr.** In a mausoleum accessible only if you have a relative buried there (or can sneak in behind another visitor), are the remains of **Jean Harlow,** as well as **Clark Gable** and **Carole Lombard.**

Holy Cross Cemetery (5835 W. Slauson Ave., Culver City; ☎ 323-776-1855) is a little bit farther afield, but it's well worth the extra effort, with a hilly landscape that holds the mortal remains of **Sharon Tate, Bing Crosby, Bela Lugosi, Rita Hayworth, Jimmy Durante, John Candy,** and **Lawrence Welk,** among others. The office can give you a map.

Dens of iniquity

Having seen many of Hollywood's final resting places, you may, if you are of a morbid, or simply curious, turn of mind, want to visit the spots where certain luminaries became candidates for cemeteries. **John Belushi** took, perhaps wittingly, perhaps not, a speedball in Bungalow 2 at the **Chateau Marmont** (8221 W. Sunset Blvd.). You probably can't see the precise bungalow, unless you rent it (and you can, if you have money enough), but you can go have a drink in the hotel's lobby and then slip into the pool area behind a guest. From there, you can peer into the foliage at the back of the bungalow. Please don't disturb the occupants, however.

Just down the street is **The Viper Room** (8852 W. Sunset Blvd.; ☎ 310-358-1880), the club owned partly by actor Johnny Depp. On the sidewalk in front of the door on Larrabee Street is where River Phoenix succumbed to a drug overdose.

Where would a tour of morbid sights be without a couple of good murder scenes? L.A.'s most notorious in recent years is, of course, the **Nicole Brown Simpson and Ron Goldman murders.** Their bodies were found at 875 S. Bundy Drive (the address has been changed to avoid looky-loos like you, but it's on the west side of the street, near the corner of Dorothy Street), while the bloody glove was found at the home of Nicole's ex-husband, football player **O.J. Simpson** (360 Rockingham, corner of Ashford). O.J.'s house was sold to pay his debts and has since been razed; you may want to time how long it takes you to drive from Nicole's house to 360 Rockingham. Here's a hint: *not very*. O.J. himself has spent his time since being acquitted in his criminal trial tirelessly searching for the real killers, down near his new home in Florida.

Prior to the Simpson case, the "Most Famed Murder Case" title was held by the **Manson murders.** Actress Sharon Tate and five others were found gruesomely slain at her rented home at 10050 Cielo Drive in Benedict Canyon north of Sunset. After years of fruitlessly trying to sell the place, and enduring Nine Inch Nails' leader Trent Reznor recording an album there (he says he didn't know of the connection; we say we weren't born yesterday), the owners finally tore it down, and a new home stands on the property. The night after Tate and friends met Charlie Manson's girls, **Leno and Rosemary LaBianca** became victims in their home at 3301 Waverly Drive in Silver Lake/Los Feliz (the number was changed to this to avoid sightseers, but the house remains the same). If you find yourself growing faint at this point, have something to eat at **El Coyote** (7312 Beverly Blvd.; ☎ 323-939-2255), as did Sharon and friends the night before they died.

The house at 722 N. Elm in Beverly Hills is where **Lyle and Eric Menendez** shot their parents and then begged for the mercy of the court because they were now orphans. (Perhaps we twist their defense, but not by much.)

Morbid souvenirs

If you need souvenirs of your special day for the folks back home, you can support those wacky folks at the L.A. County Coroner's office and visit **Skeletons in the Closet** (1104 N. Mission Rd.; ☎ **323-343-0760**) — the coroner's office . . . *gift shop*. Yes, you can pick up beach towels with body outlines, T-shirts, and more, all of it raising proceeds for a program wherein they scare the heck out of drunken teens by taking them to see the tragic results of mixing drinking and driving. A worthy cause and, of course, good conversation pieces.

Or stop in at **Necromance** (7220 Melrose Ave.; ☎ **323-934-8684**), where you can choose from a wide selection of animal and human bones (legally obtained, usually from kaput medical schools who have teaching skeletons for sale), jewelry and other ornaments, plus critters in formaldehyde, books about funeral customs, antique mourning jewelry, and other items appealing to the Goth and ghoulish crowd.

Part VI
Living It Up After the Sun Goes Down

"That's what I love about Los Angeles. It's so creative and diversified. Where else could you see Macaulay Culkin in a performance of 'La Bohème'?"

In this part . . .

*T*he nightlife scene in Los Angeles is a thriving one, with a full plate of activities for just about everyone. The city has first-class theater and music offerings weekly, big-name sports events practically year-round, and some of the most seductive bars and nightclubs in the world. If you want to dance, you can find any number of places to wiggle your toes; if you want to rock, you can discover those seminal venues where many famous bands began. If you want to sip a cold drink with the city laid out in front of you like a scattering of diamonds, you can find that, too.

Chapter 20

The Cultural Scene in Los Angeles

● ●

In This Chapter

▶ Looking for the news on the latest shows and events

▶ Finding tips on hot tickets

▶ Relaxing at the theater, symphony, and opera

▶ Choosing a show at the big music venues

● ●

*L*os Angeles has plenty of culture, thank you. It has serious, major theater, often featuring highly recognizable names. (There are a whole bunch of actors out here, for some reason — oh, right, they work in TV and movies — and they often enjoy doing a theater stint between films or during TV-season hiatus; the work keeps their acting chops up, and it's a nice change of pace.) L.A. boasts a dazzlingly staged opera and a major symphony so significant that a whole new hall is being built just for it.

Where can you find these hotbeds of cultural activity? Like the sprawling city landscape, you find them all over L.A. Los Angeles has no theater district. The Music Center downtown is host to four of the most prominent venues in town, while the rest of the arenas, clubs, and music halls are scattered willy-nilly around the city. Most small and mid-size theaters and performance spaces can be found in the Hollywood/West Hollywood neighborhoods, but they certainly aren't restricted to these venues.

The Inside Scoop: Finding Out What's Playing and How to Get Tickets

Although there aren't as many hot tickets in L.A. as there are in, say, New York City, you will need to do a little research ahead of time to procure tickets in advance for that certain something wonderful. We would hate for you to hit town and discover some great performance is playing, only to learn that everyone else in L.A. gobbled up the tickets before you arrived.

Using the Internet

The Internet is your friend when it comes to finding information and deals on live performances in Los Angeles. Just about every venue we list has a Web site, enabling you to check out their schedules as much as a year in advance. For a more comprehensive look, try www.city search.com, or better still, www.laplaz.com, which not only helps you locate productions by location, size, and genre but also makes restaurant suggestions for places near the area of each performance. The highly perusable **L.A. County Arts Commission** Web site (www. lacountryarts.org) has a number of contacts and information about performances (including free music) around Los Angeles. A week or so before your arrival, check www.laweekly.com for its comprehensive calendar.

Reading the news

Take a look at the Calendar section of the Sunday *Los Angeles Times,* which lists some events months in advance. *Los Angeles* **magazine** may also be of help.

After you hit town, get a copy of the free weekly newspapers, *LA Weekly* and *New Times LA;* both have extensive listings and trustworthy picks on what is going on that week. Although the Sunday *Los Angeles Times* is valuable, it's only available from Saturday night through Sunday night, while the *LA Weekly* and the *New Times LA* can be found at many locations (including online, though the *New Times* doesn't have as many of its listings up on the Web as the *Weekly* does) all week long.

Buying your tickets

Nearly all events sell tickets through their box offices (call for hours), and just about every venue sells them online. Some venues sell tickets over the phone. Keep in mind that when you purchase by phone or over the Internet, you often have to go through the dreaded ticket conglomerate **Ticketmaster** (☎ 877-870-4929 or 213/480-3232; Internet: www.ticketmaster.com). It's convenient, certainly (you can buy over the phone or at one of several Ticketmaster locations in the city, such as Tower Records, Wherehouse Music, and Robinsons-May department stores), but it also charges a per-ticket handling fee that can add anywhere from a couple of dollars to some outrageous sum ($15 or more) to the price of each ticket. If you want to save some dollars, buy directly at the venue's box office whenever possible.

You can almost always guarantee that about 10% of an audience won't show up, so you might take your chances on last-minute seats (unused house seats also get released just before showtime), but we advise that you arrive at least an hour before the show begins, so if others have the same idea, you'll be ahead of them on the wait list.

Theater in Los Angeles

Theater in L.A. gets a bad rap, and unjustly. Yes, it's true that the city can't compete with New York City on the level of Broadway shows (for one thing, L.A. doesn't have a theater district like the one on and around Broadway), or even on the level as theater found off-Broadway. But L.A. does have a plethora of small, 99-seat-and-under theaters that do some fine work for a modest cost to the audience member. There are too many of these theaters to mention — that's where the extensive theater listings in *LA Weekly* and the *Los Angeles Times* come in handy (see the previous section). Just browse and see what grabs you.

The big boys

Of course, Los Angeles has theater on a larger level, and that brings us to Downtown's venerable **Music Center** (the Performing Arts Center of Los Angeles County; Internet: www.musiccenter.org). Actually, it's three separate theaters: the **Dorothy Chandler Pavilion,** which usually hosts classical music and opera (135 N. Grand Ave.; ☎ 213-972-8001); the **Ahmanson,** the mid-size theater that runs about four plays a year; and the smaller **Mark Taper Forum,** with nearly in-the-round-seating (both the Ahmanson and Mark Taper Forum: 135 N. Grand Ave.; ☎ 213-628-2772; Internet: www.taperahmanson.com). Together, they are known as the Center Theater Group.

Some fine touring productions are likely to end up performing at the Center Theater Group (as we write this, *The Full Monty* is about to be, er, unveiled at the Ahmanson). But original works, some of great significance, have also been developed and debuted on these stages. The Pulitzer Prize–winning *Angels in America* was developed through the Taper, which also recently helped David Henry Hwang rework Rogers and Hammerstein's *Flower Drum Song,* currently headed to Broadway. Add to these August Wilson's *Piano Lessons, QED* (the one-man show about physicist Richard Feynman), and the upcoming revival of the reworked *Into the Woods,* and you can see that New York theater owes a debt to L.A., whether it likes it or not.

One complaint of L.A. theater is that casting often takes the form of a beauty pageant. Not literally, but it does seem to favor beauty over talent; Hollywood, and Los Angeles by extension, values looks perhaps to the neglect of greater talent, while New York theater (to pick on the

most obvious theater city) tends toward more regular-folks-type performers. The Taper seems to really enjoy having recognizable names
(with good-looking faces attached) in casts, whether those actors are
best suited to the role or not. Which is not to say that the acting is
lacking, but sometimes you can't help but muse that there might well
be some lesser-knowns or even outright unknowns who would be
better suited for the parts. Still, it can be fun to see TV or film actors
working on their live theater skills.

Productions are occasionally shifted over to the **James A. Dolittle
Theater** (1615 N. Vine St.; ☎ 310-825-4401) in Hollywood if any play
during a series becomes so popular that its run is extended.

Note that you can park at the Music Center parking garage for 30 minutes (free with validation) if you choose to buy directly from the box
office rather than over the phone or online. At all other times, the rate
for self-parking in the garage is $7, available starting at 5 p.m. for
evening performances and between noon and 2 p.m. for matinees; if
you park before noon, you're be charged $15. For information on the
free shuttle service to the Music Center from participating restaurants,
see the section on the Music Center in Chapter 11. At the heart of the
ongoing Hollywood revitalization project is the **Pantages Theater**
(6233 Hollywood Blvd.; general information only: ☎ 323-468-1700;
Internet: www.nederlander.com), a grand old movie palace (circa
1930) turned live venue. Tickets are only sold at the box office or
through Ticketmaster (☎ 213-480-3232 or 714-740-2000) or
Ticketmaster outlets throughout the city. It was recently lovingly
restored by the folks at Disney, who have made it the L.A. residence of
their smash production, *The Lion King*. The show's run may be over by
the time you read this, so check and see. (Rumors were that the road
company of *The Producers* would be finding a home here.)

Speaking of (as it seems we often do) the Hollywood revitalization project, the **Kodak Theatre** (located in the new Hollywood-Highland complex; general information only: ☎ 323-308-6300; Internet: www.kodak
theatre.com), was built primarily as a permanent home for the
Oscars. The theater is also intended to serve as a live-performance
venue, taking the place of the Shubert Theater. For many years, the
Shubert was the only other theatrical house of any size, apart from the
Pantages. It was recently shuttered to make way for office buildings.
The Kodak is still too new to say much about, apart from the fact that
it looks real purty. You can check out the schedule for the theater at
www.kodaktheatre.com. Tickets can be purchased at the box office or
through Ticketmaster (see contact information in the previous para-
graph) or Ticketmaster outlets throughout the city.

The little big guys

For smaller productions, the **Colony Theatre Company** (555 N. 3rd St., Burbank; ☎ **818-558-7000;** Internet: www.colonytheatre.org) is hard to beat. Established in 1975, it presents half a dozen or so plays (ranging from reliable classics to world premieres to revivals of overlooked and happily rediscovered gems of any vintage) annually of consistent and frequently award-winning quality. A couple of years ago, it finally left its long-time, and admittedly time-worn, small facility in Silverlake and moved to a new (and nearly 300-seat) venue in Burbank.

Ah, but let's not forget **The Actors' Gang** (6209 Santa Monica Blvd.; ☎ **323-465-0566;** Internet: www.theactorsgang.com), not that they would ever let us. A collection of theater-major friends at UCLA founded their own theater group back in the early '80s, and they just kept going. It didn't hurt that one of them was actor/director Tim Robbins, who never forgot his friends or his roots and who helped support the Gang in their quest for renegade, bold, original productions and rethinkings of classics (Shakespeare and Chekhov may never recover; but then again, even the greats can use a little shaking up from time to time). This always raucous, always bold bunch may miss as often as it hits, but the Gang reaches high — and isn't that what art and theater are all about?

Highways Performance Space (1651 18th St.; ☎ **310-319-1459;** Internet: www.highwaysperformance.com) consistently offers challenging, intriguing, controversial, or just plain good, fun performances (performance art, spoken word, dance, world music, small theater, you name it) nearly every night.

The Symphony in Los Angeles

We won't say that there is but one game in town when it comes to classical music, but it's sort of true (certainly it's hard to get anyone other than the critics to recall any other options). Its name is the **Los Angeles Philharmonic** (135 N. Grand Ave.; ☎ **213-850-2000;** Internet: www.laphil.com), led by Finnish poster-boy Esa-Pekka Salonen. The 2002–2003 season will be its last at the Dorothy Chandler Pavilion. Then it's off to a new home, the **Walt Disney Concert Hall.** Still being constructed at the time of this writing, the building, designed by Frank Gehry, has already received cries ranging from "Genius! Breathtaking!" to "Explosion in a blueprint factory!" Regardless, it is supposed to be state of the art in terms of the acoustics. Its opening will certainly introduce a new major phase in the L.A. performing-arts world. Expect the Philharmonic to continue its programs, which will include, along with its annual slate of regular performances, celebrity artist recitals, chamber music, and visiting artists-in-residence. Prices vary according to the kind of performance. The tickets can be as cheap as $12 (up in the heavens) and as expensive as $80.

Opera in Los Angeles

It may not be La Scala (but then, what is?), but the **Los Angeles Opera** (the Dorothy Chandler Pavilion; see information above) regularly stages some extraordinary shows, generally earning across-the-board raves. No wonder; besides the depth of musical talent, the company has regular access to superb visual artists who are always creating sets and staging that sparks serious talk. One complaint might be that the company relies too heavily on tried-and-true classics; but then again, it also stages and performs the classics magnificently. Placido Domingo is the opera's Artistic Director, and he has been known to turn up as guest conductor. Hollywood director Billy Friedkin (yes, *The Exorcist* guy) recently directed Bartok's *Bluebeard's Castle*, so you can see that the company does have a curious range. Perhaps this is why opera has quietly become quite a little scene in L.A.; along with the expected older crowd, you can spot a few young punks (among other non-stereotypical opera-going types) with their Doc Marten boots sticking out under their velvet gowns. (This is also one of the few true dress-up places in L.A.; half the fun is going for the fashion show.)

Another reason for the opera's increased following may be that nose-bleed seats are surprisingly inexpensive: Seats go for as little as $20 to $35, but that's for seating way up in the sky. The seats down front can go for up to $165 (suddenly distance seems like a nice thing). The theater also has a large screen showing translations above the proscenium, so don't worry about not understanding what's happening. The majority of the performances sell out, so check as far in advance as you can.

Major Music Venues

For performances of all stripes, from rock to jazz to country to comedy, L.A. has a smart selection of classic venues. Plus, you can find more rock/pop/world music/whatever at different-sized venues around town.

The Hollywood Bowl

Hollywood

One of the absolute treasures of Los Angeles, the Hollywood Bowl, inaugurated in 1922, is one of the largest natural outdoor amphitheaters in the world (seating about 18,000). The Beatles played here. Leopold

Stokowski conducted the Philharmonic here in the 1930s. The L.A. Philharmonic still holds regular concerts here. Barbra Streisand, Rudolf Nureyev, Elton John, Radiohead, Abbott and Costello, Monty Python, Billie Holiday, Judy Garland, Isaac Stern, and Leonard Bernstein have also played, danced, or yukked it up here. Summer nights at the Bowl (a distinctive shell-shaped bandbox backdrop facing out into a tiered seating level that begins with "boxes" and heads up into bleacher-type seats) is one of the best places to find entertainment in L.A., as the Summer Series (Playboy Jazz Festival, plus a wealth of shows ranging from Pops to pop, world music to movie music, classical to classics) kicks in. Tickets for regular performances, for seats way up high, can be ridiculously cheap (like $2!). Plus, dining is encouraged, making it a whole scene, as audience members bring picnics and boxed suppers (a number of restaurants around town offer special boxed meals just for Bowl-goers), with some going full-out elaborate (candles and wine) and others wolfing down burgers and the like from fast-food joints. And then everyone hangs out in the warm, fragrant night and wonders, "Why on earth don't I do this more often?"

Note: Parking for the Bowl is abysmal; there is parking, but it is limited and expensive. Nearby lots (run by the Bowl) offer shuttles to and from lots around the city where you park and ride, but these shuttles often don't leave until after the performance has ended. So if you want to sneak out early, you may get stuck. We strongly recommend taking the MetroRail, which operates a free regular shuttle to and from Hollywood and Argyle, right next to the Hollywood and Vine stop. Unfortunately, the MetroRail shuttles have the same problem as the Bowl parking shuttles — the shuttle stops during the performance. Regardless, we encourage you to visit the Bowl's Web site for parking instructions and tips — to say nothing of dining suggestions!

2301 N. Highland Ave. ☎ *323-850-2000. Internet:* www.hollywoodbowl.com.

The Staples Center

Downtown

The Staples Center is a brand-new 20,000-seat stadium that was built for the Los Angeles Lakers NBA team. This state-of-the-art arena is also the home of the L.A. Clippers (NBA), the L.A. Kings (NHL), and the L.A. Sparks (WNBA). It's a premier venue for concerts, as well, showcasing such performers as Madonna and U2. The stadium is surrounded by parking lots, both preferred seating and general public. Costs for parking start at $20; see the stadium Web site for information on the prepaid parking service and directions to each lot.

1111 S. Figueroa St. ☎ *213-624-3100. Internet:* www.staplescenter.com.

Universal Amphitheatre and the Greek Theatre

Universal City and Griffith Park

If you can't sell out a venue the size of the Staples Center, you're likely to be found playing the Universal Amphitheatre or the Greek Theatre. The difference between the two, more or less, is that the former is indoors, and the latter is outdoors. Given our druthers, we like the Greek Theatre; built in the 1920s, the graceful and pretty theater is set in the middle of Griffith Park. It's a delight, but the parking lot is a nightmare. (We park in or around Los Feliz Boulevard and walk the seven-tenths of a mile up to the theater. You will have company, so it's safe enough.) Bring a sweater in case it gets chilly. The Universal is fine, but it's located in the middle of Universal Studios, which means you have to park a considerable distance away — so you may want to forgo high heels.

Greek Theatre: 2700 N. Vermont Ave., Griffith Park. ☎ *323-665-1927. Internet:* www. greektheatrela.com. *Universal Amphitheatre: 100 Universal City Plaza, Universal City.* ☎ *818-622-4440. Internet:* www.hob.com/venues/concerts/universal.

Chapter 21

Bars, Stars, and Gee-Tars: L.A. at Night

. . . .

In This Chapter

▶ Maximum rock 'n' roll

▶ Star bars

▶ View to a thrill

▶ Viva Latino!

▶ Shall we dance?

▶ Gay clubs and drag nights

▶ Tourist faves

. . . .

*I*t's no secret that L.A.'s nightlife is *hot, hot, hot,* and you may find that getting past the velvet ropes is easier said than done. Don't worry, we have you covered. Whether you're just in town for the night or you have a few days to kick it, a trip to any of the following hot spots should give you bragging rights back home.

Before you venture out into the night, you may want to stop by such hipster clothing stores as **Blest Boutique** (1634 Cahuenga Blvd., Hollywood; ☎ **323-467-0191**), **Hot Topic** (6801 Hollywood Blvd., Hollywood; ☎ **323-462-2590**; Internet: www.hottopic.com), or the **SERIOUS store** (7569 Melrose Ave., Hollywood; ☎ **323-655-0589**; Internet: www.seriousstore.com) for the latest in lounge pants, platforms, and rock-star duds. A studded belt and Led Zeppelin T-shirt will get you more play than pleated Dockers.

Adults, do yourself a favor: Indulge in a cab if you tend to imbibe freely. Not only can you save yourself a trip to the pokey — L.A.'s finest are out en masse on weekends — but you may even save some cash. The parking rates get steeper as the week progresses (expect to pay up to $30 to park on the Sunset Strip Fridays and Saturdays).

Alrighty now, go have fun. And don't be intimidated by the too-cool-for-school folks who populate many of these clubs. They're probably tourists.

Getting past the velvet ropes

During your foray into club land, be prepared to encounter velvet ropes. But don't fret too much; the lines usually move, even if they move very slowly on weekend nights. Here are some tips for getting past the velvet ropes:

✔ **Call each venue in advance.** Ask specific questions about gaining entrance. Sometimes, if a club serves food, the surest way to get in is to make dinner reservations.

✔ **Get there early.** The biggest key to lassoing yourself in is early arrival.

✔ **Forget about attitude.** Everyone's someone in Hollywood, and seasoned door-men have heard all the lines. What almost never fails is a smile and a bit of patience.

A word to any underage readers: **Forget about using a fake I.D.** at L.A. bars and clubs. You will get busted, and you will be publicly humiliated. L.A. is very strict about its entrance policies. Some dance clubs do have special nights for all ages or 18 and over, so you may want to call and check on age limits. And hey, there's always **Club One Seven** (6800 Hollywood Blvd., Hollywood; ☎ 323-461-2017; Internet: www.onesevenhollywood.com), a *Seventeen* magazine–sponsored dance party on Friday and Saturday nights exclusively for guests 20 and under.

For Those About to Rock

Ah yes, L.A. rocks. The city is thriving with both new and veteran rock clubs, and the music scene is hotter than Riverside asphalt (ouch!). The area with the highest concentration of good rock clubs is the Sunset Strip in West Hollywood. It's well lit at night, and most venues have valet parking. The clubs listed below are open to all ages unless noted.

The Roxy
West Hollywood

Since the early '70s, this Sunset Strip club has been part of the celebrated Hollywood rock triumvirate that includes the Whisky a Go-Go and the Troubadour. Although its history includes storied superstar shows by Neil Young, Bruce Springsteen, David Bowie, and others, these days it tends to be the home of unknown local acts trying to break into the busi-ness. Check the *LA Weekly* and *New Times* concert ads to see what's play-ing here. Tickets will be scarce for big-name shows — and if you do get in, it will be crowded.

9009 W Sunset Blvd. ☎ 310-276-2222. Cover varies.

Key Club
West Hollywood

At the west end of the Sunset Strip is the ultra-snappy Key Club. This postmodern rock club was built at the site of a legendary L.A. rock club called Gazzarri's, where bands like The Doors and Buffalo Springfield started out. It's become a very popular destination for live music and late-night dancing, which is understandable. Compared with its neighboring warhorses, the bare bones Roxy and the Whisky a Go-Go, the Key Club offers first-class comfort.

9039 Sunset Blvd., West Hollywood. ☎ *310-274-5800. Cover varies.*

The Viper Room
West Hollywood

The music legacy of the Viper Room is unparalleled. Since its '93 debut, this black-hot nightclub owned by actor Johnny Depp has featured world-class talent on a weekly basis. You never know who's going to show up on stage; the club often schedules unannounced shows by big-name acts. You may find yourself taking a chance on a $10 cover only to find that the L.A. foursome Weezer is headlining. Hey, stranger things have happened. If you're in town on a Monday, check out the Viper Room's Camaro Club. Think fast bands, loose women, and loads of cocktails. It can get crowded, so you may lose sight of the stage, even in such a small club.

8852 Sunset Blvd. ☎ *310-358-1881. Cover $10–$15.*

House of Blues
West Hollywood

Fans of Southern kitsch and jambalaya will want to check out the original House of Blues, the first in the nightclub's ever-expanding chain (there's also one in Downtown Disney in Anaheim). It showcases a wide variety of live music, and the venue itself is worth taking a look at. It attracts top-flight acts from all pop and rock genres — including blues. Eric Clapton gave a special acoustic show here in the mid-'90s. Today, all kinds of not-just-blues-affiliated names pop up here. Sightlines from anywhere except the main floor can be iffy, and the chatter of Hollywood wannabes can compete with even the loudest bands, but the general quality of sound and production is high. The upstairs restaurant features a decent, Southern-derived menu, and the Sunday gospel brunch, though not cheap, is a great time, both for the food and the exuberant performances. From its colorful selection of folk art to the fanciful stage, the House of Blues offers a unique way to spend an evening.

8430 Sunset Blvd. ☎ *323-848-5100. Cover varies (there's no fee if you're dining, but you have to pay an additional charge to see any scheduled concerts).*

The Troubadour
West Hollywood

Just down the hill from the Sunset Strip is this veteran nightclub offering cutting-edge live music. The wood-grain interior is a relic from the days when this cozy Hollywood club showcased the Byrds and Eagles in the '60s and '70s. It was also a key stop for such quintessential L.A. acts as Van Halen in the '70s. In recent years, the booking has been something of a hodgepodge, but it's a good bet that some local, national, and international alternative rock acts will stop here on their way to becoming famous. There are a few rows of bleacherlike seats in the small balcony, but they get taken early most nights. Otherwise it's mostly standing room on the floor, which can get mighty crowded. The bar in front is often teaming with mid-level music-business staffers who should probably be inside watching the show instead. The all-ages venue books a wide variety of rock, punk, and alternative music.

9081 Santa Monica Blvd. ☎ *310-276-6168. Internet:* www.troubadour.com. *Cover varies; Mon free for anyone over 21, $3 for anyone under 21.*

Knitting Factory
Hollywood

The Knitting Factory, the western outpost of the New York club known for challenging, avant-garde presentations, is a high-tech, if a little aesthetically cold, complex of bar-restaurant, main performance room, and small "AlterKnit Lounge." It doesn't go as far outside the mainstream as its eastern sibling, but it still offers an impressively eclectic array of top rock, jazz, and experimental acts. Macy Gray, P.J. Harvey, and Beck are among those who choose it for special intimate performances. As of this writing, the restaurant hadn't really gotten its act together in terms of menu or service.

7021 Hollywood Blvd. ☎ *323-463-0204. Internet:* www.knitmedia.com. *Cover varies.*

The Palace
Hollywood

This Art Deco ex-vaudeville theater on Vine across from the famed Capitol Tower has been the most-used mid-sized concert site for rock acts since the early '80s. The Palace is often turned into a disco after shows or on days when no live act is booked. The floor can be a sweaty, crowded scene (music-business regulars usually stand toward the back). There is also a seated balcony if your legs aren't up to snuff.

1735 N. Vine St. ☎ *323-462-3000. Cover varies.*

The Hollywood Palladium
Hollywood

From '40s swing ballroom glory to '90s mosh-pit mayhem, the Palladium, with its chandeliers and sculpted balconies, has long been a landmark venue. Lately, though, it's been used only sporadically for rock shows. So watch listings in the *LA Weekly* and *New Times*, or check the Web site for primary rock promoter **Goldenvoice** (www.goldenvoice.com, worth checking for other area concerts, as well), and be prepared to stand — or mosh!

6215 W. Sunset Blvd. ☎ *323-962-7600. Cover varies.*

The Garage
Silver Lake

For those who like their rock down and dirty, The Garage is an excellent live music venue for *eastsidaz* with attitude. This greasy rock hang in the arty area east of Hollywood called Silver Lake has a Lower East Side New York vibe to it and a colorful interior. The cover is usually cheap, and multiple bands perform on weekends. Definitely a must-see spot for those who like boys and girls with tattoos.

4519 Santa Monica Blvd. ☎ *323-662-6166. Cover varies. 21 and older only.*

Spaceland
Silver Lake

The Silver Lake nightclub that started it all still rocks. The live-music venue born out of an old discothèque is permanently art-damaged and not terribly fancy, but that's part of its charm. Surprise guests show up often during the week. Beck, Daniel Lanois, and Fiona Apple are among the name artists who have performed spontaneous sets.

1717 Silver Lake Blvd. ☎ *323-833-2843. Cover varies. 21 and older only.*

Dragonfly
Hollywood

This way-happening rock venue in mid-Hollywood is at the heart of L.A.'s rock 'n' roll hurricane. On Wednesdays, the Pretty Ugly Club takes over, cranking up the volume to 11. Its co-host, Taime Downe, singer for Faster Pussycat and the Newlydeads, brings in stellar rock acts from around the country. On Fridays, it's Rawk House, another hot spot for new music and cute rock 'n' rollers.

6510 Santa Monica Blvd. ☎ *323-466-6111. Cover varies. 21 and older only.*

Largo
Hollywood

People are so devoted to this live music supper club, that if you duck out of the show early, you may get the stink-eye. It's understandable — musical mad-hatter Jon Brion, who produced the *Magnolia* soundtrack and such artists as Fiona Apple, performs quirky sets each Friday to a star-studded audience. On Saturdays, Grant Lee Buffalo takes over, while a variety of musical and comedy acts fill out the rest of the week.

432 N. Fairfax Ave. ☎ *323-852-1073. Cover varies.*

Snazzy Bars

There's nothing like a night on the town at one of Hollywood's gorgeous bars. We handpicked some of our favorites, narrowing the list down from many choices based on style, comfort, and easy access.

Hot, sharp, and cool

One of Hollywood's hottest bars is **Beauty Bar** (1638 Cahuenga Blvd., Hollywood; ☎ **323-464-7676**), a luscious pink confection with deejays nightly. The bar, which is designed to look like an old-school beauty parlor (the original in New York *was* an actual beauty parlor), serves martinis and manicures by appointment on weekends. No cover.

We love **Daddy's** (1610 Vine St., Hollywood; ☎ **323-463-7777**) because it's a sharp-looking cocktail lounge with no attitude, comfortable seating, and super-nice servers. Although it's only been around for a couple of years, it feels like it's been here forever. It's a gem. No cover. Open nightly.

If you like the idea of chilling like a genie in a bottle, you'll probably enjoy **Belly** (7929 Santa Monica Blvd., Los Angeles; ☎ **323-692-1068**). The artfully designed tapas bar and lounge is a favorite spot for singles on the prowl, and the soulful DJ'd music adds to the mix. Every food item is priced at appetizer rates, but the portions are plentiful — an added bonus. No cover. Open nightly.

Dive bars and hipster hangs

The **Burgundy Room** (1621 Cahuenga Blvd., Hollywood; ☎ **323-465-7530**) is a dive bar in the heart of Hollywood, just down the street from the Beauty Bar. The DJs spin rock and punk. We advise you to arrive early on weekends, or you may have to wait in line (the small bar hits capacity early). No cover; open nightly.

One of our favorite hipster hangs is the **Bigfoot Lodge** (3172 Los Feliz Blvd., Los Angeles; ☎ 323-662-9227). The bar is cleverly designed to look like a folk-art ski lodge, down to its hydraulic Smokey the Bear. But don't let the Sasquatch National Forest sign fool you: The only wildlife you'll find here are the hot chicks dancing on the bar top. Although the Bigfoot Lodge is located in Atwater Village, a quiet community about 10 or 15 minutes from Hollywood (and right next to Los Feliz) by surface streets, it's worth the drive. Cover varies; open nightly.

Swingers actor Alex Desert — the "playa" in the film who always wants to bail the second he gets into a bar — is an investor in **Vine** (1235 N. Vine St., Hollywood; ☎ 323-960-0800), one of the new breed of hipster Hollywood bars. It's located up the street from Three Clubs (see the next listing). Vine is a late-night fondue spot that also serves beer and wine. This low-key nightclub has a small dance floor and an upstairs lounge, and it is the only place we know of that serves a fondue recipe from Bo Derek. 21 and older; no cover.

At 10 years old, the **Three Clubs** (1123 N. Vine St., Hollywood; ☎ 324-462-6441) was among the first of the new wave of hipster bars that took Hollywood by storm in the late '80s and the '90s. It still has that sizzle, with its dark interior, friendly bartenders, and casual-cool clientele. Some nights you may find a DJ lurking in the back room, where it's *really* fun to lurk. 21 and older; no cover.

The legendary **Lava Lounge** (1533 N. La Brea Ave., Hollywood; ☎ 323-876-6612) opened its doors a month before the great quake of January '94, and it's still shaking. The tiki-themed bar, which has live music Wednesday through Saturday nights, once called Quentin Tarantino and Jon Favreau (of *Swingers* fame) regulars, and now it's serving up a whole new breed. The exotic drinks are adorned with plastic monkeys and mermaids, and you can't beat that with a swizzle stick. 21 and older; open nightly.

Swingers' hall of fame

The hidden gem the **Room** (1626 N. Cahuenga Blvd., Hollywood; ☎ 323-462-7196) is located at the epicenter of the Cahuenga Corridor, but you need to pay attention to find it. Forget the address and walk south from Beauty Bar on Cahuenga Boulevard, cut through the parking lot on your left, and make another left when you hit the alley. You'll see a door and a stool and, depending on the night, a few people hanging out. As this particular area of Hollywood has gotten more popular, the Room has become a more treasured bar, because it's still a quasi-secret despite its place in the Swingers' hall of fame. 21 and older; no cover.

Martinis and stilettos

What if you could shop for shoes while sipping on a cocktail? Well, **Star Shoes** (6364 Hollywood Blvd., Hollywood; ☎ 323-462-STAR/7827) can grant you your wish. The beautiful bar doubles as a shoe store, with eye-popping displays of vintage shoes enticing customers in off the street. There's a dance floor for late-night frolicking and an easy, breezy attitude-less atmosphere. No cover; open nightly.

Speaking of Swingers' hall of fame, don't forget to stop by the **Dresden Lounge** (1760 Vermont Ave., Los Feliz; ☎ 323-665-4294) and give a thumb's up to Marty and Elayne, the jazz combo popularized in *Swingers*. We have known that lovely couple for a long time, and frankly, they're tired of being asked to play "Stayin' Alive." Do us a favor: Ask Elayne to play "Autumn In New York"; she'll blow you a kiss. Marty and Elayne perform Monday through Saturday. 21 and older in lounge; no cover.

Hot Hotel Bars

Hotel bars are more popular than ever in L.A. Maybe it's the proximity to all those crispy rooms. And hey, if you decide to check yourself in, you eliminate the drinking-and-driving equation all together. Not bad.

There is nothing standard about the lobby bar in the **Standard** (Standard Hotel, 8300 Sunset Blvd., West Hollywood; ☎ 323-650-9090), a whimsical hotel bar that's a big favorite among Hollywood scenesters. From the lobby's muted space-age retro vibe to a bar lined with Wild West wallpaper, the Standard has a surreal quality that's broadly appealing. There's lots of outdoor seating. A general party ambience takes over on weekends. No cover; open nightly.

The Grafton Hotel boasts the very popular bar and restaurant **Balboa** (8462 Sunset Blvd., West Hollywood; ☎ 323-650-8383). Balboa is divided into two separate areas — a lovely modern restaurant to the left of the lobby, and a cocktail lounge to the right. To hang in the lounge, guests must enter from outside the hotel. No cover; open nightly.

Adjacent to the great Chateau Marmont lies **Bar Marmont** (8171 Sunset Blvd., West Hollywood; ☎ 323-650-0575), a picturesque restaurant and bar that attracts entertainment royalty on a nightly basis. On weekends, Bar Marmont is hosted by the famous bald drag diva, Constance, who is liable to burst into song on a whim. No cover.

Drinks With a View

The restaurant **Yamashiro** (1999 Sycamore Ave., Hollywood; ☎ 323-466-5125), one of the city's legendary haunts, still has our favorite view. The classic Japanese restaurant overlooks Hollywood in all its glory, and if you arrive in time for sunset, you can settle in for the night and watch the colors of the sky fade from pink to ink. It's terribly romantic and worth the long, winding drive up the hill. No cover; open nightly.

Cindy Crawford's hubby, Rande Gerber, knew what he was doing when he created **Skybar** (8440 Sunset Blvd., West Hollywood; ☎ 323-848-6025), a sexy indoor/outdoor bar with a poolside view. If you're a guest at the Mondrian Hotel, you're guaranteed admittance. If you're not a hotel guest, you need to call in advance to make a reservation. It's worth the hassle. You never know who you're going to see belly up to the bar, but more than likely, you'll be too busy checking out the bright lights of the city to even notice. No cover.

Latin Flava

The **Conga Room** (5364 Wilshire Blvd., Los Angeles; ☎ 323-938-1696) is a wildly colorful nightclub, featuring bands from all over the globe. You can wine, dine, and unwind on its spacious dance floor, which stays cooking all the way to closing. If you want to splurge, the club offers VIP packages, which give guests first-class treatment in special seating areas. Hey, with such investors as J. Lo and Jimmy Smits, you never know who may be shimmying next to you. Cover varies.

The **Rumba Room** (1000 Universal CityWalk, Universal City; ☎ 818-622-1226) is a crown jewel of the capitalistic mecca known as CityWalk — a shopping and clubbing area adjacent to Universal Studios. The upscale Latin dance club has live music on weekends and a hot roster of DJs. Cover varies.

One of L.A.'s best-kept secrets is **El Floridita** (1253 N. Vine St., Hollywood; ☎ 323-871-8612), a small Cuban hot spot. Despite its hole-in-the-wall status, big-time actors like Sandra Bullock and Jack Nicholson are regulars, both on and off the dance floor. Cover is $10; entrance is free with dinner. Open nightly.

Saturday Night Fever

If you find yourself in town on a Saturday night, and you're feeling frisky, the following dance clubs offer a memorable way to sample L.A.

Saturday Night Finger at **Goldfingers** (6423 Yucca St., Hollywood; ☎ 323-962-2913) is one sweet dance scene. DJ and local rock legend Coyote Shivers spins '80s glam, rock, new wave, and punk, much to the crowd's delight. Goldfingers, a trashy nightclub with a rock 'n' roll heart, is located in a section of Hollywood that's a bit divey, but there's parking to the right of the club's entrance, and everything is cheap, including the $5 cover.

The **Sunset Room** (1430 N. Cahuenga Blvd., Hollywood; ☎ 323-463-0004) is a super supper club for the well-heeled set that features hot DJs and a celebrity clientele. The cover is usually $15, but call in advance for guest-list inquiries. Dinner reservations are recommended.

Gay Faves

Tiger Heat at **7969** (7969 Santa Monica Blvd., West Hollywood; ☎ 323-654-0280) is a pop lover's paradise. This mostly boy-toy scene revels in all things Britney, Pink, Madonna, and Jacko. Fun, fun, fun. 18 and older. Thursdays only. Cover $5 to $7.

Girl Bar at the **Factory** (652 La Peer Dr., West Hollywood; ☎ 310-659-4551) is L.A.'s hottest lesbian nightclub. The spacious dance party boasts women DJs, go-go dancers, and promoters. It's a weekly girl-power powwow. Fridays only. $10 cover.

No matter what year or what day of the week, **Rage** (8911 Santa Monica Blvd., West Hollywood; ☎ 310-652-7055) rages. The long-running gay dance club in the heart of boy town is a scorcher of a scene. Rage books a wide variety of DJs, who spin everything from progressive house to alternative rock. 21 and older. Cover varies.

The hot scene on a Tuesday night for boys and their admirers is **Beige** at **360** (6290 Sunset Blvd., Hollywood; ☎ 323-871-2995), a penthouse restaurant and nightclub with a fabulous view. Its hosts modeled Beige after a New York club of the same name. It's always packed, so early arrival is recommended. Tuesdays only. 21 and older. No cover.

If you want to be absolutely fabulous, try hitting up the **Queen Mary** (12449 Ventura Blvd., Studio City; ☎ 818-506-5619), L.A.'s longest-running drag bar. The Queen Mary hosts performances nightly, wherein its stage becomes something of a spectacle, as the likes of Madonna, Diana Ross, and Britney Spears make convincing appearances. It's a simple, reasonably priced place. The only thing fancy about the Queen Mary are the ladies' gowns. 21 and older. Cover varies.

Tourist Traps

Nothing beats a mechanical bull or full-tilt karaoke for bringing out-of-towners in off the street. In these two places, a fun time is mandatory for all.

The **Saddle Ranch Chop House** (8371 Sunset Blvd., West Hollywood; ☎ 323-656-2007) has something for everyone. The country-themed restaurant serves whopping steaks, and its desserts need their own zip code. Good thing you can work it off on the mechanical bull (just try and ride that thing when it is cranked up to 10). This place gets loud and rambunctious, just like a good spaghetti western. No cover; open nightly.

The same geniuses behind the Saddle Ranch also created **Miyagi's** (8225 Sunset Blvd., West Hollywood; ☎ 323-650-3524), a Sunset Strip sushi restaurant that's actually a three-level nightclub. Karaoke heats things up on weekends, and don't be surprised to find guests doing the "wasabi" on bar tops. Blame it on the sake. No cover, open nightly.

Part VII
A Trip to Disneyland

The 5th Wave   By Rich Tennant

@RICHTENNANT

Disneyland Jungle Cruise

STOP HERE FOR
MALARIA AND TYPHOID
INOCULATIONS

In this part . . .

We give you the lowdown on the park that started it all — and no, you shouldn't miss it. We tell you how to find your way around the Disneyland Resort — which includes both Disneyland and the newer California Adventure — and offer tips on the best times to go, how to avoid crowds, which rides are best for the little ones, and how to save money on the resort's offerings. We advise you on the best places to stay and dine, and give our oh-so-humble opinion on which rides will rock you — and which ones may just rock you to sleep.

Chapter 22

Finding Your Way to Disneyland Drive

• •

In This Chapter

▶ Taking a look at the Disneyland Resort

▶ Choosing the best time to visit

▶ Deciding how long to stay

▶ Buying tickets and special passes

▶ Getting to and parking in the park

• •

*T*hey laughed when Walt Disney said he was going to build an amusement park. "Walt's Folly," they called it, just an expensive playground doomed to failure. Really. This happened. They said this. But Walt became rich, and they did not.

Disneyland opened in 1955. Although the park wasn't quite what it is now, either in content or in terms of the scary efficiency with which it runs, it was an instant hit, naysayers be darned. The bugs that plagued it in the beginning were quickly worked out, and the modern-day Disneyland is a well-oiled machine of legendary proportions, one that calls visitors "guests" and employees "cast members" and refers to off-limit areas as "backstage." See if you can catch a Disney employee — oops, we meant "cast member" — not smiling. And if you do catch one wearing a grimace, see if he or she is still working there a day later. Hey, we can mock it all day long, but we can't argue with the success of the place in terms of the lucrative dividends it has generated, the copies it has spawned (hello, Euro-Disney!), and, yes, the overall pleasant experience to be had there on all but the hottest, most crowded days.

We can, however, complain about the constant evolution of Disneyland, as many locals do. Uncle Walt's original vision remains largely intact — a microcosm of the best of America, from small-town iconic images to the wonders of futuristic utopia to the best of mythology, all by way of Disney treatment, of course. The park was fairly simple to begin with; some of the most beloved rides (Pirates of the Caribbean, It's a Small World) didn't turn up until the mid-1960s, after they were entries in the 1964 World's Fair in New York.

Disney

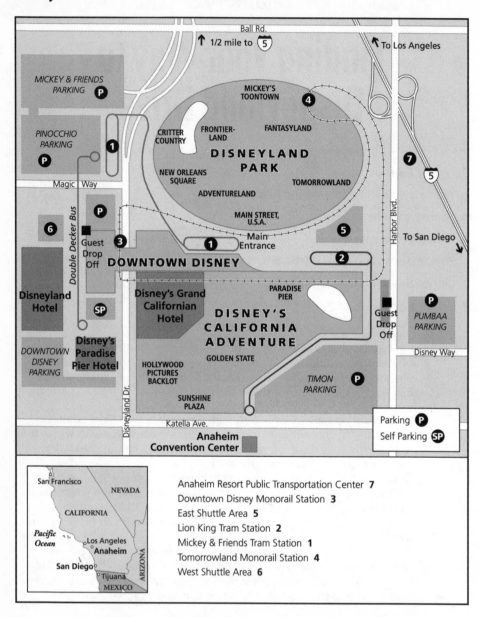

Over time, rides have come and gone — one of the favorite games of long-time attendees is "What is your favorite Disney ride from the past?" You can always tell boomer attendees, because they can still sing the theme from the House of the Future, which became history — as in completely demolished — in 1967. It is with no small measure of regret that they recall the house's space-age picture telephones, plastic chairs, and ultrasonic dishwashers.

There is even some concern among boomers, who grew up at the park and now bring their own children, about the changing face of Disneyland. It's not just nostalgia for lost rides, it's also complaints about how fast-paced it's become and how it caters more, it seems, to the short-attention-span generation, with rides that do all the work for you rather than appeal to the imagination. This may be why, when describing the park, we tend to point out the small details, the simple pleasures that can get overlooked in the rush towards mega-effects.

Introducing the Disneyland Resort

Disneyland has come a long way since its inception, from "Walt's Folly" to something so huge it spawned parks in Florida, France, and Japan. Here in California, it recently expanded into a new park, the California Adventure, which, along with the original Disneyland, three hotels, and one big shopping center, comprises the sprawling complex known as the Disneyland Resort. To lure big kids, there are clubs and late-night offerings; to lure their parents, there are fancy restaurants and shopping. It would be too easy to dismiss the park as commerce over fantasy, for Disneyland has always been about product tie-ins; it's just real slick about it. (A spoonful of sugar helps the medicine go down, don't you know.)

But to every inch of the place there is still given a tremendous amount of thought, detail, research, and, yes, imagination. No matter how it evolves, Disneyland (we still say that, even though it's Disneyland Resort) remains a place of delight where, even in the midst of souvenir stands and overpriced snacks, a kid bursts into pure giggles of joy because a mouse waved at him. And every time we go, we still play the game of "who can spot the Matterhorn first," and then shiver with pleasure when it appears, for it means that we are almost there.

Deciding When to Visit

The best time to visit may be when you are able take a vacation from your job and the kids are off from school. If you're flexible with your schedule, though, a number of factors can influence your decision, because Disneyland has seasons of its very own.

  ✔ **Busiest times:** Disneyland is busiest in summer (between Memorial Day and Labor Day), but it can also be crowded on holidays (Thanksgiving week, Christmas week, President's Day weekend, Easter week, and Japan's "Golden Week" in early May) and weekends year-round. All other times make up the off-season. During the busy summertime, Tuesday through Thursday is the best time to come; Friday and Saturday are the most crowded days.

✔ **Fireworks, shows, and parades:** If you want to see all the shows, parades, and fireworks, you'll have to come during the high season, because scheduling is sporadic on off-season weekdays. Christmas brings its own special magic to Disneyland. The park is dressed up for the holidays, complete with giant decorated trees, wreathes everywhere, visits with Santa, and the Candelight Parade, wherein carolers from all over Southern California lead visitors to a special recital of the Christmas story.

✔ **Summer scorchers:** Consider the summer heat when deciding when to go. Scorching days in July, August, and September can make waiting to board a ride feel like a death march, with everyone crowding into available shady spots to find some protection from the heat, or super-long lines to buy cold drinks. Visiting during these months can be fine; just plan to take advantage of the indoor attractions during the midday heat. Your reward later on will be a pleasantly balmy evening, when being outdoors becomes a delight — though there can still be big crowds, with a heavy emphasis on slightly rowdy high school and college kids.

✔ **Crowd-free days:** If you want to avoid crowds, visit on a weekday, preferably in November, December, or January (excluding Thanksgiving and Christmas weeks). You run the risk that some rides may be closed for maintenance (never more than three or four at a time), but visiting during this low season is the best way to maximize a single day.

✔ **First-quarter rains:** Southern California gets most of its precipitation between January and April, but only a sustained downpour should affect your Disney plans (some rides can, however, be closed on account of weather). If the forecast predicts rain, bring both a collapsible umbrella and waterproof rain poncho (or splurge on the cute Mickey Mouse ponchos that suddenly appear when the first raindrop falls). Even if you get wet, you'll enjoy the lightest crowds of the year!

The locals know the truth; the very best day to come to Disneyland is a midweek winter day with a slight drizzle. The amateurs tend to stay away — and you may find that you have the park virtually all to yourself.

Deciding How Long to Stay

You'll want to devote at least one (very) full day to Disneyland alone. If you're planning to visit during one of the peak periods, crowds and wait times will limit the attractions you're able to enjoy in a single day, so plan to spend the night and re-enter Disneyland fresh the following morning. Depending on how you feel about California Adventure, you may want to set aside two days to experience both parks.

Park Hopper Passes (see "Getting the Lowdown on Admission," later in this chapter) are a great deal for the money and don't require you to visit on consecutive days (if you want to break up your Disney stay with a day at the beach, for example). Families with small children will especially want a multiday option, regardless of the season. While surviving a marathon Disney day is a badge of honor for older kids, you all know that your toddler's naptime crankiness will eventually rear its ugly head.

All in all, we suggest allotting two or three full days for the Disney attractions, which gives you enough time to immerse yourself in the fantasy before moving on to the next leg of your California visit. (If you're staying elsewhere in Southern California and would like two days to experience the park, plan on spending the night at the park rather than driving back again the next day. Trust us, you'll be glad you did.)

Getting the Lowdown on Admission

At press time, admission to Disneyland or California Adventure — including unlimited rides and all festivities and entertainment — was $45 for adults and kids ages 10 and over, and $35 for kids ages 3 to 9 (kids under 3 enter free). These figures are given only as guidelines, because new prices can pop up at any time. This price allows you admission to one park of your choice.

Disney currently offers the aforementioned multiday **Park Hopper pass,** which allows the holder unlimited access to both Disneyland and California Adventure. A three-day pass is $114 for adults, and $90 for kids ages 3 to 9. Four-day admission costs $141 and $111, respectively. While the passes must be used within a two-week period, the days spent at the park need not be consecutive, so this is a most practical way to go. We go into further detail in the following chapters, but there are good reasons to have access to both parks, provided you don't pay full price for California Adventure.

Disney offers regular deals on ticket prices, especially during the slow winter months (when those three-day Park Hopper passes go for $99 each). However, at press time, the Park Hopper passes for use during the summer months were going for $90 each when purchased online (www.disneyland.com). So it's well worth your time to do some checking around, especially on the Internet.

Expect to pay a parking charge of between $7 to $10, which may be included in some admission packages. *Always ask* whether parking is part of the package before you buy from Disney.

Opening the starting gate

Disneyland is open every day of the year, but operating hours vary widely. Call for the information that applies to the time frame of your visit (☎ 714-781-4565). You can also find exact open hours, ride closures, and show schedules online at www.disneyland.com.

Generally speaking, the park is open from 9 or 10 a.m. to 6 or 7 p.m. on weekdays, fall to spring; and from 8 or 9 a.m. to midnight or 1 a.m. on weekends, holidays, and during summer vacation periods. If you'd like to receive a copy of the park's "Vacation Planner" brochure to orient yourself before you go, call ☎ 800-225-2024.

Buying in advance can be an enormous time-saver. If you plan to arrive during a busy time (when the gates open in the morning, or between 11 a.m. and 2 p.m.), purchasing your tickets in advance and getting a jump on the crowds at the ticket counters is your best bet. You can buy your tickets through the Disneyland Web site, at Disney stores throughout the United States, or by calling the mail-order line (☎ 714-781-4043). Many area hotels also sell tickets (including whatever special deal is being offered at the time) through an arrangement with Disney.

Discovering the art of the (package) deal

If you intend to spend two or more nights in Disney territory, investigating the available package options can pay off. Start by contacting your hotel (even those in Los Angeles or San Diego) to see whether it offers Disneyland admission packages. Some of the inclusive airline vacation packages include admission to Disneyland.

In addition, check with the official Disney agency, **Walt Disney Travel Co.** (☎ 800-225-2024 or 714-520-5050; Internet: www.disneyland.com), whose packages are value-packed time- and money-savers with lots of built-in flexibility. You can log on to the Web site and click on "Book Your Vacation" to peruse package details, take a virtual tour of participating hotel properties, and get online price quotes for customized, date-specific packages.

Hotel choices range from the official Disney hotels to one of 35 neighbor hotels in every price range (Chapter 23 has our hotel recommendations). A wide range of available extras includes admission to other Southern California attractions, guided tours (such as **Universal Studios** or a Tijuana shopping trip), and behind-the-scenes Disneyland tours, all in limitless combinations. Rates are highly competitive, especially considering that each package may include multiday admission, early park entry, and free parking (if you choose a Disney hotel), plus keepsake souvenirs and coupon books. If you want to add air transportation or car rental, the Disney Travel Co. can make those arrangements, too.

Continental Airlines.

Name: BEDDOE/ALICE
Date: 26JUL
OnePass:

BVKOW3

Flight: CO 1763Y

Gate: C-16   **Seat:** 7D

Please provide optional contact information on the reverse of this boarding pass.

0051561402102O
OAK   ETICKET

BOARDING PASS

B2 832990-1

Q   ID

72

Continental Airlines.

Name: BEDDOE/ALICE
Date: 26JUL   72
OnePass:
Mileage:

Flight: CO 1763Y

Gate: C-16 **Seat:** 7D
Depart: 858P
HOUSTON
Arrive: 1052P
OAKLAND
Board Time: 823P
0051561402102O

This portion of the boarding pass should be retained as evidence of your journey.

Esta porción del pase de abordar debe guardarse como prueba de su viaje.

Dear Customer/*Estimado Cliente:*

Thank you for taking a moment to provide optional contact information.

Agradecemos que nos proporcione información opcional sobre otra persona con la que podamos ponernos en contacto.

Name/Nombre: _____

_____ (Must not be traveling with you today. *No debe estar viajando con usted el día de hoy.*)

Phone Contact/Teléfono: _____

(Include country code, area code & number. *Incluya las claves del país y la ciudad y el número de teléfono.*)

This information is only retained for 24 hours. *Esta información se retiene solamente 24 horas.*

International Documentation Checklist (To be completed by Continental Agent only)

Destination Country: _____		Customer's Nationality: _____
Passport Required:	Yes / / No / /	Expiration: _____
APIS Completed:	Yes / / No / /	If no, ID used: _____
Valid Visa Required:	Yes / / No / /	Expiration: _____
Visa Waiver Applicant:	Yes / / No / /	
Tourist Card Issued:	Yes / / No / /	Verify forms. _____
US Taxes / Fees Collected:	Yes / / No / /	For _____ (Country)

Getting to Disneyland

Disneyland is located in the heart of Anaheim in Orange County, about 30 miles south of Los Angeles and 98 miles north of San Diego. To get there from either city, follow I-5 until you see signs for Disneyland; dedicated off-ramps from both directions lead directly to the park's parking lots and surrounding streets.

If you'd rather wing it, **Los Angeles International Airport (LAX)** serves as the region's major airport. It's about 30 miles away from the park. You can rent a car at the airport and drive to Anaheim, or you can take advantage of the many public-transportation services at LAX. Note that there are a number of shuttles just for Disneyland. They cost around $20, but haggling can be done.

If you'd rather fly directly into Anaheim from another state or another California city, the nearest airport is **John Wayne International Airport** in Irvine. It is 15 miles from Disneyland at the intersection of I-405 and Highway 55 (☎ **949-252-5200;** Internet: www.ocair.com). Most national airlines and major rental-car agencies serve the airport. To reach Anaheim from the airport, rent a car and take Highway 55 east, and then I-5 north to the Disneyland exit.

You can also catch a ride with **American Taxi** (☎ **888-482-9466**), whose cabs queue up at the Ground Transportation Center on the lower level; reservations are not necessary. Expect the fare to Disneyland to run about $26. If only two of you are making the trip, though, consider using **Super Shuttle** (☎ **800-BLUE-VAN;** Internet: www.supershuttle.com), which charges $10 per person. Advance reservations are recommended.

Before you pay for a taxi or shuttle service, ask if your Anaheim hotel offers airport transportation when you make your reservation.

Driving to Disneyland

Remember to take rush hour into consideration if you're driving to the park. The park opens fairly early — 9 a.m., in some cases — so, if you're going to be there, ticket in hand, when the gates swing open, you need to leave the L.A. area perhaps as early as 7 a.m. If you leave later, you may get stuck in traffic.

Parking

The parking is now a slightly more complicated concern at Disneyland. Before California Adventure was built, it was all pretty straightforward. Visitors simply parked in a very large lot, with designated areas named after Disney characters, serviced by a tram. But the lot became California Adventure, so now it's a whole new parking experience.

Regulars feel that the **Mickey and Friends parking structure** (perhaps the largest indoor parking lot in the country) is the best bet. It's well lit and easily accessible. However, it is also the first choice of everyone coming to the park, so you are going to have to contend with lines. Still, it's better than the **Timon and Simba lots,** which use a tram to ferry visitors to the parks. But the Timon and Simba lots are better than the **Pumba lot,** which is strictly for overflow and doesn't currently have any kind of transport. If you use the latter, prepare for a long walk (though it might be a good place to go if you fear waiting in car lines more than walking).

Chapter 23

Where to Stay and Dine in Disneyland

In This Chapter

▶ Finding a place to stay, inside and outside the parks

▶ Finding a place to dine, inside and outside the parks

*H*ere we give our advice on where to stay, both inside and outside of the parks, as well as tips on the best places to eat to fuel yet another day of Disneyland fun.

Where to Stay

There's a funny story about Disneyland. Back when Uncle Walt built his park, he knew that people would want to stay nearby, so he built a hotel, the **Disneyland Hotel,** inside the park. The park was a bit of a success, and many, many people wanted to come to it. Savvy hotel owners put up motel lodges (the predominant kind of tourist hotel at the time) right at the very edges of the park itself. But Disney, in perhaps his only misstep, only bought enough land for his more or less immediate purposes. As a result, Disney lost business. Disney corrected this error when he created Walt Disney World in Florida by buying up pretty much all the land for several states in every direction from the main park.

Up until recently, there was only one Disney-associated hotel, along with a whole bunch of tacky motor courts (many of which were themed to seem associated with Disney — "Fairy Tale Village," say, or "Robin Hood Courts"). Now, there are three (but only three) Disney-located and Disney-run hotels, but loads of nonaffiliated accommodations lie just at the outskirts of the park. These nonaffiliated hotels are mostly of the chain variety; you can pretty much close your eyes and pick one, and not go wrong. In fact, many of the hotels outside the property are very nice indeed — a Hilton, a Sheraton, a Doubletree — and they cost about the same as Disney's sensational

Grand Californian (see "Disneyland hotels," later in this chapter). But while those fine hotels offer comfortable, well-appointed lodgings, they are nothing compared with the Grand Californian.

Disney has a relationship with a number of hotels in the area. Together, they offer a package called the "Good Neighbor Package." You can purchase Disneyland tickets from the participating hotel at the regular price, thus saving yourself from having to stand in potentially very long lines at the parks. If Disney is offering any special ticket discounts during the time of your stay, the hotels will offer the same discount. (You must be staying at these hotels to purchase tickets from them.)

One of the advantages to staying at a Disney Resort hotel is that guests get early admission to the parks on certain days. About 90 minutes before the official opening, Disney hotel guests are allowed into Disneyland (and now, California Adventure) before the rest of the public. So you may be able to get in a couple rides and avoid what may normally be a prohibitively long wait in line — a cool deal, and worth the money to stay here. However, as of press time, this long-time extra's future was in doubt. Do ask about it, however.

Disneyland hotels

For a breakdown of hotel prices, go to Chapter 8.

Disney's Grand Californian
$$$ Disneyland

The Grand Californian is a thing of lavish and loving beauty, a drop-dead gorgeous hotel that has been painstakingly researched and designed. Styled to evoke Yosemite's landmark Ahwahnee Hotel (it's the "Mock-wahnee," if you will), it has incredible period detail, from the cavernous, multistoried lobby with the giant roaring fireplace, right down to the door fixtures and even the trash cans in each room. All the Grand Californian lacks is the patina of age. It will get there eventually, but you shouldn't wait until then to stay overnight. The first hotel ever built within the actual confines of the Disneyland park (well, California Adventure, which it adjoins through a special entrance), the Grand Californian is the luxury Disney Resort hotel. It's an increasingly rare hotel that invites guests to hang around the lobby and enjoy its cushy chairs, fireplace, and nightly piano player. Several times a day, a storyteller thrills kids with campfire tales; this charming, free service is just one of many kid-friendly activities (not to mention the three fun pools to play in). The rooms are Arts and Crafts smashes, with nature themes (branches and leaves), lush amenities, and even a lack of maid carts in the hallways (baskets deliver the fresh linens in the morning). All of the rooms have robes, cribs, irons and boards, and duel vanities. The beds are comfy and firm, but the towels could be a bit softer, to tell the truth. Aren't we ungrateful? In truth, we just love this place to pieces — Disney should be justly proud of themselves.

Note: Rooms overlooking the California Adventure are the most desirable; other rooms in the hotel overlook Downtown Disney (which could make for some noise at night, although it's all closed up by midnight) and the monorail (which shuts down when the park does, and besides, it doesn't make all that much noise, anyway).

1600 S. Disneyland Dr., Anaheim. ☎ *714-956-6400. Fax: 714-300-7300. Internet:* www.disneyland.com. *Parking: Free self-parking, and valet ($24). Rack rates: $200–$310.*

Disneyland Hotel

$$–$$$ **Disneyland**

The Disneyland Hotel is the original Disney hotel, bless its heart, and for a while, it was the only Disney hotel. It was once so very, very grand and fun to stay at, but now it's looking a little worn around the edges. Rooms are in the process of being upgraded, thank heavens, because that '70s decor and those tough mattresses just aren't aging well. The new rooms each have a theme, so you get to choose between, say, the Goofy room, the Minnie room, or the Donald room. Each room will have a different (bright pastel) color scheme, with the character in question showing up as a painting on the walls of the room's foyer or in prints. There is a Peter Pan–themed pool area, complete with water slide and pirate ship. Oh, face it; it's what you want in a Disney hotel, especially if you're a family with kids under 10. Still, having seen the wonders of the Grand Californian, it's hard to get enthusiastic about staying here anymore.

1150 Magic Way, Anaheim. ☎ *714-956-6400. Fax: 714-956-6597. Internet:* www.disney land.com. *Parking: Free self-parking, and valet ($24). Rack rates: $170–$255.*

Disney's Paradise Pier

$$–$$$ **Disneyland**

This hotel, the second of the Disneyland hotels and the first to get a facelift, is styled to evoke sunny California beach culture, with a little Asian mellow to top it off. It's the smallest of the three (500 rooms), and it has the lowest profile. But it does have its own entrance into California Adventure. Basically, the only reason to stay here is, well, because the other Disney hotels are full. There's nothing *wrong* with it; it is, however, the only non-themed hotel of the three, and as such, it simply remains undistinguished. Frankly, you could be staying at any high-end chain hotel for all you know. Sure, the Paradise Pier is pretty, it's more intimate, and it's more adult-oriented, all of which can be nice. But still. The rooms wearing sunny beach pastel colors (corals, blue-greens) are elegant, modern, and forgettable. The pool is rooftop, which can be kind of cool, but it pales when compared with the ones at its sibling hotels.

1717 S. Disneyland Dr. ☎ *714-956-6400. Fax: 714-776-5763. Internet:* www.disney land.com. *Parking: Free self-parking, and valet ($24). Rack rates: $140–$230.*

Hotels outside the parks

Candy Cane Inn

$–$$ **Anaheim**

In the previous section, we talk about those fairy-tale-themed motor courts that sprung up near the park in the years after Disneyland was built. The Candy Cane Inn is more or less their heir. It is a sweet, family-run place that is just this side of shabby, but in a really good way. (That is not to imply that the hotel is in any way dirty or run down.) There is something to be said for staying in a place that tries to look like an old cartoon village (complete with cobblestones, balconies, flowers, and vines), and certainly it's a fun and friendly place. Excessively floral in decor, with a little pool (and a kiddie wading pool), it feels more like a retreat than one would expect of a place smack dab on a major boulevard. Because it's independent, you will have to pay a bit more than you would for a room at its chain-hotel neighbors.

1747 S. Harbor Blvd., Anaheim. ☎ *800-345-7057, 714-774-5284. Fax: 714-772-5462. Internet:* www.candycaneinn.net. *Parking: Free self-parking. Rack rates: $72–$108.*

Holiday Inn Anaheim at the Park

$$ **Anaheim**

This Holiday Inn is the most upscale non-Disney hotel on our list. Although it's only a couple of minutes down from the park, the hotel does offer a shuttle. Rooms are large, with a separate living area, all designed in a sort of hotel-generic decor, but they feel like they are constructed with good quality wood (not like a veneer pasteboard, let's say). Bathrooms are also bigger than those found in some of the more moderately priced hotels. Basically, you pay for more space and somewhat better amenities. The pool in the newly designed tropical courtyard is bigger (and open 24 hours) than those found at similar lodgings. A limited spa offers workouts, massages, and the like; the workout room is open 24 hours. This hotel is better suited for grownups visiting the park who want only a certain amount of childhood fun — a resort hotel without a theme or any kind of Disney stamp.

1221 S. Harbor Blvd., Anaheim. ☎ *800-545-7275, 714-758-0900. Fax: 714-917-0794. Internet:* www.holiday-inn.com. *Parking: Free self-parking. Rack rates: $110–$150.*

Park Inn Anaheim

$ **Anaheim**

Of all the many hotels on Harbor Boulevard, this is the only one that has any kind of interesting architecture — a sort of old-world Tudor design (okay, prefab, but still) rather than the typical concrete block. All the rooms are in the process of being upgraded, and the new color scheme should make them look lighter and fresher. The rooms are adequately sized. All of the rooms come complete with microwaves and a small fridge, which makes this a very fine choice for families looking to save some money on dining. There is a terrace-level pool and hot tub on the third story, more or less facing Disneyland. It's an extremely friendly place (winner of the 2002 President's Award for commitment to customer service), with a fireplace going in the lobby.

1520 S. Harbor Blvd., Anaheim. ☎ *714-635-7275. Fax: 714-635-7276. Internet:* www.parkinn-anaheim.com. *Parking: Free self-parking. Rack rates: $79–$99.*

Where to Dine

Because the area outside of the parks is littered with generic chain restaurants, the same types you have too many of in your own home-town, we urge you (with a few exceptions listed below) to eat at the big dining/entertainment/shopping complex known as Downtown Disney if you don't eat at the parks themselves. Although Downtown Disney is part of the Disneyland Resort, it has no entrance fee and no gate, so it's considered to be "outside the parks." Anyone who wants to leave the resort to visit Downtown Disney can have his or her hand stamped for re-entry to the parks. Downtown Disney is not cheap (if that's a concern, go to Denny's), but the choices are so much better. Hotel shuttles will take you near the shopping area, if not right to it, so it's easy enough to go to and from a nap in your hotel room to dinner in Downtown Disney.

If you want to save some money, especially when your hotel room has a fridge and/or microwave (like the rooms at the Park Vue Inn), there is a Vons supermarket located on the corner of Chapman Avenue and Haster Street — about a half-mile from Disneyland. Stock up on break-fast items, and maybe even some easy dinner items, to save time in lines and money at the park. You can't bring food into the park, but many a parent has snuck in some snacks, and you can too.

Dining inside the parks

Most dining facilities inside Disneyland are overrated, overcrowded, and overpriced, redeeming themselves only by convenience. (The exceptions are the offerings at **Downtown Disney** and **California Adventure;** we talk more about these facilities later in this section.) It's not as bad as the days when Twinkies and "space punch" (and not much else) were served over in Tomorrowland, but hamburgers and carbs still rule the day. While the food works as fuel, it hardly works as haute cuisine (and don't get us started on those fake beignets offered in New Orleans Square). On the other hand, it tickles us that giant dill pickles are still inexplicably offered as snacks at stands in

Adventureland and the Bountiful Valley Farm section of California Adventure. Here are some noteworthy exceptions worth seeking out:

- ✔ Scattered throughout Disneyland — but thankfully plotted on the official park map — are **churro carts,** named for the absolutely addictive cylindrical Mexican donuts they sell beginning at 11 a.m.

- ✔ The food itself may be unremarkable (although its authentic Monte Cristo sandwich has many fans), but don't miss a chance to eat at New Orleans Square's **Blue Bayou Restaurant,** the only restaurant in the park that requires reservations (stop by early in the day to make yours). It meticulously re-creates a classic New Orleans veranda, complete with lush, vine-wrapped ironwork, lazily chirping crickets, and (nonalcoholic) mint juleps. Its misty, sunless atmosphere comes from being literally inside the Pirates of the Caribbean ride, so boatloads of pirate-seeking parkgoers drift by during your meal.

- ✔ For healthy snack options, head to Adventureland for refreshments at the **Tiki Juice Bar** and the **Indy Fruit Cart,** which both offer tropical juices and unembellished fresh fruit for a natural sugar boost and more diet-friendly options.

- ✔ The **Royal Street Veranda** in New Orleans Square offers imitation beignets, as well as some decent (if hardly authentic) gumbo in a sourdough bowl.

The bulk of your eating, if possible, should be done at **California Adventure,** where the options are better in terms of quality and crowds. If you have the Hopper Pass (Chapter 22 has info on passes), consider coming over here, especially if you are an adult who doesn't want hot dogs. Even the fast food seems a bit more inventive and interesting in California Adventure. Among the highlights is the **Golden Vine Winery,** which offers two dining options: a more casual, and delicious little trattoria downstairs, and a formal dining room upstairs that offers *prix fixe tasting menus* (menus providing a fixed-price sampling of food). Both are surprising entries in an amusement park. They are actual mature dining options that serve excellent grownup food. Patronize them, please, so that there is a chance that more such ventures will be added in the future. Sitting on the edge of a mock harbor is the **Pacific Wharf Café,** which is modeled after those ubiquitous tourist-trap restaurants found at Fisherman's Wharf in San Francisco. It's not a bad choice: You can get real sourdough bread (made on park premises; afterward, you can go over to the Boudin Bakery and watch loaves bake) and clam chowder — have yours served in a sourdough bowl. **Cocina Cucamonga Mexican Grill** offers decent Mexican food with fresh tortillas made on the premises. A visit to the tortilla press is riveting fun for small children.

Breakfast places fill up as soon as the park opens. Because these facilities are expensive and uninspired, we say skip them; have some cereal before you arrive, and get right to the rides. In fact, try to avoid prime eating hours as much as you can, for everyone else will be noshing at that time, as well.

Downtown Disney

You really can't go wrong dining at one of the restaurants in Downtown Disney, unless, of course, you are on a strict budget. In which case you may want to resort to the fast food/chain restaurant options, or even the supermarket suggestion we describe earlier in the chapter. Downtown Disney is located outside the resort (although it's considered part of it), but you may walk through it to get to Disneyland (on the left) or California Adventure (on the right), depending on your arrival point. Downtown Disney has no entrance fee and no gate, but you will have to pay for parking if you drive. Anyone who wants to leave the Disneyland Resort to visit Downtown Disney can have his or her hand stamped for re-entry to the parks.

In addition to the restaurants listed below, you can also try the theme restaurants (**ESPN Zone, House of Blues, Rainforest Café**), or, better still, the **La Brea Bakery Café,** where you can nibble on the best bread Southern California has to offer. All the restaurants have outdoor balcony or patio seating facing the Downtown Disney traffic, so the people-watching potential is very high.

Catal
$$–$$$ MEDITERRANEAN RIM

This restaurant, one of two Pinot Group restaurants (the Pinot Group was founded by the creator of L.A.'s Patina, which is considered one of the best restaurants in town) here in Downtown Disney, specializes in coastal Mediterranean dishes such as bouillabaisse, cassoulet, braised lamb, lots of rotisserie items, and light pastas. It's set in a lovely two-story space, with a Deco facade and a strong wood decor that emphasizes a wine and harvest theme. The first floor features casual dining; the second floor offers more formal dining. Outside, the Uva Bar is a circular, casual cafe area right smack in the middle of downtown Disney.

1510 Disneyland Dr. ☎ 714-774-4442. Main courses: $8.50–$24.50. AE, MC, V. Open: Daily 5–10 p.m.

Naples Ristorante E Pizzeria
$$ ITALIAN

This restaurant, the other of the two Pinot Group eateries here, lands squarely in fancy pasta land in a space that has a decidedly California decor. The restaurant features a large outdoor patio, a bright, colorful ambience, and a very fun atmosphere.

1510 Disneyland Dr. ☎ 714-776-6200. Main courses: $10.95–$14.50. AE, MC, V. Open: Sun–Thurs 11 a.m.–10:30 p.m., Fri–Sat 11 a.m. to midnight (note that closing hours are often based on how busy they are that particular night).

Ralph Brennan's Jazz Kitchen
$$$ CREOLE/CAJUN

New Orleans comes to Disney — well, it already did, over at the park in the New Orleans Square — in the form of a building that looks as though it was lifted straight off Royal Street in the French Quarter (in fact, they copied the iron grillwork on the outside from the Royal Street Café). The "Brennan" in the name is that of the finest New Orleans restaurant family — the same ones who bring you Commander's Palace (perhaps the best restaurant in that food-mad city). Get the *couchon de lait* (Cajun roast pork) po' boy sandwich, or better still, the BBQ shrimp, which is actually done in a peppery butter sauce and demands to be soaked up with French bread. The jambalaya, gumbo, and seafood are all heavenly. They are also fattening, but who cares, you're on vacation. The restaurant features live music nightly. If we were to eat in one place in Downtown Disney, it would be here.

1590 S. Disneyland Dr. ☎ 714-776-5200. Main courses: $12.99–$23.99. AE, MC, V. Open: Sun–Thurs 10 a.m.–10 p.m., Fri–Sat 10 a.m.–11 p.m.

Napa Rose
$$$$ CALIFORNIA CUISINE

It's elegant, but not stuffy (the architect MacIntosh designed it); all you will want to do is sit and look at the detailing, the floor-to-ceiling stained glass, the storytelling mural that lines the ceiling, the fireplace, and so on. This is Very Important Dining, with a price tag to match, but what a treat. Clearly, you're meant to think that you're in the heart of California wine country, where they take dining (to say nothing of wine) very seriously, indeed. Menus change seasonally, but here are some highlights from the most recent winter list: scallops with a sauce of lemon, lobster, and vanilla; pheasant with merlot-date essence; truffled risotto cake stuffed with fontina cheese with rock shrimp bolognese. Wasted on children, you say? Perhaps, but note that they have a children's menu, with simple things like buttered noodles, quesadillas, and pizzas. Mom and dad can have gourmet fun and avoid having to fret about Junior's finicky food habits. Oh, and they have 22 sommeliers, so you can guess what the wine list looks like. This would be a wonderful restaurant no matter where it was located; that it's here is just the cherry on top.

1600 S. Disneyland Dr. ☎ 714-956-6755. Reservations required. Main courses: $23.50–$34.50. AE, MC, V. Open: Daily 5:30–10:00 p.m., Sun brunch 11 a.m.–2 p.m.

Dining outside the parks

Casa Garcia

$–$$ Anaheim   MEXICAN

The Mexican food in this family-style, family-friendly restaurant is authentic (well, in that Southern California Mexican way). This restaurant is located in a strip mall about a half-mile from Disneyland. Nothing on the menu costs more than $14, and that's for the paella (rice with all kinds of meats and seafood in it). The award-winning menu (with the occasional charming mistake: "Barbacoa — oven cooked in a red chile sauce"; doesn't that sound like the oven itself is cooked in red chile sauce?) covers the ground from shrimps *al mojo de ajo* (in garlic sauce) to taco combo platters to Texas BBQ pork ribs. Casa Garcia is a local favorite (always a good sign), with a casual cafe style. Come early, because there will be a line for dinner. But it's also open for breakfast!

531 W. Chapman Ave., Anaheim. ☎ *714-740-1108. Main courses: $5.95–$14.95. AE, DC, MC, V. Open: Daily 8 a.m.–11 p.m.*

Millie's

$–$$ Anaheim   HOME COOKING

Do you miss home cooking? We won't say that this is like your mom used to make (or your grandma, more likely, because moms don't seem to cook like this anymore), because we don't know your mom, but we hope it is, because it's that good. For breakfast, we seriously recommend the "world-famous" cinnamon rolls. They are soft, sweet, and airy (as well as dense), with icing that is just sweet enough, and a little dab of butter. Omelets are fresh and fluffy, and come with fresh biscuits and buttermilk gravy. For dinner, try the pot roast — for $10, you get a huge portion of falling-apart meat (no knife required!) served over carrots and potatoes (both mashed and otherwise) with soup or salad and cornbread. One portion may serve an entire family, unless your family includes a whole lot of teenagers. Force yourself to eat dessert; they have an Oreo fudge berry sundae. Please, skip the nearby Denny's and IHOP, and come here.

1480 S. Harbor Blvd. (next to the Park Vu Inn, which uses the restaurant for room service). ☎ *714-535-6892. Main courses: Breakfast $4.29–$7.49, lunch and dinner $6.99–$12.99. AE, CB, DC, DISC, MC, V. Open: 24 hours.*

Chapter 24

Exploring the Disneyland Resort

● ●

In This Chapter

▶ Preparing for your trip

▶ Maneuvering throughout the resort

▶ Discovering Disneyland

▶ Cruising through California Adventure

● ●

Disneyland is no longer just Disneyland; it is now the **"Disneyland Resort,"** which encompasses Walt's original amusement park and the ambitious new theme park, **California Adventure.** It also includes three resort hotels (reviewed in Chapter 23) and a new shopping/dining/entertainment district, **Downtown Disney.** Downtown Disney is located outside the resort (although it's considered part of it), but you may walk through it to get to Disneyland (on the left) or California Adventure (on the right), depending on your arrival point. Downtown Disney has no entrance fee and no gate, but you have to pay for parking if you drive. Anyone who wants to leave the Disneyland Resort to visit Downtown Disney can have their hand stamped for readmittance to the parks (for more on Downtown Disney, see Chapter 23). Here's your guide to exploring the resort's rides and attractions.

The first thing you notice about the parks is that they're clean. Really clean. The parks are so clean that someone once did a study to find out how long a piece of paper remains on the ground at Disneyland. Although we can't remember the exact number of seconds, it is just that — seconds.

Rides get the occasional facelift to take advantage of new technology, replace a tired joke, or just follow along with modern sensibilities. (For a brief time in the 1980s, there was an attempt to add some live figures to the rides; we had a knight suddenly come to life and wave an ax in our direction on the Haunted Mansion ride, a heart-stopping moment. The idea was quickly abandoned.) Political correctness has most affected the **Pirates of the Caribbean,** which used to show pirates chasing comely lasses and one pirate being chased by a homely woman. Now, the pirate being chased holds a pie, and the woman is trying to catch the thief. But the ride is worth taking over and over to catch all the little details, jokes, and insider bits (discussed exhaustively on the Internet, naturally) — the older and longer the ride, the more the Disney design team (the Imagineers) is likely to add funny, knowing details.

The Lowdown on Visiting Disneyland

This section could also be called "things we've learned over the years that can make your trip to the Disneyland Resort as hassle-free as possible." (There are, as you can imagine, entire Web sites devoted to this stuff.) In Chapter 22, we give you tips on the best seasons to come, the best time of day to visit, and how to get deals on tickets. In Chapter 23, we share our favorite places to stay and dine. In this chapter, we offer some basic, common-sense tips to ensure that your stay at the resort is an easy, fun-filled time.

✔ **Wear comfortable shoes.** You'll spend many hours walking, standing, and putting lots of strain on your legs and feet. Running shoes or tennis shoes are best. Open-toed shoes are fine, especially on hot days; just make sure that they support your feet.

✔ **Expect a dramatic temperature drop after dark, even in summer.** Bring a sweatshirt or jacket, and perhaps even long pants; you can store them in a locker, leave them in the car, or tote them in a backpack. Too many visitors show up in shorts and tank tops, only to discover at 10 p.m. that they're freezing their buns off!

✔ **Don't forget bare necessities** such as sunscreen (the park gets a lot of direct sun); camera film (more than you think you'll want; film costs more in the park than outside of it) and spare batteries; extra baby supplies; bottled water or a sports bottle that you can refill at drinking fountains; and snacks. Although anything that you may forget is available for purchase inside Disneyland, you'll cringe at the marked-up prices.

✔ **Purchase tickets in advance** via the Internet (www.disneyland. com) or phone (☎ 714-781-4043), or through your hotel; not only do Disney Resort hotels sell tickets, so do many area hotels through an arrangement with Disney. Buying beforehand saves you from standing in what can be long and slow and ticket lines. Packages are also offered through the official Disney agency **Walt Disney Travel Co.** (☎ 800-225-2024 or 714-520-5050; Internet: www.disneyland.com). Go to the Web site and click on "Buy Vacation Packages Online" to see package details and get online price quotes for customized, date-specific packages.

Disneyland for the little ones

It's a given that all children love, or will love, Disneyland, right? Wrong. Some rides may simply be too intense (fast, dark, subtle) for certain ages or personalities. We strongly urge you to seriously consider your own child's individual tastes, phobias, and neuroses before treating your tyke to this fabulous, but pricey, destination.

Disney's own rules and regulations do some natural weeding out, as most of the rides have some sort of age or height restrictions. For most attractions, you have to be 7 years or older to ride alone. For the more active, high-speed rides, such as **Space Mountain, Splash Mountain,** and **Big Thunder Mountain Railroad,** kids are required to be at least 40 inches high and 3 years old. You can get small fries measured at certain locations, have their hands stamped to show that they're at least 40 inches tall, and then not worry about height restrictions for the rest of the day.

If you have small kids with you, concentrate on **Fantasyland** (behind Sleeping Beauty's Castle), a kids' paradise with fairy-tale-derived rides such as **King Arthur Carousel, Dumbo the Flying Elephant, Mr. Toad's Wild Ride, Peter Pan's Flight, Alice in Wonderland, Pinocchio's Daring Journey,** and the Disney signature ride, **It's a Small World.** Elsewhere in the park, little ones will enjoy clambering through **Tarzan's Treehouse,** singing along with the audio-animatronic **Country Bear Jamboree,** and doing space wheelies on **Rocket Rods,** which is tamer than the name implies (not worth a long wait for grownups). **Mickey's Toontown** is a wacky, gag-filled world inspired by the *Roger Rabbit* films, featuring endless amusement for young imaginations.

Disneyland for those with disabilities

Travelers who have disabilities are treated very, very well at Disneyland. Of course, crowds may make it difficult to maneuver at times, and the parks themselves can be formidably large. Those concerns aside, if you're disabled, you are given royal treatment, most notably in the form of jumping the line along with your family members (provided it's a reasonable number of folks). Rides that require nimbleness in boarding are halted if need be to ease passage for those requiring help. So when your "Doom Buggy" stops in the Haunted Mansion, odds are that it's because ride operators are helping a disabled person board or disembark.

Parade and show-going smarts

The park's parades and shows draw huge crowds into relatively small areas. Parades usually run twice a day, in the late afternoon and mid-evening. If a parade doesn't interest you, make a point to steer clear of the parade grounds during and immediately after the parade. You can use this time to take advantage of shorter ride lines in Frontierland (**Big Thunder Mountain Railroad**), Tomorrowland (**Space Mountain**), and New Orleans Square (**Haunted Mansion** and **Pirates of the Caribbean**).

Let's Go to Disneyland!

You've done your homework, you've packed the right park-going clothes and accessories, and you have a game plan in order. Now it's time to hit the parks.

Plan to get to the gates of either park a few minutes, at least, before opening. If you are driving there, you may want to get an early start, because you need to take into account early-morning rush-hour traffic, the drive itself, the parking, and the walk to the gate from the parking lot, all before 9 a.m. The extra time spent getting there may be reason enough to stay in the Anaheim area.

The **ticket booths** are located precisely between the entrances to Disneyland and California Adventure (one on the left, the other on the right), but you won't need to stand in those lines if you follow our advice and buy your tickets before you get to the park.

The free automated **FastPass** system, one of the finer innovations in recent Disney history, allows you to get advance tickets to certain rides. Get your FastPass tickets at the FastPass machines located at or near the entrances to the attractions where the pass is offered. (Look for signs directing you to the FastPass queue, not the Standby queue; it can be a bit confusing, so read the signs carefully, or just ask about it.) You will receive one FastPass ticket for each **Disneyland** Resort admission ticket, which you simply insert into a FastPass machine to get a FastPass ticket. You're assigned a one-hour window of time during which you can board the attraction, usually 45 to 90 minutes later. During this time, you can go on some other rides or have a snack. When you return during your appointed time, you get to bypass the regular line and more or less hop right on the ride. Not all rides have this option, but the most popular ones in both Disneyland and California Adventure do. While this system doesn't eliminate lines entirely — after all, other people have the same return time as you — it does help you do the park more efficiently. Just remember that Disney allows only a limited number of people to be in the FastPass queue at the same time. And did I mention that it's *free?*

Which park should you visit first? Disneyland, of course. It's the real reason, perhaps the only reason, you're here at all. And if you had to pick one, just one, park to visit, it would be that one. So let's go there first.

Disneyland

It's billed as the "Happiest Place on Earth," and who can say that it's true (there are places in Bali that are very happy, indeed)? But we have to admit that we get happy just writing "Disneyland."

As the clock strikes 9 a.m., the gates open, and the crowd floods into the park. You start on **Main Street**, the famous ⅔ replica of an ideal American small town — mid-19th-century Mark Twain with a little Beaver Cleaver thrown in. (Actually, all buildings in the park are ⅔ size to help make kids feel at ease and adults feel sentimental.) We urge you, even if you have never been here before, not to linger — while you dally, the lines are getting longer and longer.

But here's what you see as you race past. (You'll see it in more detail when you return later.) You first pass through the **Town Square,** where you are likely to get immediately distracted, as various Disney characters are there for greeting and photo-taking. Stop for a photo op if you must, but plenty more characters pop up later, we promise.

The rest of the street contains stores offering Disney merchandise. We suggest that you hold off buying any stuff until later, because you don't want to schlep packages around with you — although, stores and kiosks all over the park offer **free delivery of merchandise to your hotel** if you're staying in the Disney Resort.

"Steamboat Willie," the first Mickey Mouse cartoon (and thus, The One that Started It All), plays in a theater here, as does "Great Moments with Mr. Lincoln," an animatronic show wherein the Great Emancipator delivers some of his best-known lines. It's hokey, but when Disney tried to close it, protests were loud and long.

We also like the **General Store,** which has a couple of checkerboards and old-fashioned wall-mounted phones on which you can eavesdrop into an 1890s party-line conversation. Truth be told, it thrills us that these little low-tech moments still exist.

Main Street feeds into the central area of Disneyland, from which several main "lands" branch off — **Fantasyland, Tomorrowland, Frontierland, Adventure Land, New Orleans Square, Critter Country,** and **Mickey's Toontown** — rather like the fingers on a hand. Where you go at this point depends on your preferences. In the following section, we detail each area, highlighting the most popular rides, to help you decide which you should target first.

From experience, we can say that among the most perennially popular rides park-wide are the **Pirates of the Caribbean, Haunted Mansion, Indiana Jones Adventure, Space Mountain,** and **Roger Rabbit's Car Toon Spin.** All of these rides currently offer FastPass service.

Adventureland

If you turn to your left after you enter the more-or-less main hub of Disneyland, you enter Adventureland. This section of Disneyland is all jungle-themed. Here you can find the **Jungle Cruise,** where hilarious and pun-addicted "guides" take you on a jungle journey that is noted more for its terrible jokes than its thrills — everyone adores it, even if they won't admit it; **Indiana Jones Adventure,** where visitors ride in a bouncy jeep and follow Indy's adventures — it's high tech and for the short-attention-span generation, not for the faint of stomach; and the **Enchanted Tiki Room,** one of the oldest rides in the park, where the birds sing words and the flowers bloom — it's considered terribly dated by some, and adorable by others.

The former Swiss Family Robinson treehouse, now **Tarzan's Treehouse,** is a giant fake tree that kids can "climb" — actually, take stairs — and wander through while admiring Tarzan's home-decorating skills.

New Orleans Square

Adventureland leads directly to this little bit of the French Quarter. It is copied so perfectly that many people who have visited the real McCoy can't help but say "it looks just like Disneyland," when, in fact, it's the other way around.

Here you can find the **Pirates of the Caribbean,** where animatronic pirates make war on, raid, and destroy a Spanish Creole village. One of the first of the fancy rides in the park, it's hilarious and still the gold standard, even if the effects are slightly dated. It's one of the longer rides too, close to 15 minutes long. Because of the dark, the two steep drops at the beginning, and the subject matter, it may be too intense for young kids.

In the **Haunted Mansion,** you walk and ride through a house where ghosts are running amok; when we were very small and this was very new, we were terrified to go on it, but we ended up laughing our heads off and demanding an instant repeat visit. It may still be too intense for kids, even though the ride has jokes galore.

While you're in New Orleans Square, look to the right of the Blue Bayou restaurant. See a discreet #33 on a door? That's the entrance to the exclusive **33 Club;** for a hefty fee, members get year-long free admission to the park and a chance to dine amid the ambience of a gracious, wood-paneled English gentleman's club.

Frontierland

From the **Pirate Ship,** where you clamber around on a galleon, you have access to **Tom Sawyer Island** via motorized rafts; it's one of the few totally low-tech areas remaining in the park. Kids can climb rock towers, wiggle through tight caves — the latter can be genuinely creepy thanks to the low lighting — and otherwise run around like crazy.

Close encounters with Pluto

Of course, we all want our picture taken with Mickey (well, we want *ours* with Pluto), even if we're too cool to admit it. Disney characters pop up all over the park all day long, but they are most commonly found in the Town Square, as you enter the park, and in front of Sleeping Beauty Castle.

Be aware, even if your children are not, that there are real people in those (rather heavy) outfits. So in expressing your enthusiasm at the sight of them, try not to maul them (you'd be surprised how many people do). Even if you do play rough, you won't be allowed to manhandle Mickey for very long, for each character has a plainclothes handler nearby, keeping an eye on encounters to make sure that the love fests don't turn into wrestling matches.

Other attractions include the *Mark Twain* **riverboat,** which cruises around Tom Sawyer Island, and the **Indian Canoes,** where guides force unsuspecting tourists to paddle canoes around the island. **Big Thunder Mountain Railroad** is a popular runaway train–themed roller coaster.

Frontierland is also the home of an old-fashioned shooting gallery and the long-running **Golden Horseshoe Stage** (burlesque/vaudeville revue fun), which is noted for being a good place to park your grandparents, or anyone else looking to take a load off.

Critter Country

At press time, Critter Country was getting a makeover to tie in with the film, *Country Bear Jamboree* (styled after a long-running park attraction). It still houses **Splash Mountain,** a combination log-flume ride, which ends with one heck of a steep drop — prepare to get wet — and the animatronic retelling of Uncle Remus tales.

Fantasyland

You can creep up on this section around the back via Frontierland or through **Sleeping Beauty Castle,** one of the two main landmarks of the park (the other being the Matterhorn). The fairy-tale castle (styled after Mad King Ludwig's Neuschwanstein castle in Bavaria) is the perfect central meeting place for a family or group that has been split up.

Fantasyland got a major facelift right before the 1984 Olympics. Although the exteriors of the rides look better as a result, some of them lost a little bit of the magic, most noticeably **Alice in Wonderland** (your caterpillar-shaped buggy takes you on a tour of highlights from the movie), which seems to rely more on Day-Glo–painted cheap paper and cardboard cutouts than mannequins and the like (a problem found in many a newer or updated ride). Other rides include the justly popular **Mr. Toad's Wild Ride,** wherein, like Toad himself, you drive a car in a decidedly unsafe and highly amusing way; **Peter Pan's Flight,** where a pirate ship–shaped buggy flies through highlights from the story; **Snow White,** the fairy tale, which lost some of its power to scare thanks to the pre-1984 remake; and **Pinocchio's Daring Journey,** which was added during the '84 refurbishment, and which gets few riders. **Dumbo the Flying Elephant** allows you to fly around and around a pole in a small elephant (it's way more amusing than it sounds, especially because you can control the elephant, making it move up and down), and the spinning teacups in the **Mad Tea Party** have caused generations to puke. The twee **Storybook Land Canal Boats** takes you on a journey past all sorts of (we admit it) adorable little replica settings from famous tales. (We so wish we could get out and play with them.)

After you leave the main Fantasyland area — with the Alice ride on your right — you can either ride the **Matterhorn** (the park's first roller coaster, which is still a stomach-turning thrill, even if it does seem a bit tame compared with the wild rides at more conventional amusement parks), or head to your left and see if you dare take on **It's a Small World,** one of the first "new," fancy attractions added in 1966. It's hard to recall what a big deal this was for so many years. In many ways, it's Dante's Inferno, as you travel through several circles of hell in the form of internationally dressed dolls who move their heads and click their eyes, and mouth the words to *that song,* which will never, ever again leave your head. Don't say you weren't warned.

Mickey's Toontown

If you move to the left of Small World in Fantasyland, you will come to the entrance to **Mickey's Toontown,** the first major addition to the park in many a decade. Modeled after the animated world in the movie *Who Framed Roger Rabbit?,* it's largely aimed at the younger Disney visitor. They can bounce in **Goofy's Bounce House,** ride a junior-sized roller coaster, stroll through **Mickey and Minnie's** homes, or take on **Roger Rabbit's Car Toon Spin** (essentially, the same wacky idea as the Mr. Toad ride, only these cars can spin 360 degrees, if you choose). Only the latter really appeals to grownups, although there are plenty of visual gags throughout the area to help while away the time.

Tomorrowland

On the other side of the Matterhorn from Fantasyland is Tomorrowland, which got a total makeover recently, a process that is still somewhat ongoing. This is the area that causes most boomers dismay, because it has undergone the most changes over the years. Originally, it was Walt's favorite area of the park, for it was his vision of the future — remember, this was back in the 1950s, when said future was exciting, and we would all have flying cars by the year 2000. But that sort of vision naturally has a built-in obsolescence. Over the years, a number of rides and attractions have been phased out (R.I.P.: House of Tomorrow, the People Mover, the Skyway Trams), converted (people still mourn the loss of Journey Through Inner Space, also known as the Shrinking Ride, which was converted into **Star Tours,** wherein riders get to have George Lucas–designed fun with C3PO — not for the faint of stomach), or just restyled (the beloved Mission to Mars is now called the **Astro Orbitor,** even though it's still pretty much rocket ships whirling around a pole). The recent makeover abandoned the admittedly dated look for a more H.G. Wells version of the future — and how's that for irony, to go to the 1890s for a futuristic look?

Anyway, in addition to the attractions mentioned already, here you can find **Space Mountain,** an indoor roller coaster made all the more vomit-inducing because it's entirely in the dark; a 3-D production (for far too long, it was the Michael Jackson *Captain Eo* movie; currently, it's *Honey, I Shrunk the Audience*); and **Autopia,** where you drive a miniature sports car around a bucolic highway (kids love this early chance at "driving" and the "license" they get during their wait in line). The eight submarines of the Submarine Voyage ride have been decommissioned, and it's still unclear what will be done with the giant submarine lagoon. This is also the area where you can catch the **monorail,** still perhaps the longest in the United States, which takes you to and from Downtown Disney.

California Adventure

Ah, now we come to the "new" park, which opened to great fanfare in 2001. The first major new development at Disneyland since, hmm, maybe Toontown — except this is so much bigger. (Toontown was just a new land; this is a whole new park.)

After we have been going on — and on and on and on — about the general overall perfection of Disney, we now have to say California Adventure may have been a major misstep. And, unless you get one of those multi-day Hopper Passes (covered in Chapter 22), you can safely save your money and skip the California Adventure park.

Don't get us wrong; it's gorgeous. Disney design could produce no less. Every detail, as always, is extensively researched and exquisite. But did you notice the name? Do you know what the theme is? That's right: California. It's a mini version of California in (do we really need to point this out?) *California.* It boasts a mock version of Yosemite, a highly stylized version of San Francisco, and a wishful-thinking version of Hollywood Boulevard. You, the visitor, may well go, during the same day, from the real Hollywood Boulevard to the cartoon version here. And while this may be terrific for prompting discussions of the platonic ideal and archetypes, it just doesn't sit well as an amusement park, or at least not as an amusement park based in, let's just mention it again, *California.*

Look ma — no lines!

That's what *you* think. Nearly every Disney ride is fiendishly designed to look as if there is no line in front of it — either by having the line snake in such a way that its true length is obscured, or by having most of it hidden inside the ride structure itself. You walk up and think "Hey, there's no line. Let's try this ride!" only to get inside and find out there are quite a few people and a lengthy wait ahead of you. It's a clever psychological trick that we fall for *each and every time.*

The upside is that many of the newer rides have some kind of visual device — little sights, details, or other amusements (talking cars before Autopia, say, or a "set" that makes you think you are "backstage" at Roger Rabbit) — that can help while away the time. It's a good idea to bring a book or a magazine just in case. If you have kids in tow, make sure that they also have a book or comic to keep themselves occupied while they wait.

But nevermind that. A more egregious sin is that the entire park lacks the same magic of Disneyland — which is, after all, based on mythologies or faraway lands and times rather than a re-creation of something that lies right outside the gates. Consequently, it's artificial in a Vegas way, not a Disney dazzle way. Plus, it's a much more generic amusement park; there aren't many rides for the space, and those that are here often disappoint or are completely ordinary. Also, the park seems less efficiently laid out; after a couple of waits in line and a walk from one section to another, you've used up a couple of hours with little to show for it.

Which is not to say that there isn't plenty to enjoy at CA (get the initials?), but it's much more a stroll-around-and-admire park than an amusement park (much better for adults weary of lines or rides in general). And if the place didn't cost a whole separate expensive admission, we would probably think more kindly of it than we do. Which is where that Hopper Pass comes in; it pays for itself in just a couple days of Disneyland admission alone. With it, families can take advantage of the better food options in California Adventure and the smaller crowds.

Oh, yeah, the smaller crowds. As of this writing, it's clear that California Adventure is a bit of a bust. On a recent trip, admittedly a cold fall day, we found the park nearly deserted. And even when the crowds picked up a few days later, attendance was well below that of Disneyland. Disney has made some modifications, but it also conducted a Gallup poll to see if respondents would miss California Adventure were it gone for good (we participated in the poll), which just can't be good. Still, the economic repercussions from 9/11 cannot be discounted, and the park may find its footing in the near future just as other tourism attractions rebound.

You enter California Adventure through a replica of the Golden Gate, serenaded from loudspeakers by wacky versions of California-centric tunes (expect lots of Beach Boys and Jan and Dean), which play rather strangely on drizzly days. When you enter the park, you can fan out (the park more or less is in a circle, surrounding a mini San Francisco Bay) as you see fit.

Golden State

The Golden State area of California Adventure is sort of a catchall for the beauty of California. It features some lovely — and entirely uninteresting for kids — exhibits on state produce and farming (entirely in keeping with the original Disney gestalt). Here, also, is the **Grizzly River Run,** a thoroughly enjoyable water ride; expect to get either somewhat damp or soaked through. It's easily spotted, thanks to the 110-foot rock formation in the shape of California's own bear. **The Redwood Creek Challenge Trail** is part of a kid's playground area that lets little ones run around, climb on ropes or rock-climbing walls, and just generally get their ya-yas out in an area designed to look like Yosemite ("oh, it's *faux*-semite," observed one attendee).

Also featured in the Golden State area of California Adventure is the **Soarin' Over California** ride. Riders pile into rows of seats that are lifted up so that they may sway and tilt, hang-glider style, in front of an IMAX-type film. It's one of the better rides, but it's prone to long lines, and it's a tad disappointing if you thought you were going to do more actual hang-gliding-type activity. If, when you read this, the **Bug's Life Theater** is still showing its 3-D attraction (there are plans to convert it to something else), by all means, go — it is one of the best attractions in the park — but note that it is (honestly) too dark and intense for young kids.

For the adults, there is honest-to-gosh wine tasting at the **Golden Vine Winery,** where you can learn about wine-making (right out of Napa Valley) and even taste the juice of the grape. There is also a replica of the **rotunda of San Francisco's Palace of Fine Arts** (it serves the same purpose as Cinderella's Castle: It's a good meeting spot) and a copy of the **Pacific Wharf,** where you can watch bread being made or, better still, a tortilla-making machine in action (and you get a free tortilla).

Paradise Pier

This is essentially Disney's version of a traditional amusement park. It's "carnival central," with the sort of rides that fly around on chains or whiz into the air and generally make you sick to your stomach. It's nothing you haven't ridden before and, as such, it's hardly a must-do. But then again, how lovely it is that in this manic, high-tech, short-attention-span world there are still kids who get thrilled riding a merry-go-round or Ferris wheel. In between the rides are lots of gaily-colored restaurants and cartoon-styled toy shops (the dino selling sunglasses does just that — sell sunglasses, we mean; they don't sell dinosaurs, more's the pity).

Hollywood Pictures Backlot

This is possibly the most dubious portion of the park, where the sinful, back-stabbing business of show is turned into wacky fun. Sure, the whole point of Disneyland is product-placement tie-ins, but the tie-ins here seem even more grotesque and shameless. (ABC soap operas have a major presence. Need we say more?)

We mention how very odd it is to see this highly stylized, cartoon version of Hollywood Boulevard (which, as we've mentioned elsewhere in this book, has no real association with Hollywood the motion-picture industry), but it pales in comparison to the sensations experienced when riding the **Superstar Limo,** wherein you enjoy the whole panoply of stardom, from your agent bossing you around, to paparazzi flashing their bulbs, to seeing your visage on a billboard (and you get waved at by cardboard representations — what, animatronics are too expensive? — of such ABC and Disney stars as Tim Allen and Whoopi Goldberg).

This place touts a value system that is even more gross than those telling little girls that someday their prince will come. Otherwise, there isn't much to do, although the **Muppet 3D Adventure** is sweetly enjoyable.

Part VIII
The Part of Tens

The 5th Wave   By Rich Tennant

"I appreciate that our room is so near the ocean
I can hear the waves crashing, but I had to get
up to go to the bathroom 6 times last night."

In this part . . .

*E*very *For Dummies* book has the funny, quirky Part of Tens. Here our parts include the best places in Los Angeles to spot celebrities, the hairiest intersections, and, for when you need a break from the glitz and glamour, we list the spots where you think you're anywhere else but in L.A..

Chapter 25

Top Ten (or so) Places to Spot Celebrities

● ●

In This Chapter

▶ Hiking to the stars

▶ Sharing sushi with Cindy

▶ Passing the pepper to Portia

▶ Sipping toddies with Liz

● ●

*O*kay, let's all be honest (by now we're friends, right?). You want to see a star. It would be a large part of your fun to return home and say, "Hey, guess who was *right next to me* at the gas station?" Heck, it may even be a major reason for your trip to L.A. And surely, you think, the ground is thick with them. Well, that's true, but then again, they aren't going to the tourist sites — how often do you visit the ones in your own hometown? And you can buy one of those outdated Maps to the Stars' Homes, if you want to waste your money. We say forget it. Instead, listen up, *People* fans. Here are some tried-and-true Star Hangouts and some surefire ways to track those pesky famous folks in their natural habitat. Just remember, stalking is a crime. . . .

Runyon Canyon

Runyon Canyon is a nice and sometimes trying hike in Hollywood. But if the beautiful people can climb it, so can you! In one day, Drew Barrymore, Cameron Diaz, and someone who looks like Lucy Liu's agent were there. A trifecta of Angels. Almost. This canyon hike is fun, and good for you to boot.

Just north of Franklin Ave. at Poinsettia Place.

Newsroom Cafe

The Newsroom Cafe offers a nice, friendly atmosphere. This restaurant serves affordable health food the way you want it, complete with Hollywood stars sipping their fresh-squeezed juice at the table next to you. Can you say Keanu? How about Kiedis, as in Anthony of the Red Hot Chili Peppers?

120. N Robertson Blvd. ☎ *310-652-4444.*

Nobu

At Nobu, you get delicious sushi, perfect martinis, and Dirk Diggler (also known as Mark Walhberg). All Mark, all the time. Okay, also Cindy Crawford and husband, Gillian Anderson, Kelly Lynch, Adam Duritz from the Counting Crows, and a smattering of big Hollywood executives. And that was just one evening!

3853 Cross Creek Rd., Malibu, at the Pacific Coast Highway. ☎ *310-317-9140.*

Westside Pavilions Supermarket

Well, the stars have to eat too, you know, and they can't always do it at Nobu. This is the supermarket to the stars — mainly TV stars in a big rush. Look near the "15 items or less" checkout stand to see Jenny McCarthy, David Schwimmer (those sunglasses don't fool anyone), and Suzanne Pleshette, who have all pushed their own carts around this chain supermarket. Faye Dunaway insists that the store carry her favorite maple-flavored bacon.

Santa Monica Blvd. at Robertson Blvd.

Supermarkets usually have a good stock of stars, so you may want to check out these stores also:

- ✔ **Gelsons** in both Pacific Palisades (15424 W. Sunset Blvd.) and West Hollywood (8330 Santa Monica Blvd.) has had Kate Capshaw and Chris DeLuise, respectively, stroll their aisles.

- ✔ Both **Bristol Farms** in West Hollywood (9039 Beverly Blvd. and 7880 W. Sunset Blvd.) — where Drew Barrymore and the Pitt-Aniston family shop — have high star-spotting quotients.

- ✔ The **Mayfair Market** in Hollywood (5877 Franklin Ave.) is where Tim Roth and the Red Hot Chili Peppers fill their baskets.

Coffee Bean and Tea Leaf

This coffeehouse is located next to designer shopping in trendy Sunset Plaza (itself a highly predictable celeb locale). Location is everything, as they say. It's an easy place to spot a favorite celebrity sucking down a frothy drink or fat-free latte. There are too many stars to name, but we can start with Brad Pitt and Britney Spears.

8591 Sunset Blvd. Internet: `http://coffeebean.com`.

Other places to catch a star getting caffeinated:

- ✔ Balthazar Getty, Leo DiCaprio, and their friends prefer the cozy 24-hour **Coffee House** (8226 W. Sunset Blvd).
- ✔ Cameron Diaz and Portia DiRossi like to munch out and load up on coffee drinks at **Kings Road Cafe** (8361 Beverly Blvd.).
- ✔ The **Starbucks** in Malibu (30765 Pacific Coast Highway) is famous for Barbra Streisand/James Brolin sightings, along with Goldie Hawn, Kurt Russell, and Kate Hudson appearances.

Skybar at the Mondrian Hotel

Warning: This spot, which was once a hangout for George Clooney, has been way too publicized to keep the major stars coming, but the minor stars haven't gotten the word yet. Besides, with the beautiful view and poolside service from beautiful young waitresses, you'll feel like a star. Isn't that enough?

8440 Sunset Blvd., West Hollywood. ☎ *323-650-8999.*

L.A. Lakers at the Staples Center

Oh, yes. L.A. loves the Lakers. Celebrities love the Lakers. But you won't find them in the nosebleed seats. Bring a pair of binoculars, point them down toward the floor, and you may see the likes of Jack Nicholson, Dyan Cannon, Charlie Sheen, Will Smith and Jada Pinkett Smith, Matthew Perry, or Brad Pitt and wife chomping on hot dogs and cheering on the world champions.

1111 S. Figueroa St., Downtown. ☎ *213-624-3100. Internet:* `www.staples center.com`.

Fred Segal Stores

Be afraid, be very afraid. They're here, and they want that overpriced little black blouse you have in your hands. Go for lunch at the restaurant and casually glance to your left to figure out if you know that person from TV, movies, magazines, or radio. Or just camp out in the parking lot the week before the Oscars and watch the stars parade by in a buying frenzy, searching for shoes, suits, dresses, accessories, and gift items for winners and losers.

8100 Melrose Ave. in West Hollywood; Broadway and 4th Street in Santa Monica.

The Lobby Bar at the Four Seasons Hotel

It used to be that you could see everyone in the world pass by the corner of Hollywood and Vine if you stood there long enough. Now, the Four Seasons in Beverly Hills features a constant stream of Hollywood and international famous faces. Is Mick Jagger well-known enough for you?

300 S. Doheny Dr., Beverly Hills. ☎ *323-656-1010.*

The Polo Lounge at the Beverly Hills Hotel

It's a classic, and it still works, though you're more likely to spot "Old Hollywood" here than the young and tragically hip. Nancy Reagan likes to lunch here with her pals. Elizabeth Taylor is a customer, as well.

9641 Sunset Blvd., Beverly Hills. ☎ *310-276-2251.*

Chateau Marmont

All of "New Hollywood" can be found at this gothic noir Hollywood hotel. Hang out in the lobby (get a drink) or the pretty public grounds and spot Nicole Kidman, Michael Stipe of R.E.M., Ben Stiller, and many more, around for anything from a day's magazine shoot to a long-term stay.

8221 Sunset Blvd., Beverly Hills. ☎ *310-276-2251.*

Chapter 26

Eight Places You Can't Afford

● ●

In This Chapter

▶ Tasting fancy fish

▶ Getting beauteous brows

▶ Enjoying delectable digs

● ●

Sad (unless you're rich, in which case, good for you, and can we be your friend?) but true, Los Angeles is a money-hungry, money-happy, money-making city with a lot of wealthy people. Come on, it's *Hollywood,* after all. Those movie stars have to spend those $20-million salaries (and those sitcom stars their $750,000 per episode) somewhere, don't they?

Where can you and I go to feel like the rich do, if only for an hour or two? Here are a few places to check out if you're happy with your A.P.R. rate on your worn-out credit card.

Matsuhisa

Forget about not being able to afford this wonderfully creative sushi restaurant; you won't even be able to get a table — but if you call way in advance and can be happy eating before 7 p.m. or after 10 p.m. (okay, that's an exaggeration, but you *must* have a reservation), go for it. The fish and the service are so great that you won't mind too much when you get the bill. And, if you have one of their unique and dee-licious martinis, you won't really mind at all.

129 N. La Cienega Blvd., Beverly Hills. ☎ *310-659-9639.*

Nobu

This is the sister restaurant to chef Nobuyuki's Matsuhisa. It's a little easier to get a table here, in the more relaxed atmosphere of Malibu, but be prepared to eat, drink, be happy, and then get the bill. Hey, the rice is good and inexpensive . . . maybe you should go heavy on that. Nah, celebrate the good fortune that you found this spot, as it's buried in the corner of a rustic but (you guessed it) pricey shopping mall for the Malibu set.

3853 Cross Creek Rd. at the Pacific Coast Highway, Malibu. ☎ 310-317-9140.

The Golden Globe Awards

By far the most relaxed fun of all the awards shows (they serve lots of wine, and then Dick Clark televises this shindig), the Golden Globes is for the fancy-schmancy only. But you can check into the Hilton for the evening ($255 plus tax per night), dress up (Neiman Marcus is just down the street), drink up (a Heineken beer out of the minibar will set you back $6), and feel like a rich star all you want. Heck, you can even throw a tantrum when you don't win! The Golden Globes are held the third Sunday night in January.

Beverly Hilton, 9876 Wilshire Blvd., Beverly Hills. ☎ 310-274-7777.

Nonfat Yogurt with Hot Fudge at The Flowering Tree

Prices start at $4 for a small. It must be the homemade, nonfat, delicious hot fudge sauce that makes them so pricey. Okay, it's good and sorta good for you, but it's not like it's served with a complimentary engraved spoon from Tiffany's. What gives? No parking, either!

8253 Santa Monica Blvd., West Hollywood. ☎ 323-654-4332.

Barney's of New York

The chicest department store in town, this is a branch of the store so beloved by the fashionistas in New York City, laid out so that it looks like a veritable museum of clothes. Armani, Vera Wang, Christian Louboutin shoes — it's all here, and it all costs a bundle.

9570 Wilshire Blvd., Beverly Hills. ☎ 310-276-4400.

Sally Herschberger at John Frieda Salon

Sally Herschberger made her name when she gave Meg Ryan her adorable shaggy blonde haircut. Colorist Lorri Goddard keeps Jennifer Aniston, Nicole Kidman, Kim Basinger, and a host of others in the pink (or rather, blond or red or brown). There's a reason these gals and many, many others go to this chic salon — they can afford it, and they look like a million bucks afterward (arguably the best cuts and best colorists in town).

8440 Melrose Place, West Hollywood. ☎ *323-653-4040.*

Eyebrows by Anastasia

Romanian immigrant Anastasia charges about three or four times what a regular brow wax costs, but she has shaped the errant brow of many a celeb, and with good reason — she's an artist. She dyes, she pulls, she plucks, she shapes, and she draws (all at a fast pace, but don't worry, she *so* knows what she's doing). The results are so stunning that you'll gladly hand out still more dollars for some of her equipment (pencils, gloss) to try to reproduce the effects at home.

438 N Bedford Dr., Beverly Hills. ☎ *310-273-3155.*

A Room at the Hotel Bel-Air

Flat-out beautiful; the Hotel Bel-Air is discreetly tucked away in the hills above Bel-Air, on several acres of enchanting grounds full of trees, greenery, swans, and bubbling water, with the kind of service you could grow so very accustomed to. Believe us when we say that if we could afford it (rooms start at $450 per night), we would say hang the cost. Perhaps it's just as well, for if we got a room here, we would never leave. But there's no reason why you can't join us for a drink in the bar at the romantic restaurant and pretend that we're staying at the hotel.

701 Stone Canyon Rd., Los Angeles. ☎ *310-472-1211.*

Chapter 27

Almost Ten Places Where You Feel as if You're Not Even Near L.A.

● ●

In This Chapter

▶ Mayberry pies

▶ Colorado skies

▶ Ring-a-ding-ding Mai Tai's

● ●

Sure, some of these may be city landmarks, but these places are so unique that even a native can feel as if they are far, far away from the City of Angels.

The Apple Pan

This restaurant has been around since 1947. Even though the Gap, big bad malls, and pizza joints pop up all around it, the people find it and then flock here. Try the pie. Close your eyes, and chew slowly — you'll swear you're in Mayberry, RFD.

10801 W. Pico Blvd., West Los Angeles. ☎ **310-475-3585.**

Circle K Riding Stables

Take a horseback ride in Griffith Park. It's cheap ($18 an hour, and you get to take the well-behaved horse on the trail yourself), the people are nice, and the trail is lush and quiet — if you can pretend the white noise of the 134 freeway (it's just at the beginning of the ride) is a river, you may think you're in Montana . . . well, *okay*, let's just say that you won't think you're riding a horse in L.A.

910 S. Mariposa St., Burbank. ☎ **818-843-9890.**

Topanga Canyon

Travel north along the Pacific Coast Highway a few miles past the Santa Monica Pier, and you'll feel like you're in Colorado — if Colorado had Pacific Ocean breezes. Topanga is full of happy old hippies and kind New Age types — and what's wrong with that? Peaceful easy feelings abound, and all the folks you run into are happy to share the good vibrations with you, as long as you stay within the speed limit.

While you're there, try the **Inn of the Seventh Ray** (128 Old Topanga Canyon Rd.). This health-food restaurant resides in a former church. The food is organically prepared, service is friendly, and the vibe is completely Topanga.

Chez Jay

This beachfront roadhouse opened in 1959. Chez Jay's mellow, laid-back atmosphere, sawdust-covered floors, portholes, and giant schooner wheel may make you think that you've stumbled into Miami in the '60s or arrived somewhere off the beaten path in Hawaii. After you get a high-caloric, sauce-heavy meal, you'll be convinced that you're somewhere else besides L.A.

1657 Ocean Ave., Santa Monica. ☎ *310-395-1741.*

The Getty Museum

Fine art, culture, class . . . this can't be L.A., right? Wrong.

1200 Getty Dr., Los Angeles. ☎ *310-440-7300.*

Beverly Hot Springs

Yes, *of course* steam rooms, facials, and ye olde cucumber and soy milk massages are all so very L.A., but you can really feel light-years away as you relax at the city's own natural hot spring. No, it wasn't built in the 1920s by L.B. Mayer for one of his pampered contract players. Mother Nature made this one for us eons ago.

308 Oxford Ave., Los Angeles. ☎ *323-734-7000. Internet:* www.beverly hotsprings.com.

The Huntington Library, Art Collections, and Botanical Gardens

Six million books and a fabulous not-so-secret, oh-so-serene Zen garden to read them in? Sipping English tea overlooking the rose garden? Books in L.A.? It can't be L.A. Well, it is, and it's a top attraction in Pasadena.

1150 Oxford Rd., Pasadena (San Morino). ☎ *626-405-2141. Internet:* www.huntington.org.

Matteo's

It's a little bit "Old Hollywood." It's a little bit Las Vegas. Either way, with the vintage booths and decor (including clown paintings by the late comedian Red Skelton), Matteo's is not today's Los Angeles. Think Dean Martin — this was one of his favorite Italian eateries.

2323 Westwood Blvd. between Olympic and Pico Blvds., Los Angeles. ☎ *310-475-4521. Closed Mon.*

Self-Realization Fellowship Meditation Garden

This public meditation spot on the Pacific Palisades takes up several acres right along Sunset Boulevard as it winds down toward the Pacific. Wander through the park-like setting, complete with lake and dedicated to religious harmony, and wonder how the heck it came to be here. (You can find the answer in the bookshop; it was built by the late guru Yogananda and is on the site of the international headquarters for the yogi's Self-Realization Fellowship religious order.) You may also wonder how some of Gandhi's ashes came to be entombed here (a gift to the yogi). Say a little something to help the world become as peaceful as this place some day.

Mt. Washington, 5 mi. north of Downtown. ☎ *323-225-2471. Open: Tues–Sat 9 a.m.–5 p.m., Sun 1 p.m.–5 p.m. Closed Mon.*

Appendix

Quick Concierge

• •

Fast Facts

AAA

National Hotline: ☎ 800-222-4537. Internet: www.aaa.com. Roadside Assistance in California: ☎ 800-400-4222. Office locations: Westside (1900 S. Sepulveda Blvd., near Santa Monica Blvd., Los Angeles, CA 90025; ☎ 310-914-8500; Mon–Fri 9 a.m.–5 p.m. Downtown (2601 S. Figueroa St., near Adams Blvd., Los Angeles, CA 90007; ☎ 213-741-3686; Mon–Fri 9 a.m.–5 p.m. Hollywood/Wilshire (5550 Wilshire Blvd., between LaBrea and Fairfax, Los Angeles, CA 90036; ☎ 323-525-0018; Mon–Fri 9 a.m.–5 p.m.).

Ambulance

Dial ☎ 911.

American Express

Call ☎ 800-221-7282. Internet: www.americanexpress.com. Office Locations: Downtown (735 S. Figueroa St., Seventh Market Place, Los Angeles, CA 90017; ☎ 213-627-4800; Mon–Fri 9 a.m.–6 p.m.). West Hollywood (8493 W. 3rd St., at La Cienega, Los Angeles, CA 90048; ☎ 310-659-1682; Mon–Fri 9 a.m.–6 p.m. Sat 10 a.m.–3 p.m.).

Area Codes

213: Downtown Los Angeles and vicinity. **310:** West Los Angeles, Santa Monica, Beverly Hills. **323:** Hollywood, Silverlake, West Hollywood. **562:** Long Beach. **626:** Pasadena. **661:** Palmdale, Newhall, Lancaster. **714:** North and Central Orange County. **752:** Ontario, Pomona, Riverside, San Bernadino. **805:** Thousand Oaks, Agoura. **818:** San Fernando Valley, Burbank, Glendale. **909:** San Bernadino.

ATMs

ATMs are widely available at banks throughout Los Angeles. The most popular networks are Cirrus (☎ 800-424-7787; Internet: www.mastercard.com/cardholder services/atm/) and Plus (☎ 800-843-7587; Internet: www.visa.com/atms).

Baby-sitters

Babysitters Guild (6399 Wilshire Blvd., Suite 812, Los Angeles, CA 90048; ☎ 323-658-8792; Mon–Fri 8 a.m.–3 p.m.). L.A.'s largest and oldest baby-sitting service, the Babysitters Guild was recently named the city's best baby-sitting agency by *Los Angeles* magazine. Sitters are at least 21, speak English, and know how to drive; some have CPR (cardiopulmonary resuscitation) training. They serve hotels all over the city for $8 to $11 per hour (4-hour minimum) plus gas and parking costs.

Business Hours

Banks: Mon–Fri 9 a.m.–6 p.m., Saturday 9 a.m.–1 p.m. Businesses: Weekdays 9 a.m.–6 p.m. Stores/Shops: Weekdays 9 a.m.–9 p.m., weekends 10 a.m.–6 p.m.

Camera Repair

There's a one-hour photo shop about every four feet in Los Angeles, so getting your pictures developed is nothing to worry about. Getting your camera equipment repaired is another story. The biggest and best camera place in town is Samy's Camera in Hollywood. They're open 24 hours, so if they aren't convenient they can probably recommend someplace that is. Samy's Camera (431 S. Fairfax Ave., Hollywood, CA 90036; ☎ 323-938-2420;

Internet: www.samys.com; open daily 24 hours).

Convention Centers

Los Angeles Convention Center (1201 S. Figueroa St., Los Angeles, CA 90015; ☎ 213-741-1151; Internet: www.lacclink.com). Anaheim Convention Center (800 W. Katella Ave., Anaheim, CA 92802; ☎ 714-765-8950; Internet: www.anaheim.net/conventioncenter/).

Credit Cards

American Express (☎ 800-221-7282). MasterCard (☎ 800-307-7309). Visa ☎ 800-336-8472).

Dentists

DentistReferral.com (☎ 888-343-3440; Internet: www.dentistreferral.com). 1-800-Dentist (☎ 800-336-8478); Internet: www.1800dentist.com).

Doctors

The "urgent care" facilities all over Los Angeles may be a better bet for minor emergencies or health care issues than heading to the emergency room. These clinics require no appointments, and most accept the major health insurance plans. If you need a doctor but don't need a full-on hospital visit, check the yellow pages or ask your hotel concierge for an urgent care facility near you.

Emergencies

For police, fire, and ambulance, dial ☎ 911.

Hospitals

Westside: UCLA Medical Center (10833 Le Conte Ave., Los Angeles, CA 90095; ☎ 310-825-9111). St. John's (1328 22nd St., Santa Monica, CA 90404; ☎ 310-829-5511). Century City Hospital (2070 Century Park East, Los Angeles, CA 90067; ☎ 310-553-6211).

Hollywood/West Hollywood: Cedars-Sinai Medical Center (8700 Beverly Blvd., Los Angeles, CA 90048; ☎ 310-423-327). Los Angeles Children's Hospital (4650 W. Sunset Blvd., Los Angeles, CA 90027; ☎ 323-669-2178).

Downtown: Good Samaritan Hospital (1225 Wilshire Blvd., Los Angeles, CA 90017; ☎ 213-977-2121). City of Angels Medical Center (1711 W. Temple St., Los Angeles, CA 90026; ☎ 213-989-6100).

Hotlines

Los Angeles County Rape and Battering Hotline (☎ 310-392-8381). National Domestic Violence Hotline (☎ 800-799-7233). National Rape, Abuse, Incest Hotline (☎ 800-656-4673). National Suicide Prevention Hotline (☎ 800-784-2433). Los Angeles Suicide Prevention Center (☎ 310-391-1253 or 877-727-4747).

Internet Access and Cyber Cafes

Many hotels are wired for Internet access, but if you've left your laptop at home, Kinko's (☎ 800-2-KINKOS for the location nearest you) has Internet access, complete with high-speed computers for in-store use at 20¢ per minute, or $12 per hour pro-rated. The California Welcome Center in the Beverly Center (8500 Beverly Blvd., Los Angeles; ☎ 310-854-7616) provides free Internet access for travelers. Free Internet access is also available at the many branches of the Los Angeles Public Library (☎ 213-228-7000 for locations nearest you). To use their terminals, you must present a photo ID and sign up for a time slot. You are limited to 2 hours per day, in 30-minute blocks. The Santa Monica Public Library has four branches (☎ 310-458-8600 for locations nearest you), and provides free Internet access for an hour a day when you sign up for a library card. All you need for a library card is an ID that shows your address. If you prefer to gulp lattes while surfing the Web, Cyber Java (7080 Hollywood Blvd., Los Angeles; ☎ 323-466-5600) can set you up; terminals are $5 per half-hour or $9 per hour, from 7 a.m. to midnight. The Internet stations in the Knitting Factory's bar/restaurant (7021 Hollywood Blvd., Hollywood; ☎ 323-463-0204) are free of charge, but you have to order food or drink.

Liquor Laws

The legal drinking age in California is 21. Alcohol may be consumed only in establishments with liquor sales licenses (bars, restaurants, nightclubs, for example) between the hours of 6 a.m. and 2 a.m. Alcohol may be sold only between the hours of 6 a.m. and 2 a.m. Open containers are not allowed in public, either on the street or in a vehicle.

Mail

Downtown: Bunker Hill Station (300 S. Grand Ave., Los Angeles, CA 90071; ☎ 800-275-8777; Mon–Fri 8:30 a.m.–5:30 p.m.) Hollywood (1615 Wilcox Ave., Los Angeles, CA 90028; ☎ 323-464-2355; Mon–Fri 8:30 a.m.–5:30 p.m., Sat 8:30 a.m.–3:30 p.m.). West Hollywood (820 N. San Vicente, West Hollywood, CA 90069; ☎ 310-652-5435; Mon–Fri 8:30 a.m.–5:30 p.m., Sat 8 a.m.–2:30 p.m.).

Westside: Santa Monica (1248 5th St., Santa Monica, CA 90401; ☎ 310-576-6786; Mon–Fri 9 a.m.–6 p.m., Sat 9 a.m.–3 p.m.). Federal Building Westwood (11000 Wilshire Blvd., Los Angeles, CA 90024; ☎ 310-235-7443; Mon–Fri 7:30 a.m.–5:30 p.m.).

Maps

Good local maps can be found at most newsstands, many gas stations, or at the nearest AAA office.

Pharmacies

Santa Monica/Westside: Rite Aid (1808 Wilshire Blvd., Santa Monica, CA 90403; ☎ 310-829-3951; open 24 hours). Sav-On Drugs (12015 Wilshire Blvd., Los Angeles, CA 90025; ☎ 310-479-6500; Mon–Fri 9 a.m.–9 p.m., Sat 9 a.m.–7p.m, Sun 10 a.m.–6 p.m.).

West Hollywood/Hollywood: Sav-On Drugs (8491 Santa Monica Blvd., West Hollywood,

CA 90069; ☎ 310-360-7303; Mon–Fri 8 a.m.–1 p.m., Sat–Sun 10 a.m.–8 p.m.). Rite-Aid Pharmacy (6130 W. Sunset Blvd., Los Angeles, CA 90028; ☎ 323-467-4201; open 24 hours).

Downtown: Rite-Aid (600 W. 7th St., Los Angeles, CA 90017; ☎ 213-896-0083; Mon–Fri 9 a.m.–7 p.m., Sat 9 a.m.–6 p.m.).

Police

Call ☎ **911.**

Radio Station

You can find modern rock at KROQ-FM (106.7 FM), where they pretty much invented the term, pop hits at KISS FM (102.7), and classic rock at KLOS FM (95.5). Urban rules at KBT FM (100.3), and hip-hop is found at KPWR FM (105.9). The largest public radio station in L.A. is KCRW (89.9 FM), with NPR news and eclectic music. Regular news is at KFWB (980 AM), which also has traffic updates every 10 minutes.

Restrooms

Los Angeles doesn't have the kind of public restrooms you'd find in London or Paris, but you can usually take advantage of the facilities at fast-food restaurants or some gas stations. In rare circumstances, you may be asked to buy something before using the restrooms — but isn't that a small price to pay for taking care of business?

Safety

While Los Angeles does have its dangerous parts of town, by and large the average tourist isn't going to be anywhere near those sections of town. If you're staying in Downtown or in a more seedy part of Hollywood, exercise a little extra caution at night, but in general your basic street smarts apply around these parts of town. Avoid dark places in the middle of the night unless you're with a big group. Use travel wallets rather than easily snatched purses. Generally, just keep your eyes open.

Smoking

Smoking is not allowed inside most public buildings, including airports, shopping malls, restaurants, bars, and nightclubs. Smoking is only allowed outdoors.

Taxes

The sales tax on most commonly purchased items (except for snack foods) is 8.25 percent in all of Los Angeles County. You pay additional taxes and fees for travel-related items such as rental cars and hotel rooms (from 12 to 18 percent in the Los Angeles area).

Taxis

Yellow Cab (☎ 00-200-1085). United Independent (☎ 800-411-0303). Independent Taxi (☎ 800-521-8294). Checker Cabs (☎ 800-300-5007).

Cabs charge an airport fee of $2.50 in addition to their $2 pickup fee, $2 per mile charge, and additional charges when you get stuck in traffic, a common occurrence. It is customary to tip 10 to 15 percent.

Time Zone

Los Angeles is located in the Pacific Time Zone. California recognizes Daylight Saving Time from late April through late October.

Tipping

You should generally tip bartenders 10 to 15 percent; bellhops at least $1 per bag, more if you have a lot of luggage or heavy bags; cab drivers 15 percent of the fare; chambermaids at least $1 per day; checkroom attendants at least $1 per garment; delivery drivers, 15 to 20 percent of the check; hairdressers and barbers 15 to 20 percent of the bill; waiters and waitresses 15 to 20 percent of the check; and valet parking attendants at least $1 per vehicle.

Transit Info

The city's buses, subways, and commuter rail system are all operated under the heading of "Metro," a cutesy name for the Los Angeles County Metropolitan Transportation Authority. Buses run on most major thoroughfares throughout the city. The one subway line runs from Downtown through Hollywood, past Universal Studios, and ends in North Hollywood in the San Fernando Valley. The Metro operates a few light rail lines, including the "Blue Line" from downtown to Long Beach and the "Green Line" that goes near the airport (but not right to it; see Chapter 10 for more on your transportation options from the airport). For schedules, routes, and fares call ☎ 800-COMMUTE or check the MTA Web site at www.mta.net.

Weather Updates

The best source for weather information is www.weather.com, the Web site operated by The Weather Channel. If you don't have Internet access, you can call ☎ 213-976-1212 for recorded information. It'll cost you $2.00, but you'll also get all the latest California Lottery draw results at the same time, so what the heck!

Toll-Free Numbers and Web Sites

Major North American carriers

Air Canada
☎ 888/247-2262
www.aircanada.ca

Air New Zealand
☎ 800-262-1234 or 800-262-2468
    in the United States
☎ 800-663-5494 in Canada
☎ 0800-737-767 in New Zealand
www.airnewzealand.com

Alaska Airlines
☎ 800-426-0333
www.alaskaair.com

American Airlines
☎ 800-433-7300
www aa.com

American Trans Air
☎ 800-225-2995
www.ata.com

America West Airlines
☎ 800-235-9292
www.americawest.com

British Airways
☎ 800-247-9297
☎ 0345-222-111 or 0845-77-333-77
    in Britain
www.british-airways.com

Continental Airlines
☎ 800-525-0280
www.continental.com

Delta Air Lines
☎ 800-221-1212
www.delta.com

Hawaiian Airlines
☎ 800-367-5320
www.hawaiianair.com

Midwest Express
☎ 800-452-2022
www.midwestexpress.com

Northwest Airlines
☎ 800-225-2525
www.nwa.com

Qantas
☎ 800-227-4500 in the United States
☎ 612-9691-3636 in Australia
www.qantas.com

Southwest Airlines
☎ 800-435-9792
www.southwest.com

United Airlines
☎ 800-241-6522
www.united.com

US Airways
☎ 800-428-4322
www.usairways.com

Virgin Atlantic Airways
☎ 800-862-8621 in Continental
    United States
☎ 0293-747-747 in Britain
www.virgin-atlantic.com

Major car rental agencies

Advantage
☎ 800-777-5500
www.advantagerentacar.com

Alamo
☎ 800-327-9633
www.goalamo.com

Avis
☎ 800-331-1212 in Continental
    United States
☎ 800-TRY-AVIS (800-879-2847)
    in Canada
www.avis.com

Budget
☎ 800-527-0700
www.budgetrentacar.com

Dollar
☎ 800-800-4000
www.dollar.com

Enterprise
☎ 800-325-8007
www.enterprise.com

Hertz
☎ 800-654-3131
www.hertz.com

National
☎ 800-CAR-RENT (800-227-7368)
www.nationalcar.com

Payless
☎ 800-PAYLESS (800-729-5377)
www.paylesscarrental.com

Rent-A-Wreck
☎ 800-535-1391
www.rentawreck.com

Thrifty
☎ 800-367-2277
www.thrifty.com

Major hotel and motel chains

Best Western International
☎ 800-528-1234
www.bestwestern.com

Clarion Hotels
☎ 800-CLARION (800-252-7466)
www.clarionhotel.com

Comfort Inns
☎ 800-228-5150
www.hotelchoice.com

Courtyard by Marriott
☎ 800-321-2211
www.courtyard.com

Days Inn
☎ 800-325-2525
www.daysinn.com

Doubletree Hotels
☎ 800-222-TREE (800-222-8733)
www.doubletree.com

Econo Lodges
☎ 800-55-ECONO (800-553-2666)
www.hotelchoice.com

Fairfield Inn by Marriott
☎ 800-228-2800
www.marriott.com

Hampton Inn
☎ 800-HAMPTON (800-426-7866)
www.hampton-inn.com

Hilton Hotels
☎ 800-HILTONS (800-445-8667)
www.hilton.com

Holiday Inn
☎ 800-HOLIDAY (800-4654329)
www.basshotels.com

Howard Johnson
☎ 800-654-2000
www.hojo.com

Hyatt Hotels & Resorts
☎ 800-228-9000
www.hyatt.com

ITT Sheraton
☎ 800-325-3535
www.starwood.com

La Quinta Motor Inns
☎ 800-531-5900
www.laquinta.com

Marriott Hotels
☎ 800-228-9290
www.marriott.com

Motel 6
☎ 800-4-MOTEL6 (800-466-8356)
www.motel6.com

Quality Inns
☎ 800-228-5151
www.hotelchoice.com

Radisson Hotels International
☎ 800-333-3333
www.radisson.com

Ramada Inns
☎ 800-2-RAMADA (800-272-6232)
www.ramada.com

Red Carpet Inns
☎ 800-251-1962
www.bookroomsnow.com

Red Lion Hotels & Inns
☎ 800-547-8010
http://www.redlion.com/

Red Roof Inns
☎ 800-843-7663
www.redroof.com

Residence Inn by Marriott
☎ 800-331-3131
www.marriott.com

Rodeway Inns
☎ 800-228-2000
www.hotelchoice.com

Super 8 Motels
☎ 800-800-8000
www.super8.com

Travelodge
☎ 800-255-3050
www.travelodge.com

Vagabond Inns
☎ 800-522-1555
www.vagabondinn.com

Wyndham Hotels and Resorts
☎ 800-822-4200 in continental
          United States and Canada
www.wyndham.com

Making Dollars and Sense of It

Expense	Daily cost	x	Number of days	=	Total
Airfare					
Local transportation					
Car rental					
Lodging (with tax)					
Parking					
Breakfast					
Lunch					
Dinner					
Snacks					
Entertainment					
Babysitting					
Attractions					
Gifts & souvenirs					
Tips					
Other					
Grand Total					

Fare Game: Choosing an Airline

When looking for the best airfare, you should cover all your bases — 1) consult a trusted travel agent; 2) contact the airline directly, via the airline's toll-free number and/or Web site; 3) check out one of the travel-planning Web sites, such as www.frommers.com.

Travel Agency_____ Phone_____

    Agent's Name_____ Quoted fare_____

Airline 1_____ Quoted fare_____

    Toll-free number/Internet_____

Airline 2_____ Quoted fare_____

    Toll-free number/Internet_____

Web site 1_____ Quoted fare_____

Web site 2_____ Quoted fare_____

Departure Schedule & Flight Information

Airline_____ Flight #_____ Confirmation #_____

Departs_____ Date_____ Time_____ a.m./p.m.

Arrives_____ Date_____ Time_____ a.m./p.m.

Connecting Flight (if any)

Amount of time between flights_____ hours/mins

Airline_____ Flight #_____ Confirmation #_____

Departs_____ Date_____ Time_____ a.m./p.m.

Arrives_____ Date_____ Time_____ a.m./p.m.

Return Trip Schedule & Flight Information

Airline_____ Flight #_____ Confirmation #_____

Departs_____ Date_____ Time_____ a.m./p.m.

Arrives_____ Date_____ Time_____ a.m./p.m.

Connecting Flight (if any)

Amount of time between flights_____ hours/mins

Airline_____ Flight #_____ Confirmation #_____

Departs_____ Date_____ Time_____ a.m./p.m.

Arrives_____ Date_____ Time_____ a.m./p.m.

Sweet Dreams: Choosing Your Hotel

Make a list of all the hotels where you'd like to stay and then check online and call the local and toll-free numbers to get the best price. You should also check with a travel agent, who may be able to get you a better rate.

Hotel & page	Location	Internet	Tel. (local)	Tel. (Toll-free)	Quoted rate

Hotel Checklist

Here's a checklist of things to inquire about when booking your room, depending on your needs and preferences.

- ☐ Smoking/smoke-free room
- ☐ Noise (if you prefer a quiet room, ask about proximity to elevator, bar/restaurant, pool, meeting facilities, renovations, and street)
- ☐ View
- ☐ Facilities for children (crib, roll-away cot, babysitting services)
- ☐ Facilities for travelers with disabilities
- ☐ Number and size of bed(s) (king, queen, double/full-size)
- ☐ Is breakfast included? (buffet, continental, or sit-down?)
- ☐ In-room amenities (hair dryer, iron/board, minibar, etc.)
- ☐ Other_____

Going "My" Way

Day 1

Hotel_____ Tel._____

Morning_____

_____

Lunch_____ Tel._____

Afternoon_____

_____

Dinner_____ Tel._____

Evening_____

_____

Day 2

Hotel_____ Tel._____

Morning_____

_____

Lunch_____ Tel._____

Afternoon_____

_____

Dinner_____ Tel._____

Evening_____

_____

Day 3

Hotel_____ Tel._____

Morning_____

_____

Lunch_____ Tel._____

Afternoon_____

_____

Dinner_____ Tel._____

Evening_____

_____

Going "My" Way

Day 4

Hotel_____ Tel._____

Morning_____

_____

Lunch_____ Tel._____

Afternoon_____

_____

Dinner_____ Tel._____

Evening_____

_____

Day 5

Hotel_____ Tel._____

Morning_____

_____

Lunch_____ Tel._____

Afternoon_____

_____

Dinner_____ Tel._____

Evening_____

_____

Day 6

Hotel_____ Tel._____

Morning_____

_____

Lunch_____ Tel._____

Afternoon_____

_____

Dinner_____ Tel._____

Evening_____

_____

Going "My" Way

Day 7

Hotel_____ Tel._____

Morning_____

_____

Lunch_____ Tel._____

Afternoon_____

_____

Dinner_____ Tel._____

Evening_____

_____

Day 8

Hotel_____ Tel._____

Morning_____

_____

Lunch_____ Tel._____

Afternoon_____

_____

Dinner_____ Tel._____

Evening_____

_____

Day 9

Hotel_____ Tel._____

Morning_____

_____

Lunch_____ Tel._____

Afternoon_____

_____

Dinner_____ Tel._____

Evening_____

_____

Index